Kings and Propł

Emil Bock

Kings and Prophets

Saul, David, Solomon
Elijah, Jonah, Isaiah, Jeremiah

Floris Books

Translated by Maria St Goar

Originally published in German under the title *Könige und Propheten*
by Verlag Urachhaus in 1936. Fifth German edition 1977.
First published in English by Floris Books in 1989.
Second edition with minor revisions 2006

British Library CIP Data available

ISBN-10 0-86315-573-1
ISBN-13 978-086315-573-4

Produced in Poland
by Polskabook

Contents

Acknowledgments

Unless otherwise stated, all quotations from the Bible are from the Revised Standard Version with kind permission of the National Council of the Churches Christ (Old Testament © 1952; Apocrypha © 1957, 1977; New Testament © 1946, 1971).

Where the context required it, Bock's own translation has been translated into English. These are marked *B* after the reference.

Preface

The universal significance which the Old Testament possesses for all humankind is most readily discernible at the very beginning of its books where the creation, the primordial age of both the earth and the generations of people pass before our eyes in mighty visions. There we confront the mysterious womb of creation from which emerged all creatures and human beings.

Even the description of the age of Moses is still much more than merely a chapter from the history of one nation. While Genesis presented the birth of the human being on the earth, the subsequent books depict the birth of a human consciousness that is truly its own. To study Moses and his time means to watch the great turning point in the development of consciousness forming the basis for the capability of thinking and inner freedom; freedom that from long since represents the most important requirement for the life of *every* human being.

Where the Bible goes on to narrate the period of David and Solomon as well as that of the kings and prophets, it does indeed appear to be nothing more than the history of one specific nation. Offhand, it is not clear why the development of one particular ethnic group should have any significance necessitating special studies for persons other than those who belong to this group. It is particularly difficult to comprehend why the description of the history of this nation can claim to have the character of a holy scripture within the context of Christianity, hence for a completely different religious sphere.

It is the task of this third volume of Bible Studies to awaken a feeling for the fact that the Israelite-Jewish history in the first half of the last pre-Christian millennium took place in the brightly illuminated centre of humanity's history. At any given time, one nation or ethnic group stands at the centre of world history, and exemplifies and is the first to embody the then timely level of the inner development of humanity. For a while, the rays of all spiritual life and endeavours stream together there, although not always in outwardly apparent relationships and arrangements. In those particular people, the true spirit of the age seems to find its centre of irradiation; there beats the pulse of humanity of that age. This is the case for the history described in the Old Testament.

It goes without saying that it would be senseless to attribute such a central human significance to the history of Judaism for our age, for the Middle Ages or even for the last centuries prior to the Christian era. But during the period between David and Ezra, the history of the Jewish people was transparent for humankind's history.

The overall human importance of the Old Testament descriptions of history only become discernible in all their significance if we focus on the spiritual occurrences that took place behind the external course of history, namely those of the Christ history. Again, without constantly referring to it, it is the intent of the studies presented here to clarify the great extent to which Israelite-Jewish history received its content and inner form from above through the Christ-being who was on his way to his earthly incarnation, overshadowing the whole nation of Israel. Ultimately, it was this that moved the history of one people for a while so clearly into the centre of human evolution, for it was then that Christ's incarnation as man found its first beginning in a nation. Lights such as the miracles of the age of the prophets shone from another, higher sphere into earthly history and allow us to look into metaphysical processes of history which occurred on a loftier level and bestowed a greater soul impulse upon terrestrial events.

It is not only the historical writings of the Old Testament that belong in the textual material of this volume. The poetic books such as the Psalms, the books of Solomon and particularly those of the prophets had to be included. Here, corresponding to the historical character of the whole work, only the anthroposophical aspect was taken into consideration. Our description expressly leaves room for a more detailed contemplation of the text of these books, which contains the greatest artistic, religious and spiritual wealth. In the historical presentation of this volume, all descriptive details had to be omitted in order to make it possible to present the great abundance of material in a perspicuous manner. The emphasis was on working out the larger spiritual-historical aspects. In order to do this, occasional repetitions could not be avoided, either due to reference to the two earlier books (*Genesis* and *Moses*) or because they served to underline and clarify something within the context of this book. Again, it is regrettable that in order not to allow the text to become too voluminous and so as to preserve its character as a purely positive description, it was impossible to develop the viewpoints presented here step by step in the form of a debate with the theories and 'results' of established theology. Since many readers are not familiar with the viewpoints of theology, they will not notice in many instances to what extent a position is taken here in regard to problems endlessly debated, how far from the views represented by orthodox theology lie the solutions that result from the inexhaustible directions from spiritual research given by Rudolf Steiner. But in the end it is more important to write for those readers who are led by a direct human and religious interest to the subjects dealt with here than to raise theological and scientific pretensions.

As far as the method of incorporating the anthroposophical suggestions and indications is concerned, the necessary remarks were already stated in the prefaces to the first two volumes. In this book there were fewer opportunities for verbatim quotes of explanations by Rudolf Steiner than there were in the descriptions of the age of Moses. We have, however, not refrained from quoting references which might pose difficulties of comprehension for those readers who are quite unfamiliar with anthroposophy (such as in the chapter on 'The Names of Solomon'). Care was taken to include aspects calling for prerequisite knowledge in such a way that it is possible for the reader to pass over them without losing the thread of the narration.

The Age of the First Kings

CHAPTER ONE

Humanization of Consciousness

Frequently formulated in such a way as to make comprehension difficult, the books of the Old Testament are not always to be read merely word for word. The reader can also turn their pages as if looking at a picture book. Then, one after the other, the great personalities appear, who, towering over their surroundings, seem to be embodiments of Providence's intentions for the human race. The lofty sequence of the archetypal wise men, the patriarchs, the leaders, the kings and the prophets pass before our eyes.

Following a widely-held view, people usually see nothing else but devout men of God in these figures who distinguish themselves from one another only in the manner and to the degree in which they prevailed in the trials and fluctuations brought about again and again in their obedience to God.

The Old Testament, however, when understood in a spiritual-historical way reveals a certain development in the succession of its figures. If Enoch, Abraham, David and Elijah were merely examples and models of devotion, they would be but variations of one theme, different expressions of the same soul content within an unchanged structure of human nature. In reality they are much more than that.

For the biblical world view, it is one of the most important presuppositions that in the course of the millennia human nature has passed step by step through basic transformations. But the element undergoing change does not lie visibly on the surface. The bearer of evolution is not the human body but the soul-spiritual element. It is the *human consciousness* that changes from one age to another, from one historical figure to the next. For a person who views the history of consciousness, upon the change in humanity's consciousness, the figures of the Old Covenant are no longer merely variations in a coincidental juxtaposition. They reveal themselves as progressive metamorphoses, as embodied stages of a path that is arranged in a meaningful way. Through such a view, the Old Testament is recognized in its everlasting value. Instead of being just a book of edification — something that it could only be in the sense of an outdated piety — instead of merely presenting the history of a people whose original charge has been fulfilled, it emerges as the greatest document of the history of consciousness, as a divine picture book of the stations of humankind's inner path up until the appearance of the Christian impulse.

The consciousness that indwells human nature was not a human one at the very beginning. Only after passing through many other stages of development was it possible for it to arrive at the human level. These, however, did not lead up to the human stage from a primitive, subhuman or even animal level. On the contrary, it has been the purpose of the preceding studies (*Genesis* and *Moses*) to demonstrate that the evolution of humanity's consciousness started on the divine-superhuman level. From there, it proceeded by degrees to the human stage.

At the beginning of the earthly history of humankind stands the divine *primal revelation.* The human soul was the stage of the gods' thinking before it became capable of developing a consciousness of its own. From higher spheres of existence, the consciousness of superhuman, divine beings extended into the still completely open, paradisal human nature which was as yet free of any tendency towards self-isolation. If the seething cosmic processes of earth's evolution had not taken hold of the human being at one point and sucked it into the transformations, which in the Bible are described mythologically as 'the Fall,' man would have remained an ever-resting being devoid of any history and development. He would have been nothing more than a vessel in which an alien light belonging to gods either burned or became extinguished. The expulsion from paradise brought about the history and evolution of the human being as a self-sustaining being that can attain a consciousness of his own as well.

Following this, with the figures of the archetypal wise men, the brief and condensed description of the Bible opens before our eyes the realms of an epoch of humankind that began with the end of the

Lemurian age and extended into the post-Atlantean age in which the human being was still in possession of an undiminished clairvoyant consciousness. This ancient clairvoyance of Atlantean humanity represented the first rudimentary stage for the development of a human and individual consciousness, for it was the result of the first diminution which the original paradisal-divine consciousness had undergone in the soul realm. The figures of the leaders who, like Enoch and Noah, towered over humankind as the succession of bearers of wisdom were, however, more like gods than men in so far as the content of their consciousness was concerned. It was no illusion if people were permeated by the feeling retaining a recollection of it in the later mythologies that at one time the gods had actually lived and worked in the flesh on the earth.

Although the age of the *patriarchs* was determined by a further diminution and darkening of the divine consciousness which extended into human beings, and figures like Abraham, Isaac and Jacob were representative of the first clear detachment and renunciation that humanity underwent in regard to the clairvoyant legacy, nevertheless, as we have seen in *Genesis*, the patriarchal period was still illuminated by the golden afterglow of primeval revelation. An atmosphere of superhuman, almost divine dignity still enfolded the figures of the age of the patriarchs all the way to Joseph. The time was not yet completely over when gods walked upon the earth and human beings could have direct communications with them. Abraham dined with divine beings in the grove of Mamre; Jacob struggled with them at the Jabbok ford. In the age which was determined by Moses, Joshua and the judges — the figures of the *leaders* in the actual sense — the humanization of consciousness took a decisive step forward. With the attainment of intellectual consciousness, which had merely flashed up distantly and had worked as a growing tendency in figures such as Abraham and Jacob, the first truly human ingredient of consciousness came into force. As we have described in *Moses*, Moses was the one in whom the actual transition took place from the last clairvoyance to the first head-thinking. He acquired access for all humankind to that soul province where consciousness can truly become human. Consciousness was already partially human and yet still partly divine. In Greek mythology, the age of the gods is followed by that of the heroes, the demigods. In the Old Testament, this corresponds to the age of the leaders. Samson, one of the last judges, is, after all, clearly recognizable as the Old Testament correspondence to the Greek hero and demigod, Hercules.

Only in the age that we now approach for the first time in our description, in the history of the first *kings* of Israel, the consciousness that indwelt the human soul arrived completely at human level. The human being became regent of his consciousness.

Still, at the beginning of the age of the kings, we are witnesses to a dramatic transition. In the being and destiny of Saul, the first king, we observe how a soul tempest took place. It is as if man could not tear himself away from the consciousness belonging to the sphere of gods and demigods to arrive at the human level without a flare-up and a mighty upheaval in his nature. Saul had an ecstatic character. Like the disciples of prophets, he could fall dervish-like into conditions of intoxication, he could explode in heroic as well as in diabolic fury, or he could fall back into the void of desperation. The human consciousness that had slipped away from the realms of the gods appeared initially unstable, abandoned to all the storms like a ship that has lost its rudder and is tossed up by the surging waves of the sea only to crash back into the depths.

The same soul forces revealed themselves in divine majesty and greatness in the ages of the wise men and the patriarchs owing to the fact that the primal revelation shone into them then, beginning with the age of Moses, they took on superhuman form in the leaders and heroes, and now show themselves to us in ecstatic arousal. The ecstasy of Saul was the metamorphosis of the ancient spiritual force.

David represents the real midpoint in the succession of the Old Covenant figures. A process of development which was the secret guiding principle of the preceding history reached its goal: the humanization of consciousness. David was the first among the great individuals of the Old Testament who was truly a *man*. The image of the 'Son of man' shone forth in him. The element that was of divine nature in Enoch, Noah, Abraham, Moses, Joshua and Samson, the nature that revolted ecstatically in Saul, became struggling human nature and blossomed forth from the striving soul as a thinking and artistic nature in David.

The humanization of consciousness signifies the humanization of history in general and it is only this that in fact implies the beginning of what we are accustomed today to call 'history.' As long as humankind was led by figures into whom there still extended the being and consciousness of gods, the destinies of gods mingled in the destinies of men. If we could undertake to describe what took place on earth in those ages, we would really be narrating myths. The representation of those periods can be a 'historical account' only if one is aware of its indispensable mythological infusion and knows how to distinguish between 'mythical' and actually 'historical' history. We can speak of history in the normal and customary sense only from the age of David onward. Much confusion was created by the fact that the biblical descriptions of the ages preceding David were read with the same concepts and measured with the same standards as were the reports about the later epochs. It is true that the biblical books themselves do not stress this distinction in their style or language. After having described the history of the gods in human images and scenes in a form of naive mythologizing, they now describe the human history by the same means. But they count on their readers to sense such differences, such shifts in the level of history when they study them. In an instinctive manner, this was indeed possible for a long time; it lasted as long as people had a direct relationship to the Bible as a holy scripture. Today, clear-cut concepts must be coined for what was formerly experienced instinctively, to make it possible to recognize and understand the converging points and decisive moments of evolution that are described in the Bible in an implied way only. Our descriptions up to now in the first two volumes were attempts to translate the mythical reports of the Bible into a historical view and thereby, nevertheless, to comprehend the development of humanity during the epochs of cosmic and mythological history in a historical manner. Now we have arrived at an age in regard to which an actual historical description results in a direct way.

In the two figures, Saul and David, a similar transition of consciousness took place as was foreshadowed in a half-mythological realm in Esau and Jacob. In both stories a man of commanding stature stood by the side of another who was of small size. Just as Esau towered over Jacob with his clumsy, almost gigantic bodily form, so did Saul, 'a head taller than all the people' (1Sam.9:2B), rise above the shepherd-youth, David. In their case, the biblical description really does refer to a difference in the size of their bodily form; in Esau's and

Jacob's case, the picture we confront does not relate primarily to the physical facts and therefore possesses a powerfully imaginative, myth- ical-symbolical suggestion. The duality of the twin-brothers, Esau and Jacob, brought a transition to our awareness which occurred within the supersensory human nature: the ancient condition of the human etheric body to which the superhuman clairvoyant contents of con- sciousness were tied came to an end because of a process of contrac- tion.[1] The etheric body no longer towered over the physical figure by extending into gigantic proportions. Instead, it fitted and adjusted itself increasingly to the forms and organs of the physical body. Thus, all the dull nebulous elements of human nature were replaced by clearly defined ones.

In Esau, the old condition of the etheric body still continued on and therefore the old dreamlike clairvoyance remained that was not yet man's own consciousness. Jacob was one of the first in whom the new condition of the etheric body began to develop, hence he was the clev- erer, more conscious one in the sense that he was more master over his consciousness. The physical difference of stature between Saul and David was like a recollection, in purely human history, of the mythical transition symbolized in the twins of the patriarchal age. In the soul- difference of the first two kings of Israel therefore, there lived an echo of the difference between two totally dissimilar structures of human nature; the afterglow of an ancient, superhuman consciousness flashed up in Saul, the newly self-aware human nature and consciousness emerged clearly in David.

The great Greek contemporary of David, the blind bard Homer, who, as did the Books of Moses, looked back into the epochs of myth- ical history, sketched a pair of figures in his epics in whom the same change becomes apparent as in the mythical pair, Esau and Jacob, and in the historical duality of Saul and David. They are the two heroes before Troy: Achilles and Odysseus. In the hero Achilles, a half godlike element was active and extended beyond the human dimension. The courage and fury that flared up in his soul did not allow human clar- ity and presence of mind to arise. He was not yet the ruler over his con- sciousness. Instead of this he still harboured cosmic and hierarchical powers of a higher sphere in his being. The humanization of con- sciousness was symbolized in Odysseus just as it was in Jacob where it began to develop mythically, and in David where it was realized historically. He was in possession of intelligence and presence of mind, he was master over his consciousness. Owing to this, however, he was no longer the bearer of divine-superhuman powers, but, like David, he was dependent on the soul forces that are the property of human nature itself. Human history was beginning.

CHAPTER TWO

The Historical Background

The time of the first kings of Israel falls into the last millennium of antiquity. What appearance did humanity's countenance have a thousand years before the birth of Christ, when the morning mists of the mythological realm were being dispersed and the historical view gained solid clarity?

The world of the second and third millennia had been dominated by the two great magical centres of civilization on the Nile and in Mesopotamia, the land of the two rivers, Euphrates and Tigris. Egypt and Babylonia had drawn humankind under their sovereign rule. Originally, it had been the spiritual life of the Egyptian and Mesopotamian mystery centres, flowing out of old, supernatural and superhuman sources, that had radiated in all directions. The two main streams had met in the middle, where, although of unassuming size, the Jordan region was situated between that of the Nile and that of the Euphrates and the Tigris. The wanderings of Abraham and Jacob were a last trace of the spiritual stream that came from the northeast and southwest and met in the middle. At the same time, they were the first indication of an impulse that was newly developing and had to come increasingly into contrast with the mighty maternal realms.

Then, around the turn to the second millennium, at the time of the biblical patriarchs, the life of these two magical temple cultures fell quickly into decadence. The ancient spirit faculties were gripped by a twilight of the gods. The greed for power on the part of the ruling dynasties came into being as a result of the decadence of the magic spiritual life. Instead of spiritual-cultural emissions of light, masses of armies bent on conquest issued forth from the old centres. The divine greatness of the spiritual life was coming to an end, and people therefore strove to enlarge the earthly-political sphere of power as much as possible. Empires arose that waged wars against each other. Again, this time fighting one against the other, Egypt and Babylonia met in the middle. Whenever they contended for power with each other, the land of the Jordan became the indispensable marching-route for the armies of both the kingdoms. Palestine frequently turned into the battlefield of military decisions that were carried out between the two opponents.

At the beginning of *Moses*, we have seen the important position represented in these developments by the battle of Megiddo in the plains of Galilee (1479 BC). Through Pharaoh Thutmose III, Egypt at that time became master over great parts of the already divided Babylonian and Chaldean Orient as well as the lands of the middle, Palestine and Syria. The age dawned of a far-extended Egyptian empire. Egypt enjoyed a glittering culmination of power and wealth when Amenophis IV, the young sun-king who called himself Akhenaten (around 1350 BC), recognized the spiritual decay behind the external splendour and attempted to ward it off. In the period that followed, Egypt's position as a world power did not remain on this dizzy high level. Calamities of war in the Asiatic East repeatedly tore new and larger gaps into the configuration of Egypt's rule and demands of tribute. Nevertheless, the territories of the middle, in particular the Jordan region, still remained for a long while a part of the kingdom of the Pharaohs. The four hundred years of the developing Israelite nation's sojourn in Egypt fell into an era when Palestine stood under Egyptian sovereignty. Even when, led by Moses, the Israelites re-established their domiciles in the land that had been chosen by the patriarchs, they remained subjects of Pharaoh. The 'Exodus from Egypt' had not brought them out of Egypt's jurisdiction.

The Egyptian rule over the land continued in the times of Joshua and the judges. But Egypt's decay progressed quickly at that time even in political respects. Without military action, Palestine and Syria achieved a certain independence inasmuch as Egypt's rule finally was in name only and could be considered almost nonexistent.

In Mesopotamia, decadence had already set in earlier than in Egypt.[1] In the age preceding Abraham and side by side with the esoteric stream in which the legacy of spirit-nearness, belonging to the pre-Babylonian Sumerian period, was perpetuated, a culture had arisen that turned increasingly to external affairs and soon fell prey to political machinations for power. This civilization was linked to the names Nimrod and Gilgamesh. An extraordinarily colourful mixing of nations and races was the basis of the origin of frequently changing political kingdoms and configurations of power. This is what could bring about the era in which the political aspirations of the more unified Egypt could be realized all the way to Babylonia. It was then that Palestine and Syria, which were formerly linked more to the world of Babylonia and Chaldea, were annexed to the sphere of Egyptian rule. But soon after the decline and deterioration of the Egyptian world power, a people began to emerge who until then had remained in the background of Mesopotamia. They had their centres not in the south of the Euphrates-Tigris region as did the Babylonian kingdoms, but north of there. They were the Assyrians.

Everything we know concerning the characteristics of the Assyrians bears an especially sharp imprint of will. The element of gentleness and light, still possessed by the ancient Sumerian-Babylonian world, yielded here to a fanatic, blind hardness and drive. Having originated from a mixture of mid-eastern and Semitic tribes, the Assyrians became the most fanatical nation of conquerors in the ancient world. By taking advantage of the decay and chaos in Mesopotamia as well as the unrest that reverberated in the thirteenth century BC from the coast of the Mediterranean Sea eastward through Asia Minor, they began their ascent. Before too long, the spectre of the Assyrian danger was to gain a certain influence even over the history of Syria and Israel. The day had to come when Assyria would reach out towards Egypt and would require the Syrian-Palestinian region as a zone of passage. But around the year 1000, the Assyrians were still involved in the preparations for attaining their position as a world power. Their first goal was to crush all the remaining factors of power in Mesopotamia itself. Palestine therefore had as yet nothing to fear from the direction of the Euphrates-Tigris region when it had grown away from the weakening tutelage of the Pharaoh's domain. For a certain length of time, the land of the middle had escaped the enveloping pinch of the two great empires. Without being swallowed up by the two streams that had threatened to overpower it, Palestine could come into its own, collecting its senses for the purpose of its own contribution to the future of humankind.

Thus, outwardly prior to the turn of the millennium, the political situation was a particularly advantageous one for the people of Israel. Equipped with the legacy of the ancient patriarchal age which had been illuminated by the nearness of God, having absolved the school of Egypt, matured through the trials and revelations of the desert journey and having arrived at its destination, Israel was now to find the transition from its years of learning and wandering to the age of its own creative activity.

But in the Palestinian region itself, significant problems still emerged for the Israelites. They needed these obstacles and dangers in order to find themselves without absorbing too many alien elements. After their immigration into the land under Joshua's leadership, in many instances they had had to share the land and cultivate it jointly with the Phoenician-Canaanite tribes still inhabiting the territory at that time. With their still delicate, young cultural impulses, the Israelites had to live amidst nations who shared in old, often overripe cultures. Would the Israelites be in a position to hold fast to their legacy and carry out their mission in a pure manner?

In this situation, it stood the people of Israel in good stead to have to resist violent attacks on the part of a neighbouring people. These were the Philistines. The counter-pressure of this opponent required that the Israelites make a forceful stand of their own. For this reason, they arrived at the point of establishing a state which even consolidated the twelve tribes into a unity in an organizational sense and thus blocked them off from the temptation of alien, cultural influences.

Who were the Philistines? Their appearance in the Jordan region, which in fact only then received the name Palestine (meaning 'land of the Philistines') from them, was the symptom of a process that was most significant in terms of world history. In the fourteenth and thirteenth pre-Christian centuries, an agitation, arising out of mysterious depths, passed through all the peoples who dwelled around the eastern shores of the Mediterranean Sea. This excitement expressed itself everywhere in great shifts of the population, called the 'Aegean migrations.' It is probably of no avail to seek for adequate external political and economic motives regarding these migrations of nations. The process resembled a wide-ranging earthquake, shifting masses of people. The ancient cultures of Asia including Egypt had inwardly reached an end. Now it was as if a new world were close to waking up and moving and stretching in its sleep. History's focal point slowly moved to Greece, where Europe was to be born. This brought unrest and movement to the Mediterranean region between Greece, Asia Minor and Palestine, including Crete and the other Aegean islands. A whole world shook itself into position for a new epoch of humanity.

This soul-quake affected early Greek history in the so-called Ionic and Doric migrations. Where they came to an end, the first fountain-heads of Greek life came into being around the Aegean Sea. In the mythical-historical traditions of the Greeks, the memory of this struggle and movement lived in the sagas of the journey of the Argonauts to Colchis, the land of the Golden Fleece, and in the voyage of the Greek kings against Troy.

The Israelites' wandering through the Sinai region under the guidance of Moses into the land of the Jordan was also a component of these manifold movements of peoples. Israel was not a part of antiquity; it was a part of the new humanity that was just shaking itself awake. At the same time when young Greece fought its way clear of Asia's tutelage before the gates of Troy, Israel, led by Moses, separated itself from Egypt.

In the course of the same wave of migrations, the Philistines also arrived at the coastal areas of the Jordan region. A few decades before Joshua led his people across the Jordan, they had set foot on the Holy Land. They had come from the north, the Israelites came from the south. It is assumed that they were formerly settled on Crete and the coastline of Asia Minor, that they were a seafaring people like the later Vikings and Normans of the north. From the beginning, not being a part of the Semitic race, they must have possessed traits related to the Phoenician people, for as soon as they had taken possession of the fertile coastal strips in southern Palestine, they had become submerged into the language and culture of the Canaanite-Phoenician world. We must not picture them as having been lacking in culture and barbaric as is frequently the case in connection with the imaginative description of the Bible concerning the clumsy Goliath-people. Like the Phoenicians, they must have been go-betweens of the old, over-ripe cultures of the Near East; therefore, they adjusted quickly to the language and customs of the Jordan land.

Although a people of the sea and the fertile plains of the coastal regions, the Philistines nevertheless strove to make themselves rulers over the tribal groups that inhabiting the adjoining mountainous country. Particularly since soon after them the Israelite tribes with their clearly discernible cultural and spiritual differences had arrived in the area and had settled in the hill country east of them, the Philistines intensified their attacks into the interior. With great vicissitude of fortune, the Israelites defended themselves against the ever-returning Philistines. If they succeeded in repelling them, they felt that they owed their success to their dedication towards the divine power that hovered over them. If they were defeated, they had to attribute the misfortune to the fact that they had slackened in their awareness of their spiritual missions.

Finally, in the first third of the eleventh century, the efforts of the Philistines, who had at their disposal well-armed troops supported by chariots for combat, succeeded in inflicting a decisive defeat upon the Israelite bands that had been assembled in a more half-hearted fashion. The ancient holy altar which had bestowed on the people the certainty of the presence of their god during the Sinai wandering, namely the ark of the Covenant, which had been carried at the head of the fighting troops, had fallen into the hands of the enemy who was in the process of achieving the victory. As a trophy, the holy ark now stood in the main temple of Dagon down at the Mediterranean shore in Ashdod, one of the main cities of the Philistines.

The Israelites felt completely forsaken by their god. The stern divine entity whom they followed had turned away from them because of the weakness of their souls. Nothing else remained for them but to humble themselves and pay tribute to the Philistines. A Philistine governor along with occupation troops established his seat in Gibeah, a castle-like site in the sphere of the ancient high-rising sanctuary of the heights of Gibeon which had played such an important role in the Joshua stories. From the Gibeonite lookout of Mizpah, in the northern proximity of Jerusalem, the Philistines could readily overlook the hills inhabited by the Israelites as well as their own green plains located below by the sea.

The success of the Philistines also encouraged other neighbouring tribes to advance against the Israelites who were still considered to be intruders. Israel's plight grew ever greater.

It was under these conditions that the establishment of the Israelite kingdom took place. It had proved impossible to maintain the people's awareness of their spiritual guiding force strongly and consciously enough for them to remain invigorated by divine strength. Now they had at least a visible embodiment of the guiding will before them. The disintegrating multiplicity of tribes could be gathered together into a unity with strong momentum. The age of Saul, the first king, was filled with the tumult of war. Israel's aim was not directed towards conquest but it was a matter of resistance against alien oppression and of the struggle to attain breathing room for self-development. When, shortly before the turn of the millennium (in 1004 BC), David became king in place of Saul, it was not long before conditions within the Holy Land became favourable for Israel as they were for all of the Holy Land within the Egyptian-Babylonian tensions. The sphere of peace and freedom was available to the people; the external prerequisite for their own cultural unfolding was fulfilled.

A peculiar, poetic magic emanates from the land of the Israelites around the age of David about the year 1000. It resembles the magic that surrounds young Greece of the same time. The two great bards of humanity, David and Homer, are contemporaries. The Davidian and the Homeric era fall into the same age.

The peaceful radiance of the early dawn of a new epoch of humankind, which is the link between the world of Homer and that of David, is above all connected with the form in which we have to picture the human habitations of that time in which the spiritual and cultural life was nurtured and able to blossom. The period of mighty architectural creations, experienced a thousand years earlier by Babylonia and Egypt, was long since over. In the ages of the ziggurats, the Babylonian tower-structures, and the Egyptian pyramids, cities had actually existed only in the sense of temple domains. The first great representatives of the power-impulse on the thrones of both the Pharaohs and the Babylonian kings had expanded the previously modest temples into magical, gigantic dimensions. Simultaneously holding the rank of the highest priest and of absolute ruler of the state, they considered their royal palaces, which were becoming more and more luxurious and monumental, as belonging inseparably to the temples. Around the area of the temple and the palace, a city then arose quite by itself, for a priesthood belonged with the temple and a royal household with the palace.

Along with the decline of Egypt's and Babylonia's former

grandeur, a long pause ensued in architectural growth and with it a completely new era of urban development. Regions totally lacking in architecture became centres of the new cultural life. Their spiritual activity had its sources in outwardly unassuming places embedded more in nature. Except for the Phoenician and Philistine coastal regions, the Holy Land was a land marked by the absence of architecture. Instead, it abounded in nature sanctuaries, in holy hills, grottos and groves.

The new development of cities that came to the foreground around the year 1000 could in no way compare in appearance and size to the magically towering cities of gods and kings of the ancient empires. A quietly radiating, soul-filled atmosphere and charm held sway here instead, the kind that emanates from the swaying, whispering tree tops in a temple garden. The hearts of the new cities beat where a spring was located in the outer as well as in the inner sense, in a secluded place of religious instruction and worship which was established in a grove or a park near a fountain. The Greek cities on the coast of Asia Minor such as Ephesus and Miletus, which represented the background of life for the creative genius of the great blind bard, Homer, must have been such settlements. Although they possessed an external side by virtue of their harbours, their heart and soul were the domains of the mysteries enveloped in the tranquil groves — the temple-sites from which, in time, developed the schools of poets and philosophers.

The germinal formation of cities during the era of David in the region of Israel must be pictured in a similar way. When he transferred his residence to Hebron, David did after all submerge himself in a world where the atmosphere was determined by the memory of the patriarchal age. The proximity of the grove of Mamre must have been as important at the time of the kings as it had been in Abraham's days. And when David built his castle in the holy stillness on Mount Zion in Jerusalem, the echoes of the hallowed primordial past surrounded him still more. Something of the music that resounds in the swaying trees of consecrated groves pervades the songs of Homer as well as the Psalms of David.

A new epoch of urban establishments, into which then played a strong architectonic impulse once again, appeared in Greece only when the Homeric era was superseded a few centuries later by that of

Pericles. At that time, there appeared in the foreground of culture what had matured in the quiet, concealed centres in a splendid unfolding of art in the areas of architecture, sculpture and drama. Athens, the city of the Muses, arose around the shining temple of the Acropolis; other cities received a similar appearance. The corresponding transition followed in Israel immediately after the age of David, when, under Solomon, the city of Jerusalem received a completely new appearance, now also determined by larger architectural structures. If the age of David corresponded to the contemporary Homeric era, the age of Solomon was an early correspondence to Greece's epoch of Pericles. This is how quickly the world-historical advantage of the moment which in the year 1000 had come to the aid of the Israelite development became culturally fruitful.

CHAPTER THREE

Samuel, the Seer

When the Israelite tribes had to settle down in the Holy Land and were also required to set themselves apart from the culture already in existence there, the age of the judges had been dominated by a spiritual life that arose sporadically here and there.[1] The good folk spirit of the people moved about. Whenever a danger became acute during confrontations with the alien tribal groups of the land in their vicinity, an individual belonging to one or another of the twelve tribes felt himself called upon by the genius of Israel. And as he placed himself at the head of the people as their leader, it was in fact the divinity itself that guided its people, making use of a human being as its instrument and bearer. As yet, no clear configuration of a social structure had come into being. The free spiritual activity of the judges made itself evident and found acknowledgment wherever it appeared. No rigid, organizational, political institutions were therefore required.

The grace-bestowing closeness of God also enkindled less obvious, lasting fires aside from the beacon-flames of the inspiring leading figures. Communities arose that resembled religious orders and, by means of certain religious and ascetic disciplines, nurtured a continuing tradition of spiritual faculties. During the study of the Samson sagas, we have encountered the Nazirite order, a monastic movement that appeared on the historical stage in Israel at that time.[2] The story of Jephthah's daughter referred us to the origin of an order of maidens who were dedicated to a life of piety, an order that may well have resembled that of the Vestal Virgins of the later Roman era.[3]

This special condition where spiritual powers worked freely into social life could not be of long duration. It was only a transitional stage in humankind's development which as a whole proceeded in towards extinction of the ancient spiritual forces, and towards the human being's becoming dependent on himself. Something of a farewell gesture of the divine realms played into the spirit-activities of the judges' period. The more the fiery inspirational stirrings subsided and failed to appear, the more the lack of a certain social order and consolidation became noticeable in processes of disintegration and chaos. At the same time, the defence against the attacking opponents, particularly the Philistines, became increasingly weaker and ineffective. Israel relied on the aid of the lightning flashes of the divinity when the ark of the Covenant was carried into battle at the head of the troops. But the beings of the divine world no longer continued to do for human beings what they had to learn to do on their own. This is how the prostration of the Israelite tribes under Philistine rule came about.

This crisis also made itself felt in the religious orders. During the period of the special spirit-activities, the Nazirite disciplines had permitted the outpouring of clairvoyant visionary forces and magic will in human souls in superhuman abundance. Samson had become judge and leader of the people because his Nazirite affiliation had turned him to a special extent into a bearer of miracles, a sun-hero.

The Nazirite movement had been established in order that the light of supersensory consciousness could at least survive among small groups during the ages of the loss of spirit power when, along with the hardening of the physical body, the ancient clairvoyance and the special spiritual talents would become extinguished. This notwithstanding, the age of deprivation did arise which all the people now came to experience. Even in the schools of the prophets that had formed among the Nazirites, it caused a certain perplexity. No longer did the ascetic exercises readily result in the souls being borne upward in tranquil peace into the light of vision. People thought of assisting this process by artificial means and worked themselves into something resembling intoxicated stimulation. The Canaanite-Philistine surroundings presented many examples of ecstatic, cultic disciplines. An infusion of ecstatic practices thus penetrated into the Nazirite schools of prophecy. By means of dervish-like dances and rhythmic music produced by drums and cymbals, people placed themselves into soul conditions in which, in place of the dimming peaceful vision, visionary experiences were attained at least. Ecstasy, the product of the diminution of ancient divine spirit faculties, haunted the life of Israel. Due to the external attacks and dangers, the fear that frequently flamed up in a sort of panic may have lent an element of special restlessness to the ecstatic endeavours of the disciples of prophecy.

But side by side with the ecstatic deviation of Naziritism, a quieter, more sober-minded expression of an inner life also existed in a few individuals. These were the seers to whom people turned for advice here and there in the land. They represented a stage before the prophets who were to shine forth some time later like bright stars from the whole of Israel. The biblical report, itself originating in that later age, clearly directs us to these figures: 'Formerly in Israel, when a man went to inquire of God, he said, "Come, let us go to the seer"; for he who is now called a prophet was formerly called a seer.' (1Sam.9:9).

Samuel belongs to these quiet messengers of the spirit as the greatest among them. His birth, like Samson's and later John the Baptist's, was surrounded by such miraculous dispensations of Providence that, like the others, he was destined by his parents to Naziritism and was educated according to the rule of that order (1Sam.1:11). His fate brought it about that as a young boy he became completely immersed in the priestly temple centre of Israel of that time. He was appointed as a temple servant to the high priest who conducted the sacred service of the ark of the Covenant in Shiloh before it fell into the hands of the Philistines. Decadence had already crept into the official religious centres of Israel. The sons of the high priest indulged in their egoism instead of devoting themselves unselfishly to the high office. The more brightly did the soul of young Samuel shine forth in the radiance of genuine spirit fulfilment, being privileged from early on to experience wondrous revelations. Through him, the site of the tabernacle once more became a source of living, generously streaming visionary revelation of God, even during the ignominious time when the tabernacle stood empty without the altar.

It was just at this time of need that the Israelites assigned the judgeship to Samuel, acknowledging him as the intercessor of the divine will. He stands in history as the last judge; his unassuming, wisdom-filled seership is the final inner fruit of consciousness belonging to the period of the judges. If we compare him to the great Nazirite who occupied the office of judge before him, we must say: the element that burst forth in a stormy, elemental manner in Samson has turned calm and is wisdom-imbued in Samuel. Seership is no longer a superhuman characteristic which overwhelms the human dimension of the soul, forcing it into gigantic magnitude; here, the gift of seership has moved much closer to the human soul faculties and has become related to the human intellect capable of insight. The gift of seership and thinking work hand in hand in Samuel. Through him, the Nazirite vision has progressed from Samson in the direction of becoming human.

In Samson, the spirit faculties that appeared like events of nature were to a very large extent tied to physical preconditions. A certain, quite loosened and permeable relationship between his physical body and the soul-spiritual part of his nature, brought about by the Nazirite disciplines, was the source of his soul being inhabited by divine forces. This is why these forces appear in the Bible's imaginative description symbolically as physical strength. The calmer seership of Samuel must definitely be pictured as being connected to certain conditions of nature. In him, however, the elemental spirit-fruitfulness of his own body receded in favour of the more tranquil spirit influences of surrounding nature. Directed by the spirituality holding sway in him, he was led into a landscape considered to be sacred because of the ethereal-spiritual atmosphere that ensouled it. The area around the mystery-heights of Gibeon became the stage of Samuel's activity. It is the Gibeonite hill country* that abounded in ancient holy high places in the north of Jerusalem. Joshua had still been able to relate to its spiritual traditions and it was here, in league with the Gibeonites, that he had obtained the sun victory over the hostile kings. The hill of Gibeon, which even today towers proudly over the landscape north of Jerusalem, the lookout of Mizpah, characterizing the region as it arises in conical form, was chosen by Samuel as the main meeting place of the people[†] after it had had this use occasionally in the earlier period of the judges (for example, Judg.10:17 and 21:1ff).

The other places of assembly, from where Samuel carried out his instruction of the people, were also primeval nature sanctuaries which had been consecrated anew because of important events in Israelite

---

* The names of the localities situated within the radius of the mountain of Gibeon are all designations of hill sanctuaries: Gibeon, Gibeah, Gebah means 'site that arises,' Ramah means 'holy height.'

† The hill, Nebi Samuil, held today to be that of Mizpah, is considered by most experts on Palestinian history (such as Gustaf Dalman) to be the ancient height of Gibeon. Its identity is difficult to perceive in the Bible for the reason that certain of its books (Judges and 1 Samuel) only use the term 'Mizpah,' while others (2 Samuel and 1 Kings) always use the name 'Gibeon.'[4]

history. In Bethel, an ancient sun-site, stood the menhir that had been erected by the patriarch Jacob at the location of his nocturnal vision.[5] In Gilgal by the Jordan river, far down near the Dead Sea, Joshua's stone circle still remained, the monument to divine intervention during the people's entry into the Promised Land. Ramah, the quiet, elevated home-site of the seer, where Rachel once lamented over the fate of her sons, must probably be pictured by us as having been embedded into the murmuring sounds of ancient, sacred groves.

With powerful matter-of-factness, Samuel still placed the nature sanctuaries of the land with their auric magic, deriving from the influences of divine forces in the kingdom of nature, into the service of his religious activities. As yet, the rejection of these sanctuaries by the later stream of the prophets and their struggle against them was far-off. Thus, when young Saul came to Samuel for the first time to seek his advice as a seer, Samuel was just about to climb up to the holy high place. The maidens, who were going out to draw water and whom Saul queried about the seer's abode, answered him: 'Make haste, he has this day come into our city, for there is going to be a sacrifice on the holy high place. You can still find him in the city before he goes up for the holy meal.' (1Sam.9:12fB).

The hill sanctuary of Gibeon, Mizpah, which had clearly been designated by Samuel as the central sanctuary, the 'great high place' (1Kings 3:4), possessed surroundings of a universal, manifold character. On the summit above towered the holy sun column, the menhir, 'the great stone which is in Gibeon' (2Sam.20:8); at the foot was the sacred pool (2Sam.2:13). Not too far away one could see the neighbouring high place rising up with the castle of Gibeah, where the Philistine governor had established his garrison. With Saul's consecration as king, Samuel's efforts to move the sanctuary of Gibeon into the central position came to a close, for even Saul himself had been born and had grown up in Gibeah in the region of the holy mountain.[6] Saul enlarged the castle of Gibeah to become his royal residence, and finally he even had the sacred temple tent, the tabernacle, transferred from Shiloh, assigning it its place on the sacred high place of Gibeon. There it remained until it was replaced by Solomon's Temple constructed on the rock of Moriah in Jerusalem. The ark of the Covenant itself, however, was not brought into the tabernacle when it was returned to the Israelites by the Philistine temples; until David brought it to Mount

Zion, it remained at a priestly site between Jerusalem and Gibeon, in Kiriath-jearim. The brazen altar of the burnt offering stood in front of the tabernacle on Mount Gibeon. Here, lit by Israelite priests, the columns of fire and smoke now arose for many decades on the very same spot where since ancient times the smoke of pre-Israelite sacrifices had arisen. During the more recent excavations, a rock-ledge altar was unearthed on the height of Mizpah that bears witness to this. Continuations of the Sinai fire, cultic reminiscences of the fire and smoke column of the long wandering, were experienced by those who brought offerings on the height of Gibeon. Although the fire and steam processes of the still evolving earth had gradually died down in the wider surroundings, the divine element which had once revealed itself in them had not yet vanished. It had only moved inward by a degree becoming outwardly invisible. When the memory of the earth's fire was celebrated in the fire of the offering, the divine was palpably close to the souls.

After the death of the seer, this 'great high place' gained yet a new significance, for Samuel was buried there. Just as the summit of Mount Hor, the sacred rocky height of Petra, became a place of pilgrimages because of Aaron's grave, so the Mizpah-height obtained its importance for pilgrims through the seer's grave, the last judge of Israel, even after the tabernacle with the altar of the burnt offering no longer stood there. Had not Mizpah become a 'lookout' in a new sense since the visionary soul of the seer hovered above it? The prophets who turned their backs on the sacred high places in later ages often described the visionary condition of their soul by means of the picture of the scout on a high lookout-point. They transferred the sanctuaries of the high places to within, they sought the inner Mizpah. A touch of this inner intensification was always experienced on Mizpah by the grave of Samuel. Even today, where a tower puts an emphasis on this elevated site, a reflection of the seer's peaceful radiance still exists, a light which enveloped the figure of Samuel like the early dawn of the subsequent age of the prophets that was to blossom forth in great abundance.

CHAPTER FOUR

The Origin of Kingship

Heavy, dark shadows fall upon the figure of Saul, the first king of Israel. Even if we disregard his personal weaknesses and errors and his chaotic nature, an objective note of tragedy has found its way through him into the history of the Old Covenant. The fact that the children of Israel desired a king at all is seen by the Bible as a forsaking of God. Kingship is, properly speaking, considered a further step in the Fall of humankind by the Bible. The shadow that beclouds Saul's figure is caused in the main by the wrong inherent in the origin of kingship itself.

Once before, in the middle of the age of the judges, it had almost come to the establishment of a hereditary kingship, namely when Abimelech, the son of Gideon, had had himself proclaimed king by the inhabitants of Shechem. At that time, there had been no prospect that Abimelech's kingship over one city could possibly be extended to a kingship over the people encompassing all the twelve tribes. This attempt, however, not only failed because of hopeless external circumstances, it was destined to fail because — as was sensed by all the people — it represented an unheard-of sacrilege against the will of God. For the free activity of the divine spirit which, here or there, chose a human being from one tribe or another as its instrument, would have been constrained into the fetters of an institution. The founding of a royal dynasty in which the succession does not go by spiritual sovereignty but by descent would have brought an end to the people's closeness to God. Therefore, the flames in which Abimelech perished were considered the direct expression of the chastising wrath of God.

But was not the appointment of Saul as king a repetition of Abimelech's sacrilege? Was it not inevitable that the divine anger would be provoked in the same manner?

The biblical description presents us here with an apparently insoluble contradiction. On the one hand, it lends expression to the basic feeling which views kingship as an apostasy against God. Yet, on the other, with strange frequency, it speaks of events that make it apparent that Saul's selection was the will of God. As if guided by invisible hands, three different, apparently unrelated, sequences of occurrences led directly to the same goal, namely, that Saul became king.

The first story seems to possess features of a fairy tale. In vain, young Saul searches for his father's asses and finally comes to Samuel, the seer, to ask for his advice. In his vision, Samuel has anticipated the fact that this young man would come to him, and in his spirit has recognized him to be the one destined for kingship. He is on his way to the sacrificial celebration on the holy summit and immediately takes along the surprised Saul, assigning to him a superior place at the round table, a select circle of thirty men. After the meal at the high place, the seer takes the young man along to his house for an instruction in the evening. Then he lets him sleep. The next morning, he secretly conducts the anointing of Saul as king and dismisses him, prophesying to him a series of significant events.

The second story moves more into the realm of history. The people want a king. Samuel finally gives in to their urging and summons the tribal representatives to the holy high place of Mizpah. Out of the twelve tribes, the tribe of Benjamin is chosen by casting lots, and from among the tribe the lot falls on Saul. When he is brought hither, he stands head and shoulders above the others. In a wondrous manner, the lot has fallen on the one who, without anybody knowing of it, has already been anointed king by Samuel.

The third story finally leads us completely into the arena of outer events. The threat of war is in the air. The Ammonites are besieging the friendly city of Jabesh in Gilead, east of the Jordan. Messengers come and ask for Israel's assistance. Saul receives tidings of this just as he returns home from the field with the oxen. Before the eyes of the people he slaughters two of the animals and has the freshly cut pieces sent by messengers to all the tribes in order to call them to arms. Once more, the spirit miracle of the age of the judges is repeated in Saul: the spark of divine genius is enkindled in him. The spirit itself takes hold of him, makes him into an instrument of its activity and places him at the head of the quickly gathering army. After Saul has led his people to victory with the flame of enthusiasm, he is proclaimed king by all the people at the stone circle of Gilgal.

Three times, out of the supersensory sphere, the same will becomes manifest: Samuel's vision leads to a secret anointing; the lot of the gathering of the people at Mizpah falls upon Saul; and the spiritual effect, which once more interferes directly in history, makes use of the twice destined one as its instrument. How can the biblical books still say that the shadow of divine objection has fallen upon the origin of kingship?

The theology of the past decades, which had no feeling for the fact that the biblical scriptures are in the habit of pointing to deeper, more mysterious levels, especially by means of the language of contradictions, believed that it had to diagnose each apparent inconsistency in the biblical description as a confluence of different source-documents. Finally, differentiating the sources became such an obsession that in search for contradictions it was thought that breaks were discovered in the traditional texts where they simply did not exist. In the case of the three stories about Saul's selection as king, theologians were immediately ready to 'separate the sources,' for it was believed that each of the three narratives would have been sufficient by itself. It was therefore determined that two or three older tales must have been combined by a later compiler of texts. Now, as in all these cases, it makes no sense that only the later editor of the scriptures should have been the one who was not bothered by the 'contradictions' and 'discrepancies,' in this instance the superfluous threefoldness. If *he* considered something meaningful that is held to be contradictory by today's theologian, why should not those from whom the biblical texts originated in the first place already have thought so? Owing to the superficial theory of source-differentiation, the most interesting riddles of the biblical description of history remain unsolved, riddles through which the Bible itself points to more profound depths.

The threefoldness of the stories referring to the establishment of the Israelite kingship can reveal that something had happened here where the esoteric element that ran its course in the concealed background was in accord with the exoteric event of the historical foreground. The first story possesses fairy-tale quality, in allowing a glimpse into the hidden mystery-background of the occurrence. The

Bible can report on what took place esoterically only in an imaginative, symbolical manner. It presents soul developments that grew out of a concealed discipleship by enveloping them in pictures resembling fairy tales.

Regardless of whether external occurrences are *also* referred to in passing by these pictures, the tale of young Saul, who came to Samuel during the search for his father's asses and was then anointed king, conceals the fact that following a search and a development which were already active in his soul the seer accepted the young man as his disciple and led him through certain steps of an inner path. Samuel acted like the hierophants and temple sages of old who chose from among the people certain young persons who appeared suitable to their clairvoyant vision and drew them into discipleship and the initiation practices of their mystery centres. If the first of the three stories was supposed to show that Saul was not without spiritual preparation and schooling when he was chosen to be king by the people, the third story demonstrates that the choice of the people was verified. The folk genius acknowledged the decision of human beings by settling as a flame of enthusiasm upon the one who, seemingly, had been chosen by the people.

The duplications of the biblical report, which at first glance appear superfluous, in reality indicate an important turning point in the historical development, not only of the nation of Israel but of all humanity. We shall see that in David's appointment to kingship a precisely corresponding threefoldness of stories returns. A world-historical paradox becomes reality: human beings establish an institution which basically signifies a further step in the Fall, in the defection from God. And yet, such diverse co-operation on the part of Providence takes place on the occasion of this innovation that one is inclined to speak of a very special, wondrous dispensation of Providence. How could the origin of kingship be a wrong to the divine world and yet at the same time be accompanied by so many clear signs of interaction on the part of the divine powers?

The establishment of kingship was a tragedy; it increased the darkness of distance from God. In Saul's age, however, it had at the same time become a historical necessity which the powers of Providence had to admit. The time was over when the destinies of nations could stand under direct divine guidance. The inauguration of a hereditary earthly leadership, which would have been a desecration, a presumption in the age of Abimelech, was now a demand of the times.

Humanity continued on its path of terrestrial hardening, not through the evil of individual persons but because it was proceeding further in the contraction of their being, a process that had begun with the expulsion from paradise. The human being who was shrinking to his earthly form was increasingly unable to allow the activities of a higher divine world to influence his soul. More and more, he was left to his own devices, but thereby he could also reach individual human self-awareness and freedom.

After human beings in general had long since entered upon the development which separated them from the higher worlds and prepared them for self-awareness, the divine powers could still intervene directly for some time in the tribal and folk communities by means of individual, select leaders. Now this too came to an end. People now had to continue with what gods had accomplished until then. It was therefore even more important that those individuals, to whom fell the task of leadership, remained overshadowed by the light of benevolence and harmony that shone down upon them from the departed sphere of the gods. The fact that this could continue in the case of Saul can be discerned from the support by Providence which was bestowed on humankind at the turning point where it had to take yet another step away from divine existence.

CHAPTER FIVE

Saul, the King

Saul was not without the radiance that proceeds from the royal dignity that is in harmony with the will of the divine world. The magic of wholeness that surrounds a person when the genius of the greater communal whole, the angel of the people, hovers over him and enlightens him, was not lacking in the first king of Israel. Saul, however, was actually enveloped only by the very first beginning of the cloudless brightness of such kingship by the grace of God, when, through the assistance of the seer, the higher task descended upon him. Soon afterwards, the shadow of tragic necessity burdened Saul's kingship.

Saul could be the first, only because he was a human being marked by the character of transition. Only because his being also had roots in the past could he be the bridge to a new shore of the historical development.

Saul was not a person of intellectual insight. The soul forces in his nature resembled the unpredictability of the weather and the raging of the elements. The self, the inner regent of the soul's stirrings and of consciousness, had not fully awakened in him. The outer world extended into his soul and made it a stage of emotions that billowed up like the storm-tossed sea and the blazing fire. The external spiritual world also continued on into Saul's soul. He still possessed the ancient soul constitution which does not capture the supersensory element of human nature within rigid physical contours but preserves for it a certain openness in all directions. When the roaring inner tempest took hold of his soul, Saul could become the bearer and instrument of spiritual powers that were present in his vicinity. But he was born into an age of spiritual ebb-tide when the divine beings were withdrawing from human beings and were leaving them alone. In such an age, souls that resemble Saul's fare like a fish that lies twitching on the shore because the receding tide has deprived it of its element.

The Nazirite prophet-disciples resorted to the means of ecstatic soul intensification. No wonder that when Saul encountered a number of them he allowed himself to be drawn into their visionary intoxication.

After Samuel sent him back into the world following his instruction and anointing, Saul's soul was gripped for the first time by the ecstasy of the prophet-disciples. This was also part of the predictions that the seer had made to him as he departed. Samuel indicated to him that through being drawn into that ecstatic spiritual life, his soul would be transformed decisively:

> After that you shall come to the mountain of the Lord where
> there is a garrison of the Philistines (Gibeah at Mount Gibeon).
> And when you enter the city, you will meet a band of prophets
> coming down from the holy high place. Lyre, tambourine, flute
> and harp will be carried ahead of them, and they will speak
> out of ecstatic vision. And the spirit of Yahweh will come upon
> you also, and you shall prophesy like them. Thereby you will
> be turned into another man. (1Sam.10:5f*B*)

Samuel's prediction came true. When Saul met the band of prophets at the border of his home territory, he was carried along by their visionary rapture and, like them, he could speak out of the spirit. How was this possible since the Nazirite training, which had made the others capable of this form of experience, was, after all, unknown to him? As if by destiny, the ancient soul forces in Saul had developed in naive unawareness to a point where he could bring them to fruition by means of a brief schooling. Now people were astonished that Saul was suddenly counted among the prophets and could conjure forth from his soul the same things (1Sam.10:11ff).

The ecstatic experience resembling intoxication that is not directed by the self, need not always bear a person upwards into pure, spiritual heights. Herein lies its ambiguity. It can also cause a fall into dark, obscure and demeaning depths. And the ecstatic element remained alive in Saul in its dark, shameful or demonic form when the radiance of kingship had departed once again from him.

In later times, when Saul's soul was again and again brought to a state of vehement rage, particularly through David's presence, the ecstatic condition took hold of him once in an especially grotesque way. David had fled from Saul's persecutions to Samuel who was staying in Ramah with his disciples. When Saul had discovered David's whereabouts, he dispatched messengers who were to fetch him. No sooner had they entered the sphere of the seer's school and influence, however, they became infected by the ecstasy of the disciples of the seer and could not help participating in their frenzied, rhythmic dance movements. Saul sent messengers after messengers, but they all succumbed to the same suggestive spell. Finally, Saul himself made his way there, but before he had quite reached the boundaries of Ramah, the ecstatic condition overcame him. Speaking in visionary rapture, he arrived at Samuel's abode. In his ravings, he stripped off the clothes from his body, and sank down naked and speaking in tongues at the feet of the seer where David had found refuge (1Sam.19:18–24), a condition that lasted all that day and the following night. The pursuer had become a helpless man whose own experience humiliated him most grievously before the one he was pursuing.

Incessantly, the land resounded with the din of war as long as Saul was king. One cannot picture Saul as a king who leads his people in a time of rest and peace to the heights of truth, beauty and fraternal sentiment. An age without great upheavals could only have produced lame ill-humour in him. Saul was not a sanguine person who responds to joy, he was a choleric. The magic key to his soul was rage: either the noble anger in which, enkindled by opposition, the stormy will to do good flamed up, or the sinister fury fed by selfishness.

In particular, Saul had to wage defensive wars in which Samson's battles against the Philistines were continued. The Philistines were Goliath-people. Because of their ancient soul nature, they possessed a dully-gigantic element in their being. Magic, ecstatic faculties dominated their lives, faculties which were no longer irradiated by the sanctity of the old consciousness of the gods but contained a gloomy, eerie character. As a bearer of divine-cosmic forces, Samson also towered above human stature and because of it was equal to the Goliath element of the Philistines. In him, the son of the sun, however, the superhuman nature was illuminated by the light of spirit-consciousness. With divine authority of spirit, he overcame the dim, giantlike soul nature of the Philistines although he met his death that way. Saul was directly related to the Philistines. In his ecstatic temperament, he was a giant of rage — something of which his bodily size was only an external symbol — and he bore an inner Goliath-element within himself. If he was able to withstand the Philistines, it was due less to his difference than to his resemblance to them. In fact, it was a constant swaying struggle until Saul met his death in the battle against the Philistines when, wounded and desperate, he plunged upon his own sword.

In the battles that he had to lead, it soon came about that Saul inwardly forfeited the kingship because of the ambiguity of his nature. Under the advice of Samuel, he moved against the Amalekites. The seer had revealed to him that the divine will demanded the total extermination of the enemy who had evidently fallen into the worst black-magical degeneration. Saul achieved a complete victory but he was not obedient to the divine command since he spared Agag, the hostile king, with all that appeared useful to him of the latter's property.

In his spirit, Samuel beheld the blazing fire of the divine wrath. For one whole night, he struggled to comprehend the will of God clearly. Had the attempt which the spiritual world made when it permitted the kingship failed already? As the messenger of wrath, he had to come before Saul and proclaim to him that God had taken from him the charge of the kingship. Before Saul's eyes, the seer hewed the vanquished Agag into pieces with his sword. In Saul himself, a tragic transformation took place: 'Now the Spirit of Yahweh departed from Saul, and an evil spirit began to torment him ceaselessly' (1Sam.16:14B).

The significance of this biblical report, which is interspersed considerably with imaginative elements, remains incomprehensible without penetrating the external events to behold what took place in the soul sphere. At the outset of his kingship, gripped by the fire of the spirit, Saul had overpowered a hostile king, namely Nahash, the Ammonite. Nahash means, 'the serpent.' The name of this king points to the spiritual direction that existed in the Ammonite nation. We have seen[1] that the ancient world designated the atavistic clairvoyant forces with the symbol of the serpent; the forces which had remained from the age when the etheric body extended serpent-like beyond the head and the feet of the physical body and thus could form the basis of a dreamy vision. Outwardly as well as inwardly, Saul could readily master the forces of the serpent, because he himself had passed beyond this point in his development.

He faced the world of Agag, the Amalekite, in a different manner. Agag means 'the giant.' It was possible for Saul to vanquish King Agag outwardly, but this did not mean that he had overcome the Agag element, the Goliath nature of his own being. In the battle against the Amalekites, which had been waged following the divine command, Saul was supposed to have conquered the giant in himself. He was unsuccessful in this. Agag's world somehow fascinated him, because he felt himself related to it. He was unable to separate himself in his own mind from the element of the past which extended into him as the 'shadow of the giant;'[2] this is the reason why he was not ready for a total annihilation of Agag's world. Saul was not able to take the step of self-effacement, of renouncing the ancient ecstatic soul intensification, which, although it would have made him more insignificant in his conduct, would have allowed him to enjoy inner harmony. Samuel, therefore, did not confront Saul with his devastating judgment because of outward disobedience. As he pronounced the ban against him that signified the loss of his royal office, Samuel made Saul realize that he had not passed an important test. Only if he had overcome the giant in his soul, would Saul have remained illumined by the genius of the people. With the dismembering of Agag, Samuel outwardly placed a picture before Saul of the task that had inwardly remained unsolved.

The point where Saul foundered has caused much misfortune in the history of humankind. He could only have achieved the true greatness demanded of royal dignity if he had renounced what he bore in his personal nature of ancient faculties. Instead, he allowed himself to be misled by his sovereign stature to proud self-aggrandizement. This is the reason why, in the figure of Saul, and at the first beginning of kingship, an archetype of Caesarean deviation, which is the degenerate opposite of kingship, is found in the history of the Old Covenant. The Bible points to the inner formula of Caesarean aberration when it says that the good, divine spirit had abandoned Saul and that an evil spirit had gained entrance into him, causing havoc. A true king is the bearer and servant of the good genius of his people; one who has degenerated to a Caesar has made himself into a vessel for the demon of the nation. Prior to the war against the Amalekites, Saul's soul could blaze in holy wrath and fervid activity. Afterwards, we see it erupt in demonic fury that is mixed with egotistical fear. Scenes come before us as if they were previews of the Roman Caesars' period of insanity. When, driven by jealousy and fear to excesses of brutality, Saul hurled his spear against David, we feel as if we are confronting a picture of the Caesarean insanity of a Caligula. And we can ask, when he, who was increasingly falling prey to sinister darkness, who, out of fear of what they might proclaim to him, had driven all prophets and sooth-sayers out of the land, stole away at night to the sibyl of Endor: was this really Saul or was it Nero who descended at the nocturnal hour to the grotto of the Cumaean sibyl to receive spiritual guidance from her? When Nero felt that his end was coming, he too gave orders to a slave to kill him with a sword. Nero's order was carried out; Saul's armour-bearer, however, refused, and the first of the Israelite kings therefore fell upon his sword himself, overcome by the dark abyss of fear.

As Rudolf Steiner has pointed out,[3] the demonic mental derange-ment in the Caesars of Rome came about because, misusing their power, they obtained initiation into decadent mysteries by force. Correct training and transformation of self would have led to an initi-ation, whereby the soul would have been capable of being the bearer of benevolent divine forces. Coerced initiation had to lead to demonic possession and insanity.

The biblical description of sparing Agag and his most valuable pos-sessions may perhaps conceal the fact that Saul allowed the hostile king to live in order to gain access through him to the mysteries of the Amalekites. The abnormal shift amounting to demonic derangement which henceforth led to Samuel's strict avoidance of him would become historically comprehensible by a degree.

The Saul tragedy also drew dark clouds around the summit of the ancient holy height of Gibeon. It was no coincidence but a benevolent spiritual concurrence that in Saul a human being had been elevated to the royal throne who, by virtue of birth and background, belonged to the ancient sun-height. When Saul had been king for one year, his son Jonathan was able to defeat the foreign occupying troops settled in Gibeah east of the Gibeon mountain in the shifting battles against the Philistines, thus purifying the area around Gibeon from Philistine ignominy. From then on, Saul's royal residence stood in Gibeah. When

Saul's demonic possession began, he found himself in essential contradiction to the traditions of the area — held holy by Samuel as well — in the confines of which he dwelt. The Gibeonites, still representing a small free state within the territory of the Israelite tribes thanks to the old defence agreement concluded with them by Joshua, continued the mystery traditions of the site. They appear clearly to have sensed the contradiction that increasingly emerged in Saul's nature. Saul also interfered directly in their protected rights. Perhaps he was misled by his Caesarean mania to gain access to the ancient Amorite Gibeon-mysteries by means of force and the shedding of blood.

Later this came to light. When a famine broke out towards the end of David's reign, and David inquired after the inner reason for it through questioning the oracle, he received the answer that the guilt incurred by Saul in regard to the Gibeonites had not yet been atoned for. The puzzling reference by the oracle to the 'house of blood in Gibeon,' which still attested the violation of the Joshua agreement by Saul, moved David to grant the demand of the Gibeonites: seven descendants of Saul had to forfeit their lives as atonement for the old guilt (2Sam.21).

When David had reason to believe that the ancient wrong had been compensated, he sent messengers to Jabesh in the eastern Jordan land where Saul and Jonathan lay buried. He asked for the mortal remains of the first king and his first-born. He then had his former persecutor and his best friend buried side by side at Gibeon in the hereditary tomb of the family of the House of Benjamin from whom Saul had descended. Henceforth, high up on the summit of the holy mountain, the seer rested in his grave and nearby, at the site where the royal castle had stood, rested the first king. The holy heights of Jerusalem had already begun to replace the height of Gibeon. The ark of the Covenant stood on Mount Zion, and the foundation stone for the Temple was laid on the rocky plateau of Moriah.

CHAPTER SIX

The Young David:
Shepherd, Minstrel, Hero

The transition from the first to the second king of Israel signifies a much greater change than is normally sensed in reading the biblical story. Even the fact that the barely established office of royalty passed over to another tribe although Saul was not without descendants, poses a difficult historical riddle. More than that: with David a completely new stream of humanity moved into the foreground of history.

The great historical turn originated in Samuel's soul. The seer was led to a decisive spiritual experience. We find that this is only hinted at; the description conceals rather than emphasizes it. In order to recognize it clearly, we must take into consideration that the Bible generally recounts supersensory experiences very imperceptibly in the form of conversations between two people (1Sam.16:1–3).

Through Saul's aberration and failure, Samuel found himself in a torturous quandary. Having withdrawn himself from the office of judge, he had pursued the establishment of kingship in accord with the will of the spiritual world, as he was justified in believing. There existed no other means of restraining the chaotic disintegration of the people and securing their future. The attempt had failed. The quick degeneration of kingship into Caesarean mania threatened to lead into far worse chaos and a much faster decline than the lack of leadership which was due to the withdrawal of the spirit that had permeated the age of the judges. The seer's anxiety for the future of Israel was not, however, concerned only with the external welfare of the people. It reached far beyond into the tapestry of cosmic secrets. As a Nazirite, Samuel was deeply imbued with the holiest task of the people: to help bring about the eventual incarnation of the Messiah, the divine being that was in the process of descending to earth. Along with the future of his people, the Messianic future of all humankind was at stake.

The sorrow-filled focus upon the Messianic secret elicited a vision in Samuel's soul which showed him a way out of the tragic dilemma. He felt himself dispatched by the divine will itself to the tribe and house from which the divine-human being was one day to receive its earthly body. He realized: henceforth, in the external affairs of state as well, the Messianic lineage itself was supposed to lead the people towards their future. At the same time, the Messianic vision directed Samuel's steps to the paradisal, lovely island in the midst of the desert which since time immemorial had been graced by an early radiance of the divine future of humanity, namely to Bethlehem.

Samuel beheld that the history of Israel was to take a decisive turn; it was to be a Messianic turn. From here onwards, as in the days of the patriarchs, the kings were once again to be the fathers of the Messianic lineage. A human being was to continue the task, left unfulfilled by Saul, in whom something like an earthly reflection could be discerned of the divine being that was descending from heaven.

In Bethlehem, Samuel entered the house of Jesse whose name itself is like a prophecy: Jesse is the same word as Joshua or Jesus. Belonging to the tribe of Judah, Jesse was perplexed by the appearance of the seer. He did not know what the latter's coming signified and yet was filled with premonitions of significant events. Perhaps he also recalled the break between Saul and Samuel that had become public knowledge and feared that something was imminent whereby the wrath of the king could turn against him too.

Samuel invited Jesse and his sons to participate with him in a solemn sacrifice. He knew that during the execution of the sacrifice the light-signal of divine predestination would reveal itself in the soul configuration of one of the sons. The seer kept silent about the fact that the one whom he would choose would be destined for kingship. He left it open whether he merely wanted to draw him into his circle of disciples or whether he had special plans for him. One son after the other went up to the altar to offer up his sacrifice; the verification on the part of the spirit failed to materialize. Finally, so the Bible describes it, Jesse had to admit that he had one other son who was out in the pasture as a shepherd. David was fetched and when he was ready to give his offering, the light of the Messianic future shone forth above him. As a sign of having been chosen, Samuel poured the sacred oil on the head of the young shepherd. By virtue of the seer's silent action, the youth stood in the midst of his family members as the 'anointed one' — the Hebrew term 'Messiah' means the 'anointed one.' Samuel left the people of Bethlehem without an explanation for what he had done. Wordlessly, he departed to go back to his home. Everybody realized that a great future had been predicted for the youth, but nobody could guess what destiny had in store for him. In a strange way, David was changed. It was as if he had awakened from a deep sleep; a higher, spiritual keenness of mind moved into his soul (1Sam.16:13).

At a divine behest, Samuel had sown a seed, had enkindled a new spark of life. Now he had to stand aside, although his heart beat in tense expectation, and let destiny take its course. He could be confident that the one whom he had anointed would prove himself if he were the right one and would follow the beckoning call of his genius. A new tribe, a new branch of humanity, which, so far as external political life was concerned, still lived in the hidden background, had secretly been destined as the bearer of the future. Now it would be up to him whether he would be able to fit into the causalities of the foreground.

To start with, no outward achievements were demanded of David. If it had only been a matter of those, there would have been no reason for Saul, a member of the tribe of Benjamin, to be replaced by another of the same tribe, for Saul had certainly not been lacking in outward achievements. The new leader of the people had to be of a different soul nature and spirit. A time of probation had to ensue. Only in this manner could David move into the position intended for him in an external sense as well.

As the Bible now describes the sequence of soul transformations and soul achievements that young David had to undergo, it resorts to a picturesque, half imaginative form of representation. A poetic suggestion of fairy tales thereby slips into the stories. It is as if, out of the treasure of fairy tales of all the nations, we were told once again of the shepherd youth who, in order to win the princess for himself, fulfils all the tasks that are posed to him; who, after he has vanquished the giant and many other opponents, finally becomes king himself. Humankind's history once more starts from the very beginning in an inconspicuous manner, passing again through the land of childhood where fairy tales originate.

The miracle of a quiet new beginning had as its stage a landscape perfectly in accordance with its nature. External and inward elements were in the purest harmony. We are transposed into the cosmic childlikeness of the pastoral meadows of Bethlehem. Since distant ages a radiance overshone Bethlehem. When, owing to universal conflagrations and fire catastrophes ending with the destruction of Sodom and Gomorrah, the Desert of Judah and the world of the Dead Sea came into being — a landscape of the Fall and of death, Bethlehem with its sphere of influence was spared like a sun-island pleasing to God.[1] It was as if the memory of the lost paradise was to remain alive there in a special, concrete manner, evoking at the same time the longing for its restoration by the Messiah. In this way, the echo of paradise and the presentiment of the Messianic future were interwoven from ancient times in Bethlehem. On the green shepherds' meadows of Bethlehem's slopes, on the golden wheat fields in the 'House of Bread,' the Arcadian innocence of soul and the blissful assurance of divine promise came together. It was the piety of the shepherds lasting all the way to the night of Christmas, when the glory of the angelic choirs appeared to them.

Bethlehem was always virginal and maternal at the same time. It was virginal because of the reflected cosmic radiance of innocence; it was maternal because of the love-filled longing for the divine child that was to be born there. In Ruth, the gleaner, the Mary-secret of the Bethlehem landscape had taken on form. The golden Messianic Bethlehem-thread in the tapestry of the Israelite folk history had become visible in her unassuming destiny.[2]

The shepherd-childhood of David took place in exactly the same locality as did the Christmas story of the shepherds and the angels. At the same time, it was most closely connected with the still recent memory of the pious, loving soul of Ruth whose grandson was Jesse, David's father.

The devout picture of shepherdhood has accompanied the history of Israel since its mythical beginnings. David is described to us as a shepherd, as was Abraham and Moses. But in each epoch, the same picture is an expression of a different historic set of facts. In the case of Abraham and the other patriarchs, the description reaches furthest beyond external reality. The picture is transparent for a lofty consecration and office deriving from divine, superhuman sources. When mention is made of shepherds in that mythical age, priests are referred to who are at the same time the kings of the people who are led by them. Although the group of people, taken out of the Chaldean-Babylonian sphere by Abraham, may have been small in numbers, we still have to picture him as a priest-king.

Then, in the age and figure of Moses, a transformation of the shepherd motif occurs. As the son of the house of Pharaoh, Moses had at first a share in royal dignity. Only when he turned away from Egypt and the splendour of the court, the world of shepherdhood took him in. The king became a shepherd. Again, no pastoral activity in the outer sense is referred to. The picture conceals Moses' entrance into the obscure priestly realm of Jethro, where, for forty long years, he was prepared for his great mission of leadership.

Abraham was both shepherd and king. Moses was a king and subsequently became a shepherd. David was first a shepherd and then became king.

In David's youth, which fell into the age when myth transformed into history, a physical realization of the formerly imaginative, supersensory picture took place. The symbol became earthly reality and in Bethlehem entered upon the physical plane. For this very reason, the shepherd-youth of David was still surrounded by an unearthly magic. Lights of the holy ancient past condensed into an outwardly insignificant destiny which nevertheless was to become the starting-point of a great development.

People paid little attention to the shepherd youth. Even his father overlooked him when he presented his sons to the seer. Jesse did not love his youngest son as much as Jacob loved Joseph. With that much greater love and expectation, the beings of a higher world must have looked down upon the youngster who tended the herds of his father in the meadows of Bethlehem. Thus, miracles were woven into the early experiences of David. Outer events took place which appear like fairy tales, because they were nothing else but revelations of the changes that occurred in David's soul with the help of the angelic realms. If David could later relate how he had overpowered the lion and the bear that threatened his flocks, he basically spoke of how he was brought to an awareness of the power which is lord and victor in the human being over the lower nature.

What Samuel had done to the youth with his mysterious anointing was like the pulling aside of a curtain, the disenchantment and awakening of a slumbering soul. Henceforth, in a variety of ways, miracles of the higher human nature blossomed forth in David. Especially one aspect of this was that David revealed himself as a minstrel and player of the harp.

Like the other shepherds, David captured the melodies indwelling the pastoral fields with his flute and shawm. But in him, this produced a high form of individual artistry which finally made him become the singer of the Psalms, the worthy contemporary of Homer.

His harp-playing became the reason for David to emerge from the obscurity of a shepherd's life into the world. Since the break with Samuel, the soul of Saul, the king, was subject to eerie moods and rages. Periods of dull apathy alternated with wild fits of raving madness. The people around him were helpless in the face of these instances of possession that remained after the wastage of prophetic ecstasy. They hit upon the idea to counter the madness of the king, when it threatened to erupt, with the soothing magic of music and they sought for a harpist.

David's name was mentioned, who in his tranquil pastoral world had nevertheless drawn people's attention to himself because of his singing. This was how the shepherd of Bethlehem came to the royal court at Gibeah. Every time the sinister clouds of mental tempest arose in Saul's soul, he was fetched. Just as Orpheus, the bard, turned the wild beasts surrounding him into a tame flock with the sound of his instrument in immemorial ages, so David calmed the wild element in Saul's soul with the magic of musical sound.

What feelings must have moved the seer Samuel in his seclusion as he watched the course of events! Without his having had a hand in the matter, guided by invisible hands, the destinies moved towards each other in the direction of the goal, envisioned and hoped for by him. Since David had been led into the vicinity of the king, the bridge to kingship for the tribe of Judah had come into being without anybody being able to realize it except the seer. But the soothing effects of the harmonies were not always a match for Saul's demonic rage. Then there were occasions when the huge king hurled his mighty spear against the youngster. And if David had not evaded it watchfully, so that the spear penetrated the wall, quivering, the incipient Messianic beginning of Israel would have been aborted.

In successfully banishing the demon of Saul with his playing on the harp, David experienced anew the power within himself that vanquishes the lower nature as if under a higher assistance. It proved itself as a power that orders and harmonizes. David's harp had the opposite effect of Joshua's trumpets: The latter caused the world of Jericho to fall, bringing the soul chaos that reigned there to a culmination even externally, while David's singing gave composure and form to the wildly raving element, healing the chaotic unrest. Whereas the ancient soul nature's conditions of intoxication and ecstasy degenerated in Saul, the early dawn of an Apollonian power emerged in David which worked out of the soul's centre. To begin with it was still delicate, and yet, owing to this, the human being gradually began to become lord over his consciousness and destiny.

A new level in David's development commenced with the militant attacks by the Philistines flaring up anew. Just as David's flock had earlier been endangered by lions and bears, so his people were now threatened by the magically powerful rulers of the coast who were experienced as the race of giants. Fateful events brought it about that David was moved another step out of his pastoral world into his nation's history. When for some time the fighting had come to a deadlock and there was no prospect on the side of Israel to withstand successfully the crushing pressure of the enemy, David accomplished a deed which grievously affected the army of the Philistines.

Precisely how David's heroic accomplishment developed and took place is a great riddle. The Bible gives a detailed but thoroughly imaginative and symbolic description of it in the story of the battle with Goliath that really refers more to the events taking their course metaphysically in the soul realm, and it is difficult to say to what extent they include what happens outwardly. For forty days, every morning and evening, a giant bristling with armour stepped out of the ranks of the Philistines and faced the troops of Saul, challenging them to a duel. Was he a man of flesh and blood or a fearful phantom that showed itself in the twilight before sunrise and after sunset? Each time, a terrible dread passed through the lines of the Israelites, as if the whole unpredictable, sinister might of the enemy surging towards them were gathered up in this figure. No Israelite risked the battle, although the victor had been promised great wealth and the hand of the royal princess. It appeared that the Philistines might overcome the armies of Saul and become rulers of the hill country merely through instilling fear, without having to resort to their weapons.

This is when destiny led the shepherd youth of Bethlehem to the campsite of the troops. He was sent by his father to bring fruits of the field to his brothers in the army, and so he too heard the challenge of the giant. The Philistine suggestion had no power over him, the image of the giant did not frighten him. He felt himself spontaneously called to battle. Saul finally had to yield to the youth, who said to him that since he had killed both lions and bears, he would be able to prevail in the battle with the giant. Saul wanted to put his own armour on him; but David refused it. He could not and did not want to give himself the appearance of a giant. He did not want to fight with forces that resembled those of the giant. He could muster a new human faculty, clearly aiming awareness and reasoning power, against the dim nature-force of the Philistines.

Unprotected, the youth stepped up to the opponent and hit him squarely in the middle of his forehead with a well-aimed stone from his sling. As the Homeric saga of Polyphemus shows, that is where the giants had their eye, the organ of ancient dim vision; but in the same spot, clear thought dwells in the person whose 'I' is awakening. Just as Odysseus, the clever one, overcame the giant, Polyphemus, by robbing him of the Cyclops-eye, David was victorious over Goliath by hitting him on the forehead.* The shepherd and singer became a hero when the power, with which he had protected his herds and had calmed the raving Saul, now proved itself as I-imbued self-confidence, alert lightness, as a faculty of clear aiming and finding its mark. With the giant's own sword, he severed his head from the body and approached the king with the gruesome trophy.

* Cyclops means, 'he who sees around in a circle.'

Does the Bible describe nothing more to us than a grotesque, outward duel? It indicates the imaginative quality of its description by relating that towards the end of the years of David's royal reign, a whole number of giants had been vanquished in newly arising battles with Philistines (2Sam.21:15–22). Among them was Goliath once again; he is described exactly as in the stories from David's youth and again it was a man from Bethlehem who defeated him: 'and Elhanan ... the Bethlehemite, slew Goliath the Gittite, the shaft of whose spear was like a weaver's beam.' We are supposed to realize that David was the first bearer of a new, victorious power, which, after he had led the people as their king, had already passed over to many others.

Regardless of whether individual traits in the story of David's battle with Goliath are intended to refer to physically real events or not, we have in them a picture of the collision of two soul-natures. One belongs to the past, the other is just appearing on the stage of history. Perhaps the main point in the sequence of outer occurrences was also that the magic spell of fear with which the Philistines tried to overcome the Israelites was broken by David's clear power of thought, and that owing to David's cleverness the enemy's army was brought to the point of destroying itself — something that would be expressed in the picture of Goliath's being beheaded with his own sword.

The young David was a favourite subject for the artists of the Florentine renaissance, above all for Michelangelo and Donatello. They represented him again and again with the sling or with the cut-off head of the giant in his hand, as if he were the Perseus of the Old Testament with the deadly head of the Medusa or the Gorgon. Like the head of the Medusa, the head of Goliath was not human, for the light of thinking and freedom had not arisen on his forehead. Powers of nature that had turned demonic became visible in a ghostly, frightening manner in the distorted countenance of the giant. In David, Michelangelo and Donatello saw the embodiment of the modern spirit of freedom, which at that time was fighting its way into the light of day with the weapons of thinking and art in Florence and other free city states. The Medusan head of Goliath was to them the mask of terror of the now victoriously overcome tyrannical darkness of the Middle Ages. It is indeed true that in David, a thousand years before the turn of time, a crucial juncture of history became embodied that was similar to the one experienced at the end of the Middle Ages in the Renaissance, only to a much greater extent. The overcoming of Goliath by David was the victory of the present over the once great past which had become demonic.

When destiny confronted young David with the world of Goliath, this was only an intensification of the task that had been posed to him in the encounter with Saul. Was the Goliath spear — as large as a weaver's beam and similar to the spear that the furious king had hurled against him — not an expression of the blind nature force of the magic will which had darkened into an egotistical instinct and thus roused all the abysses of evil?

In Goliath, a world of forces confronted young David that Saul had been unable to overcome because they extended into his own nature. Before he became king, David was supposed to pass the test in which Saul as king had not been successful. David's victory over Goliath, the giant, was at the same time the final defeat of the world of Agag, whose name means 'giant.' In David, humanity reached a new level: the age of the *giants* was over, the age of *man* had begun. The epoch of the ecstatic sentient soul, which had still turned the human being into a setting for non-human powers, was henceforth being replaced by the epoch of the intellectual or rational soul in which the 'I' made its entry into the human being.

The legends outside the Bible liked to spin the imaginative thread of the Goliath tale further and even intensified its grotesque vividness. They relate how, during a hunt, David followed a white stag deep into the forest. Finally he lost the trail of the mysterious animal and discovered that he had gone astray in an unknown wilderness of the Philistines' territory. In front of him he saw a tower with decaying walls. When he opened a door within the tower, he found an old woman giant of gruesome ugliness sitting by her spinning wheel. Unsuspecting and fearfully, he replied to her question by giving his name. He did not know that he was confronting Orpa, the mother of Goliath.* The old woman flew into a rage against the murderer of her son. She let her spindle drop and from behind grabbed hold of David,

---

* The legends bring David and Goliath together as blood relatives, which emphasizes their soul-spiritual difference that much more. As David descended from Ruth, Goliath was supposed to have descended from her sister Orpa. But Orpa did not move with her mother-in-law to Bethlehem, but submerged back into her Moabite folk heritage.

who was bending down, threw him on the ground and tried to crush him with a heavy bedstead. Only because David happened to find himself lying in a hollow on the floor underneath the boards of the bed, did he remain alive. After a while, the giant Jesbi, Goliath's brother, came trudging in. He smelled the scent of a human being and when he discovered David, he grabbed him, foaming with rage, and carried him outside. In front of the tower, he planted his spear, which was also the size of a weaver's beam, into the ground with the sharp end pointing upwards. Then he threw his victim high up in the air so that when he fell back down he would be pierced through by the point of the spear. But a miracle happened: the hands of angels held on to David and kept him firmly aloft. At this moment, Abishai, David's warrior, who had looked for him everywhere, came riding up on his horse, having been guided there by divine signs. He slew the giant and invoked the holy name of God whereupon David sank unharmed down to the ground.[3]

With all their resemblance to fairy tales, such legends demonstrate that the task of overcoming the giant could not be solved all at one time. It included a constant, vigilant endeavour of soul, an everlasting battle to escape the spell of the past and to strengthen the new power developing in humanity.

David's victory over Goliath was after all the pictorial expression for a transformation of consciousness which would come true all the way in humankind only in the course of millennia. In the mythological realm, the tension between Esau and Jacob had been a first preparation of this evolutionary advance. In David the rational soul which brought with it the self-imbued intellect emerged out of the womb of the myth to the light of actual history. But then it took long periods of time until the new ferment could fully penetrate civilized humanity. It is therefore not surprising that even more recent folk fairy tales could not do enough to confront Goliath and David with one another in changed, amusing forms.

The fairy tale of the 'Giant and the Little Tailor' shows that it is not always certain who wins. The tailor is clever but he is not much to brag about otherwise. This is why, when he is threatened by the giant, he allows himself to be propelled into the air by a reed on which he sits down. Unfortunately, he proves to be so light that he remains afloat in the air and cannot find his way back to the earth. He fares as did David with the rough brother of Goliath. Only, no Abishai comes to his aid with a pious word. So it can happen to the clever person that all his cleverness makes him completely lose the ground under his feet. The giant is not threatened by this danger; he instead is clumsy and stupid. This is why most fairy tales know that owing to his cleverness the 'brave little tailor' will succeed in overcoming the giant by letting them get at each other in a furious fight. Thus, the battle between David and Goliath continues through all the ages in many different versions.

CHAPTER SEVEN

The Young David: Homelessness

Thanks to his help in warding off the danger of the Philistines, David became a permanent member of Saul's royal court. Henceforth, he left behind his pastoral home of Bethlehem. Although a difficult time of suffering and persecutions began for him now, destiny had nevertheless led him to where he could transform the task received in secrecy into activity visible to all the people.

Three sequences of events that were unrelated to each other brought David to the king's court: the anointing by Samuel in Bethlehem; the appointment as Saul's musician; the victory over Goliath. Here too, since the various stories do in fact appear to contradict each other, the theology of the past decades has been involved in distinguishing between different sources, and believed that it could identify three independent threads of tales that were later woven together. Behind the multiplicity of legendary reports that are historically useless, the only one acknowledged as historic was that Saul, in order to win the tribe of Judah for his dynasty, had admitted a 'Judean prince,' the son of an influential Judean family, to his court, having no idea that the latter would one day oust him and his house from the throne.*

An important light is thrown on the threefoldness of the reports if we notice that they correspond exactly to the threefoldness that we have encountered in the descriptions of Saul's ascent to royalty. The first stage is in each case represented by the anointing enacted secretly

---

* Here too, it must be emphasized that it is not the author's intention to deny the research of textual criticism all justification and value. Doubtless, important and correct observations were produced in many cases concerning specific questions that relate to the original form of the Bible text. But the significance that was attributed to textual criticism for a long time and the conclusions that were drawn from these critical observations must be considered by us as a basic misunderstanding of scripture.

by Samuel; the second step is taken by virtue of the fact that the attention of the public is directed to a larger extent on the one who has been called: Saul is elected king, David is appointed to be the harpist. Finally, as a historic verification, a deed is added that overcomes a need and leads the whole nation forward: Saul defeats the Amalekites and is acknowledged as the leader; David overcomes the giant and henceforth occupies a leading position in the king's surroundings. This analogy is no coincidence. A secret of composition comes to light here in the face of which the theological theories concerning the differentiations of sources collapse. We see into the structural wisdom of the Bible which is never satisfied with merely representing the events in the foreground, but always allows one to sense the emergence of history out of the mystery of divine providence and co-operation.

In the three stages of David's coming into prominence, the powers that intervened supportively from outside were more reserved than in Saul's case. After his initial action of arousal, Samuel remained completely in the background. Everything that happened subsequently appeared to fall into place in a much more accidental way; the seer, after all, left David without the instruction which he gave Saul. With his artistic and thinking abilities, David participated in a much more self-aware, active manner in the dispensations of destiny, whereas Saul was borne up as if from outside by the swells of his fate.

Henceforth, Saul was no longer the sole centre of his court and people. An opposite force was present as a spiritual potential, although without interfering to begin with in the outer course of events but the latent tension made itself felt ever more clearly. Indeed, owing to David's presence, Saul was increasingly driven to the extremes of his Caesarean madness. David's playing on the harp failed in its purpose; more and more frequently, the king hurled his spear at the minstrel in a sudden fit of fury. The more David's inner nobility and the growing capacity of leadership were perceived, the more vehemently the royal jealousy and fear, changed suddenly into rage, broke forth from Saul, who, in quiet and sane times, actually felt a deep sympathy for David.

The king did not keep his promise that he had given to the victor over the giant. David fared as had Jacob long ago in Mesopotamia, who served many years for Rachel, Laban's daughter, but was always confronted with new tasks. One could also compare him to the heroes of fairy tales who are denied the hand of the princess, the reward of their deed, until they have passed additional difficult trials. Saul hesitated to make David the husband of his daughter. He tried to humiliate him with ever new tasks until he finally had to allow him to marry one of his daughters. But from then on, Saul's outbreaks of hate and rage against David became more violent and dangerous than ever before.

What was David's reaction to the king's unjust raving? Did he not give vent to anger, something he would have been justified in doing? Or did he play out his calm, superior faculty against Saul's brutality as he had done against Goliath's dull power? After all, he could have counted on many of the people to take his side immediately, for they had long been uneasy about the king's Caesarean madness. Guided by the sense of his higher mission, David did not allow himself to be carried away by any hostile emotion against Saul. He faced his outbreaks of rage as if they were an act of nature. He possessed a faculty in his soul by means of which he could always restore his equanimity of mind and will, namely clear thought. He could not be angry with the one who tormented him. Through the mask of insanity he could see the man, Saul, for whom he rather felt sorrow and even more than simply compassion. For David could do what Saul was unable to do: he could bridge over the abyss that gaped between the two.

In the tribulations that arose for him through Saul, destiny gave him a helper. Jonathan, Saul's son and heir to the throne, became David's friend. The bond between David and Jonathan stands in history like the archetype of all friendship. It was in fact only at that time that the star of friendship arose on the horizon of humankind. Something became historical reality which the Greek Dioscuroi myth of Castor and Pollux had contained more as a prophecy and which had found a realization, still submerged completely in the sphere of mythology, in the friendship of the heroes Achilles and Patroclus before Troy. Ancient humanity knew only blood relationships as the one bond that united souls with each other. It was not until the awakening of awareness of self that the miracle of friendship became possible, the free congenial harmony between two souls. Thus, the morning-light of a first beginning, of a dawning new age of humankind, shone upon the friendship between David and Jonathan. The experience of friendship was one of the compensations bestowed on humanity when the ancient supportive blood ties were loosened and the individual became lonely and homeless as they acquired awareness of self. Therefore, the sorrow and persecutions brought upon him by Saul were easier to bear for David because of his friendship. How could he have been hostile to the father of his friend? From the love and friendship for the son, a seed of love for the enemy arose towards the father.

David had to flee. A time of troubled and ceaseless roaming to and fro began for him. The rugged landscape of death, the Judean Desert with its precipitous gorges and haunted caves became the stage of the next chapter of his life. He had exchanged the pastoral fields of Bethlehem with the life at court in the castle of Gibeah. The world into which destiny now expelled him was not only lacking in the luxury of the royal court. It was the most direct opposite of the paradise of Bethlehem — a true hell, an inferno on earth. He was driven into the mountainous dross-heap of the Sodom-conflagration, into the sphere of the hostile breath of death that arises from the Dead Sea.

But this most desolate, uninviting area did nevertheless belong to David's homeland, for it was a part of the territory that had been assigned to the tribe of Judah. In Gibeah, David had left the realm of his tribe and had entered upon the ground of the tribe of Benjamin. Now, the fugitive made his escape into his own tribal land. The cosmic strangeness that held sway there could not but be experienced by him in a bitter way. Just like anybody who came there, he too must have felt that he was not only banished to a hostile land but on to an alien planet, a dead lunar world.

In its netherworld-quality, the Judean Desert has an unusual effect. Ties are loosened there that elsewhere make the human being a member of a greater whole. No elements of nature are encountered there that can enfold, embed and support us with stirring life forces. The dead earth rejects us in an unmotherly way so that we cannot but feel alone in a cosmic sense and left to our own resources. Any feeling of having emotional roots to the land withers away or does not arise in the first place. For this reason, however, this landscape is in fact a realistic symbol of impoverishment and loneliness, the only means through which the human being finds his way to freedom. When David had to escape, he went into the desert, just as all the children of Israel went into the wilderness under the leadership of Moses.

As were all genuine shepherds, David was integrated with his whole being into a supportive, maternal cosmos when he was a shepherd in Bethlehem. As a fugitive in the desert, he passed through a number of inwardly justifiable and yet guilt-filled, tragic stations of emancipation.

Thus he comes to an oracle centre, to the colony of the priests at Nob. The questioning of the oracle that was practised there must be pictured as functions that we would label spiritualistic-mediumistic ones today. We must not assume, however, that the conceptions will suffice that can be acquired from the phenomena still existing today, which are final symptoms of decadence. The nature of the oracle of Nob was a continuation of what Moses and Aaron undertook in the tabernacle during the Sinai journey, when, in order to question the deity, they caused the revelation-bearing columns of smoke and fire to arise from the partly volcanic nature present there.[1] Perhaps the oracle of Nob was linked to certain peculiarities of that region which were related to the earlier processes of fire.

The priests at Nob knew David as the one who had become the king's son-in-law because of his victory over the giant. When they consulted the oracle for him, indications of his great future may have been presented to them. In order to aid the fugitive, they were therefore even willing to break their own temple laws. They offered the consecrated bread from the holy table to David who asked them for provisions for his journey — perhaps the bread had just been a certain factor in the execution of the oracle — and, after all, could only be sustenance for consecrated persons. And when David asked them for protective weapons, they gave him Goliath's sword, which, having been dedicated to the sanctuary, should no longer have come into the hands of the profane. Inwardly, the priests committed no wrong, for they saw David as the consecrated one. Had not the seer in fact anointed him? But according to the letter of the law, David did not possess the rights of those who were consecrated. Thus, by its action, the priesthood of Nob created the basis for its own doom. A traitor informed the furious king of what had taken place, and he himself had to kill the priests of Nob, eighty-five in number, before Saul's eyes. Only a single one escaped, joined up with David, the fugitive, and placed the secrets of the oracle of Nob in his service.

This was the first emancipation that was carried out by David: the dissolution of the obligation to the temple law. The glimpse of the future human freedom and sovereignty that could flash forth for an instance was attained through guilt-ridden, tragic disaster.*

For a long, eventful time, it was David's lot to roam about in the face of Saul's persecutions. Soon, a group of men gathered around him composed partly of those who wanted to serve him because they sensed his destiny, partly of men who were fugitives like him. A colourful, fantastic picture arises of a horde, armed with haphazardly acquired weapons, which finally numbered several hundred men who roamed through the rugged mountains. How did they sustain themselves? Since they shielded the Israelite towns at the edge of the desert from the Philistine danger with their daring bravery, they felt that they had the right to levy a tax on those whom they protected. The story of Nabal demonstrates that wherever their demand was not met they were willing to obtain redress by force of arms. David and his companions could believe that they were not committing any wrong, as did Nabal's wife, Abigail, who acknowledged and fulfilled the demand rejected by her husband. David, however, had not received the right to make an appearance as he did from anybody but himself. He stands before us as the archetype of a freebooter and captain of brigands who only follows the rules of an inner sense of justice. Under the duress of privation, he carried out a further emancipation inasmuch as he placed himself above the communal laws governing the country to which he belonged.

Finally, more and more hard pressed, David was driven to a last, desperate step. With his troop that had grown in numbers, he went over to Philistine territory and became a vassal of the enemy just at the time when Saul was in danger of having to give up his resistance to the hostile attacks. From the Philistine town of Ziklag, which was assigned to him and his horde as a dwelling place, he ventured forth on his military expeditions. He made use of a most daring ruse. He led the

---

* It is revealing that in the New Testament this particular story is referred to where it is a matter of demonstrating the sovereignty of the 'Son of man' over the law of the past. When Jesus was accused of breaking the law of the sabbath, he made a point of the fact that David had eaten the consecrated bread of Nob (Mark 2:25–28).

Philistines to believe that he was fighting on their behalf against his own people whose defences were weakening. But in reality, he put down the furtive attacks of the neighbouring nations who wanted to take advantage of Israel's predicament. Were his actions right or wrong? Seen from outside, he was a traitor by siding with the enemy of his people. Nevertheless, he did more for the defence of Israel than Saul was in a position to do. To the emancipation from the temple and state-laws he also emancipates himself from the law of patriotism. The homeless one disengaged himself from one bond after the other; he placed himself above the law and yet remained faithful to the genius of his higher destiny and task.

Once before in the history of the Old Covenant, a ruse had a significant effect, namely, when Jacob directed the blessing of the first-born by aged Isaac upon himself instead of upon Esau. But Jacob's ruse must still be understood in a mythical sense, symbolizing the first emergence of thinking in the head and the slowly developing separation of the human being from the ancient orders and laws. As humankind advanced from Jacob to David, the ruse moved out of the mythical realm into history. The Fall progressed in so far as it included a guilt-ridden, tragic detachment of the human being from the original ties. But the freedom of the human personality that stands above the law continued also. And the correspondence between Jacob's and David's destinies, to which we have already been directed repeatedly, becomes especially evident here: from a profound necessity of fate, did David not prepare to acquire for himself the first-born's right to be king which belonged to Saul, just as Jacob appropriated for himself Esau's right of the first-born?

A sequence of images is woven into the reports concerning the period of David's flight which remind us of themes from Germanic sagas of heroes and which, by a comparison with the latter, can perhaps become more clearly discernible. The legend of Dietrich, the mythical rearrangement of the history of Theodoric, the king of the Ostrogoths, relates to us how the hero acquired his armour piece by piece through combat and victory. In the battle against the giants he gained possession of the miraculous sword, Nagelring, and the golden helmet of magic, Hildegrim. The hero Heime, who had been defeated by him and thereby had become his loyal retainer, presented him with Falke, the finest horse from the stud of his queen. Many other precious signs attest to successfully passed trials. In each case, the trophy is the pictorial expression of a soul-spiritual faculty. Step by step, Dietrich of Bern proved that he too mastered the faculty with which his opponent hoped to overcome him, indeed, he availed himself of it in a superior manner. His full armour represents him finally as the bearer of the sum of all the various faculties which had confronted him individually in his various opponents. He bore within himself the quintessence of his surroundings turned inward.

The sequence that one could call 'the saga of David's armour,' already began when Saul put his own armour on him in order to equip him for the battle with Goliath. David made it obvious by his refusal of the king's weaponry that he intended to overcome the giant with faculties other than those that resembled Saul's, but he did not refuse Jonathan's gift of weapons. When, after the victory over Goliath, he had taken up residence in the imperial palace, Saul's son and heir came to pay homage to him as the future leader of the people. He placed his own armour, tunic, sword, bow, belt and mantle at the feet of the stranger, for he had recognized the superior spirit in him and the fact that he was sent by God. David was able to accept the gifts and seal his friendship with him, for he and Jonathan were soul-mates; the faculties that distinguished the friend lived in him as well. Henceforth, David used Jonathan's bow. In contrast to Saul's coarse spear, the faculty that is expressed in this nobler device for a sure aim lived in his soul as an exact and significant force from the innermost self, something that he gave proof of in the battle against Goliath.

The priests of Nob added the sword of Goliath to David's weapons out of their temple treasure. Had David not proven his right to this weapon? If the magic faculty of the Philistines had not dwelt in him in a transformed and inwardly deepened manner — something of which the sword is a pictorial expression — how could he have vanquished the giant!

In the moments of his greatest need it happened that David became master over Saul's nature and weaponry in a new way, thus reaching a most important stage of his inner path. Inserted inconspicuously into the flow of the narrative, this story is the very centre of David's inner development.

Twice, the one who was pursued got the better of the pursuer. The first scene plays in a cave in the Valley of En-gedi on the western shore of the Dead Sea. A tributary with sweet water runs from the mountains through this valley down to the salt lake and — something that can still be detected faintly today — is the only area where a vein of life extends from the Bethlehem-Hebron region into the netherworld of death. In the final years of the Old Covenant, the Valley of En-gedi held an important place, for the order of the Essenes had established their central settlement there during the period of John the Baptist and Jesus of Nazareth.

David stayed in hiding there in a cave and Saul, who was furiously pursuing him, entered the cave at last himself. The darkness concealed the fugitive from the unsteady sight of the king. Before Saul got ready to depart from the cave, David cut off a piece of his cloak. With this trophy, he could do more than show that Saul had fallen into his hands. He now possessed a symbol for the fact that he had elevated the soul force, which was dull and dark in Saul, into inward lightness and consciousness in himself.

Some time later, an intensification of this experience occurred. Now we find ourselves in the region of the stark desert which is not mitigated by any traces of life. Upon two mountains, facing each other, the army of Saul and David's horde were encamped. During the night, David along with Abishai, his companion-in-arms, stole into Saul's camp. Abishai wanted to slay the defenceless Saul with the spear that had so often been hurled against David, but at this moment David's superiority over Saul was more than that of a physical battle. It was as if the picture of how the wide-awake David stood next to the deeply asleep Saul in the nocturnal desert was supposed to demonstrate the difference of their spiritual natures with ultimate clarity. David did not allow his pursuer to be killed. He took for himself the spear and the drinking goblet which lay at the head of the sleeping king. Then, from the other mountain, he roused his enemies from their sleep with his call. As proof of the fact that the king's life had been in his hands, he lifted up the spear and the goblet. And what happened before, when David had shown Saul the piece of the mantle that he had taken from him in the cave of En-gedi, happened again now: for an instant, Saul was free of his demon. Once again filled with his prophetic genius, he himself proclaimed David's royal future in ecstatic words.

Although still pursued and banished, David had now won the greatest spiritual victory over Saul and the whole world of the ancient faculties. Significantly, even though inconspicuously, this breakthrough is symbolized in the two objects which he took from the slumbering Saul. The spear and the goblet are none other than the duality of symbols which were venerated later on in the Christian era as the Holy Grail of the sacred chalice and the holy lance. The image of the young David, who called across to the still sleeping Saul and lifted the two trophies of his spiritual superiority into the rays of the rising sun, is like an Old Testament prelude to the moment when Perceval entered the Grail castle with the Grail's spear that he had won back from Klingsor, then uncovering the sacred chalice.

The dual symbol of the Grail reveals an important secret of human nature. As long as the human being was still an unfree member of the cosmos, his nature remained the stage of superhuman forces. Surrounding nature extended into him unchanged. Natural man only turns into the spiritual man who bears the selfhood's noble attribute of freedom within him when, out of the central point of his own being, he transforms within himself the forces of the outer world. One can behold the finest quintessence of the forces of outer nature, if one watches how the sun's rays immerse like light-spears into the open flower-cups of the kingdom of blossoms, begetting life. In an archetypal way, nature sums up all the principles of its life in this allegory and through it attains its nearness to the Grail. To serve the sacred lance and chalice of the Grail, to be a knight of the Holy Grail signifies to draw nature in its archetypal life-principles into the inner sphere of self-awareness, so that in the human being too, the allegory is repeated in the life-begetting power of the spirit and the pure receptivity of the soul that is like the chalice of the blossom.

Like Goliath's spear that resembled a weaver's beam, the spear in Saul's hands was nothing but the expression of the blind, oppressive forces of outer nature which extended unchanged into the human being. Only in David's hands, Saul's spear and goblet became symbols of the Grail. They represented the element that was maturing in him as a new factor of humanity: the inward intensification of nature's forces into the active generative power of the spirit and the tender receptivity of the soul. An early dawn of the Grail mystery threw its light into humankind's history. That was the result of David's homelessness.

In a way, the whole period of David's flight from Saul's pursuits was one great temptation for him. Would it not have been humanly understandable if he had lost his patience and had reacted to the king's unjust fury with his own outburst of rage? Since he could avail himself of a large troop of armed men, would it not have been a simple matter for him to force Saul, who was hard pressed by the Philistine attacks, to give in? In the cave of En-gedi and at night within Saul's encampment, was he not tempted to rid himself of his pursuer since he could be sure that the people would hail him as their saviour?

A thousand years before the Judean Desert turned into the stage of Jesus' temptation, it saw the temptation of David; but David remained steadfast as did the greater one later on. It was far from David's nature to suffer a relapse into the ancient characteristics of rage that he witnessed in Saul. More than that, David struggled through to a healing humaneness, at rest within itself — and in this too he was illuminated by the approach of the Grail element. Was not Saul healed of his demonic possession for brief moments through his subsequent awareness of having twice been spared? Was he not healed similarly and better than before through David's harp playing?

David not only harboured no hatred against Saul and his ways. He confronted his pursuer with a sense for the tragedy of the latter's destiny, having become compassionate through insight and knowledge gained through pity. He looked into the doom of a world that was destroying itself. How could he be angry with those whose tragic fate was being fulfilled? His humaneness, which proved itself most in the Judean Desert when he liberated himself from all laws, was like a Messianic prophecy. A thousand years later, the words were spoken: 'Love your enemies ... bless those who curse you!' There is scarcely another pronouncement of the Gospel that addresses itself more to the new human being, the 'I'-man who has become free of the laws of the past. In David, it found a prophetic, early realization.

It was not long before a messenger, an Amalekite, came to him with the report — thinking that he was bringing David joyous news — that, following Saul's own request, in the hopeless battle he had killed Saul. But David cut down the messenger who was greedy for a reward. It was genuine, deep pain that turned him, the minstrel, into the psalmist and evoked from his heart the most sublime elegy, not only for his friend, Jonathan, but also for his enemy, Saul.

Step by step, doom closed in over the house and party of Saul. Not for a moment did David, the king, feel that he was thereby free to proceed. He even tried to set himself against the inevitable tragedy but he could not stop his henchmen, who, in the belief that they were serving him and the people, became instruments of this doom. When David's commander-in-chief, Joab, had slain Abner, Saul's army commander, David struck up the lamentation over him too. David's elegies sound to us like the proclamation of a twilight of the gods, like the lamentation over a whole world of soul forces.

David had an unhappy love for the house of Saul, notwithstanding the suffering that had befallen him from it. When Ishbosheth had been murdered by followers of David who felt that it was their duty to guard the interests of the state more than had the king, David immediately had the murderers executed. And just as he had caused Saul's body to be buried finally in the region of the ancient sacred high place of Gibeon, he also saw to an honourable burial for Abner and Ishbosheth. And since he could not prevent the fate of the seven descendants of Saul, whose death was demanded by the Gibeonites as atonement for the desecration of their sanctuary, he even had them laid to rest with all honours in the royal tombs next to Saul and Jonathan.

Even as king, David remained true to his soul's achievements attained during the period of his suffering and homelessness.

CHAPTER EIGHT

Jerusalem and its History

When David still went back and forth between the shepherds' fields of Bethlehem and the royal castle at Gibeah, his life resembled the beat of a pendulum around an important centre: Gibeah is exactly as far north of Jerusalem as Bethlehem is south of it. On each of his walks he saw the ancient city lying on its sacred hills, the city to which so many lofty mysteries were linked. As was true of all Israelites of that age, in David the feelings of awe were combined with the puzzling question: why are we prohibited from entering just this central point, when all the land is ours? Is the land without this city not like a person without a head? Emanating from the soul of Israel, the longing for the hills on which the divinity dwelled may have moved the heart of young David.

As long ago as that, every glimpse of Jerusalem evoked the memory of unfathomable past ages. We have reliable historical documents from a period four hundred years earlier than David's age. The archives found in Tel El Amarna, the city of the Egyptian reformer, Akhenaten (Amenophis IV), contains letters in which Abd Khiba, a king of 'Urusalim,' 'falls seven times seven at the feet' of Pharaoh and beseeches him for military aid. But when David went on this ancient path on the water-shed from Bethlehem to Gibeah and in so doing described a curve towards the west around the hills of the mysterious city, his thoughts were occupied with times of the far more distant past. The image may have passed through his soul of the exalted priest-king, Melchizedek, who had once emerged out of the silence of his mystery sanctuary in Salem to offer bread and wine to Abraham, the king. And pondering the past, his thoughts need not even have stopped with Melchizedek. Out of the very depths of time, sagas and reminiscences were woven around the heights of Jerusalem. Had they not become the centre and navel of all creation when God had created the world there? The sacred rocks were the foundation from which the earth had solidified in all directions out of the waters. And they had also become the keystone which kept the waters of the primal Flood locked up. In them, the miracle of the floating stone was contained, which, like the whole earth in the universe, keeps itself afloat without a solid foundation underneath.*

For David, Jerusalem must have been surrounded by a golden brilliance which had its source in all the epochs of creation and humankind. Cosmic grandeur from divine beginnings combined with solemn sanctity from the times of Melchizedek. But what must have caused people's feelings the greatest suspense was that it was said that on the heights of the primordial city stood the gate of heaven as well as the portal of hell. How could it be that the most extreme opposites of existence adjoined each other and were linked in neighbourly fashion?

In as much detail as possible, we must try and pursue the question of the historical configuration and significance that Jerusalem possessed in the age preceding David and the transformations the city experienced because of David and Solomon after it had become the capital of the kingdom. All the deeper secrets of Israel's history are consolidated in the mystery of the city of Jerusalem.

The riddle of Jerusalem is a profound one. Whole libraries of texts have been amassed merely about the question concerning which of the ancient city's hills originally possessed the name, Mount Zion, the term which at all times was experienced as being filled with the sound of the most intimate inspiration by God. But the problem of Jerusalem is of significance far beyond the contexts of the Old Testament. If it is

---

* In later ages, these ancient mythological conceptions pertaining to Jerusalem were written down. But they were doubtless related with the view of the city in very ancient times and bestowed on it the awe-inspiring nimbus which distinguished it from all other cities of the world: 'God created the world like an embryo. Just as the latter develops from the navel, so God began to create the world from the navel from which it spread in all directions. Where is the navel? It is Jerusalem. The navel itself is the altar. And why is it called the foundation stone? Because, beginning from it, the world was founded.'[1] 'What did the Holy one do, praised be he? With his right foot, he set in the stone all the way to the depths of the primordial Flood and made it the keystone of the world, just as a human being who places a keystone in a dome. This is why it is called, 'the foundation stone,' for there is the navel of the earth and from there, the whole world was made to extend, and on it stands the Temple.'[2]

possible anywhere on earth, it must be possible to rediscover archetypes of earthly existence in the landscape of the Holy Land, and especially in its primeval, holy centre. The phenomena that appear to the
external senses must be especially transparent here for the sphere of
the archetypal phenomena. If all apparent coincidences were not an
expression of innermost necessities of being here, if in this place it
were not true that, as Goethe expressed it, 'all things transitory but as
symbols are sent,' how could these sites have become the stage of the
events whereby the divine-heavenly being submerged into the realm
of earthly-human existence? What spiritual archetype attained terrestrial form in Jerusalem?

The archetypal character of the whole Palestinian landscape has
occupied us already on several occasion in the descriptions up to now.
It shows in a purely external sense in the Jordan region's location
which leads to the lowest point on the earth's surface. In the Jordan
depression, that mighty rift valley, the largest and most conspicuous
scar in the countenance of our earth, descends into the greatest depths:
it is the so-called Syrian/East African Rift, the main part of which runs
from the Syrian plains southward between Lebanon and Anti-Lebanon
until it loses itself in the Ethiopian highland. Together with its northern and southern offshoots it is more than 7 000 kilometres long (4 500
miles). We have already mentioned once that this rift, and especially
the Jordan Valley, the section of its greatest depth, is the sign of the
mightiest cosmic processes of creation and the developments which
first shaped our planet Earth as it appears today.[3] From here, we have
access to the ancient mythological traditions which saw in the Holy
Land the centre of the world and the point from which terrestrial creation proceeded. Not in a geometrical, spatial sense, but in a dynamic
sense of time, the Holy Land with its centre in Jerusalem has been
called the midpoint of the world. This land was seen as the centre of
developments, of the labour pains and tempests of creation of our
planet Earth, and it is possible to experience this through the transparency of this landscape.

A revelation of the archetypal character of the Holy Land, concerned less with the tangible geological and geographical facts than
those more fundamental for a comprehension of the Old and New
Testament, is the polarity between Judea and Galilee that refers us to
the sphere of ethereal geography. In a relatively small area — the

distance between the Dead Sea and the Sea of Galilee amounts to not much more than one hundred kilometres (sixty miles) — two worlds collide. Even today, after the desolation has exercised its levelling influence, their topographical contrast cannot be pictured strongly enough: a landscape of death and a landscape of life. In Judea, the clearest expression of which are the Judean Desert and the surroundings of the Dead Sea, a person finds himself more in an unearthly, cindery lunar landscape than on the maternal ground of our earth. It is as if the Jordan Valley and the great cosmic rift to which it belongs were a trace of the prehistoric catastrophes during which the moon tore itself loose in a tremendous eruption from the body of the earth. One could imagine that at this point of separation, remnants of the moon had been left behind on the planet Earth. In Galilee, on the other hand, particularly at some places by the Sea of Galilee or on the summit of Mount Tabor, one can inhale in landscapes that have such a joyful, heavenly atmosphere, an unearthly, sunlike element that it is as if traces could still be encountered there of far more distant epochs in which the earth was as yet united with the sun into one cosmic body: traces of the long-lost sun-home of our existence, the pre-physical sun-earth, of which a faint recollection has been retained in the paradise myths of the various peoples.[4]

The Holy Land does in fact encompass landscapes which are terrestrial reflections of the inferno and paradise, of hell and heaven. It is perhaps from this direction that we can find a key to the mythical tradition that Jerusalem contained within the portals to heaven as well as those to hell. If we penetrate further the landscapes of the region, we repeatedly encounter smaller repetitions and cross-overs of the great polarity of Judea and Galilee. As is apparent already from the previous descriptions, the surroundings of Bethlehem could be termed a Galilean enclave within Judea. Similarly, there exist Judean reminiscences in Galilee, for example in the vicinity of Nazareth.

Jerusalem is a quintessence of the Holy Land. The same archetypes that can be discerned from the topography of the whole land are revealed again in an extreme concentration within the smallest area. It should be permissible to approach a solution of the Jerusalem riddle from such qualitative, ethereal-geographical starting-points. This does not imply any disregard for the tremendous archaeological and topographical work which up to now has been applied to this subject. The results that we try to describe here can also be found and corroborated by archeological discoveries and by ancient textual traditions.

Despite the changes that the ground has experienced through the systematic human efforts or the frequently towering rubble of the many storms of destruction which have passed over the city, even today it can be recognized at first glance that Jerusalem is constructed mainly on two rows of hills that run parallel from north to south. Just as ancient Rome was a city of seven hills, so Jerusalem was and is a city of two hills. The two elevations nestle into the sharp angle that arises between the Kidron Brook and the Hinnom Valley in the south. The Kidron runs from north to south on the eastern side of the city at the foot of the steep elevation. The Hinnom Valley runs southward from the north-west, then turns off to the east and at the southern end of the two rows of hills it enters the Kidron Valley. The city's domain is thus cut off steeply by the approaching valleys in the west, south and east; only towards the north, the city has access to the neighbouring hill country that spreads out in undulating shapes. The higher, western hill of the city is traditionally designated as Mount Zion, a tradition that we consider genuine and very ancient. This hill has its most significant characteristics in its southern parts. The eastern elevation bears the flat summit of the Temple site, its most important feature, on its northern, broader end.

It is understandable that the Temple Mount with its wide rocky plateau has in most cases attracted the exclusive interest of those who wanted to form an idea of ancient Jerusalem in their minds. Although it is the lower of the two hills, it is a site of commanding majesty that cannot but cast its spell over everybody. This must certainly have been the case throughout the ages, at least since Solomon built his Temple there. Today, the eastern hill is topped by the Muslim Dome of the Rock with the external splendour of its Arabesque beauty. But that stern majesty touches us especially in the wide expanse outdoors and on the broad stone surface of the Temple site. This eastern hill of the city has even managed to cast its spell over science during the past century, for a number of scholars searched for sacred Mount Zion, the original hill of Jerusalem, on the narrower southern extension of the Temple Mount, distrusting the local tradition which designated the western hill as Zion.

It is not possible here to undertake a detailed exposition of the various theories which have surfaced concerning the topography of the Holy Land in reference to the location of Mount Zion. The conviction that the local tradition is correct has been arrived at by us in the first place because of the more intimate archetypal, total impression of Jerusalem; in what follows, the attempt will be made to describe it. The most recent excavations on the south-eastern slope of the Mount Zion clearly confirm the authenticity of the local tradition.*

The distrust of the local tradition and the attempts to place Mount Zion on the eastern hill have their source in many instances in an overestimate and misinterpretation of the descriptions which Josephus gives of the city prior to the Roman destruction in AD 70. Josephus does not mention the name Zion at all. One need not be led astray by his terms, 'upper town,' and 'Akra.' They refer to sections of the city into which the part designated as Zion does not fit at all.

It becomes clear from the books of the Maccabees that around the turn of time, a usage of terms was prevalent which obscured the ancient tradition, for in Maccabees, the whole elevation of Jerusalem inclusive of the Temple site was designated as Zion. The more ancient Old Testament scriptures, among them the Psalms, distinguish between Zion and the Temple Mount. In the book of the prophet Micah, this is especially clearly recognizable. 'Therefore because of you Zion shall be ploughed as a field; Jerusalem shall become a heap of ruins, and the mountain of the house [the Temple] a wooded height.' (3:12).

The traditional Mount Zion harbours no less a miracle than does the Temple rock. One can still encounter this miracle today.† Leaving behind the area of the actual Old City, which overflows with the colourful, noisy life of the Orient in its narrow, steep alleys, and turning towards the south-western part of the city, one enters a region of stillness and silence. It is as if one had not only left behind the clam-

---

*   These lines were written in 1936. Archaeological research today locates David's city on the southern extension of the Temple Mount (*Translator*, 1988).

†   In the new edition of 1953, the text of this passage, written in 1936, has been left unchanged although there can be no doubt that many of the atmospheric wonders in Jerusalem and the whole country, which could still be encountered in the thirties, have fallen victim to the destinies of the age. In Italy as well, many of the auric sites, such as Trefontane near Rome, cited here as an example, have to a large extent forfeited their soul-magic.

orous stir of the bazaars but had been removed from the whole world
of the present. Very old, quiet streets are laid down between high walls
and in many instances certainly offer a sight resembling that of the
time of the Apostles since this part of the city was spared during
Jerusalem's destruction in the year 70. The dark columns of the
cypresses, the tops of huge, ancient cedars which look over the walls,
intensify the dense atmosphere of a saturated silence that dwells there
and even extends its effect into the settlements, such as the Armenian
quarter, which are concealed behind the walls instead of the large gardens as one would like to believe. No eye-catching sight of interest
draws the curiosity of the traveller upon itself as is the case on the
Temple Mount. And yet, what can be encountered on Mount Zion by
a receptive heart can almost make a deeper and more vivid impression
in memory than even the Temple site. The Christian pilgrim, who has
been disappointed by the strife of the different faiths, the commercial-
ism and the lack of taste at the site of the Crucifixion and the Holy
Tomb, will also frequently come to the realization in his recollections
that on peaceful Mount Zion he was close to the spirit after all which
he sought in the Holy Land. The touch of a soul element, radiating
down from the beyond, that one can sense, for example, before the
gates of Rome in Trefontane, the marvellous, soulful oasis where Paul
died a martyr's death, this is what dwells in a more intense form on
Mount Zion in Jerusalem.

The meaning of the name, 'Salem,' which the city bore in the age of
Melchizedek and which is still contained in the name, 'Jerusalem,' the
'city of peace,' can be encountered in a clear reflection even today on
this western hill of the city. The traditional hill of Zion is a 'dwelling
place of peace;' there, the blessed atmosphere of a higher sphere
extends into the terrestrial realm.

A deeply devout longing and loving faith resounds from the
Psalms whenever mention is made of Zion, the mountain on which
dwells God's mercy and grace. Directing his glance upon Zion, the
longed-for goal, the pilgrim sang: 'I lift up my eyes to the hills ...' In
that quiet section of Jerusalem, one can still enter into the blissful happiness that pilgrims from afar must have felt when they arrived at the
goal of their pilgrimage there and felt themselves welcomed into the
sphere of higher peace and divine love. An ancient flight of stone
steps, which has been completely excavated in recent times and

which ascends from the pool of Siloam in the Kidron Valley all the way to the southern part of the western hill, evokes images of processions of Zion's pilgrims of long ago. Just as those who made pilgrimages in Greece to the sanctuary of Apollo on the hills of Delphi, purified themselves first at the Castalian spring and then ascended in a solemn procession up the 'holy path' paved with flagstones to the Temple district, so, in pre-Israelite times and in the age of David when the Temple of Solomon was not yet built, the pilgrims may have walked up the sacred steps to the grove and dwelling-place of peace, singing Psalms, after having washed themselves at the spring of Siloam.

It is only through this contrast that one becomes really aware of the difference of the experience evoked by the Temple site. There too, sanctity holds sway but not in the sense of peace and divine grace. The stern majesty prevailing a person there seems to demand and exercise justice exclusively. There dwells the strict, judgmental Yahweh god who does not envelop the human being with forgiving mercy but denudes him of all his disguises and places him before his penetrating, relentlessly searching eye. The Temple Mount with its hard stone countenance harbours God's love less than his wrath.

It is always thought that everywhere the Old Testament only knows and reveres the stern lunar Yahweh god. This, however, is only applicable to the age of the prophets following Solomon in which the specific element of Judaism emerged from the totality of the Israelite character. As long as the twelve tribes still formed a unity, Israelite faith in many instances had an inkling of what lay beyond the sphere of Yahweh, since it affiliated with the nature sanctuaries of the land. Rays from the sphere of the higher solar divinity, whose servant was Melchizedek, 'the priest of *God Most High*,'[5] still penetrated the souls of the people. As the 'site of peace,' adorned by the rustling of a sacred grove, was Mount Zion perhaps the dwelling place of this highest god, the 'El-elyon,' the sunlike god of love? And did the abode of the moon-like god, who had given the Law and watched judicially over humanity, perhaps confront Zion in the bare rock of the Temple Mount as the 'site of justice'? The Letter to the Hebrews in the New Testament indicates to us that in the figure of the sage and priest king, Melchizedek, the duality of 'peace' and 'justice' was combined into one. 'He is first, by translation of his name, king of righteousness, and then he is also king of Salem, that is, king of peace' (7:2). In the external realm, Jerusalem may have been a replica of the duality that Melchizedek encompassed in a spiritual sense.

We have tried to grope our way towards the polarity which Jerusalem harbours within itself to this day. We are convinced that we are thus on the track of the riddle of this city. This polarity is the key to a comprehension of Jerusalem. Scant attention has been paid to this up to now. But in the long run, even one who does not agree with the details of our descriptions or the conclusions that we draw from them, will not be able to close his mind to the recognition of this polarity.

Countless times, the attempt was made to picture the origin of the city from economic or strategic points of view. It was really due to such considerations that the whole chaos of topographical theories and discussions arose in which the literature on the Holy Land abounds. One should desist from projecting such external interests, indeed decisive today, into ancient times as the sole causes for the construction of cities. As one of the oldest cities of humankind, Jerusalem in particular reaches back far into the mythological past. If the reasons for building it had been strategic-economic ones, Jerusalem would have never arisen in the form in which we picture it according to the topography of today. On the surface, a city could hardly have been laid out in a more 'unsuitable' way than appears to have been the case with Jerusalem. Its location is not even strategically as protected as was always emphasized, since it has no natural defences to the north. And was the city not in fact conquered and destroyed many, many times from this direction?

The reasons for Jerusalem's origin rest in the mythical-religious sphere, in the spiritual significance of the locale. We can approach the original spiritual element, although only as if from afar, when we recognize the fundamental cosmic polarity by which the city of the two hills is dominated. The greater polarity of Galilee and Judea finds a concentrated repetition, compressed into a small area, in the two elevations of Jerusalem, solar Mount Zion and the moonlike rock of the Temple hill. All at once, this casts a light on the Hebrew name of the holy city. Yerushalayim is neither singular nor plural, but a dual form. Even through the name one can perceive that Jerusalem is a twin-formation, a city of duality and cosmic opposites that meet here.

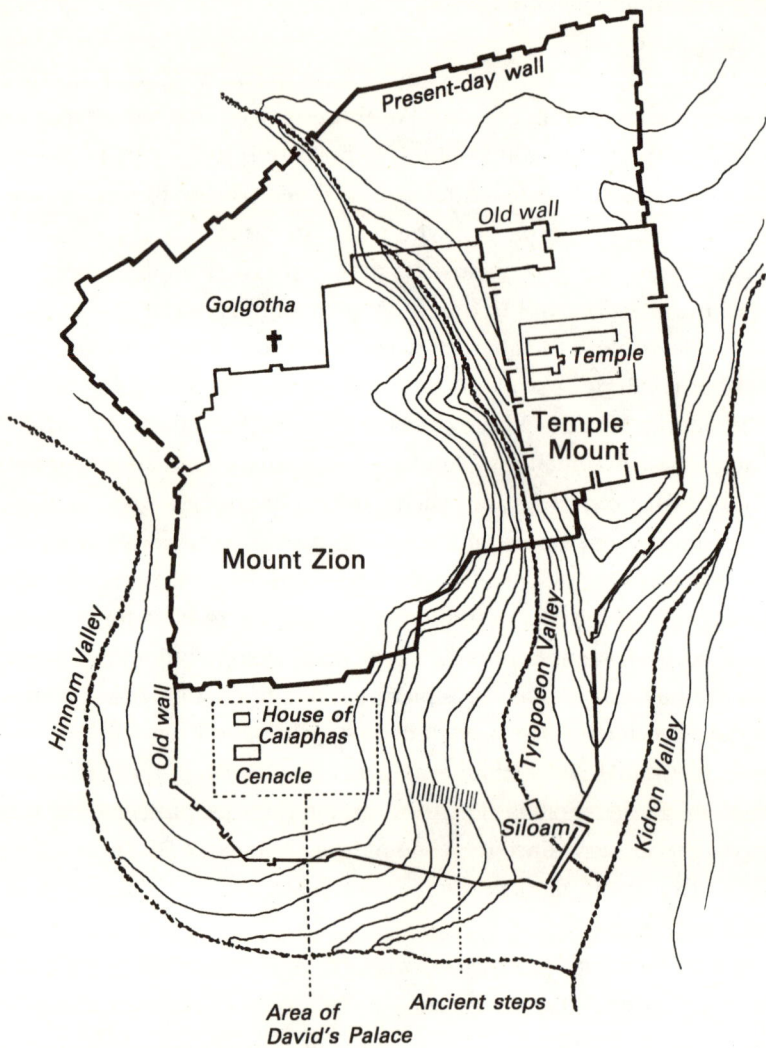

Present-day wall

Old wall

Golgotha

Temple

Temple
Mount

Mount Zion

Hinnom Valley

Old wall

House of
Caiaphas

Cenacle

Tyropoeon Valley

Siloam

Kidron Valley

Area of
David's Palace

Ancient steps

Plan of Jerusalem

Like the lifting of a curtain from the duality, there now appears a discovery concerning which it is incomprehensible that its epochal significance has not been recognized and applied.

Until the age of David and Solomon, the topographic appearance of Jerusalem was totally different from what we confront today and from what is taken more or less for granted by all topographic studies. Between the city's two rows of hills, there once gaped a deeply incised rock-bound ravine which, running from north to south, cut into two parts the region that rises there wedged in between Hinnom and Kidron. In connection with the extensive transformations, which we have yet to discuss, that Solomon undertook with the whole city of Jerusalem, he had this crevice-like gorge filled in. As the Bible puts it, he 'closed up the breach in the city of David his father' (1Kings 11:27).

Scattered here and there, one can find traditions concerning the filling of the Tyropoeon Valley by Solomon. Josephus mentions it repeatedly but unclearly. As late as in the thirteenth century, the scholarly Dominican monk, Brocardus, having returned from a pilgrimage, described what he had seen: 'Since the concave side of the semi-circle fell away steeply in the direction of the city so that the fortification offered no convenient site for construction, the kings of old went to much trouble to fill up the ancient gorge ... the gorge is completely filled up but traces of the earlier depression have remained.'[6]

A flat depression, going from north to south, is marked in the customary maps where the Jewish Quarter Road runs its course today in the Old City. And following Josephus, who, as a contemporary of the destruction of Jerusalem in the year 70 and a participant in the battle, gives a description of the city as it looked then, this depression is customarily called the Tyropoeon Valley, the 'Valley of Cheese Makers.' This, however is a completely senseless name if one does not trace it back to its original form. The latter is not difficult to find, and it is merely surprising that only a few isolated scholars have hit upon it, although the solution to the Jerusalem riddle is contained in it.*

---

* In a footnote to the Pool of Amygdalon, mentioned by Josephus, the Swiss theologian Furrer[7] for example, quite coincidentally mentions the meaning of the word Tyropoeon as well: 'The Greeks made the Hebrew name *Hamigdalim* palatable in the form *amygdalos* and thus changed the "Pool of the Tower" into an "Almond Pool" (*kolymbethran amygdalon*), just as they reshaped the Hebrew word *Teraphon*, "tear, ravine" (from *taraph*, meaning, to tear, ...) into the Greek Tyropoeon and happily declared it to be the 'Valley of Cheese Makers.'

Tyropoeon is a popularized etymological Greek inflexion of the Hebrew term *teraphon*, 'the tear, that which has been torn.' The original name, denoting the rocky gorge, became incomprehensible in the times when this valley no longer existed and its former presence had fallen into oblivion. The ancient Hebrew word was expressed in Greek and thus could arise the total and senseless distortion of 'Valley of Cheese Makers.'

Now the picture of ancient Jerusalem as it appeared even in David's time takes on graphic proportions. If we imagine, for example, that we had been standing on the high-lying surfaces of the eastern hill where Solomon's Temple later rose up and had looked up to the still higher summit of Zion, the gaping, deep rock gorge in front of us would have been part of the view that would have spread out before us. We would have stood in front of a deep abyss that separated us from the celestial summit of peace.

Father Mommert, who was not taken very seriously by science, but who, thanks to his long stay in Jerusalem and the almost pedantic manner in which he dug into the traditions of antiquity, has become one of the most knowledgeable experts of the city's history, was probably the first to define clearly the conception of the Teraphon Gorge and to put it forth as a corroboration of his view that even in regard to pre-Christian times, the western hill had to be identified with Zion. He used the insight thus gained to decipher the strange, mutilated report that the Bible gives of the seizure of Jerusalem by David.

In the Second Book of Samuel it is written: '.. David took the stronghold of Zion, that is, the city of David. And David said on that day, "Whoever would smite the Jebusites let him get up the water shaft [*çinor*]" ...' (5:7f). Although the Books of the Chronicles leave out the word, water shafts, they offer a rendition that fills the gap remaining here: 'David said, "Whoever shall smite the Jebusites first shall be chief and commander." And Joab ... went up first ...' (1Chr.11:6).

If the Hebrew term, *çinor*, is correctly rendered as 'water shaft' — and the Vulgate and the Septuagint, the Latin and Greek translations of the Old Testament, use similar words — then the biblical text remains obscure. Doubtless, Mommert is correct in identifying the word *çinor* as a name for that crevice-like rock gorge — and here he can quote the one passage where this word occurs in the Hebrew Bible a second time — called Tyropoeon Valley, and which, during the time of

the winter rains, carried the water in fierce falls into the Kidron Valley.*
It was due to Josephus that Mommert hit upon this interpretation, for
Josephus paraphrased the Old Testament report in the following manner: David was supposed to have promised the reward to the one 'who
would be successful in the ascent through the gorges that extended in
front.'† And because Joab managed to climb through the gruesome
gorge, the Israelites finally conquered Jerusalem.

> The *Çinor* channel ... is the narrow ravine which in ancient
> times ran between the upper and lower city ... from north to
> south ... This narrow gorge ... at one time represented one the
> strongest bulwarks of the upper city and remained in existence
> as 'the tear in the city of David' until Solomon had it filled
> with great effort for the purpose of a more convenient connec-
> tion between the upper and lower city. This is the same ravine
> (φαρανξ, *pharanx*) which, according to the description of the
> city by Flavius Josephus *(Bellum Judaicum* 5.4.1) separated the
> hill of the upper city from that of the lower city. In order to
> make the Hebrew term, *teraphon,* meaning gorge, tear, palat-
> able to the Greeks,‡ it was called Tyropoeon by Josephus ... Just
> as the *Çinor* Gorge represented the key to the fortification of
> Zion in David's days, and Joab only conquered the stronghold
> after the *Çinor* lay behind him — so, today as well, the correct
> determination of the *Çinor* or Tyropoeon Gorge is the key to
> the question of Zion. With this magic key, a person who has
> correctly solved the riddle of the Tyropoeon ravine will be able
> to solve all the riddles ... of the topography of ancient
> Jerusalem with ease.[8]

Mommert is right. All at once, the idea of the rocky ravine which
tore the city apart into its archetypal duality moves ancient Jerusalem
into an luminous clarity. At the same time, innumerable new questions
emerge that force us to penetrate to a deeper level of the events.

One such problem is how the seizure of the gorge by Joab, David's
commander-in-chief, may be pictured. The Bible makes no mention of

---

* The Forty-second Psalm (verse 8) also contains the word *çinor,* translated as 'cataract,'
'waterfall.'

† Τω δια των ‘υποκειμενων ‘επι την ‘ακραν ‘αναβαντι. *(Tô dia tôn hypokeimenôn
pharangôn epi tên akran anabanti).*

‡ Most likely, the change of this name dates back to earlier times than Josephus.

a battle when the city, which had never opened its gates to the Israelites, finally became Israel's capital. Legendary tradition says that since the days of Abraham there existed a sacred agreement whereby the Israelites had given the Jebusites, the inhabitants of Jerusalem, a solemn pledge never to take possession of the city. Although this agreement is denoted as Abraham's way of returning a favour for the relinquishment of the tomb at Hebron by the Hittites who are here referred to as the ancestors of the Jebusites, this pledge by Abraham which promised to spare Jerusalem can perhaps be traced back originally to the relationship which the patriarch himself entered into with Melchizedek in Jerusalem.

Legend now describes in a grotesque way how David supposedly freed himself from this treaty of Abraham's and acquired possession of Jerusalem. A large reward was promised to the person who would let himself be hurled into the city by means of a catapult, and once inside, would destroy the tablets with Abraham's pledge and make the city accessible from within. Joab himself agreed to do it, solved the task assigned to him and thus secured for David and his people entry into the long desired city.

Perhaps the puzzling biblical report as well as such grotesque elaborations are an indication that the conquest of Jerusalem was by no means merely a military action but that in addition tests had to be passed which, in the sense of antiquity, could be denoted as mystery trials. It is possible that the Jebusites opened their gates to the Israelites in a peaceful manner after they saw that the latter were in possession of certain soul faculties and secrets of courage. Indeed, it is said later on that the Jebusite king, Araunah, in a peaceful way relinquished to David the location where subsequently the Temple was to arise.

A reference to such historical possibilities must remain unclear as long as we have not come across a further secret of ancient Jerusalem following the picture of the city's gorge. In the pre-Solomonic age, not only the external topographical form of the city must have been fundamentally different but the whole configuration of nature's forces as well. It is impossible to solve a number of individual problems that arise for us there without taking into consideration that Jerusalem was originally the source of very special planetary processes of evolution which in the course of time came to a standstill and were extinguished. Without considering this, all the mythical characterizations are also meaningless which designate Jerusalem as the centre of the world, as creation's point of departure, and as the portal of heaven and hell.

The Tyropoeon ravine must be pictured as having been filled during pre-Israelite times with the same half-volcanic fire and steam phenomena that billowed and flamed up most powerfully around the biblical Sinai.[9] For a long time, creation did not come to an end there, and for this reason reminiscences remained alive that made it seem as if it had been possible at one time to observe the creator beings in their activity. The mountain of the revelation of the Law in the wilderness, so the Bible leads us to believe, was also dominated by a significant duality and polarity that is expressed in the two names, Horeb and Sinai, which were kept apart by the cave-like rocky ravine,[10] from which, two centuries before David, Moses emerged, gifted with divine revelations, and two hundred years later, Elijah.

Pre-Israelite Jerusalem probably belongs into the same category with the great oracle sites of antiquity that drew their power from partly volcanic processes of evolution and — as was the case with Jerusalem — with the conception that the Omphalos, the navel or centre of the world was located there. The gorge of Castalia near Delphi, once filled with the clouds of smoke rising from the earth's interior that inspired the Pythia, corresponds to the Tyropoeon Valley between Zion and the Temple Mount. The Phrygian Hierapolis in the vicinity of Paul's cities, Colossae and Laodicea — Paul mentions this in the Letter to the Colossians (4:13) — possessed in Plutonion a rocky, fissure-like oracle gorge from which still in relatively late ages arose vapours that were poisonous for the intruders, but revelation-bearing for the Cybele priests who were active there. For the Israelites as well as the earlier inhabitants of the Holy Land, what was represented for the Greeks in the Castalian spring at the foot of the Pythian Gorge was present in the spring of Siloam at the junction of the Teraphon Gorge and the Kidron Valley. The fact that by David's time no mention was made any more of fiery vapours does not prove that they had become completely extinguished, since the Bible conceals this abyss in the veil of secrecy. And if, as appears to have been the case, the activity of these forces of nature was still only rarely observable at that time, this had its plausible parallel in the gradual extinction of the vapours arising from the ravine near Delphi.

Until the age of Solomon, those who were allowed to enter the sphere of Jerusalem stood before the deep gorge as if they looked down into the open jaws of hell. If they had been able to absolve the journey through hell and the abyss's trial by fire, heaven descended on them on yonder side of the gorge on top of Mount Zion. The portals of heaven and hell were truly next door to each other. Ancient Jerusalem represented a picture of creation torn asunder.

To this day, the city's region is filled with reminiscences of this. The western border-valley outside the city is still called Ge-Hinnom; but this is none other than the Arabian name for hell, Gehenna. And the gruesome fire altar of Molech, which stood down there as an instrument of infernal rituals until the age of King Josiah, probably only retained in a black-magical form the memory of the subterranean hell-fire which had once blazed up there from within the earth. When it is said that Herod the Great was driven back by flames that suddenly blazed forth when, in order to plunder David's grave, he had penetrated into the tomb of the kings; when it is told that even in later centuries flames flared up when the servants of Emperor Julian, the Apostate, wanted to proceed with the reconstruction of the Temple, we may well be dealing with late and last flickers of the forces of the depths which manifested there once upon a time continually. The custom, perpetuated to this day by the Eastern Churches, to conduct on every Easter Saturday the ecstatic ceremony of the sacred fire that falls from heaven, is perhaps also a reminiscence of the ancient nature of the Jerusalem heights.

On the other hand, we encounter the name 'paradise' on the western hill of the city in a variety of connections. Also, the Arabs oddly enough still retain the name, el Ferdus, the paradise,[11] for the ancient Potters' Field in the south, later called Aceldama, 'Field of Blood,' which is mentioned by the Gospels. In his description of the devastations brought about by the Roman troops of Emperor Titus in the garden district of the northern part of Mount Zion where the garden of Joseph of Arimathea was also located, Josephus bemoaned the fact that the city had become quite unrecognizable because of the destruction of the trees and the 'paradise.'[12]

The innumerable corridors, grottoes, caves and halls that exist in the subterranean rocky ground of Jerusalem pose the greatest riddles and at the same time offer the most splendid corroboration of the

Tyropoeon aspect. To an enormous extent, the city is hollowed out underneath — something that has been given insufficient attention by scholars. The city as a whole is indeed what is said of the sacred rock of the Temple site: the stone that floats freely over an abyss. These spaces within the earth's interior which extend far in depth and width, are not created by human hands, although from a certain time, they were appropriately called the 'stone quarries and stables of Solomon.' In rocky petrification, they are witnesses of the fire, steam and liquid processes of planetary evolution which in prehistoric times must have emerged there with original force. The Teraphon Gorge, the rift between the polar opposite elevations, is only the main vein of a whole system of fissures and gaping chasms. In later ages, the subterranean Jerusalem occasionally emerged into history in a terrifying manner; for example, when, after the storming of the city, the Romans under Titus discovered two thousand dead defenders of Jerusalem in one of the large caves alone. One can only dimly imagine what kind of mysteries and rituals took place in ancient times in these grottoes.

Finally, the riddles connected with water, which existed there until recently, also testify to the former telluric activity and elemental distinctiveness of Jerusalem's nature. The Gospel of John describes the pool of Bethesda (Beth-zatha) in the north-eastern part of the city as an intermittent spring. Its former significance is revealed by the ruins of large structural enclosures. Heated and impelled by subterranean fire, the curative waters of this pool boiled up like a geyser at periodic intervals. In like manner, the Well of the Virgins or the Well of Steps in the Kidron Valley south-east of the city, called Gihon in the Old Testament, dispensed its water in a rhythm resembling high and low tide — as reported by the Fathers of the Church and the pilgrims of the Middle Ages and still observable until a short time ago — thus bearing witness to the activity of the subterranean forces. For many centuries, this Gihon well has been the only remaining active spring in the immediate vicinity of Jerusalem. The drying up of the original abundance of the Holy City's water supplies is also expressed in the gradual coming-to-rest of the formerly vehement elemental vitality of nature in that region.

Since antiquity, the spring which was the most important water sanctuary of ancient Jerusalem, namely the Siloam pool, was fed from Gihon. An artificial rock tunnel, more than half a kilometre long, has connected Gihon and Siloam since very early times. Many guesses have been made concerning the question of Siloam.* Here too, the key is found in the change brought about by the filling up of the Tyropoeon ravine. Without doubt, the pool of Siloam at the southern tip of the Teraphon was not always a secondary spring. Its significance is much older and surpasses that of the Gihon spring. When the rocky fissure still gaped between the two elevations of Jerusalem, water must have emerged from it and the whole system of subterranean rifts and fiery chambers which, since it was saturated with the vehement evolutionary forces of the earth's interior, possessed special curative quality. The pilgrims to Zion must have experienced the greatest feeling of sacredness when they washed themselves there prior to ascending the holy mountain. Evidently, the subsequent filling up of the city's gorge must have obstructed the subterranean inlets of the pool of Siloam and forced the water to seek a path to the well of Gihon through the network of crevices. But in order to prevent the sanctuary of Siloam from drying up, Solomon had the rocky tunnel dug, which, as shown by its winding, almost arch-shaped course (it was 533 metres, 1 750 ft long, although its starting-point and end were only 335 meters (1 100 ft) apart in a straight line) and its alternating height (between 1.15 and 4.5 metres, 4–15 ft) could be driven into the rock by utilizing natural crevices and rifts. In the story of the one who was born blind, the Gospel of John still knows and reports about the curative force and sacredness of the water of Siloam.

Frequently, the ancient world thought that it heard the rushing of mighty waters in the interior of the mountains of Jerusalem, especially underneath the rock surfaces of the Temple Mount. It considered the springs of Siloam and Beth-zatha merely as the most negligible manifestations of much greater subterranean forces of nature. The sacred

---

* The most frequently held opinion is that King Hezekiah (around 700 BC) had constructed the tunnel during the threatening siege of Jerusalem by the Assyrians in order to direct the water of Gihon, which flowed outside the city walls, to a location within. A fact that speaks against this is that although an ancient Hebrew inscription at that site states that the tunnel was dug from both sides, the time of construction required was seven to eight months. Mommert is doubtless correct in stating that the construction of the tunnel already falls into the time of Solomon.[13] Strangely enough, the key thought of the filling of the Tyropoeon Gorge, which is elsewhere so clearly employed by him, eludes him here. [Modern archaeology concludes a tunnel built at the time of Solomon along the bottom of the hill of the Kidron Valley; at the time of Hezekiah this was closed and another dug through to Siloam from Gihon.[14] *Translator*]

rock was, after all, considered to be the stone that kept the wells of the abyss sealed in which the first Flood roared. The ancient mythical designation of the sacred rock, *Even Shetiyah*, actually means 'stone of watering,' but has in most instances incorrectly been understood to mean 'foundation stone.' A legend relates that when David wanted to lay the foundation stone for the Temple, he had to dig deeper and deeper until, at a depth of 1 500 ells, he came upon a shard of clay on which the holy name of God was inscribed. Astonished, but not having been warned, the king lifted up the shard and lo, the buried waters of the abyss gushed up irresistibly. The hitherto banished primal powers of creation emerged threateningly at the centre of the world. And if David had not found a helper in Ahithophel who, having been initiated into the secrets of Jerusalem's nature, could speak the magic word over the unleashed depth, he would have been unable to prevent the end of the world.[15]

In the final analysis, all such traditions are not without foundations in nature. Real reminiscences play into them, although they have become all but unrecognizable. At the time when Joab paved the way to Jerusalem for his people by climbing through the Teraphon Gorge, the nature of that region may well have still been such that human beings who dared venture into the depths had to absolve — as in the mysteries — true journeys through hell, fire and water trials.

In quick alternation, the two hills of the Holy City became the sites of the sanctuary and the residency of the king after the history of Israel had arrived in Jerusalem. David chose the summit of Zion with its cosmic atmosphere of benevolence and peace on yonder side of the gaping rift. But as early as Solomon's reign — and nothing can illustrate more clearly the great turning point which thereby occurred in history — the centre of Israelite life moved over to the rocky eastern hill where it remained until the end of the Old Covenant. The ravine was closed and the great cosmic polarity, which made up the character of Jerusalem, was concealed as if behind a curtain.

When David built his palace on the hill of Zion with the aid of Phoenician architects and then also brought the ark of the Covenant there in a solemn procession from the region of Gibeon, this signified a link to the hidden mystery stream which had emerged out of its obscurity at one time in the figure of Melchizedek.

The temple-like room that became the home of the sanctuary — just as the palace itself which must be pictured as being quite unpretentious — was probably connected to the residence of the king as a kind of castle-chapel. But in view of the customs which were decisive in the ancient world for the construction of sanctuaries, this room containing the ark could not but occupy the same locality where the concealed mystery-site's centre of worship had existed since earliest times. The name Zion (*çiyun* means the 'erected stone monument,' from *çawah*, to erect) points to an ancient holy menhir, a sun column of stone, a site where the spiritual sun's sacred uplifting forces were worshipped. Under David, the ark of the Covenant assumed the legacy of the sacred stone of Zion.

According to an almost uninterrupted tradition, which we consider well founded, particularly because of the inner logic of the sequence of stories as well as the concurrence of the various segments of tradition, (a more detailed description will follow in the volumes on early Christianity) the site of the ark on Zion had an important history even later on. When the sacred ark had been brought to the eastern hill into the Holy of Holies in Solomon's Temple, David was buried under the temple-chapel of his royal castle and the tombs of all the kings of Judah until Hezekiah were added to it in the course of time. After a number of desecrations of David's grave, in the final instance by Herod the Great, it was on this site that during the lifetime of Jesus the house stood in which he celebrated the Last Supper on Maundy Thursday with his disciples. (As we shall show in the later volumes, this was the house of the religious order of the Essenes.) In the same room, the disciples experienced the event of Pentecost. Thus, this became the first Christian place of worship, the 'mother of the churches.'

The locality and surroundings of the Cenacle, which was enlarged into a beautiful Gothic hall during the period of the Crusades, but has been claimed and guarded fanatically by the Arabs for several centuries as part of the mosque above the grave of David, permits graphic conclusions concerning the constructions by David in the Zion region, if the inner consistency of religious building traditions can be utilized as a means of historical research. Close by the site of the Cenacle, the Armenian Christians show the locality of the palace of Caiaphas. The Roman Church contest this and claim that the house of the high priest was situated a bit more to the east (about 250 metres, 800 ft), where, in place of the early Christian church of 'St Peter at the Crowing of the Cock,' they constructed a pompous, new Petrine Church. This is a place where the slope of Mount Zion drops off steeply to the Kidron Valley and to which the ancient steps, mentioned earlier, lead up. The Armenian tradition is probably in the right as compared with the Roman. The site of Caiaphas' palace was not chosen at random. This structure was, after all, the dwelling of the family and Order of the Sadducees, the temple-aristocracy from which descended all the high priests and which insisted on the old traditions with special emphasis. The first ancestor of the Sadducees was Zadok, one of the two high priests who, under David, conducted the service at the sanctuary. Just as the houses of the priests were next door to the Holy of Holies later on in the precinct of Solomon's Temple, Zadok's dwelling most likely stood near that part of David's castle which contained the ark of the Covenant. It then becomes comprehensible why the palace of Caiaphas, built at the site of the house of Zadok, was situated so close to the Cenacle in Jesus' time. We arrive at an approximate picture of the establishments erected by David on the southern part of Mount Zion: above the ancient steps that led up from Siloam, at the site of today's Roman Church of St Peter, the entrance was located to the castle's confines. David's royal palace complex extended westward from there and ended in the room of the ark of the Covenant at the site of the (later) Cenacle. The neighbourhood of this chapel was composed of the priests' dwellings, among which the one belonging to Zadok must have been situated north of the room of the ark at the site of the (future) Armenian garden of Caiaphas (see the city map on page 82).

What, then, was the reason that Solomon erected the Temple as well as his royal residence on the rocky eastern hill of the city, completely departing from the location chosen by David and his constructions? This change was already prepared by David. In a supersensory experience of punishing and shattering severity which overcame him there, David had been ordered to leave the celestial area of Zion and to begin construction of the Temple on the other side of the infernal gorge on the stern rocky plateau which was called 'the threshing floor of Araunah.' Solomon finally fulfilled the command given to his father; he completed the change which David must have experienced like an expulsion from paradise.

We go wrong if we assume that the 'threshing floor' of the Jebusite, Araunah, was nothing more than a place for threshing wheat. Like Mount Zion, the eastern hill also had its religious, cultic past. When the Old Testament speaks of a 'threshing floor,' it always refers to rocky high places of sacrifice from the sphere of pre-Israelite cults, regardless of whether the expression is only meant in an imaginative sense, or whether localities are indicated which served as both threshing floors and places of sacrifice.

We have already encountered the picture of the threshing floor more than once. During the sacrifice to Baal on the threshing floor of Ophra, Gideon received his calling to become Judge.[16] On the threshing floor of Boaz at Bethlehem, Ruth, the gleaner, betrothed herself to the Messianic lineage.[17] The Old Testament abounds in cultic scenes that occur on threshing floors. The lamentations by Joseph for his father Jacob, lasting seven days, were held on the threshing floor of Atad (Gen.50:10f). When the solemn procession was on its way, by means of which David had the ark of the Covenant brought to Jerusalem, a sacrilege occurred: Uzzah wanted to stop the sanctuary on a pagan site of sacrifice, Nacon's threshing floor (called 'Chidon's threshing floor' in Chronicles), but he collapsed dead on the ground, the reason why the threshing floor was henceforth called 'Uzzah's Doom' (Perez-uzzah, 2Sam.6:6–8). And when the prophet Hosea had to accuse his people of being unfaithful and turning to the worship of Baal, he summed up his call of reproach in the words: '... you have played the harlot, forsaking your God. You have loved a harlot's hire upon all threshing floors. Threshing floor and wine-vats shall not feed ...' (9:1f). To this day, one can observe in Greece how the people in the country celebrate their religious ceremonies and festivals on the *halônes,* the threshing floors outside the villages.

The Bible points out clearly that when David acquired Araunah's threshing floor, this was more than a scene of a profane purchase. When Araunah, the Jebusite, saw David coming, he prostrated himself before him and offered gifts of sacrifice to him. The biblical text permits us to take a look into real mystery backgrounds by indicating who Araunah really was: 'Araunah, the king, gave all this to the king' (2Sam.24:23B). Araunah was more than a peasant who sold his threshing floor; as king of Jerusalem, he was the successor of Melchizedek. Behind the scene of how he bowed before David emerges the picture of the encounter between Melchizedek and Abraham. At that time, Abraham, who did obeisance before Melchizedek, received bread and wine. Now, Araunah bowed before David as the higher one and opened the ancient place of sacrifice to him. The name of the Jebusite king (Chronicles calls him by the related name, Ornan) is itself an expression of what gave the rocky plateau on the eastern hill of Jerusalem its actual content and at the same time is a premonition of what is now to be erected there by David and Solomon: Araunah means, 'the altar.' The sacred rock, which to this day can be viewed in the Muslim Dome of the Rock on the Temple grounds, must have served for thousands of years before David's age as a sacrificial altar. It was the very centre of the sacred 'threshing floor.' The king of the Jebusites may well have received his name from the service he conducted there. In Solomon's Temple, it was extended to be the altar of the burnt offering. It is the one site on earth, where it can be proven that since thousands of years, from primeval ages until the present, sacrificial rituals have taken place without interruption.

Araunah's threshing floor is the rock of Moriah on which Abraham prepared his son Isaac for sacrifice outside the sanctuary of Melchizedek.[18] The picture of the whole of ancient Jerusalem can round itself out for us now: during the age of Melchizedek and Abraham, the duality of Jerusalem had its significance. Mount Zion carried the hidden mystery site of Melchizedek, the sun sanctuary of the 'God Most High,' the source of esoteric wisdom to which Jewish legendary tradition pointed with the pictorial expression of 'the School of Shem.'[19] The rock of Moriah on the stern, moonlike stone surface east of the gorge was the exoteric place of sacrifice, the locality for the cultic service in which the uninitiated could participate and the site of preparation for the actual mystery. Just like Abraham and Isaac, many were those who had to absolve the trials whereby the secret of Zion finally was revealed to them. Thus, between David and Solomon lies a great turn from the esoteric to the exoteric, from a world of hidden consecrations to a splendid culture unfolding itself to the outside. This came to expression in the fact that the centre of Israelite-Jewish life no longer existed in Zion but on Moriah. The turn to the exoteric realm corresponded exactly to Solomon's nature and gave its stamp to all his accomplishments. Even the filling up of the ravine in the middle of the city belonged to them. Wherever he could, Solomon removed from the ancient Holy City the ominous element, the traces of the forces from the earth's interior, but along with it he also stripped the city of its secrets.

When, after the lunar pole in Jerusalem's duality had been moved exclusively into the foreground following Solomon's Temple construction, and Zion, the quieter, hidden pole of the sun, was consigned to obscurity, all the mythological characterizations that originally related to the whole of the city were thought to refer to the Temple Mount. All at once, the sacred rock altar on Moriah was reputed to be the centre of the world. But one of two polarities cannot be declared the centre without an element of one-sidedness. In the age following Solomon, in genuine Judaism which arose only then, a historical one-sidedness did indeed make its appearance.

It was not until a thousand years later that an event took place, which suddenly revealed the true centre again that lies between Zion and Moriah, and rent the curtain which had not only been woven over the secret of Jerusalem but all cosmic secrets. The Cross of Golgotha stood over the ancient, no longer recognizable central tear of the city. It is a historically proven fact that the earthquakes, which took place between that significant Good Friday and Easter morning, again tore apart the old cosmic-mythical crevice, above which also lay the tomb of Joseph of Arimathea. There is a report by a pilgrim, one Antonius Placentius, from the middle of the sixth century with an exact portrayal of the Holy City. There, we find the startling description of a crevice in the rock next to the Holy Grave, underneath which one could hear the waters of the ancient Teraphon Gorge rushing along in the depths: 'Directly by the altar there is a fissure. You put your ear to it and you hear the streaming of water; and if you throw an apple into it or something else that can float and go to the Siloam spring, you will discover it there again.'

If Christian tradition relates to Golgotha all the attributes which together make up the cosmic myth of Jerusalem: that there is the centre of the earth, the seal of the primeval depths with its Flood waters, the entrance to heaven and the portal of hell, these legendary traditions were not transferred after the fact from the Temple Mount to Golgotha as believed by the scholars.[20] In reality, the true centre of Jerusalem and the world, mistakenly sought by Judaism on the Temple

Mount, has been revealed again on Golgotha. In the life of Jesus and the Christ events, the polarity between Galilee and Judea as well as between Zion and Moriah was brought into balance and reconciled. The archetypal character of Jerusalem as the quintessence of the Holy Land has found its redemption and fulfilment. In like manner, Mount Zion around the Cenacle came into its own again in the era of early Christianity as the central point of the Apostolic experiences and the first establishment of a Christian community.

CHAPTER NINE

The Splendour and Trials of the King

After Saul's tragic end, David chose Hebron to begin with as his residence, having advanced from fugitive to king. In this way, the first seven-and-a-half year segment of his reign, which lasted forty years (1004–965 BC), became a living connection to and a reawakening of the age of the patriarchs. Hebron, along with the grove of Mamre, had been the city of Abraham and Isaac, and Jacob had also proceeded from there. David did not continue in the direction that had begun with Saul. He fell back far into the past. And before Jerusalem was accessible to him, which enabled him to have a link to Melchizedek's ancient stream of wisdom, he placed himself at first into the direction and world of the patriarchs. He thus sealed the Messianic turn of Israel's history which withdrew the kingship from the tribe of Benjamin and imposed it upon the Messianic lineage in the tribe of Judah. In it, the lines of the patriarchs and kings flowed into one.

In Hebron, David was also once again in the sphere of influence of his Bethlehem youth. After the long period of his flight in the Judean wasteland, the part of the Judean tribal region, which possessed Bethlehem and Hebron as its focal points and was an oasis of life in the midst of the desert, opened to him, who to begin with was acknowledged as king only by his own tribe of Judah. When all the tribes of Israel finally professed him as king and turned away from the sons of Saul, the part of Judah at last opened itself to him which, despite being situated in the centre of the territory, had remained closed off to all the people, namely Jerusalem. The acquisition of Jerusalem and the transference of the king's seat to Melchizedek's Mount Zion represented the solemn culmination of the union, now actually extending into a political state, of the people of the twelve tribes. The cosmic harmony of twelve which had overshadowed the nascent nation like a prophecy at the end of the age of the patriarchs was now realized historically around Jerusalem as its centre.

When David had become king and the union of the people gradually took place, it was as if a glorious sunrise were breaking through mists and clouds. First, however, step by step, the tragic fate of Saul's lineage came to be fulfilled, and David, trying in vain to avert the tragedy, beheld in it with deep emotion the shadow of his own ascent. Also the conflicts and the sounds of war which had raged around Saul's throne were not over all of a sudden. But it was not long before David, who had assumed his royal position at first as a vassal of the Philistines, was acknowledged as a bright, leading star far beyond the confines of the twelve tribes. Particularly from the time he reigned on the sacred hill of Zion in his royal castle in the ever-present vicinity of the sanctuary which had been transferred there, a special radiance emanated from him over Israel and all the neighbouring nations. Soon, his power extended far into the north and the south. Damascus became the centre of a new, large northern province of David's kingdom, which extended close to the region of the Euphrates and Tigris. South of the Dead Sea — as if the strife between the sons of Jacob and those of Esau was now to be settled once and for all in favour of Jacob — the mighty nation of the Edomites had submitted to him, whose territory reached far into the deserts of the Sinai and the coast of the Red Sea.

The Davidian kingdom did not really become great through military might. No desire for conquest emerged from Hebron and Jerusalem. Saul's armies had been involved throughout his reign in defensive actions and these continued into the first years of David's rule. The basic reason why more and more regions in the surrounding areas entered into alliances or relationships as vassals to Israel was that in David and the twelve tribes the neighbouring nations encountered a spiritual life and a civilization in its most fruitful early stage that evoked deepest admiration. Perhaps another reason was that people were inclined to pay homage to the one who was king of Jerusalem because of the traditions which, going back into mythological pasts, retained recollections of the priest-king Melchizedek.

Purified by trials and persecutions, David's nature must have shown a most uncommon majesty, an element reminiscent of gods.

Had the beauty of his countenance, which had so delighted Saul in the his youthful harp-player, now changed into dignity of soul? Or did the nearness to the divinity, which Samuel had called down upon young David once upon a time with his secret anointing, come visibly to light?

In a whole number of passages, the biblical report states that David was addressed as an 'angel of God,' not by those who were close to him but particularly by those who, being different themselves, recognized the special quality of his character. During his flight from Saul, the Philistine king Achish had said to him: 'You are as pleasing to my eyes as an angel of God' (1Sam.29:9B). Later, the prophetess of Tekoa, who was supposed to incline the king towards forgiving his son, Absalom, said the same thing: '... my lord the king is like the angel of God ...' and '... my lord has wisdom like the wisdom of the angel of God to know all things that are on the earth' (2Sam.14:17, 20). Finally, the last descendant of the house of Saul, Mephibosheth, the crippled son of Jonathan, whom David accepted among those who ate at his table, said to him: '... my lord the king is like the angel of God; do therefore what seems good to you,' (2Sam.19:27). Many kings and powerful men among the surrounding nations may have felt and thought similarly.

The effect evoked by his own nature made it possible for David to expand his kingdom by peaceful means and spiritual politics. When Araunah, the king of the Jebusites, paid homage to David by prostrating himself before him on the sacred rock of Moriah and was willing to relinquish the ancient sanctuary to him, this may be the most significant example of an event several times repeated.

In the history of nations, it has often happened that one looked up to the figure of a great leader of humanity as to the bearer of a divine nature and consciousness. The further one goes back in time, the more it was a matter of course in the life of people to know that they had gods in human form in their midst. The new element that entered into history through the impression that David made upon his age as king was this, that he resembled a being of heaven although he was truly only a human being. In him, a humanization of soul forces had taken place that formerly had been divine and superhuman. Just because of this, David was enveloped by the supersensory, divine shining radiance of true humaneness.

The level that humankind attained in David was a most important and characteristic one. Rudolf Steiner once pointed this out when he placed David's achievements and culture into the course of evolution which wisdom has undergone on earth. Originally, not yet having awakened to selfhood, humankind received the gift of a sunlike revelation from the realms of the gods. Wisdom streamed from outside into the culturally advanced branch of humanity as does the light of the sun, which gives itself to the sprouting, blooming and fruit-bearing plant life. The last great historical form in which the divine sun-wisdom became effective on earth was the sacred Hermes-wisdom from which emerged the beginnings of the Egyptian culture a few millennia before the turn of time. Then, for the sake of the developing selfhood and freedom, humanity was increasingly left alone by the gods. Humanity was supposed to take the sun-wisdom it had received and utilize it as earthly wisdom. Thus transforming it, humankind was to let it reflect back step by step as the fruit of growing human independence. This reflection sought the path to a new sun element, now beginning to shine forth from the human kingdom, and in the process passed through stations similar to those designated in a spatial sense in the universe between earth and sun by the cosmic bodies of moon, Mercury and Venus. The Mosaic wisdom, which in the course of history had derived from the sun-wisdom of Hermes perpetuated in Egypt, represented the moon level of wisdom on its course of reflection. As a disciple of the Egyptian and Jethro-Sinai mysteries,[1] Moses had to bring to his people and to humankind something that was no longer a divine wisdom merely streaming in from outside, but it was not yet earthly wisdom originating purely from the human being. The Mosaic wisdom was akin to what moonlight is to sunlight; it was divine wisdom reflected in a moonlike manner by the earth.

During the spiritual life of the Davidian age, the wisdom that was being reflected by the earth entered its Mercury stage. For the first time, a wisdom shone forth on earth that originated from the personal being of a man. In the lofty, prehistorical figure of Hermes or Mercury, the Egyptians had revered the last superhuman messenger and bearer of divine wisdom. In David, the first human Hermes or Mercury lived on the earth. The transformed 'stream of the Moses wisdom ... moved towards the sun from which it had originated ... inasmuch as in the age of David, it inaugurated a direct Hermes element, a science and art of its own.'

This is how we can view:

> ... the time and reign of David; he is described as the royal psalmist, as a divine prophet, as a man of God, an armour-bearer and also a player on the harp. David is the Hermes, the Mercury, of the Hebrew people who had now developed to a stage of being able to produce an Hermes or Mercury-wisdom in an independent form. At the time of David, therefore, the Hermes-wisdom, once assimilated by the Moses-wisdom, had reached the region, or stage, of Mercury.[2]

The magic of an adolescent age of humanity overshadowed that turn of the millennium and especially the form assumed by the spiritual life of Jerusalem. In the Homeric poetry, the mature radiance of old age still held sway which had remained as an afterglow and echo of the ancient wisdom of the gods. In the Davidian spiritual life, which found its classic poetic expression in the Psalms, the struggling self-awareness of the human personality could be felt which in itself could now become culturally creative. The figure of David shone like the planet Mercury when it lights up in the young glow of dawn that precedes the sun. The radiance of his creative spirit communicated itself to his kingdom and caused the tribes all around him to turn into vassals or friends.

In David's case, the resemblance to the planet Mercury now also extended to the course of his destinies. Since he was no longer protected and supported by divine forces, his fate could not be one that took its course on the height of existence, remaining immune to all adversities. The dependence on the personal human forces had to become evident in that David had to pull himself up from the depths ever and again. In the true sense, his destiny was mercurial and eventful.* Just as the path of the planet Mercury circles the sun quickly, frequently changing from the morning sky to the evening sky, so an element of ascent and descent was inscribed into his destiny. In Saul's case, the quick, weather-like change had occurred in the sphere of consciousness, where blazing ecstasy alternated with deep depression. David could set the constant power of a thought-imbued capac-

---

* In medieval alchemy, quicksilver (mercury) played an important role as the mercurial basic element.

ity against these mood swings that raged in Saul's soul, but in his case, the upward and downward trends became a law of his destiny's course.

From the insignificance of the pastoral life in Bethlehem, young David had been propelled into the splendour of the royal court and he had already begun to attract much of the enthusiasm and veneration which really was due to the king. Then commenced the painful period of persecution. And although there were a few small uplifting instances and breakthroughs of happiness in the desert, David's degradation went so far that he finally had to turn into a vassal of the enemies. Then, however, fate quickly carried him up again to the shining height, visible far and wide, of royal splendour. Henceforth, was he spared the descent into the depths? Even as king, David had to pass through difficult trials and dark depths. Three times, he was overtaken by grievous blows of fate. The first misfortune befell him personally; he brought it about through his own guilt when he made Bathsheba, the wife of Uriah, his wife. The second concerned his kingship when he had to flee from Absalom, his son, having been deprived of his throne. The third concerned his people when heaven responded to the aberration in his reign with an epidemic of pestilence.

During the period of his flight in the desert, David, the wanderer to freedom, had placed himself above the external laws, only keeping faith with the inner law. Along with the priests of Nob, he freed himself of the Temple law when he took the consecrated bread. When he offered his services to the Philistines, he gave the appearance of betraying his people. During that time, he could at least have the feeling of inner justification when he turned himself into a lawbreaker. When he desired Bathsheba, the wife of another man, and added blood-guilt to adultery by placing Uriah in a position in the battle where he would be killed by the enemy, there was no more excuse for him. He had allowed passion to carry him away so that he transgressed against the divinely decreed moral law and became entangled in grievous guilt.

The fact that human beings were now beginning to be dependent on themselves, that they had to transform into the personal and human realm what had formerly extended into the soul as a divine element, this now exhibited its reverse aspect. Not only did the former divine wisdom turn into human wisdom and personal artistry; the soul stirrings that held sway between man and woman and led them together, something that up to now had been guided in unconscious or half conscious depths of being by powers surpassing the personal level, now moved into the sphere of personal experience. The quite personal sexual desire now arose. We see it enter into history in the figure of David. When he beheld Bathsheba, this aroused a longing in him, against which the imperativeness of the moral law appeared as if it had been extinguished. The will of the desirous personality thrust itself above the claim of the law.

It may be that David's encounter with Bathsheba occurred during a low point of his frame of mind. The homelessness, which had been his lot in an outer sense earlier, must now have returned frequently in an inner sense after he had become king. Free, proud self-confidence could not always be the fruit of the human personality's independence. Often, a sense of abandonment and hopeless loneliness had to predominate until the struggling soul could once again lift itself up to the idea of the divine power's benevolence. In Bathsheba an image of the long lost home and community may have suddenly arisen before David.[3]

He incurred guilt and when the child that Bathsheba bore him lay dead before David, he was cast into the depth of sorrow and recognized the stern hand of retribution. Nevertheless, his guilt was a necessary link in his and his people's destiny. After the death of this first child, did Bathsheba not become the mother of Solomon and, like Ruth, one of the progenitors of the Messiah whom the world awaited?

It is one of the most profound universal riddles that in the course of Providence and history, human transgression is counted upon. The divinely ordained destinies are not fulfilled without human co-operation, even through his incurring guilt. Even if man breaks the law that has been given him, it is possible that he thereby fulfils a law of destiny on a deeper level. Man cannot derive any excuse from this, but, if he recognizes it, he can sense the mysteries of grace that are involved in the guidance of his destinies.

The Bathsheba episode in David's life has often caused people to puzzle over the questions concerning the more fundamental guidance of destiny. The legends try in a childlike manner to cope with this riddle by relating that Bathsheba was originally intended to become David's spouse, but that he relinquished his right to Uriah when the latter helped him loosen the strap on the helmet of the slain Goliath.[4]

By means of subtle but clear indications, the biblical scriptures themselves, however, allow one to sense the deeper level of destiny. They show how the Bathsheba scene is only one link in a sequence of strange dispensations of Providence in David's life. Prior to Bathsheba, Abigail, the wife of Nabal, and Michal, Paltiel's wife, had become David's wives without his having committed any transgression.

During the period of his flight, when David had wandered about in the desert, he had once demanded a tribute from the wealthy cattle-owner, Nabal, for the military protection that his bands represented to the region. Nabal, the name means 'the fool,' concerned short-sightedly with the undiminished preservation of his riches, rejected David's demand, but Abigail, his wife, acknowledged David's right and brought forth gifts in abundance. Impressed by David's dignity, she was willing to serve him further. During an immoderate feast, Nabal was overtaken by death; Abigail was free and David made her his wife.

After David had become king, he also demanded that Michal, Saul's daughter, be returned to him. She had been given to him in marriage at one time but had been taken from him again during the period of his persecution and had been wed to a man named Paltiel. Those who were left of Saul's lineage had to fulfil his just request. Tearfully, Paltiel accompanied his wife when she returned to David. David's adulterous union with Bathsheba only occurred after this. When David married Abigail and Michal, he did not infringe upon the law. In this regard, these destinies differed from that concerning Bathsheba. And yet one is led to believe that a similar mark of destiny can be discerned in all three stories, a hidden law of David's fate that emerged repeatedly in different form. We see David complete the circle of his existence into the depths of guilt and its tragic consequences.

After Bathsheba had borne David the son who lived, Solomon, the destiny of the king took a strange course. On one side, it seemed that through the transgression a whole stream of sorrow and misfortune had been unleashed. On the other, it appeared that all the events played the great future into the hands of Bathsheba's son.

Among his older sons there was one whom David loved above all

others: Absalom. A Syrian princess was his mother. He resembled
Adonis, the youthful, handsome god; with his beauty and the suggestive charm of his nature he cast everybody under his spell. David
loved him as Jacob once loved Joseph. Absalom possessed a magic
similar to Joseph's. And yet he was completely different from him.
Whereas Joseph was of chaste purity and innocence, Absalom was
unrestrained in his enjoyments, passion and ambition, in a Dionysian
manner. He was aware of the power of fascination that he exercised
over people and he enjoyed making use of them as if in a game. He let
his hair grow long but how far removed he was from the ascetic training to which the Nazirites subjected themselves who also did not cut
their hair. Like a Lucifer incarnate, he proudly strode about.

A whole world separated David and Absalom, so different were
their souls. Did David, the earnestly striving and struggling one, perhaps love the son, who was so completely given up to beautiful illusion, with the same unhappy love with which he had loved the house
of Saul? Like them, did Absalom arouse in him the wistful sorrow over
the twilight of a world of ancient soul forces?

It was inevitable that destinies became intensely agitated around a
will-o'-the-wisp soul like that of Absalom. David's first-born son,
Amnon, fell madly in love with Absalom's sister, Tamar, and did not
rest until he had brought her under his power through trickery.
Absalom allowed some time to pass but then he took bloody revenge.
During a festival, he had Amnon killed and then fled into the homeland of his mother. When David had forgiven him, he returned to
Jerusalem, but now an untamable fire had been enkindled in him. He
himself strove after the highest power and prepared a revolution in all
the regions of the land. Taking advantage of the magic power he had
over human souls, he succeeded in turning large numbers of the people from David over to his side. Even Ahithophel, who, drawing from
ancient faculties, was active at David's court as a seer and magician
and whose advice David had always heeded, went over to Absalom.
As Bathsheba's grandfather, he could not forgive the king for his tres-
pass.

Absalom had himself declared king, and David, betrayed by his
people, had to flee before his own son whom he loved. Even as king,
he had to suffer the degradation and insecurity of flight. He had to
drink the bitter cup of sorrow to the last drop.

In the midst of the lamenting procession of those who still were on his side, David went down from Mount Zion into the valley, crossed the Kidron stream and, arriving at the foot of the Mount of Olives, went to Gethsemane. There, he sent the priests back to the city with the ark of the Covenant. 'But David went up the ascent of the Mount of Olives, weeping as he went, barefoot and with his head covered; and all the people who were with him covered their heads, and they went up, weeping as they went' (2Sam.15:30).

A moving picture unfolds before us that appears like a precast shadow of what is supposed to take place there a thousand years hence, when, in the dark of night, another would go on the same path from Mount Zion down to the Kidron Valley and then up to Gethsemane together with the group of disciples who would remain faithful to him. The story of the Passion in the New Testament finds a foreshadowing here in the Old Testament. Ahithophel gave Absalom counsel, observance of which was to heap disgrace on David and was designed to make him fall into the hands of the insurgents. Only the ruse of a man who, in order to serve David, claimed to be a follower of Absalom, succeeded in foiling the advice of the magician. And just as did Judas, when he saw that the expectations he had linked to his betrayal had been frustrated, so Ahithophel now went and hanged himself.

In the ensuing battle between David's and Absalom's followers, David's troops miraculously repulsed the superior number of their attackers. Destiny again stepped in. With his long, flowing hair, the source of his magic allure, Absalom became entangled in the branches of a terebinth tree; the mule he was riding ran away from under him, and although David had given explicit orders to spare Absalom's life, Joab, David's army commander, took it upon himself to kill the insurgent, just as he had earlier believed that he would serve the interest of the people best by terminating Saul's party against David's will. David's sorrow over the death of the son who had caused him such bitter suffering was beyond comprehension. It was far from his thoughts that he had now regained his royal throne. Only with difficulty could his people tear him away from his mournful lamentations over Absalom.

After David had now lost his two eldest sons, his love turned increasingly to the still young son of Bathsheba. His heart placed him between Absalom and Solomon, the two sons whose names both speak of 'peace,' but who related to one another as the old world does to the new. In Absalom, the dying flame of the human soul's divine content, which once had been peace, flickered up one more time. The peace-filled substance of the gods that the human being is able to bring forth out of his own being was to have its beginning in Solomon. Fate decided against Absalom in favour of Solomon, although he was the fruit of a guilt-laden marriage. Mourning over a dying world, David saw the future emerging from his transgression.

David's greatest peril was still ahead of him. While the first period of his royal reign had resembled an ever-increasing splendour of a rising sun, the culmination of the forty years were like nightfall after the sunset. The tragedy of the aging king is something, however, that is difficult to understand for modern-day cultural sentiments: David had a census taken of the people and, as a result of his action, pestilence afflicted the Israelites throughout the land, claiming many thousands of lives.

Today, when statistics have long since become the most matter-of-fact and indispensable means with which social conditions are regulated and improved, it must seem strange that the Bible, without even questioning it in the slightest, represents the epidemic of pestilence as heaven's answer to the David's census. Did he not have the best interest of his people in mind when he dispatched the overseers into all the regions in order to produce a true overview of the condition and the life of the whole population? And if by means of this census David became the inventor of statistics, would he not deserve fame and humankind's gratitude rather than heaven's severe punishment?

The Bible knows of the dual countenance of evil. It does not only look upon the impure Luciferic fire of personal sinfulness, which emerges from human self-love and sensual desire. It also knows of the cold, insidious poison of that other evil for which our modern age is so blind: the Ahrimanic power of soul-less calculation, which is active not so much in the personal as in social life.

This was the great transgression of the old David, namely, that he allowed a spirit to enter into humanity, which, although seemingly useful for bringing about the greatest progress, entailed infinite peril as well: the cold, soul-devoid spirit of numbers.

As long as the wisdom of the gods dwelled among people, the poisonous touch of calculating cleverness had remained distant from them. Now, the heavenly beings left the human being to his own devices. With the soul and thought-faculties left to him by the gods, humankind thus became capable of producing an art and science of its own, like the kind which, in its beginnings, gave rise to the splendour of David's age. But at the same time, there arose the danger of a world of thought with which the human soul could not relate and which developed in a cold direction of its own, finally producing the tyranny of the mechanized age of the machine which in our time pushes aside the human soul-bearing being and turns him into the slave of his creations. The Bible sees the beginning of this development in David's census. The human being allowed the reins of thinking and intelligence to slip from his hands, and the first threads were spun of the Ahrimanic web in which humanity became enmeshed as the centuries went by.

Today, one hardly gives it a thought that illnesses could have causes other than hygienic ones, namely spiritual causes: that the wrong spiritual behaviour by people can produce epidemics. The Bible originated in times in which a direct, instinctive comprehension for this was still alive. It is not so long ago either that the biblical report of the pestilence at the end of David's reign was generally considered to be plausible. Along with that census, which degraded the living individual human being for the first time into a mere number, something so unfamiliar and foreign gripped the people that a chill dismay and horror spread about, that extended under the threshold of consciousness deep into the physical body. The souls became estranged from their physical incarnation as in a shock, and terrible processes of decay invaded the bodies.

Naturally, neither the Bible nor he who confronts it here with positive understanding, means to imply that humankind should have never allowed reason and statistics to enter their cultural life. Otherwise, in the face of modern life, the Bible would only institute a helpless, pitiful form of prudery. The cold spirit of statistics has a perilous and ominous effect only when it is put to use in a wrong, premature manner before the soul has grown strong enough to tolerate and compensate for the chilling influence.

'Saul's sin,' whereby the benign spirit of the divinity had departed from him, had consisted in the fact that despite the victory over Agag he had not wanted to divorce himself from the realm of the giants, from the soul forces of the past. He became the victim of a spiritual relapse. David's great mistake was the premature utilization of a faculty, to the mastery of which humankind would only advance in the future. A spiritual anticipation cast him into the tragic wastage of his kingship.

When the pestilence had been arrested among the populace, David himself still presented a pitiful appearance which seemed like the condition that had to overtake humanity through incorrect application of the intellect: he lay on his bed, freezing; no garment, no warm cover could dispel the cold chills that had gripped him. Only the warmth of devoted human kindness could ease the suffering of the aging king. A turn for the better occurred that is similar to the one in the medieval epic of Poor Henry, *Der arme Heinrich,* which, like the biblical report of David's last period of life, describes a historical event but in fact only reveals the tragic mythos of the I-bearing human being. Just as the leprous knight, 'Poor Henry,' of the Middle Ages could only be healed by the pure devotion of a virginal maiden, so David too, the Poor Henry of the Old Testament, only found relief through the Shunammite virgin, Abishag (1Kings 1:1–4).

When the pestilence broke out in Jerusalem and the whole land, David himself had a supersensory experience of commanding greatness. On the sombre rock of Moriah he beheld the archangel with the flaming sword, the Michaelic power that guards against humankind's misuse of the forces of thinking which have been entrusted to it by the worlds of the gods. The entity otherwise revealed as Israel's helping and protecting genius now stood as a stern judge before the king in order to expiate the fall into sin of thinking. There, in the centre of the world, where the gates of hell and the portals of paradise were situated side by side, a new expulsion from paradise had to take place after the Fall of human perception. Just as Adam once beheld the angel with the flaming sword, so David now beheld him as well.

It was this experience that commanded him to give up the blissful height of Zion and to lay the foundation stone for the new Temple construction on stern Mount Moriah. David acquired the threshing floor of Araunah. The great turn commenced from the esoteric to the exoteric sphere. Humankind had to take its leave of the last blessed place of proximity to the gods and paradise. Henceforth, Mount Zion stood deserted, for the stern divinity had decreed it to be thus. Where David had cared for the sanctuary, solemn stillness of tombs held sway. David's grave found its place there.

With sorrow and longing, the devout from then on looked across to Zion, ringed by evergreen trees, the visible expression of the lost paradise. It seemed that what had still been present during David's reign would have to return in the future. One day, the 'son of David,' who would bring back the paradise, would have to appear. On that day, when the great longed-for being would come, it would be as if the tomb of the great king had opened and his golden age had returned in new, divine radiance.

Thus, after David's death, Mount Zion, from whence the stern angel had driven Israel away, became the Kyffhäuser Mountain* of the Old Covenant. Down in that vault, so it was believed, the king awaited the dawn of a new day. But when the fulfilment of this great expectation came, when the 'son of David' washed the feet of his disciples in the house above David's grave and gave them bread and wine; when he appeared to them there as the resurrected one and poured the flames of the spirit of Pentecost over them, the world did not recognize him. The fulfilment did not come in the manner in which it had been expected, namely as the re-establishment of the Davidian kingdom; it came inconspicuously as the sowing of a cosmic-divine power into the souls of men.

---

* According to the German legend, Emperor Friedrich I, Barbarossa, (1122–90) sleeps inside the Kyffhäuser Mountain, awaiting the time when there will no longer be any strife in the German lands, at which time he will re-emerge and lead the country once again. [*Translator*]

CHAPTER TEN

The World of the Psalms

In the Septuagint, the Greek Bible, the Book of Psalms does not end with the song of praise which we commonly know as Psalm 150, but the ringing conclusion continues into Psalm 151, into a concealed 'final word of David,' which once again sums up the significance and wealth of David's age in the image of the victory over Goliath:

> Hallelujah!
> Praise God amidst all beings sanctified to him
> Praise him in the firmament of his power,
> Praise him throughout the kingdoms of his reign,
> Praise him and all the wealth of his glory,
> Praise him with the sounds of trumpets,
> Praise him with the sound of lute and harp,
> Praise him with the beat of drums and choir song,
> Praise him with the lyre's strings and the sound of flutes,
> Praise him with the cymbals' pleasing sound,
> Praise him with the cymbals' battle cry.
> Let everything that breathes praise the Lord! (Ps.150B)

Now here is David's special Psalm, concerning his battle with Goliath:

> The smallest one was I among my brothers,
> And the youngest in the house of my father.
> I tended the sheep of my father,
> My hands carved an instrument for playing flute,
> My fingers played upon the harp.
> Who brought the message to my Lord?
> He, the Lord, heard the message.

He sent his angel; he took me away from my father's sheep
And anointed me with his holy oil.
My brothers were handsome and tall,
But they did not find favour before the Lord.
And I went to confront the stranger.
He cast his curse against me in the name of his gods.
But I took hold of his sword and cut off his head
And freed Israel from its ignominy. (Ps.151*B*)

In the spirit of the picture consciousness from which the biblical scriptures originate, it is an expressive indication of the inner nature of the Old Testament's Psalm-poetry that David, the great psalmist, appears once again here at the end as the vanquisher of the giant.

In the age of the giants, to which Saul also paid his tribute, the Psalms could have never originated. They are the classic document of a new spirit that subdues the natural forces, extending dimly and titanically into the soul, with the light of clear-thinking self-awareness. The actual singer of Psalms is the personality struggling for its 'I,' the personality liberated from the dreamy spell of ancient fetters. In the Psalms, there arises not only a new form of poetry; the striving personality itself is born in them.

The name and image of David stands above the whole psalter, although the Bible attributes only a part of the hymns actually to him. And if it were ever proven — something that we do not believe will happen — that even the so-called 'Psalms of David' were not composed by David, it would not change the fact that the Book of Psalms is the most wonderful expression and result of the stage which David embodied in the history of humanity.

Approximately four hundred years earlier, young Pharaoh Amenophis IV, Akhenaten, far ahead of his time, had composed psalms: his radiant hymns to the sun. But they had actually only imbued Heliopolis' traditionally existing odes to the sun with a touch of an especially inspired enthusiasm, and as yet had not added any expression of the praying soul's quite personal emotions to the cultic song of praise dedicated to the sphere transcending the personal level.

At the same time as David's reign, Homer, his great contemporary, composed his immortal epics on the Grecian coast of the Sea of Asia Minor. But even though a great human soul offered up the colours and nuances of its inner being, the Homeric songs are really composed more by gods than a man. The mythos composes itself in them but now before all humankind, whereas earlier it had been expressed in the inspirations of the mysteries to a few elect. In order to be the mouthpiece of the gods, the poet who was the bearer of a personal life receded into insignificance to such an extent that the scholars have even been of a mind to doubt his existence.

By contrast, the Psalms of the Old Testament are already personal poetry through and through. Just as the 'Song of the Bow,' David's song of lamentation over Saul and Jonathan, was born out of personal suffering, so all the Psalms have originated from a concrete experience. Particularly those hymns that are attributed to David himself are in many cases connected with certain situations in his personal destiny. A number of Psalms are cries for help in the duress of persecution: 'when he fled from Saul, in the cave' (57); 'when Saul sent men to watch his house in order to kill him' (59); 'when the Ziphites went and told Saul, "David is in hiding among us"' (54); 'when he fled from Absalom his son' (3); 'when he was in the Wilderness of Judah' (63); 'When he was in the cave. A prayer.' (142*B*). In other Psalms, the soul seeks to free itself of the suffering and burden of guilt: 'a Psalm of David, when Nathan the prophet came to him, after he had gone in to Bathsheba' (51).

The religious and poetic expression in which David clothed the pain and relief of his own personal conflicts of soul nevertheless is of universal validity in every instance. David experienced archetypal destinies. In his suffering and trials, in his elevations and inklings of salvation, he absolved the paths which henceforth had to be under-gone by human beings, who struggle to attain their true self, every-where and at all times. Dismissed from the protective bosom of the gods and left to his own devices, human beings plunge into abysses, flee into deserts and caves, and yet call again and again for the help-ing hand of God which has let go of them for their own sake. For per-sonal devotion and prayer to be born in the human soul, this presupposes the separation of the human being from the cosmic total-ity, a process that culminates during David's age. Only a human being who is developing into an unfettered, free personality can place him-self before the deity, struggling and pleading for help in his needs, for mercy in his transgressions: 'Out of the depths I cry to thee, O Lord!'

(130). Only out of the terrors born of being far away from God, something that man as an individual being comes to experience at a certain stage of maturity, the cry can be heard: 'My God, my God, why hast thou forsaken me?' (22). Only one who has struggled through the abysses of transgression and, in sensing a new closeness to God, also acquires an awareness of the path lying before him can pray: 'Create in me a clean heart, O God, and put a new and right spirit within me' (51:10, Bathsheba Psalm). David's Psalms document the birth of personal devotion, of personal prayer.

Specifically in Israel's spiritual development, the sound of the poetic psalms contains the magic of a new beginning. From the start, the world of the Old Covenant had possessed a basic attitude which consciously turned away from beauty. The inner task of Israel, which consists in distilling the ancient dim soul faculties from human nature and replacing them with the clearness of thinking in a consciousness that originated in the human being itself, had necessitated the renunciation of art that had been the fruit of clairvoyant vision and inspiration in humanity of antiquity. The stern law of Sinai had even expressly forbidden any pictorial art as a transgression against the Yahweh deity. Nevertheless, in David's age, we see the flower of art bloom on the tree or harsh sternness. Although the commandment was not broken that excluded any form of sculpture, painting and architecture, something not of material substance, namely word and sound that stream out of the inner being, became the means of art. There arose a marvellous inner unity of poetry and music. It is a form of poetry which, by means of the vowels in its words, brings to expression the melody for the intonation of singing, because when they are included in the writing, the vowels in the Hebrew text of the Psalms are at the same time notes. An art was born, distinguished from the art of the great magic civilizations of Egypt and Babylonia by the fact that it was not brought down from supernatural spheres through clairvoyant faculties, but instead blossomed forth from the young inwardness of the human heart, the personality seeking and finding itself. The humanization of consciousness created for itself an artistic and poetic expression. Poetry and music appeared on the stage of history as ancient clairvoyance turned inward. The element of Saul's either prophetic or demonic ecstasy, which was only just bidding farewell to the divine sphere and tore itself loose towards the human realm, actually arrived in the Psalms of David on a human level and in the sphere of human-ness. It is only the alternation between the songs of suffering and repentance, resulting from the personal struggles of the soul in the Psalms, that appear to us like a faint reminiscence of the stormy swings of mood in Saul.

The poetic and musical element of the Psalms was a fruit of the new relationship in which the human being, developing towards per-sonalization, confronted nature. As long as he was still interwoven as a dependent link into the life of nature as is the child at the breast of the mother, psalms of nature such as those contained among the Old Testament's Book of Psalms could not come into being. The human being first had to lose something of the ancient closeness to nature, experiencing himself cut off and opposite to nature, his mother, in order to marvel over the wonders of creation in songs of praise. The resonant longing contained in this amazement, which wanted to renew the experience of the old unity and fusion, is a main source of poetry and music. A nostalgia clothed in admiration produces hymns in the human heart such as Psalm 19 or 104:

> The heavens are telling the glory of God;
>> and the firmament proclaims his handiwork
>
>> ...
>
> In them he has set a tent for the sun,
> which comes forth like a bridegroom leaving his chamber,
>> and like a strong man runs its course with joy.
>
>> ...

> Bless the LORD, O my soul!
> O LORD, my God, thou art very great!
> Thou art clothed with honour and majesty,
>> who coverest thyself with light as with a garment,
> who hast stretched the heavens like a tent,
>> who hast laid the beams of thy chambers on the waters,
> who makest the clouds thy chariot,
>> who ridest on the wings of the wind
>
>> ...

> O LORD, how manifold are thy works!
> In wisdom hast thou made them all;

the earth is full of thy creatures

...

These all look to thee,
to give them their food in due season.
When thou givest to them, they gather it up;
When thou openest thy hand, they are filled with
good things.

In the historical development of Israel, David's relationship with nature represents an important mean. Moses, who because of his hymn of praise at the Sea of Reeds is known as the poet of the first psalm, still looked into the kingdom of the elements as into the wide open sphere of divine revelation. The fire and steam-clouds of the Sinai-nature were his element. Later, under the leadership of the judges, a development commenced that turned away from nature. The divine was no longer supposed to be sought outside but exclusively within the soul. Elijah no longer experienced the deity in the elements of earthquake, fire and windstorm through which it had so clearly spoken to Moses.

David represents the midpoint between Moses and Elijah, between Moses and the prophets. He was no longer so closely united and linked to the divine element in nature as was the Hebraic primeval age. But as yet, he was also not as separated and withdrawn from nature as was the age of the Jewish prophets. The inward intensification of nature, which found its poetic expression in the Psalms, lies on the path that began with an experience of nature saturated with revelation and culminated in an extreme inner devoutness. Nature and the inner world of human beings find their balance in the art of David, the bard carrying the harp.

Here, we come close to the solution for the strange historic riddle that we encounter in the heading of a large number of Psalms. There, not David but the 'Sons of Korah' are designated as the poets and singers. Does this fit in with the dark role that the company of the Korah people had played during the Sinai journey, when we now meet them again as singers of those Psalms in particular which we would want to count among the most beautiful and melodious ones? To the songs of Korah belongs the Psalm of longing:

> As a hart longs
>> for flowing streams,
> so longs my soul,
>> for thee, O God.
> My soul thirsts for God,
>> for the living God. (42*B*).

The hymn of faith, Psalm 46, which Martin Luther composed into his song of faith and courage, 'A mighty fortress is our God,' also belongs to the children of Korah:

> God is our refuge and strength,
>> a help in the great troubles that have come upon us.
> Therefore we will not fear though the earth should perish
>> and the mountains would sink into the middle of the sea
>> ... (*B*)

Finally, Psalm 84, the hymn of love for the Temple, is a song of Korah: 'How lovely is thy dwelling place ... My soul desires and longs for the courts of the LORD.'(*B*)

Did not the company of Korah rise against Moses in the wilderness, presumptuously laying claim to the performance of the sacrificial service, and did not the earth's depths open under them to swallow them up? How could it be that the former malefactors now share in David's fame as creators of the most intimately religious hymns?

During Moses' age, the spiritual nature of the children of Korah represented an element in history that was far ahead of its time.[1] As bearers of a principle of personality not yet valid at all, they took offence at the fact that Moses and Aaron led the people instead of granting the same privileges to every individual, especially in regard to conducting the sacrificial service. It was just this, their abstract anticipation of an selfhood to which humankind could only mature later on, that deprived them also of the living relationship to nature which in their time was still enjoyed by the other Israelites. This was why Moses could confront them with their own abstract spiritual nature by giving in to them and allowing them actually to conduct the burnt offering. The flames enkindled in the censers awakened the forces of fire and steam, slumbering in the rocky clefts of the Sinai

Desert, into frightening activity. The Korah people saw themselves helplessly abandoned to the spirits they had called forth. They no longer possessed the instinct that would have guided them to conduct themselves properly in relation to the forces of nature. The fact that the biblical report, which claims that the gaping abyss had swallowed the company of Korah, must be taken imaginatively and cannot be interpreted as referring to their physical annihilation, becomes evident here where the Bible once again mentions the Sons of Korah as psalmists along with David. In the age of Moses, they had been rejected. In David's era, the form of mentality that would have had to produce fatal consequences during the period of the desert wanderings was now timely and had been reached in humanity's development. The age of the Sons of Korah had arrived. We must probably picture them as a progressive community,* resembling a religious order, which, as temple minstrels, stood in service of the artistic and cultic life. So, in David and the culture inaugurated by him, a stream of Israel's spiritual life found its salvation which had earlier been experienced as standing under the ban of a transgression. The almost abstract relationship was now justified in which the human being, who was developing into an individual personality, confronted nature. In David, whom one could call the 'true Korahite,' as well as in this whole group, this relationship became the source of a rich artistry, a music and poetry lending wings to the spiritual-religious life.

It was a quite specific relationship to nature that wove in the world of the Psalms. The psalmist did not confront nature in general, intensifying it in his soul and transforming it into landscapes of the mind. A landscape of special archetypal character lay before his inner view, which was transparent for the ever-present soul-landscape of man who struggles for divine mercy: the nature in the Psalms is in many instances the earth that is still coming into being, moved by the primal forces of creation. A Sinai-nature, transferred within the soul, with its thunder and lightning, its fire and earthquakes and its trials of the wilderness, turned into the realm of human struggles of soul.

---

* The name (*korah* means bald) is indicative of the fact that the Korahites adhered to an attitude of mind that was opposite that of the Nazirites, who retained their hair in order to be able to preserve certain ancient soul faculties.[2]

The voice of Yahweh breaks the cedars of Lebanon ...
The voice of Yahweh flashes forth flames of fire ...
The voice of Yahweh shakes the wilderness of Kadesh.
> (Ps.29B)

The cords of Sheol [hell] entangled me

...

Then the earth reeled and rocked;
> the foundations also of the mountains trembled
> and quaked, because he was angry.
Smoke went up from his nostrils,
> and devouring fire from his mouth;
> glowing coals flamed forth from him.

...

He rode on a cherub, and flew;
> he came swiftly upon the wings of the wind.

...

Out of the brightness before him there broke through
> his clouds
> hailstones and and coals of fire.
> (Ps.18B; see also 77 and 144)

In David's age, however, the of the elements extended even into Jerusalem. An atmosphere resembling that which surrounded the heights on which Moses had received the revelation of the Law enveloped the rock fissure which was still open then and which drew a symbol of torn creation into the city's appearance. The archetypal character of Jerusalem coincided here with the archetypal nature of the smoke-filled wilderness of Sinai; in terrestrial images, the obscure, unpredictable forces of destiny could be sensed, and the soul which the human being was supposed to overcome by means of the deity's grace. After all, the Judean Desert, the ravines of which could be overlooked from the Mount of Olives, bordered on the sphere of Jerusalem as a physical reflection of the soul-landscape that the self-endowed human being had to traverse in the trials of loneliness and abandonment by God.

Thus, we finally recognize Jerusalem itself in the archetypal nature that turns inward in the Psalms. The Teraphon-Gorge itself, the *çinor* fissure, filled with the roaring cataracts, appears before us in Psalm 42, which is also a Korah-hymn:

> Thy floods roar towards me,
>> one primeval chasm calls to the other,
> and the cataracts in the cleft of hell [çinor]
>> pour over me. (42:8B)*

Once we have rediscovered the subterranean, Sinai-like pole of archetypal Jerusalem in the Psalms, we become aware with happy surprise how the hymns abound in sounds relating to Zion. The Korah-Psalm of the çinor-Gorge allows the complete primal image of Jerusalem to arise before us, and therefore also passes on to the view of the blessed hill of Zion. The psalmist stood on the stern rock-elevation of Moriah at the edge of the dividing abyss and looked across to celestial Mount Zion which still harboured the sanctuary. Oh, if only his soul could pass across the roaring gorge!

> I pour out my heart,
>> for I would like to pass across
>> in a procession to the site of thy wondrous tent,
> to the dwelling place of God,
>> with jubilation, songs of praise and festive sounds
>> ... (Ps.42:4B)

> Oh send out thy light and thy truth;
>> let them guide and lead me,
> let them bring me to thy holy hill
>> and to thy dwelling,
> that I may go in to the altar of the deity,
>> to God who is my joy and bliss,
> so that I may thank thee with the harp,
>> thou, my God. (Ps.43:3fB)

Out of all the terrors of hell, the thunderous raging of the angry deity, out of the sternness of the rock of justice, men's glance always

---

* See p. 84.

turned again to the miraculous mercy of Zion. The name, Zion, could not be invoked at all without all sounds of wrath or judgment being silenced immediately. From there come mercy, help and consolation: 'May he [the LORD] send you help from his sanctuary, and give you support from Zion!' (20:2 and, for instance, 14:7). From there resound the quiet, blissful songs of praise: 'One praises thee in the stillness on Zion, O God' (65:1*B*). The beauty of heaven itself dwells there: 'Great is the LORD and wondrously radiant in the city of God on his holy mountain. Mount Zion rises up beautifully, whereby all the land is consoled' (48:1f*B*).

In the Jerusalem of the Psalms, the expulsion from the paradise of Zion had not yet taken place; the sanctuary had as yet not been erected on the rock of Moriah. This is why, through the Psalms, there shines the first dawn of the heavenly Jerusalem as described in the Revelation to John. The Mount Zion of the Psalms still possesses the union of the external and the inner landscape. And it is this archetypal character that allowed Mount Zion to shine its light all the way to the Apocalypse in the New Testament as a prophetic picture, the longed-for view of the eventually coming Messianic life of the spirit.

CHAPTER ELEVEN

Solomon, Favoured by Destiny

When Solomon, Bathsheba's son, ascended to the throne of his father, the trinitarian archetype of the universal trinity, proceeding from the divine-spiritual womb of being and determining all existence and evolution according to its laws, found a human reflection in the trinity of the first kings of Israel just as it had once before, a thousand years earlier, in the trinity of the patriarchs. In Abraham, Isaac and Jacob, the trinitarian law was reflected in mythical-superhuman form; in Saul, David and Solomon, it emerged fully out of the sphere of mystery into the realm of human personalities as a historical fact.

The countenances of the kings were more distinct in their selfhood's character than those of the patriarchs. Only in Jacob, the third of the patriarchs, the tension-filled drama of a personal destiny tended to emerge from the cloud of the myth. In the case of the kings, this cloud had retreated without a trace and had made way for the bright light of day, which allows for a clear discernment of the human outlines of the figures and the personal motives and directions of their fate. Here, it was above all David, the figure in the middle, who revealed the law of the struggling personality in his nature and life. The selfhood of Saul and Solomon had also emerged from the twilight of the mythos, but Saul's 'I' was overcome by nature which still extended into his being, and Solomon's personal being was completely eclipsed by his creation, the happy success granted to all his undertakings.

An important step of evolution comes to expression in the fact that in the human trinity of the first kings, the emphasis moved completely to the figure in the middle. The patriarch in the middle, Isaac, was still quite enveloped by silence. The Bible is sparing in what it reports concerning him, and lets his father Abraham as well as his son Jacob arise in much greater detail before our mind's eye. In the case of the kings, on the other hand, it is in particular David, the middle one, in whose description — between the brief episodes referring to Saul and Solomon — the Bible rises to its greatest and most classic piece of narrative presentation.

The human trinities of the patriarchs and kings are reflections of the divine trinity: the element of the father, the son, and the spirit. The emergence of the middle in the time from Isaac to David discloses humanity's approach to the son-principle from which selfhood flows forth. A thousand years after Isaac and a thousand years prior to the actual, full human incarnation of the 'son,' the son-principle, which was drawing closer to humankind, took on form in David in a special way. In him, the 'Son of man' wore the crown of the Old Covenant after the decline of the ancient father-forces of humankind had become evident in Saul's figure.

In the human realization of Solomon, the spiritual principle lit up, shining forth brightly but then quickly sinking back into obscurity. The element that had become 'man' in David seemed to try to become 'world' in Solomon, who, like his father, was king for forty years (965–926 BC). The beginnings of a new culture, now born completely out of human faculties, which David struggled to attain from his destiny in the areas of art, science and political leadership, were quickly lifted up as through a miracle to an advanced, mature level. The Hermes element of the Old Testament unfolded after the death of its creator in the most splendid wealth and abundance to the outside during the age of Solomon.

Despite his youth, Solomon appeared on history's stage as the born leader. He did not owe his royal authority to a secret, direct charge by God; in contrast to the cases of Saul and David, no seer sent by God came to anoint him. He also did not owe the crown to the old law of the first-born's right. Solomon was a younger son of David, David himself being the youngest among the sons of Jesse. Although Absalom was no longer alive, the second-eldest son of the king was Adonijah. And the highest-ranking dignitaries of the court were those who, against the will of the ailing David and following the old law, were determined to name Adonijah king, namely, Joab, chief armourer and commander-in-chief, and Abiathar, the highest priest, who once had been the sole survivor of the oracle of Nob and had placed the oracle's power into David's service. Supported only by the will of David, expressed one more time on the deathbed, Solomon was able to raise uncertainty in the adherents to the law and to overcome them by means of the royal self-assurance of his nature. In Solomon, the right of the first-born, which would make the future emerge solely from the continuing legacy of the past, was once more explicitly moved aside. Solomon was preferred by destiny over his brothers Absalom and Adonijah, as was Abel-Seth over Cain, Abraham over Haran-Lot, Isaac over Ishmael and Jacob over Esau. The balance between heredity and the new impact of the impulse of personality was to appear in him, realized in a specific way.

Throughout the ages, all traditions in and outside the Bible have considered Solomon as the embodiment and quintessence of wisdom that can emanate from a human being. Narrators could never do enough to praise Solomon's wisdom:

The great King Solomon, on whom the Eternal One has bestowed dominion from one end of the world to the other, was beloved by God and chosen by him when he was still in his mother's womb. The Lord let him know all the mysteries and revealed all that is hidden to him. He gave him wisdom and insight into the things of the world as they have unfolded since the time of creation. When people came before him who had disputes with each other, he only had to look at them searchingly to know immediately who was the guilty one and who the innocent one, and none dared speak an untruth before him. In his hand was the great key with which the portals to all wisdom are unlocked. He understood the language of the birds and the speech of the tame and wild animals. Deer and antelope ran before him, and lions and panthers fought for him. He was fluent in the tongues of all the nations, and knew an answer to all questions.[1]

In Solomon, the clairvoyance, which had inspired human beings in earlier times with divine wisdom, had ceased to exist; instead, it had been transformed into insight. Human wisdom took the place of divine wisdom, but Solomon's wisdom was not laboriously acquired, born of suffering and wrested from destiny as was David's poetry. It was simply present as a wondrous natural talent. Just as the clairvoyant perception once shone forth in the human being as a gift of nature owing to a certain condition of the physical and ethereal organisms, so, in Solomon, the intuitive ideas and insights arose as a gift of nature owing to an especially fortunate, inherited talent, as if from outside.

In the classic scene of 'Solomon's judgment,' often artistically portrayed, the Bible illustrates the spiritual nature of Solomon. Quarrelling with one another, two women appeared before the royal judge with two infants to whom they had given birth at the same time in the same house. One child was alive, the other dead. Each of the women claimed the living infant as her own. One woman maintained that during the night the other had taken the living child and put in its place the dead one. Solomon could no longer clairvoyantly spot the guilty one as could judges in ancient times. But a genius of thinking was available to him that allowed him to make a decision with smooth effortlessness by means of which the truth had to come out. He gave the order to have the living child cut in two with a sword. The king ruled for the woman who was willing to waive her claim in favour of the other merely to save the child's life, for the maternal love that spoke out of her demonstrated that she was the mother of the infant.

If Solomon had become wise in old age, his wisdom could have been interpreted as being the fruit of rich experience. This is what was so astonishing, namely, that he could avail himself of it when, following his father, he ascended to the throne, still being a young man. The miracle of talent, of genius, entered through him into humanity's history of consciousness. Solomon was the prototype of the 'gifted' human being. A new metamorphosis of soul faculties had been reached. The human nature which was alive from Abraham to Moses as a remnant of the old clairvoyant vision and in Saul ebbed away in ecstatic intoxication, which began to develop in David as a spiritual life of the personality struggling with its destiny and with itself, this made its appearance in Solomon as brilliant genius and talent.

In a fundamental experience that he was privileged to have at the beginning of his period as king, Solomon realized that his divinely decreed mission consisted specifically in the development of the wisdom bestowed on him. On the ancient height of the gods, on Gibeon-Mizpah, where at that time still stood the tabernacle with the bronze altar of the burnt offering — David had already taken the ark of the Covenant to Mount Zion — Solomon conducted his royal inauguration-sacrifice amid the tribal heads of the nation (1Kings 3:4; 2Chr.1:6). During the night following this event, a wondrous dream descended into his soul as the divine reply to his attitude of sacrifice. The deity appeared before him and allowed him one great wish for his life. The young king did not ask for riches and worldly success, but for wisdom. And he received the answer: 'Behold I give you a wise and discerning mind, so that none like you has been before you and none like you shall arise after you.' Henceforth, Solomon went his way with proud assurance.

From the very beginning, Solomon's nature and accomplishments appeared with the greatest cosmopolitan breadth, and it was here that the external good fortune of the Solomonic age came most clearly to expression. Whereas, until now, the Israelite development had mainly consisted of acquiring inward composure, of a separation of oneself from the temptations of a rich surrounding world, a regular reversal of the goals seemed to commence now under Solomon. Did the inwardness, which Israel was supposed to develop, really possess such secure strength and an assured future that the great turn to the outside and the distance could be directly executed?

Solomon took as his wife the daughter of the Egyptian Pharaoh. In a political sense, this was a most important and promising step. For many centuries Egypt had been ruler over the Holy Land. Despite its decline, which prevented the actual execution of this rule, it had remained one of the most powerful kingdoms of that period. Through Solomon's marriage, Israel freed itself from the nominally continuing vassalage and became a friend and ally of Egypt. For the Holy Land as well as for Egypt, this alliance became a fundamental protection against the Assyrian danger, already emerging on the distant horizon.

But was the political advantage not attained at the expense of relinquishing the innermost vocation of the people? Along with the Egyptian princess, the spiritual and cultic life of Egypt, still saturated with the magic legacy of ancient traditions of wisdom, entered powerfully into Israel's sphere. Was it not out of the most weighty necessities that Moses had removed his people from the spell of the Egyptian life which had turned decadent? Solomon threw open all the doors to the forces against which Moses had guarded the people in the strictest manner possible.

Likewise, Solomon concluded a treaty of friendship with the richest neighbour in the north: the Phoenician king, Hiram of Tyre. This alliance also offered protection against the Assyrian threat. But it too changed Israelite life profoundly. Henceforth, there existed a powerful fleet of Israelite merchant ships, which, together with those of the long-trained seafaring nation, sailed to the most distant coasts. Israel's horizon expanded immeasurably. Together with their Phoenician friends, Israelites looked on to the Atlantic Ocean from the coasts of Spain in the distant west. The fabulous riches of the south and the east, heretofore only sensed as in dreams from fairy tales, now suddenly moved within their reach. The legendary treasures of India, Arabia and Africa accumulated before the amazed eyes of Israel; the returning ships brought along precious stones, pearls and gold in abundance. Ophir, the land of gold, was no longer a fairy tale. The ancient gold mines of Africa, in Ethiopia and further south, which travellers and explorers came across again and again in the past decades, may well have been built and exploited by Solomon's workmen in company with the Phoenicians.

Again, it was not merely a matter of external changes that came about in Israel as a result of the Phoenician friendship. While the foreign treasures could not help but alter Israel's vital consciousness significantly, the customs and perceptions which streamed into the Holy Land through the sailors returning from foreign lands and continents contributed even more. In particular, it was the cultural life of the Phoenicians themselves that came into vogue. When, in order to give his capital a completely new appearance and to execute the construction of the Temple which had only been planned by David, Solomon asked King Hiram for the architect Hiram to be the head and teacher of the Israelite construction workers, this signified a break with the principle which, until now, had been strictly adhered to in the whole development of Israel. Since Abraham had turned away from Babylonia and later on also from Egypt, filled with disgust over the cultural conceit of the construction of the 'Tower of Babel,' and since he had settled in the quiet, insignificant land of the Jordan in the middle between the ziggurats of Mesopotamia and the pyramids of Egypt, the life of Israel had taken its course, consciously disregarding any architecture. The development of such a skill would have diverted the faculties, which were to capture the realm of inwardness, to the external sphere. During David's reign, the first Phoenician construction workers had come to Jerusalem, but under Solomon's rule, an actual irruption of architecture occurred into a people and a realm lacking all architectural tradition. Only now, Jerusalem attained the appearance of a real city built by human hands, something it had never possessed until then. Visible far and wide, the splendid palaces of Solomon covered the stern, formerly bare rock-summit of Moriah. Amid such splendour-oriented, external developments, could the inward-leading impulse of Israel still be maintained at all?

The ancient world knew well how to treasure a magnificent royal court where the palace and Temple-structures were not only an expression of power and wealth but also the source of a rich cultural life. Solomon's royal court, however, drew the amazed attention and admiration of the world upon itself in a completely new manner. Perhaps the reason was that all this splendour arose so suddenly out of nothing and replaced a condition of the greatest possible unpretentiousness. But what spread Jerusalem's fame far and wide was the life of wisdom that emanated from Solomon himself. The attraction of an unheard-of modernness was inherent in this wisdom. The royal courts of Memphis and Thebes, of Ur and Babylonia had certainly emitted wisdom in abundance. But the messengers of this wisdom, the kings and priests, had always experienced themselves as organs and bearers of divine forces and had designated themselves accordingly. Now there existed a wise king who was truly a man, who did not want to be anything else and therefore demanded for himself no function at all in priestly service.

Kings from the most distant lands, themselves in possession of the greatest wealth and traditions of wisdom, left on pilgrimage to Jerusalem. Not only as an example for that, but actually as a symbol, there appears in the biblical scriptures and in history the journey of the Queen of Sheba who came from her South-Arabian kingdom to marvel at Solomon's wisdom and to venerate it. A thousand years later, following the directions of the stars, three kings travelled from the same regions with precious gifts on the same path to pay homage to a child that had to bring humanity a completely new impulse for life. The journey of that queen, perhaps also occasioned by the star-wisdom of her land, was an expression of adoration as well to a spiritual impulse, newly arising in humankind.

In the age of the patriarchs, the Israelite development had eliminated in Ishmael a cultural stream that would have hampered the developing nation in concentrating on its mission, directed within. Since then, from the roots of Ishmael, nations had come into being who had attained to the true pinnacle of culture in Arabia. Among them, a high flowering of astrology and arithmetic had been achieved in transforming the Egyptian-Chaldean star-wisdom. As late as in the middle ages, the Sabians of Arabia were known as bearers of ancient astrological traditions and the wisdom of numbers.* In the age of Solomon, Israel turned again to the stream of Ishmael which had earlier been eliminated, just as it did to the once abandoned Egypt. In the course of time, many stories have been told about how the Queen of Sheba not only listened to Solomon's wisdom, but how, through Solomon, she also became Israel's teacher of Sabian wisdom.†

When the many different relationships are studied that were entertained by cosmopolitan Solomon with foreign countries, it might appear as if the still tender inwardness, which Israel was supposed to develop, had been completely sacrificed to outward development. In reality, the law of the Old Testament development only emerged here to one side with particular clearness. Periods of breathing in and breathing out, of involution and evolution, succeeded one another. When Abraham left behind the cultural realms of Babylonia and Egypt which were experiencing pronounced external expansion, he brought about a period of involution, of concentration directed within. Then, when Joseph entered into the centre of Egyptian life and finally also drew his people into the sphere of the Egyptian spirit, the involution of the patriarchs' age was replaced by an evolution, a submergence into the alien outer world. When Moses led the people into the wilderness, he introduced a new period of concentrated involution. The Sinai Desert was the stage for a mighty introspection of the folk soul. Now, Solomon had once again to turn around the Moses-direction. The most

---

* When the magic world of Hadhramaut in southern Arabia was thrown open to travellers and scholars in recent times, the numbers of those quickly increased, who interpreted the finds in these legendary cities of towering buildings as the remains of the advanced civilization of Sheba.

† In Jerusalem, for instance, the tradition has survived through all the ages that the construction of the 'Golden Gate,' the gate-sanctuary in the eastern city-wall of Jerusalem, originally dated back to the Queen of Sheba.

abundant view to the outside and a process of learning from alien elements followed the Sinai-severity. This lasted until the great prophets called again for introspection, particularly at the time when the splendour of the Neo-Babylonian kingdom surrounded the people in the foreign land. The process of inward intensification progressed, but from time to time, new nourishment was given from outside and it was confronted with new, greater tasks.

Israel drank deeply of the wider world in Solomon's age. As the rich fruit of looking all around, as a moulded quintessence of all humankind of that era, Solomon's *work* stands before us. Whatever the king undertook succeeded. He did not belong to those people who plan and start on a lot of things and yet accomplish little. With brilliant aim, effortlessly as if it were a game, all his endeavours worked out well as do those of creative nature itself.

David had erred in a tragic way when he made a first attempt at organizing the people and the state by means of the census. In Solomon's case, it was quite different. He divided the land into twelve regions which were put under the rule of overseers, and it was not long before he had a method of taxation running in such an easy, copious manner that from this direction too, great wealth accumulated in Jerusalem. At strategic locations of the land, such as in Megiddo and Gezer, he built exemplary fortifications. To this day Solomon's Pools, south of Bethlehem, resembling river dams, bear witness to his ingeniously invented method of water-supply. Under Solomon, Israel obtained a splendid army although this time of abundant peace was not interrupted by any wars. It was Solomon in particular who introduced the horse to a greater extent, which the Israelites had mainly come to know from the Philistines. The foundation walls of large stables were unearthed, for example, in the ruins of the citadel of Megiddo and in the subterranean halls on the south side of the rocky hill of Moriah. The large numbers of cavalry and mounted men must have contributed in special measure to the feeling of an uplifting, modern life in Israel.

But the core of the Solomonic accomplishment, its fame spreading far and wide, was the magnificent building which arose in Jerusalem under the direction of the Phoenician architects, chiefly the palace constructions on Mount Moriah that surrounded the Temple, which in itself was inconspicuous. The new appearance of the ancient city — it was only now that it really took on the look of a city in the sense that we are accustomed to use the word — was the signal for a completely new epoch of urban construction in general. Ancient Rome of the seven kings, Athens of Pericles, and Babylon of Nebuchadnezzar as well — even if they adhered in one way or another to the traditions of the old sacred construction of temple-cities — in fact now followed the more mundane impulse of construction entering for the first time into history under Solomon in Jerusalem. The transition from the Davidian to the Solomonic Jerusalem was like the dawn of a new world. It is understandable that David still failed in the task posed to him of constructing the Temple on Moriah. The mood of Mount Zion, which, like a murmuring sacred grove, maintained the memory of ages of paradise, held him under its spell. Solomon no longer had any ties to ancient times; rather, he felt liberated when he could shake off the mystery-filled twilight of the past. With alert determination, he strode towards a less secretive future, illuminated by a more distinct light.

As little as the Bible reports on the personal destiny of Solomon, it grants much space to his accomplishments. For the scriptures are not content with a mere description of them, but as a literary expression of them also exists, it included them among the sacred texts. No less than three Solomonic books are contained in the canon of the Old Testament: Proverbs, Ecclesiastes, and The Song of Solomon. The Wisdom of Solomon, which is usually included in the apocryphal appendix of Old Testament scriptures, is only one example of a whole number of apocryphal books which are attributed to Solomon. The Davidian poetry of the Psalms has been metamorphosed by Solomon in two directions: as an abundantly streaming wisdom of proverb-like verses to help the human being to master life, and as priceless songlike poetry which no longer seems to derive from religious struggles but appears to capture presentiments of the spirit in pictures of blissful love.

The Bible also indicates that besides his activities as a teacher of wisdom concerning life, an organizer, an architect, and a poet, Solomon also accomplished deeds as a pioneer of scientific insights. The beginnings of a natural science of botany and zoology that not only describe and list the wealth of creation but comprehend it as well, must surely be meant when it says Solomon 'spoke of trees, from the cedar that is in Lebanon to the hyssop that grows out of the wall; he spoke also of beasts, and of birds and of reptiles, and of fish' (1Kings 4:33).

The world that Solomon built up was of grandiose uniformity and consistency. But it should not be overlooked that it could be like this only through an inner one-sidedness which is difficult to recognize today, because what has become established as a matter of course for the past three thousand years only originated through the great Solomonic cultural turning point.

Solomon has become one of the greatest creators of a purely exoteric culture, because he no longer possessed nor wanted to have any positive relationship to the sphere of the esoteric life which at that time was dying away and becoming extinct. His joy in developing and conquering new fields in the area of outwardly directed culture was based on an abhorrence of all that was concealed, veiled and filled with mystery. Here lay the limits of his nature. After all, the fact that he could avail himself of such great talents and successful good fortune did not signify that he would necessarily have possessed solid inner strength and force of selfhood. In his innermost being, there dwelled a certain weakness and fear. Everything that was reminiscent of the world of the mysteries upset him and made him unsure. His human wisdom was not free of jealousy of divine wisdom which still re-echoed here and there from the realm of the mysteries. On the surface, he proudly rejected the old as superstition. Uncertainty was concealed underneath. Looking at his essential nature, one can describe his untiring cultural creativity, which was crowned with the glory of success, as an escape of a still weak selfhood into external affairs.

When, to Solomon's satisfaction, the appearance of the city of Jerusalem was utterly changed by the constructions on Moriah, the traces of the old mystery site could also be erased and consigned to oblivion. The shift of the royal residence from the western to the eastern hill suited him well. Mount Zion with its atmosphere of the past was not to his taste. Let it become the graveyard of the kings, and for the rest, allow the sprawling city's buildings to cover it up. Consciously methodical, Solomon must have proceeded with the effacement and changes past recognition of what was reminiscent of the ancient Jerusalem of the Melchizedek era. It suited him perfectly that stones were needed for the constructions. He had them broken out in the extensive corridors and grottoes, which had once been the stage of mysteries in the subterranean rock of Jerusalem. In converting them to stone quarries, he introduced into them the vapidity of external life, banishing the remnants of the mythos, which he interpreted as pure superstition. The summit of Moriah alone was by no means large enough for the palace and Temple complex as planned by Solomon. Was this not a welcome opportunity to change the whole eerie topography which pointed back not only to the age of the mysteries but far beyond that into eras of fiery elemental tempests? Many abysses were filled up and this is how it came to the most drastic transformation of the old Jerusalem: the filling-up of the gruesome Teraphon Gorge, which tore the city in two and made it into a symbol of the world's duality. 'Solomon closed up the fissure in the city of David his father' (1Kings 11:27B). All this brought about much work. A time of most industrious activity ensued. The clang of hammers never ceased, the columns of workmen carrying debris and stones never stopped. In order to keep alive the flow of the spring of Siloam, the famous waterway was hewn through the rock. Large grottos within the Temple rock were converted to stables for horses, a thousand other similar projects followed. The result was a splendidly smoothed-out Jerusalem completely deprived of its ancient secrets.

Only if the hidden inner weakness of Solomon, the fear of the mysteries, is discovered behind the facade of the magnificent work and never-failing success, the inglorious end of this glorious life can be comprehended. How was it possible that Solomon's radiance became extinguished even more quickly than it had come into being and that after the death of the wise king, the kingdom immediately broke apart into factions? The biblical description presents the sinking into oblivion of the formerly brilliant development by narrating how, at the end of his life, Solomon became a victim of his polygamy. More than a moral failing is concealed behind this. Polygamy as such was not considered a wrong in that age and was definitely customary in the reigning houses as it had been in David's court.

A tragedy emerged which had imperceptibly intruded already into Solomon's years of fortune-filled glory. Solomon was not only the first-born of humanity's gifts of genius. Also through him, the tragedy of the gifted person was fulfilled.

The destiny of Solomon poses a problem to us, the recognition of which is not readily faced. Even today, the view of life prevails in which talent and success are everything. Generally, a person is judged according to what heredity and destiny allot to him of material possessions, natural talents, fortunate circumstances of life and connections. The human being is given credit for something that does not constitute his own being, for it does not originate from his present, striving 'I.' In the same way, people are inclined to consider a person inferior who is haunted by misfortune, afflicted with illness and has not been richly gifted by nature. The true being and value of a human being are neither identical with his gifts nor with his external possessions. The true worth of a person only consists in what they make of their talents, what they accomplishes through striving effort in inner transformations of the inherited natural character, and what they struggle for and attain through truly selfless sacrifice and commitment.

Viewed from an inner standpoint, the so-called 'good luck' of a person can be their misfortune because it does not stimulate them to inner alertness and activity. People are too readily inclined to give credit to themselves for something that they have only brought along but that is not self-acquired, and thus they conveniently allows themselves to be deluded concerning the true requirements of inner being.

As a ruler whose fame had reached into all the world, Solomon could deceive himself concerning the fact that he neglected to be regent of his own inner development and fate. For him, the favourite of fortune, everything worked out too easily; it was all so matter-of-fact, even his wisdom, that it never occurred to him to admit to duties of inner self-discipline and to the necessity of changing himself.

Although the notes of deep resignation, which, as the teacher of his people, made him sing the song of transiency and the disconsolate return of sameness,* they demonstrate to us that the riches of life that had merely been given to him were becoming used up even for him and finally had proved to be empty illusion. But how could a breakthrough be possible into the higher self's hidden sphere of fire for one who drew curtains and built walls before the mysteries?

The superabundance of the rich outer world over which he merely needed to rule became Solomon's doom. When the Bible mentions his

---

* In Latin, the beginning of Ecclesiastes, 'Vanity of vanities, all is vanity,' goes: *Vanitas vanitatum et omnia vanitas,* which can be rendered as, 'illusion and transiency is the nature of all existence ... There is nothing new under the sun; none can say: lo, this or that is new; in the centuries before us, it already existed.'

polygamy, it indicates that Solomon became involved in ever new relationships with foreign nations and cultures. Each one of his women, whom he took from all the different countries, represented a further alienation from Israel. Just as Solomon gave the Egyptian spirit entry into his nation when he made the daughter of the Egyptian Pharaoh his wife, he brought a part of the alien surrounding world, which had everywhere fallen into decadence and decay, into Jerusalem with each following wife. Solomon wasted and lost himself. The glorious wealth finally turned into a chaotic glut. Solomon himself inflicted the most grievous injustice on the holy Temple, which he had built on the ancient sacrificial rock of Moriah, fulfilling the wish and plan of David, when, all around on the hills of Jerusalem, he constructed altars to the gods for the alien princesses whom he had brought into his harem. On the Mount of Olives, for example, from where people had the best view of the splendid Solomonic Jerusalem, Solomon built an altar for the Moabite god, Chemosh, where the Moabite princess, who lived in his harem, had gruesome blood rituals performed. Was it not as if hordes of demons were being called into the confines of Jerusalem from the red Moabite hills on the distant horizon, and from the infernal depths of the desert and the Dead Sea into which one could also look from the Mount of Olives? The spiritual atmosphere of Jerusalem, which had so quickly shone forth in the brightest light, fast became gloomy and impure. Immoderately intensified, the beauty and splendour, which had appeared as if by magic, turned into formless, chaotic disorder. This was the inglorious end of the Solomonic age. It had only lasted forty years.

CHAPTER TWELVE

The Names of Solomon

The far-reaching effect that the figure of Solomon exercised on all the following epochs of history originated by no means from the hidden tragedy that became evident towards the end of his life. It actually cannot be traced back either to the rich, success-filled work that he was permitted to create. The reason for this effect is that, in Solomon, an image of the human being appeared which henceforth could serve as the ideal for the striving soul. It is not as if he could have been exemplary as a human personality. He himself did not fill the image of man at all that came into view through him. After all, he did not bear it as an acquirement of his striving innermost self but as a wondrously ordained gift of heredity and destiny. Nevertheless, later humanity knew by looking up to him what it would actually signify to be human according to the manner of divine creation and intention. In the most diverse forms and expressions, it has been humankind's inner aim to achieve through conscious effort what was present in Solomon as a natural gift and to raise it to the level of attainment.

In David, history had entered into the sphere of personal humanness; in Solomon, the full image of man, the image of the perfect human being, flashed forth like the picture of a deity in its temple.

We are led to this secret of humankind's history, when we pay heed to the strange and manifold traditions that exist concerning the names of Solomon. At first, such mentions give the impression of eulogies that are added together by chance, since the ancient narrators could not do enough in lavishing praise on Solomon.

At one point, it says:

During the first days of his kingship, he was called *Yedidyah*, a name which the prophet Nathan has given him because he was the beloved of the Lord Zebaoth (Lord of the Heavenly Hosts).

He was called *Solomon* because of the peace that reigned
during his time. He was also called *Master Builder,* because he
had built God a dwelling. He was called *Ithiel* because the
Lord was with him. He also bore the name *Jakeh* because he
was the supreme ruler over all the lords of the Orient and the
Occident ...[1]

Occasionally, a more discernible order and form appears through
these mentions. Once, when the character of the number three in
Solomon's nature and life is mentioned, three names are placed in a
relationship with the three Solomonic scriptures, included in the Old
Testament canon:

He was called by three names: Yedidyah, Solomon and
Kohelet. Three works were written by Solomon: The Book of
the Proverbs, the Book of the Preacher, and the Song of Songs.
He composed the Song of Songs first. Then he wrote the
Proverbs of Wisdom and finally, he wrote the Book of Kohelet.
For this is man's nature: in his youth, he sings songs; as a
grown man, he coins wise sayings; as an old man of advanced
age, he proclaims that all is vain![2]

Solomon is to bear the name Yedidyah, 'beloved of God,' as the
poet of the Song of Songs. He is called Solomon, 'bearer of peace,' as
the creator of the proverbs of wisdom. He is called Kohelet, 'preacher'
or 'teacher,' by the Bible itself in the title of the third book.

From the traces and traditions which we find in and outside the
Bible concerning the names of Solomon, it is not self-evident what is
actually meant with them, much less what an important indication is
concealed here. Only an explanation, given by Rudolf Steiner inde-
pendently of the biblical or other texts, can throw light on the significance and range of these traditions. But before approaching what he
outlined concerning the names of Solomon, we shall complete the survey of the riddles and problems connected with them.

It is a fact that attention is only drawn to certain passages of the
Old Testament, if the secret of Solomon's names has been recognized.
Through these insights, the beginnings of the last two chapters in
Proverbs, for example, which are ordinarily the subject of hopeless
confusion, become clearer. In the customary Bible translations,
Chapter 30 begins: 'The words of Agur son of Jakeh,' and Chapter 31
begins: 'The words of King Lemuel, the oracle, which his mother

taught him' (RSV alternative). Who are the strange figures, Agur, Ben Jakeh and Lemuel who seem to replace the wise King Solomon here as poets of proverbs at the end of the book? The reference books give only a perplexed indication of unknown persons whom the Book of Proverbs names as the authors of its last chapters. It is obvious that we are dealing here with other names of Solomon himself. He uttered the final proverbs not as Solomon but as Agur, Ben Jakeh and as King Lemuel. What is the meaning of all these names?

Our survey is still not complete. The beginning of Chapter 30 of Proverbs continues with the words: 'The man says to Ithi-el ...' Here another name of Solomon is concealed, namely, Ithiel, which means, 'God is with me.' So we have three names of Solomon side by side here:

Agur	the gatherer
Ben Jakeh	son of devout obedience, or discipline
Ithiel	the one who bears the divine within him.

The whole of the chapter beginning therefore says: 'These are the words of Agur (the gatherer), of Ben Jakeh (son of devout discipline). It is the teaching and the saying of the man, Ithiel (with me is God), for only because God is with him he can speak like this.' The name Lemuel, which Chapter 31 adds as a fourth name means, 'the one consecrated to God.' Solomon speaks the last verses of his book of wisdom as the 'consecrated king.'

In the seven names of Solomon:

> Agur, gatherer,
>
> Ben Jakeh, son of devotion
>
> Lemuel, the one consecrated to God,
>
> Ithiel, the one filled with God,
>
> Solomon, bearer of peace,
>
> Kohelet, teacher, preacher,
>
> Yedidyah, beloved of God,

A segment of ancient Hebrew esoteric doctrine extends like a fragment into the biblical texts as well as the traditions outside the Bible, according to Rudolf Steiner. In a lecture which deals with the New Testament's Sermon on the Mount, he gave the key to the solution of the secret of Solomon's names without reference to the textual problems of the Old Testament.[3]

He finds that, together, the seven names of Solomon form a figure that refers to the members of the human being, similar to what applies also in a different way to the ten sephiroth of the cabbalistic scriptures. A differentiated view of the sensory-supersensory human being, similar to the one coined in modern conceptual terms by anthroposophy, already forms the basis of the Solomonic texts and the apocryphal, legendary interpretation found in early theology. In a more pictorial, sentient and to begin with unsystematic manner, people then knew of differentiations, such as are made and put together in a clearly outlined form by anthroposophy when the members of the human being are described, namely,

> the physical body,
> the etheric body (life body, formative forces body),
> the astral body (soul body),
> the 'I,'
> the spirit self (manas, spirit-permeated soul body),
> the life spirit (budhi, spirit-permeated life body),
> spirit man (atma, spirit-permeated physical body).

The reason why the seven members of the human being were designated by the seven names of Solomon was that the total image of man shone forth at a certain degree of perfection in Solomon. For the Hebraic secret doctrine, Solomon was not only a historical personality but at the same time an important symbol of teaching. Perhaps, his picture with the seven names was sketched when the teachers wanted to instruct the advanced disciples concerning the true and complete being of man.

Such pictorial instruction was a central part of the Messianic theology which found an expression later on, for example, in the genealogy of Jesus at the beginning of the Gospel of St Matthew, but it was also nurtured in the era of the Old Testament. It was known to be the most noble task of the Israelite nation to make possible the human incarnation of the Messiah. The human sheaths, in which this divine being was supposed to be able to clothe itself one day, had to be brought to a certain level of perfection by means of regulating the hereditary relationships.

Definite focal points in the sequence of generations had to be absolved in this development. The beginning of the Gospel of Matthew subsequently indicates two such stages clearly. There, the sequence of forty-two generations between Abraham and Jesus is divided into three times fourteen segments, so that a significant turning-point is created between David and Solomon as well as at the time of the Babylonian exile (Matt.1:17). The degree of perfection attained after the first great turning-point stood pictorially before ancient theology in the figure of Solomon. For the first time, the image of the complete, sevenfold human being shone forth. The true perfection of the sheaths, which was to be offered to the descending divine being on the part of the human stream of heredity after another two-times fourteen generations became discernible as a predisposition and ideal.

In the above-mentioned lecture, Rudolf Steiner describes this in the following manner:

> In an ancestor of Jesus, the predisposition existed, as it were, for the correct development of the seven members of the human nature ... Although it is not brought out in the external tradition, this fact was known in the ancient Hebraic esoteric teaching ...
>
> Thus, the 'I' in this ancestor was called *Ithiel* by them so as to indicate that it had to possess the power, — for the word Ithiel would mean something like 'Bearer of Power' — had to have the daring which, having been inherited by generation after generation, would become the right I-bearer of that lofty being who then ... was supposed to appear in Jesus of Nazareth. Thus, they termed the *astral body* of that ancestor, *Lemuel.* This would approximately denote an astral body which is developed in such a way that it feels that it bears the (moral) law, the configuration of laws, not only outside itself, but within. They termed the *etheric body* of that ancestor *Ben Jakeh.* This would signify an etheric body which has been worked through to the utmost within itself and can incorporate habits at a certain stage of perfection.* And the *physical body* of this ancestor was called *Agur* for the reason that the

---

* The literal meaning of the name *Ithiel* is 'with me (in me) is God.' Therefore, one can probably also say that through this name the power is indicated that will eventually enable the 'I' to receive a divine being into itself. *Lemuel* means 'consecrated to God;' it therefore denotes a soul condition devoted to the divine law. *Jakeh* means: the devout exercise, devout obedience, the regularly practised prayer; it therefore indicates a life-body which has learned to develop habits in life oriented toward the spirit. (Bock).

physical activity, the capability of this ancestor on the physical plane, consisted in the fact that he gathered together what existed of ancient traditions; for Agur would mean 'the Gatherer.' All the world views and teachings were gathered together in Jesus,* and this predisposition had also developed already in that ancestor.

And what was active in this ancestor as *spirit man* was expressed with a word ... that would mean 'Beloved of God, or *Yedidyah* by them, for ... the love of the divine-spiritual beings works on this predisposition of the 'spirit man' with special care. And what worked into this ancestor as *budhi* or *life spirit*, of which they said, 'in this ancestor, a kind of life spirit must be active so that he can have the effect of being a teacher of the whole nation, so that the content of this life spirit can pour itself out on all the people,' this they designated as *Kohelet*. And finally, they called the *manas* or *spirit self* of this ancestor by a word that means 'inner balance,' or *Solomon*,[†] because they said: Such a spirit self must contain within itself the predisposition to be inwardly enclosed, to be in balance within itself. Therefore, this ancestor, whom one normally only knows under the name 'Shelomo' or 'Solomon,' had those three first names: Yedidyah, Kohelet, Solomon; and he possessed the four extra names, Agur, Ben Jakeh, Lemuel, Ithiel; for these denote the four sheaths, whereas the three first names designate the divine inner being.

The fact that, in Solomon, the image of universal man became visible as a Messianic predisposition is by no means negated by the other fact, as Rudolf Steiner adds, that as a historical personality Solomon

---

* What is meant here is that Jesus of Nazareth represented a quintessence of all the streams which had been produced in humanity. In a sense, the physical body of every human being is a 'gatherer.' By means of what is introduced into it through the sense perceptions, breathing, the intake of food, and so on, the body bears within itself a quintessence of the external world. (Bock).

† Literally, Solomon means, 'bearer of peace.' Here, as in the religious sphere everywhere, what is referred to is inner harmony that comes into being through the indwelling of a divine-spiritual force in the soul realm of man. The fact that the name, which indicates the spirit self or manas of man, is at the same time the historical, customary name of Solomon, shows us that in ages that still experienced the significance and expressiveness of a name, Solomon was considered a manas-man. He sustained himself on a spirituality bestowed on him by destiny and nature, which can only become fully imbued with the 'I' in future humanity. (Bock).

was far from filling out this image with accomplishments directed by his 'I.' Here too, one must recognize that

> the individual human being, who is on a certain level of devel-
> opment, by no means always needs to represent in his outer
> life what he is to pass on as a predisposition to his descendants
> — that just because lofty faculties are contained in him, he is
> perhaps more susceptible to err against the direction of such
> faculties than another person who does not possess such
> potentials.

Just because of the all-embracing wealth of talents on which he could sustain himself, because of the cosmopolitan reach to so many nations, attained seemingly on its own by the radius of his life, Solomon signifies an important preparation of Israel for the future accommodating of the cosmic Christ being who encompasses the whole of humankind.

CHAPTER THIRTEEN

Solomon's Temple

'There exists only one temple in the world, and that is the human body. Nothing is more sacred than its upright form. Bowing down before human beings is paying homage to this revelation in the flesh. One touches heaven when one touches a human body.' In these words, Novalis indicated the body-mystery of every true temple. This relationship also resounds in the words of admonition that Paul directed to the Corinthians: 'Do you not know that your body is a temple of the Holy Spirit ...?' (1Cor.6:19).

When the creator powers of the universe fashioned the human earthly body, a sacred archetypal image, belonging to the highest spheres of the gods, found a terrestrial, visible realization. Particularly through the body, the deity bestowed on the human being, to carry along on his earthly path, the secret of his likeness to God. Subsequently, in the course of the millennia, when human beings erected temples as earthly abodes for their gods, in doing so and corresponding to the spiritual nature of their peoples, they sought the same celestial archetype from which the human being too has received his secrets of form and harmonious proportions. The history of ancient architectures shows us a rich sequence of shapes into which the divine archetype was mysteriously incorporated through clairvoyant ability or artistic instinct; the archetype that was originally the basis for the human experience of his body, supposed to be present in his mind with increasing awareness.

Like a central point of history, *one* temple, however, emerges above all other temples built by human hands: the Solomonic Temple in Jerusalem. In it, those who constructed it not only symbolized the archetype of creation, the likeness to God that is common to all humanity. It was at the same time a new archetypal idea inasmuch as it was the classic symbol for Israel's Messianic mission. Before a body could be born of the hereditary stream of that nation, which was to become a temple of God in a special, unique sense by receiving into itself the Messianic, divine being, an image, translated into architecture, was created of the Messianic, divine-human body out of wood, stone, brass and gold on the rocky hill of Jerusalem. It reflected the Christ being's approach to the sphere of earthly incarnation and gave a distant inkling of the glory of the new spirit body that was to be implanted into the being of man by the Christ being.

Solomon's Temple itself had had fore-stages in Noah's ark and in the ark of the Covenant constructed by Moses.

Noah's ark, the descriptions of which refer more to a mythical image than a physical fact, descended together with the waters of the great Flood from the misty heights of clouds and reached the solid ground of the earth on the high mountain summit. In the same way, every human being descends at birth out of the supersensory worlds into incarnation, and humankind as a whole has also descended with the earth out of pre-physical realms into the dense earth body. The ark, the first fore-stage of the Temple, therefore represents the mystery at the level of primal beginning and birth.

The ark of the Covenant, no longer a mythical but a historical fact, was built during the journey through the wilderness and carried ahead of the people, with the smoke, fire and storms of the earth's depths raging and blazing around it. It represents the mystery of the body on the level of the earthly path of destiny that is filled with trials.

In the end, the ark of the Covenant found its home on the sacred Gibeah-height of Mizpah until it was replaced by the Temple, which was constructed by Solomon on the highest point of Moriah's rock-plateau. The development of the Temple led from the summit of the mountain into the depths of the wilderness and again up to the mountainous height. Solomon's Temple represents the level of redemption and the future nearness of God. Solomon, who, as a historical figure within the Messiah-nation, signified an emergence of the complete image of man, also had to establish a prophetic picture of the coming temple-like perfection of the human body by means of building the Temple.

If the narrow Phoenician-Philistine realm of culture on the Mediterranean coastline is disregarded, the Solomonic constructions in the Holy Land represented something completely new. Owing to the peculiarities and polarities of its nature, the Jordan-region, the unpretentious middle between the great temple civilizations of Egypt and Mesopotamia, was predestined for a spiritual life lacking any architecture and related more to the grotto-element or the ethereal atmosphere of mountainous summits. Abraham, for instance, had settled there when he rejected the tower-building impulses of Babylonia.

Nevertheless, at one time, the construction of a mighty sun temple in Jerusalem had been planned and had perhaps been started in its initial phases. This was when, a hundred years before Moses, Pharaoh Akhenaten (Amenophis IV) wanted to carry out his reformatory efforts in favour of the sun god, worshipped in Heliopolis, not only in Egypt but also in all the tributary states. It was his plan that temples like those he had built in Tel El Amarna, his newly established capital, should also arise at important points of the remaining world. And one of the selected sites, perhaps even considered above all others, was Jerusalem which at that time stood clearly under the cultural influence of Egypt.[1]

But even if the construction of the Akhenaten temple had really been carried out, no antecedent of Solomon's Temple would thus have come into being. The structure that would have been erected would have belonged in the ranks of the temple buildings of the ancient civilizations of the Nile and Euphrates-Tigris regions, which, pointing back to the past like Noah's ark, symbolized the divine mystery of the body of creation's beginnings. Solomon's Temple represented something new also in the sequence of the great, ancient monuments inasmuch as it revealed in an architectonic sense the Messianic corporeality-secret, newly coming to the earth, thus pointing prophetically into the future.

Whole erudite libraries have been written about Solomon's Temple. Since scholars began to acquire a conception of the temple architecture of the Near East from recent excavations, particularly of the Euphrates-Tigris region, they have unceasingly endeavoured to classify the Temple in Jerusalem, as we know it from biblical construction reports, in an architectonic-historical sense and to trace it back to its prototypes. Now, the Bible itself by no means claims architectural uniqueness and originality for Solomon's Temple, for it describes how Solomon undertook the construction from the very first only with the support of Phoenician workmen. Even the expressions, which the Old Testament uses for the individual parts of the Temple (for example: *Ulam,* vestibule; *Hechal,* long room; *Dvir,* Holy of Holies) are foreign terms of Akkadian or Phoenician origin within the Hebrew tongue. For a time, in reference to the Bible itself — the trail-blazing excavations carried out by Koldewey and some others in Mesopotamia and Asia Minor could not yet be included in the considerations — the Temple and palace of Solomon were thought to be monuments of Phoenician art.[2] Later, since we actually do not know much about the architecture of the Phoenicians, scholars abandoned the thesis of the Phoenician origin. Solomon's Temple was compared with the wealth of structures from the ancient civilizations which have now become known through archaeological excavations. It was found that while no significant link to the temples of ancient Egypt and Babylonia existed, there was one to that of the Assyrians. For the triangular arrangement of Solomon's Temple, for the manner in which it was connected to the neighbouring palace structures, as well as for a number of other details of construction, obvious parallels can be found in the Assyrian temples.[3]

Aside from the question of what could be gained by ascertaining dependencies, it would have to be noted in reference to such research that the temple structures of northern Mesopotamia, which are cited for the Assyrian origin of Solomon's Temple, all stem from a more recent age than the latter. In Solomon's period (965–926 BC), Assyria was still engaged in consolidating its power and could only devote itself later on to the development of a new phase of its culture, for example, in regard to architecture.

The attempts to classify the Temple in the history of architecture will probably only arrive at more illuminating results when it will have been recognized that generally, around the age of Solomon, a completely new building-impulse arose in history.

To clarify the fundamental turning-point, which the beginning of the last pre-Christian millennium signifies in the history of architecture, would require a separate, detailed treatise beyond the scope of this book. But since the significance of Solomon's Temple would remain obscure without any insight into this turning-point, it is here simply aserted and may be considered as a hypothesis and tested accordingly. This is done in the conviction that research in the history of architecture is in any case on the verge of penetrating in one manner or another to this crucial idea. No headway will be made with the concept of simple linear evolution; in view of the striking pause in architecture prior to the year 1000 BC and the new impulses commencing then, the idea will have to come that, like any organic development, the history of architecture too passes through sudden important leaps.

In their monumentality that pointed back to primordial ages, the great temple architectures in Egypt and Babylonia had at that time long since become exhausted. As far as creativity and size was concerned, a pause of several centuries had already ensued in the development of architecture. Around the year 1000, a new will to build stirred in many different regions, something that we can probably view as an effect of the same agitation in humankind that became evident in the migrations of people in the eastern Mediterranean region.

In contrast to the edifices of ancient Egypt and Babylonia that were based on primeval traditions and exuded ancient greatness, what came into being now was imbued with a sense of urgency, with a progressive spirit of the future. A new age worked its way out of ferment and unrest. The tension-filled premonition of an impending world event reverberated in everything. The wave of agitation which passed through the humanity of Asia Minor in the last pre-Christian turn of the millennium can well be described as the beginning of a Messianic excitement, which assumed increasingly clear form. Looking at it from this direction, the temple structures that now originated also took on a prophetic, futuristic impulse. They were not born of fulfilment but of expectation.

This new building impulse found its purest expression in Solomon's Temple in Jerusalem. Here, the artistic ability that had been developed in other nations could unite with a clear, calm Messiah-concept and with an inner attitude of feeling concerning the supersensory-sensory human being that flowed out of this concept as if by itself.

Among the Phoenician national groups, the Adonis cults were active and, filled with Messianic tension, brought into being architectural elements which, without being compressed into a homogeneous form, gave expression to the spirit of the new era. In Assyria, which was in the process of becoming the most powerful empire of the world, an architecture, stormily pressing towards the future, came about in the next few centuries in monumental, homogeneous concentration. But there, the Messianic expectation was completely transformed into political will for power, and the building impulse also assumed a sinister gloom. Assyria could be denoted as a gigantic wraith of prophetic Judaism. Thus we can comprehend the parallels in the history of architecture between the Assyrian temples of the eighth pre-Christian century and the Temple of Solomon. The architectural replicas of the new spirit of the age that originated in Phoenicia in a disunited manner and in Assyria in gloomy structures, found their classic, homogeneous correspondence, exclusively turned to the spiritual archetype, in Jerusalem.

How did Solomon's Temple appear to the eye? The ideas customarily formed and based on the feeling for the central human significance of this structure, can hardly give credence to a description of the actual external set of facts. The Temple of Solomon did not possess any outer magnificence and beauty: its forms were plain in the extreme, its dimensions unpretentious. If we go by the specifications of the Bible, we arrive at a picture of a rectangular external structure lacking any significant divisions and ornamentation. It was between seventy cubits long (about 37–38 metres, 123–127 feet), twenty cubits wide (about 11 m, 36 feet), and thirty cubits high (about 16 m, 55 feet).* These are the proportions of a large farm-house or those of a somewhat larger village church, which, omitting the divisions and walls of the inner space, would just hold a small congregation. The reconstruction illustrated here may help to form an idea of the Temple. We believe that the exterior of the Temple was even plainer. It must also not be assumed that the building had as much space around it as the sketch would suggest. Other structures reached quite close on all sides.

* The values of the metre fluctuate because it is not known whether the royal Egyptian cubit (52.5 to 52.8 cm) or the Babylonian cubit (55 cm) should be taken as the basis. In the inscription of Siloam (see p. 90), the measurements are based on the common Egyptian cubit.

Reconstruction of Solomon's Temple, from Moehlenbrink, Der Tempel Salomos.

    If Solomon's buildings on Mount Moriah's offered a splendid appearance, visible far into the distance, the reason was not the Temple itself, but the surrounding palaces which were far more impressive in size, as we discern from the biblical specifications. South of the Temple, which together with its courtyards was surrounded by walls and priests' dwellings, but forming a structural unity with the Temple complex, there stood the royal palace, the living quarters of Solomon, with the separate seraglio for his Egyptian wife; the Hall of the Throne or Judgment Hall, the Hall of Pillars with the 'place of the threshold,' and the House of the Forest of Lebanon, a majestic hall with three rows of fifteen splendid cedar wood pillars. The unassuming rectangle of the Temple was situated on the highest point of the stone surface of Moriah, on the ancient sacrificial site, the rock that was experienced as the foundation and corner-stone of all earthly creation, the *Even Shetiyah*. Steps may have led up to the entrance, located in the narrow eastern wall. Inwardly, the Temple towered over all its surroundings; outwardly, however, it certainly remained concealed behind the taller adjoining walls and edifices. It could have seemed, like a simple chapel of a castle or a palace, to have been added to the far larger and more splendid royal palace.

    The palace buildings were the bearers of the continuing architectural development in history. It is believed that Saul's royal castle at Gibeah within the realm of the ancient sun-height of Gibeon, the location where young David played his harp before the raving king, has been rediscovered through the excavation of the ruins on the height of Tell el-Ful. The structure that stood there must be called downright primitive. A wall of rough stones enclosed a number of small chambers and rooms into which, through openings resembling arrow slits, very little light could come in.

Even though workmen from Tyre and Phoenicia participated in its construction, the castle that was built by David on Mount Zion must also be pictured as having been quite plain and unpretentious. The new element in David's castle was that, in all probability, a room was added on to it on the western side at a point to which ancient Melchizedek-traditions may have been attached. This space harboured the sacred ark of the Covenant. The tabernacle itself, the actual precursor of the Temple structure, still remained on the height of Gibeon. Only the altar that could be carried, the most important Temple content, was freed by David from its condition of homelessness and housed in a certainly very modest addition of the royal castle. Not until Solomon's palaces was the plainness, the castle-appearance of the earlier royal seats, left far behind. But we observe how the role, played by the space which the Temple occupied — the Temple which now, once and for all, took the place of the tabernacle and caused the fame of the Gibeon-height to sink into oblivion — developed out of the earlier condition: the sanctuary remained embedded in the confines of the royal seat. Now, however, it became quite clear that the location of the Temple determined that of the palaces, not the other way around; for only the ancient rock of sacrifice on the 'threshing floor of Araunah,' where David had beheld the stern angel of judgment, came under consideration as the starting-point. The palace buildings with their splendour surrounded the austere, plain-looking sanctuary in a protective manner as well.

Since the Temple was, after all, no gathering place and intended only for conducting the priestly functions, its location within the courtyards of the royal palace was the reason that its external form could be seen by the populace only at fixed times of the year and then from a certain distance. The feelings of awe and devotion, which Israel offered up to its Temple were not occasioned by outer sumptuousness; they were only the fruit of the idea that here was the actual abode of the deity and the source of the divine proximity.

The plain, almost box-like exterior of the Temple could have led to the assumption that all riches and display had been reserved for the interior. But anybody who entered with such ideas would have been surprised anew. Except for a few simple cultic and symbolic objects, the Temple's interior, which was lined in gold foil, contained nothing. The actual reality of this Temple was not to be sought in the sensory realm but in the sphere of the archetypes. After all, when constructing the ark of the Covenant, Moses had received the direction to reproduce in earthly shadows and reflections what he had beheld in the spirit realm (Exod.25:40, Heb.8:5). A whole stream of symbolism started from the Temple of Solomon. The freemasons, for example, trace their symbolism back to Solomon and refer to their ritual premises as Solomonic Temples. A few masonic lodges hold meetings to this day on certain days of the year in Solomon's quarries in Jerusalem. But it would be an error to assume that the symbols of the first Temple in Jerusalem were contrived symbols, arbitrary pictorial representations of some abstract thought. As yet, they did not belong to the intellectual symbolism which alone remained in later ages; they had still been deciphered from the sphere of the archetypes, a symbolic script of inner necessity and objectivity.

The concept, from which the Temple-symbolism proceeded, viewed the human being as an image and symbol formed by the cosmic artist himself. In the human being, there was a quintessence and concentration of the whole creation, a 'little world,' a 'microcosm' in which the 'great world,' the 'macrocosm' was reflected and repeated. If now, in the Temple and its symbolic signs, a kind of microcosmic reproduction and artistic intensification was created, the same archetype and cosmic secret was once again depicted which had also taken on form in man. Out of the external existence in nature, there were brought into the inner existence of the cultic sign: the seven planets through the seven lights of the candelabrum, the zodiac-images of the heaven of fixed stars through the twelve loaves of consecrated bread, the four elements through the four colours of the curtain. By placing the secrets of the universe under seal, the human being was unsealed. The contemplation of the Temple's symbolism was supposed to lead man to the rediscovery of the effects in his own nature of the great cosmic forces, the fixed stars, planets and elements and to the recognition of himself as the image and abode of the deity, thus once again freeing the divine element, cast under a spell in himself, by means of the sanctification of his life. And in the expectation of the Messiah, he was to look up to those forces that would come to his aid in this endeavour.

Like Noah's ark and the ark of the Covenant, the Temple was divided into three rooms. The entrance, located in the east, led first into a vestibule (*Ulam*), which was only half as deep as it was wide (10 by 20 cubits, about 5 by 10 m, 16 by 33 ft); then followed the long room (the *Hechal*), which was twice as deep as the width (40 by 20 cubits, about 20 by 10 m, 33 by 66 f) and contained the altar of the burnt offering as well as the seven-armed candelabrum and the table with the consecrated bread on each side. The third, innermost room, to the west, the Holy of Holies (*Dvir*), was hidden by a wooden wall which had a five-cornered door that was covered by the curtain of the four colours. To stand in front of this curtain and to sense behind it the ark of the Covenant with the figures of the cherubim, representing the throne of the invisible god, was the high point of the cultic life in Israel, reserved for only a few individuals. From Philo to Thomas Aquinas to Martin Luther, we always find it expressed as an assured insight that the Temple in its threefoldness reflected the perfect human being, the 'man of God,' of body, soul and spirit. To pass in mind through the three parts of the sacred edifice, led from the physical world through the soul world to the threshold of the spirit world, illuminating the mystery of the threefold human being.

The room in the middle, which represented the soul's sphere, was filled with the miracles of faith. The corporeal world where things only speak their everyday language and reveal nothing more than themselves had been left behind. Now, turning into symbols, things began to speak a priestly language. External form was assumed by something that otherwise only took place invisibly in man's inner being.

From the altar in the centre, sacrificial smoke arose. The human being, who along with his breath bears within himself the whole aeriform sphere of the earth, could watch the symbolic image of incense in devotion and veneration, sanctifying his breath and his word. Faith carried the soul beyond its own confines. The soul world expanded to the starry world when one's glance fell upon the candelabra and the consecrated breads. The forces of the planets and the signs of the zodiac worked formatively on the organs of human beings even if they did not pay heed to these forces. But if they experienced themselves in conscious devotion as creatures and handiwork of God, it was as if the planets enkindled lights in them and the fixed stars nourished them with bread from heaven.

The soul wanted to go further. It found itself in front of the curtain that concealed the spirit world from it. The world of earthly substances, of the earthly elements, weaves an impenetrable veil before the seeing eye. This was expressed in the four hues of which the curtain consisted, as theologians of old always depicted it. The earth element was expressed in the byssus, the white linen; the water element in the purple, the air element in the hyacinth-coloured part and the fire element in the scarlet. For the human being who stood in front of the curtain, it remained to exercise with devout longing the virtues that transform the earthly elements. Thomas Aquinas described how an inclination towards the spirit was enkindled from the four colours: purity from white, the sense of sacrifice from purple, meditation from the hyacinth-coloured material, and love from the scarlet hue.

It was a sombre and serious secret that the devout Israelite sensed behind the curtain in the Holy of Holies. It was not without reason that this actual abode of the deity, lacking even the smallest window-opening, was located in the west where the light of the sun is extinguished. When the Temple was completed, Solomon also mentioned the divine darkness in his words of dedication: 'The LORD has set the sun in the heavens, but has said that he would dwell in thick darkness. I have built thee an exalted house, a place for thee to dwell in for ever.' (1Kings 8:12f). Only once a year, the high priest entered the section behind the curtain. Was not the sacrifice of atonement that he offered up there reminiscent of the dark cloud of divine wrath? In his temples, the Greek knew of the radiantly beautiful image of the deity in human form. Therefore, conscious of being alive, was he not also able to feel the divine form in his human nature? Through the symbol of the curtain, the Israelite was made aware that the spirit world had turned dark and that man had lost his divinity. Death is God's answer to the sin of man. To behold God is synonymous with death. He who would have gone behind the curtain would have met death in encountering God. First, the divine being itself, namely the Messiah, had to gain entrance into a human body and thus descend into the realm of death. Otherwise, it could not become light behind the curtain. As yet, God dwelt in darkness and, since he was drawing ever closer to human incarnation, he descended into increasing darkness.

The dark sanctuary behind the curtain had the shape of a cube. We shall leave it unresolved whether this was achieved by having a low, upper storey above this space which would have filled out the difference between the width and the height of the Temple (the width and length of the *Dvir* was twenty cubits, as was the width of the Temple itself; but the Temple was thirty cubits high), or whether the floor was higher than that of the rest of the Temple, perhaps on account of the shape of the ancient, sacrificial rock. The second possibility sounds very probable.

Just like the black Kaaba of the Muslims at Mecca, it was thus fashioned as an expression of creation that had become dark, heavy and earthly. The time had not yet arrived for the clear view that John's revelation opened up to the new heaven and the new earth by describing the heavenly Jerusalem as a light, golden, crystalline cube (Rev. 21:16–18). The Temple of Solomon was a yearning for the Messiah become architecture and visible symbol, because it contained as its most profound secret the darkness of death that had descended upon earth and humankind.

Thomas Aquinas stated that it was a presentiment of Christ's death that the Holy of Holies was situated in the west. The Temple of Solomon was indeed the most concentrated expression of Israel's Messianic mission. But the people of the Old Covenant could only prepare a sheath for the Christ that bore within itself the destiny of death: the physical body. Just as that part of the Christ being, who was incarnated on earth, added resurrection to death, so that part of the Temple-symbolism, which contained a prophecy of resurrection, was added from the non-Jewish mysteries to the Solomonic architecture.

Among the workmen whom Hiram, king of Tyre, made available to Solomon for the Temple construction, the one who bore the same name as the king, the master-builder Hiram, stood out in first place. In him, a messenger of the mysteries, a bearer of initiation, came and stood alongside Solomon. The Bible makes this clear by calling the architect a 'son of the widow' (1Kings 7:14). In the Osiris and Adonis cults those individuals were called 'sons of the widow' who, in under-going initiation, had experienced how through the 'death of Osiris' — the divine forces extending into the human being — the Isis-forces of the soul were widowed, and how the spirit element can arise in the impoverished womb of the human soul through the birth of the son, the Horus-like higher 'I.'[4]

In Solomon's time, the Adonis mysteries of Phoenicia had not fallen into decadence as completely as they did a hundred years later when, in the age of Elijah, the Sidonian princess, Jezebel, brought the decadent Baal cults to Israel from the same country from where Hiram, the builder, had been dispatched to Jerusalem. Hiram could still come to Solomon as a genuine messenger of the mysteries in which the prophetic Messianic knowledge of the death and resurrection of the god lived and was cultically nurtured.

Like Tubal-cain, the son of Cain, Hiram is described as 'a worker in bronze; and he was full of wisdom, understanding, and skill, for mak-ing any work in bronze' (1Kings 7:14, compare Gen.4:22). Down in the plain of the Jordan, Hiram built the smelting ovens in which he poured those parts made of brass which he had to add to the symbolism of the Temple.

Above all else, Hiram was the creator of the two pillars, Jachin and Boaz, which found their place at the left and right sides of the Temple entrance and of the mighty, lily-shaped 'molten sea,' resting on twelve bull shapes, which was to be erected to the south between the palace and the Temple.

Hiram's symbols were not withheld from the sight of the populace as was the interior of the Temple. They were to press like mighty seals into the souls of those who could only associate with them an obscure sensation and inkling. Images that indicated matters of the far-off, dis-tant future were to shape the soul of the people in such a way that thereby also, the path was made ready for the divine being, in the process of descending to earth.

In the two brazen pillars of the Temple gate, the mystery signs of universal duality were included in the Solomonic symbolism that could frequently be encountered in the mystery sites of Asia Minor. Herodotus, for example, reports to us that he saw two columns at the Hercules-Temple in Phoenicia's Tyre, which, designed in contrast, emitted light day and night, one during the day, by its golden radiance, the other at night because of its phosphorescence: 'There were two pillars there; one made of pure gold, the other as if of emeralds which shone with a strong light at night.'[5]

We must picture Jachin as having been fashioned in brightly shining metals, Boaz as dark and stern-looking but luminous at night. Jachin was light as day, Boaz with its radiance evoked a mysterious feeling as does the night. Jachin was the pillar of birth and life, Boaz that of death. If two such powerfully impressive pillars, cast in brass, formed a portal, they had to evoke from deep within the soul the presentiment of a force that stands above the opposites, combining the world-duality into divine unity. This symbol of the portal pointed to far-distant future times, to a being who, having been resurrected, is elevated above the opposites of death and life and can say of himself: I am the door.

The molten sea, formed by fire, destined to hold water within itself, placed a grandiose symbol of the divine incarnation into the Temple's vicinity. Fire forged earthly substance into a receptive chalice; water signified the heavenly content which pours into it. Thus, humankind, glowing in the flame of sacrifice, was to form the sheath which could receive into itself the divine being, descending to the earth to become man.

The initiated Phoenician master-builder, Hiram, added Messianic, prophetic symbols of the incarnation and resurrection of Christ, forged in brass, to the sombre, stern Solomonic Temple. Lights of divine salvation, lights of Easter, lit up on the rocky hill of the god passing judgment on Moriah, lights that played around the Temple in which the deity had its 'abode in darkness.' The connection between Hiram, the builder, and the mysteries of resurrection, pointing far beyond the age of Solomon, has been experienced again and again. Thus, according to Josephus, the Greek poet Menander, in a description of Phoenician history, attributed the resurrection festival of the Tyrian god Melkart to Hiram and denoted the erection of the Temple as a symbol of the resurrection ('εγερσις, *egersis*) of the god. In his later, Christian fragments, Friedrich Schlegel, the Romantic poet, interpreted the word Hieram (the German spelling), obviously in reference to ancient Christian-masonic traditions, by showing that it is composed from the first letters of those Latin words, meaning, 'He is Jesus who rises from the dead.' 'In all probability, the slain master Hieram (*hic Iesus est resurgens a mortuis)* is the dying death-god of new life, known and venerated in the ancient mysteries — Dionysus or Osiris. He is Christ as an idea before and outside Christianity.'[6]

In Hiram and Solomon, two worlds confronted each other that had become estranged in the course of time. The initiated messenger of the mysteries stood by the side of the one who had turned his back on all esoteric life and everything reminiscent of mystery practices and had dedicated himself to the development of an exoteric culture. It was inevitable that in this confrontation, the tragic, historic weakness of Solomon, his fear of all occult elements, would emerge. The 'Temple Legend,' retained in all occult traditions to this day, tells about this.[7] It relates that in Hiram and Solomon, descendants of the lineage of Cain and Abel-Seth confronted each other; the Cainite with spiritual courage of achievement, the son of Abel-Seth with timid force of self. It goes on to say that especially because of the daring forging of the molten sea, Hiram had on one hand earned the admiration of the Queen of Sheba, who was still familiar with ancient traditions of wisdom, but on the other hand had provoked the jealousy and enmity of Solomon. Finally, Solomon was supposed to have ordered the slaying of master Hiram by three evil apprentices who earlier had wanted to disturb the forging of the molten sea by prematurely pouring water into it. An ancient tragedy was fulfilled. As yet, Cain and Abel could not be reconciled. Abel still took his revenge for the ancient fratricide by having the Cain son killed. The mystery principle and the principle of an exoteric culture were hopelessly split apart. The age of the mysteries was over. Only through the Christ event, to which the Phoenician initiate pointed with his prophetic brazen creations, a reconciliation would begin between Cain and Abel, between the mystery principle and the life of people in the external activity of civilization.

CHAPTER FOURTEEN

The Song of Songs

When, stricken by serious illness and close to death, Thomas Aquinas interrupted his last journey — he was on his way to a council in Lyons — the monks at the monastery where he sought refuge asked him for an interpretation of the Song of Songs. On his deathbed, in his transfigured consciousness, the great teacher dictated his thoughts concerning the brief Old Testament text which is the most poetic part of the whole Bible, thus bestowing on his rich life's work the most beautiful crowning point of faith.

Oh, how far away modern theologians have moved from such feelings of greatest admiration, love and most ardent faith, with which the great Christians of earlier times looked upon the Song of Solomon, when they confront this text in a completely helpless way and claim that a bit of mundane poetry of love has accidentally been misplaced in the domain of the holy scriptures!

At first glance, the Song of Songs does in fact oblige us to ask what significance it might have in the Bible. In it, we do not find any directly religious motifs as in the Psalms, in the Book of Proverbs or Ecclesiastes. It does indeed appear at first to be nothing more than a dialogue, abounding in poetic pictures, between two lovers who at times are separated, at times united, now filled with longing, now filled with bliss.

This question is not resolved even when we go into the details of the lyrical beauty of the images and the sound of the melodies slumbering in them. But now we become aware of the hundredfold similarities which, verse for verse, the Song of Solomon possesses to the realm of folk songs. All the folk songs of the world seem to encounter each other here with their dreamy, touching images in which nature's floral beauty turns into the language of the loving heart. We begin to understand the name: 'Song of Songs.' It is truly a sort of archetypal song. All the songs of the different nations find their epitome here. Is it perhaps also their origin and source? Was this perhaps the first time that the well poured forth its gifts from which, through all the centuries, all people have henceforth obtained their songs?

The riddle and wonder of the Song of Solomon must be related to the riddles and miracles of folk songs and song as such. What does the magic of a genuine folk song consist of?

In an authentic song, not only the earthly element holds sway. It has a strange, emotional transparency for the unearthly sphere. Bright and dreamy prophetic forces, filled with feeling, pervade it and have the effect that the soul element within becomes clear like a prism so that one can see through it into another world. Colourful joy of spring and longing for spring determine the poetic picture, but the forms and colours of blossoming nature do not refer to themselves; instead, they are pictures for the flowering of the soul through love. Again, the love of one human heart for another is not the highest form of love. Another, higher world resonates in it and, through it, shines its light. We sense that spring and love harmonize so well with each other because they are two different revelations on earth of the same archetypal activity.

A deeply hidden interplay exists between the soul realm and the spirit sphere. Everywhere, soul longingly seeks spirit and is filled with bliss when it is allowed to draw close to it. This mysterious alternation of seeking and finding pervades all the kingdoms of nature and of human beings. In nature, it is concealed in the miracle of the seasons: the earth seeks and finds heaven in spring and summer, and is separated from it again in autumn and winter. The seeking and finding of human beings who love one another is a revelation of the interplay between soul and spirit, holding sway in all creation. The love of the devout heart for God directly reveals this secret, but earthly love is only another aspect of the same phenomenon. In and above all earthly love, the longing, seeking and finding can become visible which guides the soul in the spirit and thereby, in a higher form, to itself.

Thus, every genuine song, even if it is 'only' a love song, possesses a religious nuance because, in the images of earthly love, it allows heavenly love to shimmer through. And it is only accurate in a very limited sense when one distinguishes between the minnesongs of lofty and ordinary love as, for example, in the Middle High German song-poetry, in the poems by Walther von der Vogelweide, or in the 'Minne Song's Spring' *(Minnesangs Frühling)*. Behind the image of the beloved, the song's vision always allows the mystery of the Madonna to shine, even if the text of the song reveals nothing about it.

The archetypal image of the soul that seeks the spirit, in all songs the cause of the transcendental, religious radiance, is the essential element in the Song of Solomon, the archetypal song. Here, the pictures of spring and love are completely transparent for the higher mystery. While the Temple construction was the most sublime, sacred crowning point of the Solomonic work, the Song of Songs was its loveliest, most beautiful flower. Like the Temple, the Song of Solomon in its own way makes visible the total image of man, the archetype of spirit man.

The texts that are included in the Bible under Solomon's name are not only attuned to very different soul nuances; they actually originate in quite different soul and life spheres. Owing to the universality of his nature, Solomon could give vent to the wealth of wisdom, which was conveyed through him, by letting it stream forth out of the depths of the different parts of the human being.

The teachings of the Book of Proverbs were gleaned by him from his actual 'Solomon' or Manas-nature, the actual spirit self, the inner harmony and peace, the effects of the higher self in his soul being (see p. 142). Only at the end, Solomon twice gave the sayings of wisdom a special phrasing. As we have discussed, he actually did not utter the verses of the chapter preceding the last one as 'Solomon,' as bearer of the spirit self, but as 'Agur,' 'Ben Jakeh' and as 'Ithiel,' — as the physical human entity who struggles for his 'I'-being (Prov.30:1, see pp 139f). In him, earthly man who has lost the spirit calls out:

> Surely I am the most foolish among men, devoid of all human
> wisdom. I have learned nothing wise, the knowledge of the
> holy ones is closed to me. Who can ascend to heaven and come
> down again to earth? Who holds fast with his hand to the
> spirit in the wind? Who gathers the waters in a garment? Who
> can arouse the ends of the earth? What is his name, and what
> is his son's name? Do you know that? (Prov.30:2–4B)

Solomon wrote the verses of the last chapter as 'Lemuel,' the soul human being who is devoted to the divine (see pp 141f). The soul speaks, the part of the human being that appears to imagination in the form a feminine being. For this reason, the end of the Proverbs is a 'golden alphabet for women,' a number of teachings and words of praise, beginning in each instance with another letter of the Hebrew alphabet, concerning feminine virtues; instruction not merely for a woman but for the feminine aspect in all human beings.

Finally, the wise king became the poet of the Song of Songs, not out of his Solomon-nature but as 'Yedidyah,' the 'beloved of God,' as bearer of the 'spirit man' (see p. 142). The soul of man moves into the vicinity of the greatest fulfilment prepared for it by the loving deity. Here, all chastising seriousness and judgmental sternness are far removed. The mysteries of love between God and his beloved, the spirit man — the love, of which all earthly longing and bliss of love are only shadows and images — unfold and cast rays into the realm of the soul that longs for the higher self like the bride for her groom. Here, the stern, serious words that instruct and train could no longer suffice for what was to be proclaimed. Solomon, the teacher and preacher, had to turn into the poet, and thus the Song of Songs was born; the beautiful dialogue of love began between the soul and the higher 'I,' the spirit man.

Spring's miracle of flowers is transplanted from external nature into the sphere of the soul when, like the sun's rays, the breath of love of spirit-nearness awakens the soul to new life: 'Lo, the winter is past, the rain is over and gone; the flowers appear on the land, spring is here ... Arise, my love, my fair one, and come to me!' (S.of S.2:11–13B) Is it not the song that all peoples of the earth sing in their own manner and yet always in the same words?

The soul in love knows that the glance of her longed-for beloved does not see her weaknesses and failings. This is what makes her so joyful and allows her to blossom: that the eyes, now resting on her, only see and want to lift the spell of enchantment from her beauty and radiance. She hears the beloved voice say: 'My sister, my bride, you are a garden locked, a hidden spring, a fountain sealed' (4:12B). And of herself, she can say: 'I am a flower of Sharon, I am a rose in the valley' (2:1B). A strange, darkly shining beauty always emanates from folk songs when they speak of the 'rose in the valley.' It is as if an immemorial word of the heart were uttered. It touches the heart in a special way to look down from a hill and see the red roses shining in the glow of a sunset. It is a picture that directly brings to mind everything that a person bears within as love. The image of the loved one arises, but as if it were the essence of one's own being; as if one beheld the heart shining in love like a red rose in the dusky depths of one's own being.

And how does the soul behold the one she loves?

> My beloved is white and red,
> > distinguished among ten thousand.
> His head is the finest gold;
> > his locks are like the tops of palms
> > and black as a raven.
> His eyes are like doves
> > beside springs of water,
> washed in milk;
> > the most abundant streams flow past them.
> His cheeks are like garden-beds
> > on which fragrant spices are sown.
> His lips are like lilies;
> > the finest myrrh pours forth from them.
> His arms are like golden rings,
> > adorned with turqoise.
> His body is ivory,
> > encrusted with sapphires.
> His legs stand like alabaster columns
> > that rest on golden feet.
> His form is like rising incense,
> > noble like a cedar.
> His voice is sweet beyond all measure;
> > he is altogether graceful.
> Thus is my beloved, my friend,
> > O daughters of Jerusalem. (5:10–16B)

Is it not as if this image is composed of nothing but seeds of songs and fairy-tale pictures? When the beloved is called 'white and red,' for example, it seems that all the spirit-presentiments become audible that have found an expression in the songs of the lily and the rose, in the fairy tale of 'Snow-White and Rose-Red,' and in the sagas of 'Flos and Blancheflore'? Above all, however, this song of longing and adulation is the most beautiful, poetic parallel to the mighty spirit-vision of the Son of man, the Christ-vision, with which the seer John begins his apocalypse (Rev.1:13–16). The ardour of the love song veils the apocalyptic element which is nevertheless contained in it, for the soul beholds the form of spirit man whom she longs for.

The search of the loving soul for the beloved permeates all the spheres of poetry. There is a Frankish folk song that begins with the question: 'Shepherd, tell me, where do you pasture your flock?' And the reply is: 'Out on the green meadows, the cheerful shepherds pasture their flock.' This song appears to be a simple shepherd-song, sung to the accompaniment of a bagpipe or a shawm in which nothing but the joy of a shepherd's life is expressed. But the shepherd with his flock is himself poetry, an archetype that has taken on form and reveals something of the secret of the higher human self. It therefore need not surprise us that the seed for this song is also encountered in the Song of Songs: 'Tell me, you whom my soul loves, where you rest at noon, so that I do not have to wander back and forth among the flocks of your companions' (1:7B). As a shepherd is to his flock, the higher 'I' is to the content of his soul.

Does the soul now find him whom she seeks? Does she cross over the threshold of the world in which he sojourns? The wistfulness of separation, the pain of loss is woven ever and anew into the bliss of love. A threshold experience must be absolved again and again, a fact which the Middle High German minne-poetry and the German folk songs with their great transparency for the archetypal element have captured in the so-called 'Day Songs.' Night harbours the mystery of union. Freed of the body, the soul is then united with the spirit. But then, when day dawns, the hour of separation strikes. The red glow of morning is a stern guardian who drives everybody away from the blissful nocturnal town and reminds those in love to part.

> The guardian on the rampart began a song and sang:
> If one remains within still, he should go home forthwith!
> I see the day a-dawning, through clouds already clear.
> O guardian on the rampart, you torment me so hard.
> I lie in deepest sorrow o'er the dearest, gentle one.
> My heart endures such pain that I must part from her ...[1]

All the sorrow of leave-taking and being apart, of which the songs
are full, originates here:

> The morning red is already high,
> It spreads its roses wide,
> Farewell, you lovely maiden.[2]

The threshold drama of the 'day song' breathes through the Song
of Solomon. The transparency for the destinies of the spirit-seeking
soul is remarkable. The guardian on the wall turns into the guardian
of the threshold. If the soul is successful in crossing the threshold, the
miracle of union opens up to it:

> Upon my bed by night
>   I sought him whom my soul loves;
> I sought him, but found him not
>
>   ...
> I will rise now and go about the city
>   in the alleys and in the street
> I will seek him whom my soul loves.
>
>   ...
> The watchmen found me,
>   as they went about in the city:
> 'Have you seen him whom my soul loves?'
> Scarcely had I passed them,
>   when I found him whom my soul loves.
> Now I hold him and will no longer let him go (3:1–4*B*)

But the soul is never spared the pain of separation. The miracle of
the night, when the body sleeps but the soul is awake, is always followed by day, during which the soul is not strong enough to maintain
itself near the spirit:

> I sleep, but my heart is awake.
> There sounds the voice of my beloved. He knocks:
> 'Open to me, dear friend, my sister,
>   my dove, my pure one!
> My head is wet with dew,

my locks with the drops of night.'
[The soul answers:] I have taken off my garment,
 how can I put it on again?
I have bathed my feet,
 how could I soil them again?
But my friend put his hand to the latch;
 and my heart was thrilled within me.
I arose to open to my beloved.
 My hands dripped with myrrh,
precious myrrh ran from my hand
 upon the handles and the bolt.
But when I had opened to my friend,
 he was gone.
Was not my soul beside itself when he spoke?
I sought him, but found him not.
 I called him, but he gave no answer.
The watchmen found me,
 as they went about in the city;
they beat me, they wounded me.
 They took away my veil,
 those watchmen on the wall.
I adjure you, O daughters of Jerusalem,
 if you find my friend,
that you tell him
 I am sick with love ... (5:2–8B)

The New Testament speaks in a stern, apocalyptic manner of the soul's chymical wedding with the higher being, namely in the parable of the wise and the foolish maidens who expect the bridegroom. In the Song of Songs, immersed completely in melodious beauty, the Old Testament catches the first prophetic rays of this secret of humankind.

Solomon's share in the lofty mystery of the spirit man was like a gift possessed without effort, as a special favour of destiny, which the human being, in possession of the 'I,' must first struggle with much effort to attain unless he is to forfeit what life bestows on him as did Solomon's wealth which vanished in the end. What is important is to find the true dimension of the Song of Solomon, where all that is transient is but an allegory, where earthly love becomes more and more transparent for divine love; where natural man with his potential and talents is increasingly permeated by spirit man and the latter's actions of transformation.[3]

The Age of the Prophets

CHAPTER FIFTEEN

The Division of the Kingdom

Never was the bright radiance of a royal empire extinguished more quickly than Israel's splendour after Solomon's death. Overnight, the Solomonic kingdom crumbled which had appeared to be the human spirit's triumph over the darkness of matter. The kingdom and the nation split into two parts; the cosmic integrity and harmonious whole of the configuration of the twelve tribes thus fell into ruin.

No sooner had Rehoboam, Solomon's son, emerged before the people as king when the far greater segment of Israel broke away from him and founded a kingdom of its own, composed of the ten northern tribes. The splendidly altered and perfected city of Jerusalem was suddenly only the capital of a very small region. Only the two tribes of Judah and Benjamin remained faithful to the royal house of David and Solomon, and the major part of the Judean territory consisted of the awesome landscape of death, the Judean Desert and the Dead Sea. Henceforth, the two kingdoms faced each other like two feuding brothers: the rich kingdom of Israel consisting of the ten northern tribes, and the outwardly unassuming kingdom of Judah in the south around Jerusalem.

The first king of the northern empire, Jeroboam, was a mysterious figure. From early on, Solomon's attention had been drawn to him and, recognizing his potential despite the fact that he was only a youth, Solomon had kept Jeroboam near him and had allowed him quickly to attain to high honours and influence. At one point, it came to an irreparable dissension between them. Jeroboam faced Solomon with great self-confidence and only by escaping to Egypt could he save himself from the king's wrath, the king having decided upon his death.

The Bible indicates that Jeroboam's stubborn protest had a connection with the alterations in Jerusalem undertaken by Solomon, particularly the elimination of the Tyropoeon Gorge (1Kings 11:27). It is possible that Jeroboam made himself the spokesman of the ancient mystery sites of the city, the traces of which were now to be entirely eradicated. The Bible appears to denote him as a representative of the mystery and initiation-principle by calling him a 'son of a widow.' If this is correct, then it is understandable that one day the rupture had to come between him and Solomon, the more exoteric.

Jeroboam also had had experiences that gave him the courage to confront the king. As in Saul's and David's case, he had been privileged to experience something that had been denied to Solomon. A seer had come to him and had prophesied a royal future to him.

After Solomon's death, it was as if everywhere all kinds of diverse and opposing forces which Solomon's figure had held in check now followed their own inclinations. This is why the special interests of the northern tribes dared to emerge and recklessly override everything that spoke for maintaining the unity of the nation.

Jeroboam must have been an overwhelmingly impressive, hypnotic personality. The people had not forgotten him during the years of his Egyptian exile. Now, those who did not wish to be under the leadership originating from Jerusalem, fetched him back from Egypt. The ten northern tribes appointed Jeroboam king and he made the ancient city of Shechem in Samaria his royal seat, thus into the city opposing Jerusalem. But after his return from Egypt, Jeroboam by no means considered himself to be merely the representative of a political mission. He became decisively involved in the religious and cultic life of his people. He opposed the Yahweh-worship's concentration in a single location of the land, which had been initiated by Solomon through the construction of the Temple; and he did this not only because, following the division of the kingdom, the northern tribes had forfeited their share in the sanctuary. He established two cultural centres in his royal territory — one in the north in Dan and the other in the south in Bethel — which represented something totally different from Solomon's Temple in their spirit as well. The heart of each of these two sanctuaries was the golden image of a bull. Jeroboam clothed the Yahweh-worship that was to prevail in his realm into the forms of the Egyptian Apis cult.

Once before, the Israelites had put up a golden, bull-shaped image of the deity: the golden calf at the foot of Mount Sinai. At that time, Aaron had assisted those who had wanted to give the Yahweh cult this Egyptian stamp. But as if he were the very embodiment of Yahweh's fire and wrath, Moses had smashed the golden bull and nullified the temptation of a relapse into the Egyptian past in favour of the spirit of the future. Coming from Egypt, approximately three hundred years after Moses had destroyed it, Jeroboam re-erected this image of the deity in a twofold and splendid manner, thus bestowing on the newly arising kingdom of North-Israel its sanctuaries.

The symbol of the bull was also encountered in the vicinity of the Temple of Solomon: the molten sea of Hiram rested on twelve bulls arranged in a circle. But the molten sea was at the same time the classic expression of the fact that the ancient spirit forces, which had been venerated particularly in the Egyptian bull cult, were to place themselves now into selfless service of a new task of humankind: the bulls carried the mighty chalice, opening up to heaven in lily-like form, in which the Messianic expectation of Israel was symbolized. In Jeroboam's golden bulls, the spirit forces of a bygone age regained a value of their own.

The division of the kingdom after Solomon's death was an event of unforeseeable consequences. It almost seemed as if everything that had been achieved in regard to a new impulse of humanity in the Israelite development, all the foundations that had been erected for the Messianic future, had been for nothing. Magic powers of the past broke forth chaotically. Could the laboriously nurtured seeds of the future withstand this onslaught?

The approaching tension of great upheavals also influenced the catastrophe of the division. The Assyrian danger increased from the north like a sinister, giant spectre. With magic speed, the Assyrian Empire grew in power. The forces, newly arising in humanity and striving towards a future as yet veiled but nevertheless ardently awaited, which found their purest self-expression in Israel through the Messiah-expectation, assumed a sinister counterpart in the emergence of the Assyrian kingdom. The Assyrian civilization was like the growing terrestrial shadow of a great, approaching heavenly force. The fear and panic which issued from it reverberated also into the Israelite tribes. It was obvious that the Assyrians would soon reach out in conquest to Egypt. If Syria and Palestine were not to be in their way in this endeavour, they had to be taken over first. The fact that Solomon paid no heed to the Assyrian danger and instead consolidated his cultural work as if no world existed outside of Jerusalem was one reason why the northern tribes, together with the bordering Syrian vassal-states, became restless and dissatisfied while he was still king. Solomon's death was the signal for Syria, which became independent immediately under the leadership of Rezin, one of the greatest enemies and haters whom the wise king had had. The secession of the ten northern tribes was directly related to this. Instead of being allied to Jerusalem, which was self-sufficient, the part of Israel that appointed Jeroboam as its king wished to be allied with Damascus, the Syrian capital, in order to be able to form a block with the northern neighbour as a defence against the Assyrians. Despite its treaty with Jerusalem, Egypt favoured Rezin and Jeroboam. It had to welcome the Syrian, North-Israelite block as the most valuable bulwark in case it might itself be attacked by the Assyrians.

The tear that split the nation of Israel into two did not occur at an arbitrary location. A duality now became outwardly visible that had already existed as a polarity earlier and was linked to the mighty, basic contrast of Galilee's and Judea's topography. The north of the region around the Sea of Galilee and the upper Jordan with its abundance of sunlike etheric formative forces had to favour and give rise to a completely different form of soul and consciousness in the Israelite tribes living there, from that of the moonlike south with the Judean Desert and the Dead Sea. The Galileans were close to nature, imbedded in the etheric weaving of forces in their landscape, thus still gifted with the remnants of ancient clairvoyance. And their character of soul continued in altered form all the way into the region of the middle, into Samaria. Only in Judea — because there the dominant etheric forces gave way to a desert-landscape poor in etheric life forces — there was an abstract, intellectual manner of soul, alien to nature, into which intruded no remnant of the old clairvoyance. Between the inhabitants of Galilee, Samaria and those of Judea, there existed a more pronounced difference in the nature of soul and consciousness than held sway between the Galileans and the non-Israelite, Syrian neighbours in the north. Galilee and Samaria could not be anything else but sites of nature rituals with pagan nuances. The rejection of nature-religions and thus a radical isolation from the ancient pagan civilizations was possible only in Judea.

In David's and Solomon's kingdom, a duality, extraordinarily full of tensions, had been integrated into a unity: the very one corresponding to the topographic polarity of Galilee and Judea. The pressing contemporary constellations could only increase it, in so far as they caused the northern tribes to seek support increasingly from the pagan Syrian neighbours, and inasmuch as they drove the inhabitants of Judea more and more emphatically into developing their culture, which, turned away from nature, flowed purely out of human forces.

It was *Judaism* that had developed in Judea and now suddenly stood there as a uniform configuration after the division of the kingdom. Until Solomon's time, no specific Jewish element existed as an independent cultural factor. There was only the totality of Israel; within it, the spiritual life of the tribes of Judah and Benjamin existed as one pole of the whole. Through David and Solomon, the tribe of Judah gained a leading position and Jerusalem, its centre, became for a time the capital of all the people. But the Jewish cultural element still remained imbedded as a segment in the whole of Israel. After the secession of the ten northern tribes, the kingdom of Judah was suddenly placed on its own as the realm of the Jewish people. Rehoboam was the first king of the Jews. The rejection of Jerusalem by the Jeroboam-tribes signified at the same time the rejection of Judaism by the majority of the people.

The transfer of the royal seat and the Temple site from Mount Zion to the rock of Moriah and the transformation of Jerusalem must have had an important effect in the preparation of the division. The hill of Zion with its mysteries as well as the spiritual life nurtured on it were related to Galilee, whereas the rock of Moriah was the quintessence of Judea. The establishment of the Temple signified the specific beginning of Judaism and was indeed experienced as such by the northern, non-Jewish tribes of Israel. It was not without good reason that the Bible depicts Jeroboam, the exponent of the northern tribes, as the one who protested against the changes conceived by Solomon in the appearance of the city of Jerusalem. Solomon could ally himself as much as he wanted to with the pagan nations of his surroundings and befriend them, building altars to their gods on all the high places around Jerusalem, but by transferring the main Israelite sanctuary to the eastern hill, he became the creator of Judaism, alienated from nature, whereby the tribes in Samaria and Galilee, who were close to nature, felt excluded.

Seen outwardly, the initiative for the division of the kingdom originated from the tribes which then established the kingdom of Israel under Jeroboam. But if we look at the inward directions taken by the development of the Old Covenant, it can dawn on us that it was the progressive genius of the people itself who, through the division, had undertaken a purification, eliminating the no longer suitable northern tribes. As if to isolate and crystallize in the purest way possible those forces that were required for the promised future, the circle of the Messianic development was concentrated on the small southern kingdom.

A new stage commenced in the alternation between involution and evolution that dominated the history of Israel (see pp. 130f). Even in the age of the patriarchs, it had often been necessary to eliminate from the stream of Messianic heredity elements that were unsuitable, although as such valuable: Ishmael, Esau and Joseph had to become progenitors of hereditary branches outside the Messianic line. These ages of early selection and involutional concentration were then followed by periods where the alien outer world was directed in great measure into the Israelite evolution so as to be absorbed. This evolutionary expansion of the nation's horizon had experienced its greatest intensification under Solomon. Immediately after his death, a significant epoch of renewed contraction and concentration ensued. The external expression for that was the elimination of the sphere belonging to the ten tribes and the tightening of the circle around Jerusalem. Henceforth, Judaism, which had become independent, the tiny kingdom of Judah, turned into the bearer of the Messianic mission.

CHAPTER SIXTEEN

The Genius of Elijah

The sequence of the four kings of the Grail, Titurel, Amfortas, Perceval and Lohengrin, is the pictorial expression for a law asserted on a number of levels in the development of spiritual life. Titurel, the ancient one, carries heaven's lofty wisdom into the circle of his people as if he were the human incarnation of the divine revelation itself. Amfortas, the ailing one, demonstrates how, after the extinction of the gods' wisdom, the human being must traverse the dark abysses of guilt and suffering in a spirit of sacrifice, filled with longing for redemption. Perceval is the one who is able to ascend to the light again on yonder side of the abyss of suffering.* He is the transformed human being who can make himself the bearer of the healing and redeeming love of God. Lohengrin is the messenger of the spirit, a living link between the divine and the human world, who has grown beyond the merely human and personal level.

The sequence of the figures in the Old Testament is also secretly determined by this law of descent and reascent as revealed in the above four individuals. Titurel figures stand at the beginning in the great ancient teachers, Enoch and Noah. Job, the Amfortas of the Old Testament, is only the most distinct embodiment of the sacrificial stage, which, however, is also absolved by the patriarchs, since, in them, humanity learns suffering. As we have seen (pp. 70f), reflections of the Perceval destiny flash across the life of David. He penetrates through the valley of trials and, like a king of the Grail, holds up the lance and the chalice, even though he resembles the ailing Amfortas again in the end.

The Old Testament finds its Lohengrin figure in the prophet Elijah.

---

* One of the possible translations of the name Perceval is 'through the valley.'

In him, more than a mere human being spoke and acted. In him, an angel, a messenger from the spirit world, seemed to have appeared among men. First here, then there, he emerged as if borne on the wings of the spirit, be it as a helper and protector of those in need, be it as the warrior against the adversaries of good.

Since the division of the kingdom (926 BC), life had become quiet in Jerusalem. The splendid city of Solomon, now merely the capital of little, politically insignificant Judah, settled back to the rank of a provincial town. Its inhabitants continued to live for a long time on the slowly subsiding cultural wealth created by David and Solomon. History seemed to stand still at the 'centre of the world.' In undisturbed succession, the descendants of David, Solomon and Rehoboam took their places on the throne of the kings of Judah.

Things were different in the larger kingdom of the ten tribes in the north of the land. There, storms and upheavals raged incessantly through the soul realm; for, after all, the unrest of that period, caused by the Assyrian threat, also surged directly against this region. Jeroboam's successors, the kings of Israel who resided in Shechem, did not follow one another in tranquil dynastic sequence. One ruling house superseded another, for the kings were not always followed by their sons; instead, their thrones were mostly usurped by their murderers. The dramatic agitation and confusion of forces seemed endless.

Approximately half a century after Solomon's death, a king assumed the reign in the northern kingdom who made an all-out effort to adopt the Adonis and Baal cults from the neighbouring north-western kingdom of the Phoenicians of Tyre and Sidon. This was Omri (886–875 BC). At the time of the Temple construction, it had been from Tyre that Hiram, the master builder, had come to Jerusalem as a last representative of the genuine mystery impulse. Particularly in the age that followed, the Phoenician Adonis mysteries that had their centre in Byblos north of Tyre and Sidon on the Mediterranean coast must have rapidly fallen into pronounced decadence. Owing to the worship of the dying and re-arising god, the Baal cult possessed a strong Messianic quality, but for that very reason it was particularly exposed to the cosmic unrest and impatience of the tension-filled epoch. By means of wildly ecstatic rituals, people attempted to speed up the longed for arrival of the god.

Omri betrothed his son Ahab (875–854 BC) to the Sidonian princess Jezebel who herself played a fanatically active part in the context of the Baal and Astarte cults. No sooner had Ahab become king when Jezebel found a way to push the Egyptian bull cult, introduced to Israel by Jeroboam, into the background by means of a large contingent of Phoenician Baal priests. The high tension of soul, which held sway in any case among the ten northern tribes, was increased to the utmost by this alien, ecstatic element. Ahab transferred the residence of the kingdom of Israel from Shechem, located between the ancient mountains of the deity, Ebal and Gerizim, into the city of Samaria, which had been erected to the north by his father Omri on an old Canaanite holy high place.

There, he remodelled the former unassuming sacrificial altars into magnificent temples and surrounded them with splendid palaces with which he drew the attention of the world on to himself. One part of his royal palace that became especially famous consisted entirely of ivory. A rival centre to Jerusalem was to arise; Solomon in all his splendour was to be outdone.

The feverish unrest of this time erupted in military involvements. Battles raged between Israel and Syria, the two countries that had in fact wanted to form an alliance against the Assyrian danger. The Syrian, Ben-hadad, was obviously afraid that Israel with its new, glorious capital city would become too powerful and would want to extend all the way to Syria as had been the case in Solomon's age. Although Ahab was successful in repelling the armies of the opponent, the inner unrest increased rather than subsided. Prophets emerged who uttered serious reprimands against the alliance that Israel renewed with vanquished Syria. They predicted terrible misfortune because they saw a repetition of the sin which Saul had incurred by his leniency towards the Amalekite king, Agag, in Ahab's compliance to Ben-hadad.

Simultaneously with the upheavals of war, another calamity broke in upon the land: a long spell of scorching heat, of the heavens denying the earth the revivifying rain, made all the fields dry up. The fertile plains of Galilee soon resembled the frightening regions of the Judean Desert. Boundless dearth and famine afflicted the people. Was doomsday already approaching?

This was the condition of Israel when, spreading like wildfire, rumours circulated which gave rise to unexpected premonitions and visions in the souls of the excited populace.

There was somebody about of whom it was felt as soon as the rumour was heard, that a truly great person was active and appearing among the people in the name of God. There were many prophets in the land; to those who had originated from the Nazirite stream, the ecstatic Phoenician prophets had been added. But soon people sensed that this mysterious, great being who had now begun to be active was not just any prophet; he was *the* prophet, belonging to a quite different class, hailing from the same world from which, so it was ardently hoped, the Messiah himself would appear. Was he the forerunner, whose coming had likewise been predicted, who now let his voice resound and who would prepare the way for the One, longed-for and awaited by all?

For some time people had been speaking of the divine messenger. It was claimed that he had been seen in various places. Nobody knew where he came from and where he belonged. Nobody succeeded in following him. Scarcely had he been seen and laid people under his spell when he had disappeared again. Then it happened one day that Ahab, who had also heard of this mysterious personage, saw him in the flesh before him. In stern words, the apparition predicted to the king that the scarcity of provisions would last for years.

Ahab was accustomed to having some prophet appear before him who predicted some calamitous event. After all, following the battles against the Syrians, a prophet had foretold his own death. But what he heard now was more. Although it appeared to relate to a definite earthly event, in it, also a vision of the whole future of humanity seemed to reverberate. The prediction of a long-lasting drought really sounded like the proclamation of a mighty turn of time, of a Last Judgment that would break in upon a world grown old and decayed. Like everything that the mysterious messenger of God had said, what he had to announce to the king was uttered as if spoken to all the people. By means of a strange magic, it spread quickly everywhere and its effect was so direct that everybody believed that he had heard it with his own ears. Merely the awareness that this great being was present had an effect that penetrated and transformed the souls.

He was a man like all other men; yet he was more. The soul-spiritual power active in him was not exhausted within the confines of the human personality but extended into another world, being filled and borne by the beings of this higher plane. If he revealed himself to people, the 'words uttered by his mouth and the actions performed by his hands' did not originate only from the earthly but the celestial part of his being; 'they were manifestations of divine-spiritual Beings in the background.'[1]

The great admonisher's soul being, reaching up into the spiritual world, appeared to conceal its human bearer entirely so that he could neither be recognized nor grasped. People only experienced that aspect of him which was 'more than a personality, which hovers over the individuality like an aura but has an efficacy that transcends it, something alive like an atmosphere ...'[2] As if, in him, the folk-spirit of Israel itself went about, and as if the Yahweh deity revealed itself through him in its direct, intrinsic being, this is how Elijah appeared to those to whom he showed himself. The name that was used to speak of him indicates something of this mystery. 'Elijah' means 'Yahweh's divine bearer of forces.' When, three hundred years later, Gautama Buddha lived in India, it filled the souls everywhere with reverence and piety to know of his existence, for he was more than a Bodhisattva, a great teacher: he had acquired the rank of Buddha, having attained to complete permeation with God. In him, a divine being walked over the earth. The effect that emanated from Elijah was similar and at the same time completely different. Elijah had nothing of the corporeal-spiritual unity of the divine and human, present in Buddha, which radiated peace. Instead, in him, there dwelled a divine power which had the effect of a fire, a windstorm or a force of nature. A reflection of the forces that had spoken to Moses on the summit of Mount Sinai were present in Elijah and called forth the fear of God, awakening the tremulous sensation of God's nearness.

Everywhere in the land, only a few episodes were related concerning Elijah. But they were conveyed in such a manner that it did not remain merely a matter of listening and passing the story on. By hearing them, people had a nearly visionary share in the prophet's destiny. It was as if by relating these stories they attained to waking dreams in which the images were revealed directly like events experienced by the listener himself.

Miracles occurred in and through the person of Elijah; this was the content of what people related and believed they had seen. Two scenes in particular made the rounds after the prophet had confronted the king publicly. Through them, people followed him into the distant seclusion that now harboured him. He was seen far from human dwellings in a narrow, gorge-like valley of the Judean wilderness by the side of a dried-up course of a brook. No nourishment, no fresh drinking water as far as the eye could see, but lo, ravens flew to him who was deep in pious prayer and brought him sustenance. The image of the ravens around the head of Elijah bestowed a faint inkling on the souls of the people that even in times of greatest need and seeming abandonment by God, the deity nevertheless does not cease caring for human beings.

The other scene led into the midst of the bustle of a populated city at the coast of the Mediterranean Sea. The prophet was seen entering the house of a widow who, together with her son, was just eating her last, meagre provisions, soon having to face death by starvation. Miraculous sustenance had been bestowed by the ravens on the prophet and now, through him, on other people as well. But then, as it was related, events took a strange turn. Despite the preceding miracle, the son of the widow died, but through the power indwelling him, Elijah was victorious over death as he had been earlier over need: he called the son of the widow back to life.

A strange geographic riddle gathered together the images in which the people participated in Elijah's fate. The brook, Cherith, where the ravens had been observed flying around the head of the prophet, flows into the Jordan in the Judean south of the land near the Dead Sea, emerging from the rifts that are cut into the desert like canyons. Today, this rift valley is called Wadi Kelt. At the spot where Elijah is said to have stayed, a small monastery, dedicated to St George and cared for by Greek monks, is attached to the steep slopes of the rocks. Zarephath (Sarepta in Greek), the town where Elijah sojourned in the house of the widow, is situated in the north between Tyre and Sidon on the Mediterranean coast. Already these two images embrace the whole territory of the once undivided Israel.

In a very special way, the tragedy of the nation's division can be sensed, when the paths on which the Elijah destiny took its course are traced. Was it not as if the genius of Israel was wandering homelessly around over the members of its body that had been torn asunder, woefully seeking the lost unity?

Three years of most dire need went by. Then the unheard-of occurred: Elijah emerged from his seclusion and again appeared publicly before all the people and the king. His concisely coined words penetrated powerfully into the souls when he challenged the nation to decide either for Baal or Yahweh. Then, suddenly, in dramatic intensification, the scene changed. On Mount Carmel, from where one can look far over the Mediterranean Sea, Elijah appeared, as if transported there by magic, in the midst of the Baal priests who, in Carmel's temple confines, were engaged in wild, ecstatic rituals, trying to conjure forth spiritual powers to end the privation. To the people and to the king, Elijah had spoken in words. Here, he was silently effective through his action. Out of twelve rough stones, as if he wanted spiritually to reunite Israel's twelve tribes, he erected an altar that appeared insignificant and unaffected compared with the splendid terraces and halls of the Baal and Astarte temples.

Even in theology, the ideas that were formed concerning the scenario of the spiritual contest on Mount Carmel were in most cases incorrect from a religious, historical standpoint. Only Elijah's figure and his altar may have given a primitive appearance. Quite certainly, the Baal priesthood together with the temple structures and altars, where the ritual functions were carried out, must be pictured as having been cast in rich, monumental splendour. Descriptions such as those by Franz Werfel that originated through poetic imagination, may often-times be more accurate historically than the picture gained by theological and scientific essays.

Werfel describes a monk who gives the following account in visionary retrospection:

> The path sloped up gently to the knob of the hill. Here, the
> gigantic sanctuary stands in the strong, scorching sun, the two
> altars and statues close together. The images represent the lofty
> pair, the brother and sister, the husband and wife: Baal and
> Astarte. The altars arise on a round, circular terrace from
> which steps lead down to the clearing. Each of the altars has a
> base twelve feet high, on which the history of the deity is

engraved on raised lines. A door, fashioned of dull metal, leads
into the interior of each of the bases. The sacrificial stones
themselves are hewn squares of polished, transparent quartz
that absorb the rays of the sun and moon in a special way and
then transmit that light again, something that has a mysterious
effect on the human senses. The outline of the statues of the
deities, each of which may well measure thirty feet, becomes
blurry in the light ...

On the terraced staircase outside, on the platform of the
sanctuary, a whole army of priests in yellow robes moves
around in a sacred order, ascending and descending. I do
notice, however, that the altar of Astarte is being attended by
priestesses who also wear yellow gowns, but with long
trains ...

These priestesses have purple sashes, resembling belts,
around their hips, whereas the priests of Baal wear sashes that
are a deep blue like the Mediterranean Sea. The great round of
the steps is continuously circled by two rows of temple
dancers ...[3]

Elijah stood before his stone altar in the plain hermit's garb
which contrasted with the colourful robes of the priests, and
looked up to heaven: the archetype of the priest. And lo, he
was successful where the wild ecstasy of the Baal priesthood
had failed: the atmosphere was set in motion which, for many
long years, had been stifling and still. The souls of the people
all around were touched by the breath of the spirit. A vision
was born: they beheld the spiritual power that Elijah was able
to call down from heaven; they saw it descend on to the twelve
stones in the form of mighty, blazing flames. And it was not
long before clouds rose on the horizon and wind began to
blow; the sky at last opened its long closed locks and bestowed
refreshing, life-giving water. The time of want had come to an
end.

The same individuality, who had been pictured as the bearer and
bestower of miraculous nourishment during the years of privation,
had now broken the spell of nature so that all the people could find
sustenance again. Whereas drought and famine had been experienced as a sign of the decline and end of an ancient world of forces,

the fire and rain now seemed to proclaim that one day in the future heaven would open in order to lavish new life and strength on devout humanity.

The end of the famine, however, by no means signified escape from the Judgment Days of the turn of time for which it had been an admonishing symbol. The chaos and destructive upheavals not only continued but intensified. The conflagrations of war and religious conflict, which had finally only smouldered faintly during the years of the drought, were once again rekindled into unrestrained flames. It goes without saying that the Baal priesthood was imbued with furious hatred after its devastating defeat on the summit of Mount Carmel and, under the queen's protection, commenced on a cruel persecution of all those faithful to Yahweh.

Again, Elijah, against whom the Baal faction's most vehement hatred was directed, vanished from the public scene. Again, in the powerful after-effect of his appearance, the soul of the people followed him into his seclusion in visionary images, which this time were more far-reaching and therefore only like distant premonitions. Now also, the direction of the paths taken by the prophet resembled the wistful search of the territory of Israel by the genius of the people who had become homeless. The pendulum swung first from Galilee's north into the distant south far beyond the Cherith Brook into the rugged hills and ravines of the Sinai-Horeb, where Moses had once received his mighty revelations. Then it swung northward, far past Zarephath all the way to the paradisal oasis of Damascus in Syria.

Whereas a blessed healing and sustaining element had emanated from Elijah in his seclusion at the Cherith Brook and in Zarephath where he had gone after his first public appearance, now, all those who could follow him into his solitude with their thoughts, had to experience him as the mighty fighter, the relentless herald of a new epoch of humankind. His path led him to the site of the Moses revelation, for the age that had begun with Moses had run its course and had to make way now for something completely new. Elijah had to take the place of Moses.

Four hundred years after Moses, the Sinai mountain became the stage of a solitary scene far removed from the world, but one that was most significant for humanity's evolution. No human beings were

now camped at the foot of the sacred mountain. Infinite, ultimate loneliness held sway far and wide. Above, on the summit, surrounded by
raging elemental forces, the sacrificial site, which had still been in use
in Moses' age as part of the Jethro mysteries, had become dilapidated
and weather-worn.[4] As if human beings had never stayed there nor
could ever have been there, the elemental greatness surrounded Elijah
when, in the early dawn of a stormy day, he left the rocky cave in the
canyon where he had spent the night. He felt himself called upon by a
divine power and voice, and he sensed the mystery of God's proximity. But a frightful surging of the elements confronted him. First, the
airy realm spoke in its fierce language. A storm resembling a hurricane
roared and screamed across the bare, cold summit. The deity did not
reveal itself to Elijah out of the rushing of the wind. Then the earth's
depths replied; first with thunderous quaking. The divine did not
reveal itself to Elijah in the earthquake. Finally, the forces of fire and
steam from the earth's interior pushed their way out into the open air.
Thick clouds filled with blazing lightning covered everything. But the
divine was not revealed to Elijah in the fire. How strange this was!
Once, Moses stood at the same location and the deity revealed itself to
him with clear-cut power and infinite wealth out of the tempest of the
atmosphere, the quaking of the earth and the clouds of fire. What sort
of change had taken place here?

Had human nature already become so hardened and incapable of
experience that it could no longer penetrate behind the external surface of natural phenomena? Certainly, the human being and consciousness had become fundamentally different in the centuries
between Moses and Elijah. But after all, Elijah bore within his soul faculties that extended far beyond human potential. The fact that he
could not find the deity in Sinai's nature forces could not only be
caused by the shrinkages which had occurred in the human being with
the loss of the ancient clairvoyance.

Since the age of Moses, a decisive change had occurred in the spiritual world itself. A transformation had taken place, similar to the one
which in his time had extinguished the ancient divine radiance in
Egyptian spiritual life.

Looking up to the starry spheres, ancient Egypt had beheld the
eternally young, creative light of Osiris. Then, the tragic twilight of the
gods had set in. The light of the youthfully fair deity was extinguished

in the star-studded heights, and on earth, the mournful dirge over Osiris' death was intoned. But the divine being had not disappeared. He had only passed over into another sphere. Moses experienced and pointed him out to his people during the Sinai journey in the Yahweh realm of the earth's forces, in the elemental forces of the fire and steam pillars of the wilderness. In the transition from Egypt's Osiris-light to the Yahweh-revelation of Moses, it had been demonstrated in a grandiose manner for those who could have deeper insight that the divine being, who, since the beginning of creation, had been on his way to earth from the highest cosmic spheres, had come closer by a decisive step in his approach to the earth.[5] When Elijah stood on the summit surrounded by lightning and thunder, this highest divine being, whom we call the Christ being, had taken another step on his path. The twilight of the gods had been extended to the Sinai elements because the divine entity, whom Moses had still beheld there in Yahweh's radiance, was no longer in this sphere either. Where was he now?

When the raging of the elements had ceased and suddenly a great stillness held sway all around, Elijah became aware of mysterious sounds, reminiscent of the harmonies of the spheres, as if he heard a soul echo of the thunder and lightning. The Bible calls it a 'still, small voice.' It was no external noise that Elijah became aware of. It originated from listening within. His own soul realm became like a sea shell in which the inner rushing sound could be heard. The gentle beating of wings of a divine being became audible in the human soul sphere. Elijah now felt touched in an inward manner by the divine element which had not been revealed in the wind, the earthquake or the fire. In deepest reverence, Elijah covered his countenance with his cloak and turned from the expanses of outer existence by stepping into the entrance of the cave of Horeb. The fact that he turned his covered face to the dark interior of the mountain was only an outward symbol for his having given up his whole being to the inner sphere. There, the deity revealed itself to him and appointed him to his task.

After this hour, Elijah had to be the herald of a new cosmic age, of a completely new experience of God. All the nature religions of the pagan nations that sought for the divine in the outer world now belonged to the past and with them also the form in which Moses had still received his revelations. A time of a more inwardly oriented soul religion began with Elijah. The radical opposition arose to all pagan religions which was to intensify into the mighty prophetic movement and its militant rejection of all nature sanctuaries.

With Elijah, the world-historical antithesis between paganism and Judaism made its appearance. It is not true that in principle and from the beginning, the piety of the Old Testament stood in opposition to any form of nature religion. This opinion is encountered almost throughout those Christian factions which believe that Christianity is as incompatible with paganism as is Judaism. A correctly understood Christianity stands as the synthesis above the contrast of paganism and Judaism, that of nature and soul religions. Christianity's focus and object of worship is, after all, the lofty divine being who, on his journey to the earth, first revealed himself through the kingdoms of nature, and then, when the time of his human incarnation was already drawing closer, revealed himself out of the human soul realm. When it will be clearly recognized that not only did Judaism originate quite late (after the division of the kingdom), but that only beginning with Elijah the anti-pagan, Jewish piety replaced the nature faith that extended far into the Old Testament, then the path will probably be cleared for the view that sees in Christianity the fulfilment of the prophetic Jewish as well as of the pagan yearnings and premonitions.

So long as the members of the Old Covenant sought the divine in the external forces of nature, so long, the outer course of destiny had to appear to them also as a direct mirror of the divine will. When times of happiness and prosperity held sway, they believed that the deity was close to them and well disposed. When periods of misfortune and want came about, they viewed this as a sign that God had turned away from them in anger. Owing to the fact that Elijah appeared to his contemporaries as the pioneer and herald of an inner experience of God, he paved the way for the discovery of the divine, loving will in the midst of unhappiness and suffering. One who had been able to sense God's nearness in his own soul realm could maintain this experience even when external events of destiny were hard and painful. Elijah's call for inwardness laid the foundation for a new faculty in the human being: the belief that there was meaning even in suffering and misfortune, the acceptance of destiny, the inward independence from the outward course of fate.

Moses had become Israel's mentor through a broadly conceived teaching which he integrated into the abundance of the laws and the structure of the ritual. Elijah enkindled the fire of a certain force in his people. He embodied and actualized not only a teaching but an impulse of being which, like a burning fire, was conveyed to those who were able to be the first-born of a new attitude of soul. The spirit of Elijah was a spirit of inner strength. In reference to the apocalyptic picture of the two witnesses (Rev.11), the two main columns in the temple of humanity, Rudolf Steiner once characterized the difference between Moses and Elijah and at the same time gave a spiritual inter-pretation of the two names: 'Elias [Elijah] was the one who brought to man the knowledge and message of the one pillar, the pillar of strength, Moses was the one who brought the message of the pillar of wisdom. Moses means wisdom or truth; and Elias means the directing force, that which points the direction, that which gives the impulse.'[6]

The divine mission which Elijah received on Mount Horeb and which led him from there far into the north to Damascus, signified a pro-found intervention into the destinies of the future. On behalf of the deity, a chain of events of bloodshed and destruction were mercilessly brought about by the prophet. The divine voice that was heard by Elijah as a 'still, small voice,' announced no peace but only terror. This is one of the greatest world-historical paradoxes. We only comprehend the seeming contradiction if we recognize that the word of the deity that reveals itself in the quiet soul interior is at the same time the power which bestows courage in the face of any necessary destiny, even in case of decline and death.

In Damascus, Elijah was supposed to put mandatory powers for the immediate future of Israel into the hands of three persons. He was to make Hazael king of Syria, Jehu king of Israel and Elisha the succes-sor of his own prophetic mission. It was basically not the execution of outward deeds that Elijah was asked to perform, but the enkindling in his soul of an unheard-of courage in regard to destiny. The fact that he was supposed to nominate Elisha as his successor signified to him the certainty of his imminent death. And the appointment of Hazael and Jehu, the arch-enemies of the present royal house of Israel, had to bring about unending battles, catastrophes and destruction for all the people of the northern kingdom: 'And him who escapes from the sword of Hazael shall Jehu slay; and him who escapes from the sword of Jehu shall Elisha slay. Yet I will leave seven thousand in Israel, all the knees that have not bowed to Baal, and every mouth that has not kissed him.' (1Kings 19:17f). These are the words that Elijah heard from the 'still small voice.' It would be the will of God and yet correspond to his hidden love if, henceforth, the history of Israel resembled the conflagration of a fiery furnace just as long as the shiny core of the precious metal could be refined out of the slag in the end! The only thing that mattered was the end which would contain the meaning of what was happening now;* the well-being or misfortune of those living now did not matter.

When the Sinai fire blazed around him, Elijah no longer beheld the countenance of the deity. Instead, he himself was the fire. The fire of God had become the human flame. In his impulse of inner strength, in his merciless, determined courage of destiny, Elijah resembled a torch which had enkindled a fire of the future in humankind. This was how the teachers of the Old Covenant saw and described him:

> Then the prophet Elijah arose like a fire,
>> and his word burned like a torch ...
> By the word of the Lord he shut up the heavens,
>> and also brought fire down to earth
>>
>> ...
>
> You heard the coming judgment of the world on Mount Sinai,
>> and the judgment of vengeance on the height of Horeb
>>
>> ...
>
> How glorious you were, O Elijah, in your wondrous deeds!
>> Who is as marvellous as you? (Sirach 48:1,3,7,4 B)

After his appearance in Damascus, Elijah's activities changed in a puzzling way. To begin with it seemed as if he had vanished altogether. People excitedly asked themselves: Is he still alive at all, or has he already fallen victim to his enemies who hate and persecute him?

---

* The number seven thousand, similar to the number three thousand that refers to the number of people who, through Moses, perished after the destruction of the Golden Calf, or similar to the five thousand and four thousand who, according to the New Testament, partook of the miraculous feeding, must be understood qualitatively, not quantitatively. It is not meant to refer to the number of Israelites, namely seven thousand, who remained alive in the end. Seven thousand is the number of the ultimate goal, the Seventh or final Epoch of humanity.[7]

Then he showed himself again. But while he had earlier resembled a being extending beyond the human and terrestrial realm, it now seemed as if he was revealed from a totally different world. Now, everything benevolent had disappeared from his being; he was experienced like the countenance of the wrathful deity itself. One who saw him had to be shaken, for he could be sure that his life had come to an end. This is what happened to Ahab, the king. In the vineyard of a man, Naboth, whom Queen Jezebel had ordered killed out of unaccountable hatred, the figure of the prophet appeared to Ahab. Frightening insights pierced his soul; the sudden certainty overpowered him that his death was imminent. Not long afterwards, he was killed in battle.

For some years, Elijah did not show himself. Then a message was brought to king Ahaziah, Ahab's son, who lay on his sick-bed, that Elijah had reappeared and was staying on a mountain top. Twice, upon beholding him, a group of soldiers, whom the king had dispatched to fetch Elijah, were consumed by flames of fire which suddenly blazed forth on the mountain's summit. Just as Moses at one time had experienced the deity in the fiery forces of the earth's interior, so the bailiffs of the king now experienced the spirit form of Elijah in this fire. But to behold him signified death. Only the third group that was sent out was spared from the consuming fire. And now Elijah appeared before the ailing king. But to him also, he proclaimed and brought only death.

Henceforth, the people no longer saw Elijah. Nobody could answer the question of where he had gone. Elisha, the disciple of the prophet, had already begun his activity. And such astounding effects emanated from him that soon rumours circulated that Elijah with his power worked through him. How could that be? Was Elijah himself no longer on this earth? Nobody had heard anything about his death. What had taken place?

An answer spread about that certainly was appropriate for the nature of the prophetic genius through reports about a wondrous experience of Elijah at which a number of the prophet's disciples had been present: henceforth, people talked about Elijah's ascension to heaven. It was said that Elijah had appeared within the circle of the disciples of prophecy, engaged in their exercises, and, together with Elisha, he had ventured off on a special path. At the end of this road, by the Jordan, Elisha then had beheld a fiery chariot with horses blazing like the sun, and before his eyes, Elijah was supposed to have been born up into the heights of heaven. As he vanished, the prophet, having turned into a flame himself, was supposed to have let his robe slide down upon Elisha, who was sunk into spiritual vision, as a sign that henceforth, he would continue to be active on earth by means of it.

This truly elevated Elijah above human existence — not to have died but to have ascended to heaven. Had the divine nature of the primordial era returned, so that, as in Enoch's case, it could be said of Elijah that the deity had taken him up directly?

Sensing the element of genius in his nature, the pious of all ages have seen a spiritual power in Elijah with which on can feel connected and united at any place and in any age. If he was more than a human being on earth, exalted above space and time, so that he could appear like a being of the higher world, this was that much more true of him after the conclusion of his earthly life. Even today, at a Jewish Passover meal, an extra cup of wine stands on the table, the 'cup of Elijah,' for according to tradition the prophet Elijah walks about like an angel and may enter any house uninvited during the eve of Passover.

In the mystical communities within Judaism, for example among the Hasidim, the focus on the prophet Elijah as a being that is a guardian angel had an important influence. The encounter with him was one of the first experiences that came to the practitioner of cabbalistic exercises. Thus, legend relates that the mystical path of the Baal Shem, whose birth had been announced to the father in an Elijah vision, began by an encounter with the prophet in the form of an old man.

The Old Testament contains the most impressive indication of Elijah's effectiveness, outlasting death, at the end of its canonic scriptures. The brief prophetic text that has come down to us under Malachi's name, concludes with the words in which the deity itself proclaims the return of Elijah: 'Behold, I will send you Elijah the prophet before the great day dawns of cosmic reckoning' (4:5*B*). The sentence that speaks of Elijah as of a superhuman angel being is interpreted in the Gospels as the fulfilled prophecy concerning John the Baptist as the returning Elijah: 'Behold, I send my angel to prepare the way before me' (Mal.3:1*B* and Mark 1:2). Through this sentence the heading of the whole text is unsealed: Malachi means 'my angel.' The

name, under which the scripture has come down to us does not indicate the author of the text, as is usually assumed, but contains the
angel-mystery of the Elijah entity. The Old Testament concludes by
indicating the future activity of the genius of Elijah. In the end, it
makes that figure of the Old Covenant arise once more in his superhuman glory who inwardly could lead one most closely to the Christ
event and the beginning of the New Testament.

CHAPTER SEVENTEEN

The Drama of Elijah

Elijah's figure can be studied in different ways. At first glance, the prophet's demeanour seems like that of an apparition flashing through an aroused era, the harbinger of evolutionary tempests of a new age. Up to now we have followed the viewpoint that tries to survey the totality of the events of that time as if from above and that also predominates in the Bible to begin with.

In so doing, however, the question remains open concerning the human personality from whom emanated the mighty effects. How do we arrive at a conception of the man, Elijah, his circumstances in life and developments in the realm of external facts, causes and effects?

The loftiest secrets in the narrations of the biblical books are not, as is readily assumed, the great supersensory relationships and occurrences, but their terrestrial embodiments and realizations. Especially on the earthly level with its outer course of history, the deepest mysteries hold sway. Increasingly, it will have to be recognized how superficial and wrong it is to believe that the physical, historical set of facts can simply be read off from the reports of the Bible. In the first place, what the Bible relates has to do always with what has taken place soul-spiritually in human beings and the different periods, even though it appears to be otherwise owing to the matter-of-fact, pictorial description. A task that has to be solved each time is to penetrate through the psychic-spiritual sphere down to the physical ground of the earth. The Elijah stories are a classic example of how the Bible itself challenges us to question the special mystery concerning the terrestrial, human foundation of the super-earthly, superhuman event. The description of the historical Elijah secret does indeed belong to the trail-blazing deeds with which Rudolf Steiner pointed the way to a new comprehension of the Bible.[1] With the key offered there, we shall now approach the question concerning the human being and destiny of Elijah.

An episode is inserted into the sequence of the Elijah stories and it is at first inexplicable why it is placed into this context at all. We are told about a man from Jezreel in Galilee named Naboth. King Ahab made the demand on him either to relinquish or to sell to him his vineyard that bordered on the territory of the royal palace. When Naboth refused to give up the legacy of his fathers, the king was profoundly displeased. At this point, Jezebel, the queen, intervened. She knew a way to bring about the convening of a folk festival at which Naboth presided at first, but subsequently was defamed and stoned. Although Naboth's death brought the king fulfilment of his wish, it was at the same time the beginning of his doom, as he was soon forced to realize. From now on, a tragic misfortune broke over him and his whole house.

The Naboth episode is the more puzzling because, precisely at the point where it is inserted into the Elijah stories, something entirely different should be expected. It is preceded by the scene of the mighty spiritual battle on Mount Carmel. The fire of Elijah had vanquished and annihilated the world of the Baal priests. In boundless hatred, the queen, who felt personally hit by the blow directed against the Baal priests, let herself be carried away by a wild oath of revenge. She vowed to kill Elijah. Then, however, instead of reporting how she put her oath of revenge into action, there follows the story of Naboth's vineyard. How was it possible that Jezebel, determined to execute an extraordinary, demonic deed, was finally content with an intrigue against an insignificant, unknown vineyard owner?

Once again, by means of the quiet language of gestures, the Bible indicates a profound secret in the dramatically artistic composition of its reports. Through the murder of Naboth, Jezebel did execute the oath of revenge that she had uttered against Elijah, for Naboth was none other than the human personality in whom the Elijah genius was incarnated and from whom he blazed forth like a fire when he spoke and was active among the people.

If a special mystery were not connected with this, the Bible would not conceal the connection between Naboth and Elijah. It was a mystery of incarnation. Naboth and Elijah were one and yet were different from one another. Naboth was Elijah to the upper limit of being human. When Elijah appeared only in ordinary human contexts, he was Naboth. Elijah, however, was more than Naboth; this was revealed when he appeared before the world in fulfilment of his prophetic mission. Then, a power far surpassing all human elements vibrated through his words when he spoke; a fire and brilliance shone forth from his human countenance as if a world were aflame; the human form then grew to spiritually gigantic dimensions, surrounded as if by a cloud and atmosphere of power that made people think they still beheld him when he was actually long gone on his way. It took a very special faculty of perception and knowledge, capable of penetrating into the supersensory, to realize that Naboth and Elijah were one and the same. People were familiar with Naboth, the quiet, humble Galilean; they knew about the prophet Elijah who went about like a tempest or a force of nature, having either seen him once themselves or having heard of him. Who, however, could know that Naboth was the bearer of this spirit, the tower, from the windows of which this blazing fire flamed forth on occasions?

Once attention has been drawn to the identity of Naboth and Elijah, indicated in veiled form in the Bible and clearly revealed by Rudolf Steiner, we see how a deeply moving human drama is entwined into the sequence of scenes, which, viewed only from the Elijah aspect, appears to be nothing but a grandiose historical apparition. The attempt is now made to sketch the outlines of this drama.

In his youth, Naboth must have felt an impulse of spirit in his mind, often overpowering him, that led him into solitude or transported him into soul conditions where he was lost in dreams and posed a riddle to those around him. Although he need not have taken the specific vows of the Nazirites, inner necessity made him arrange his life as ascetically and meditatively as the Nazirites were in the habit of doing. He may still have been young, perhaps no more than twenty, when the chaotically aroused events of the time, the fantastic expansion of the city of Samaria, the pretentious demeanour of Jezebel and her ecstatic priesthood kindled the divine wrath in him that made him come forward as the prophetic herald of the approaching misfortunes and catastrophes. Naboth was changed into Elijah.

Perhaps he himself was the most shocked and astounded over the cosmic force with which the spirit had spoken through him when he had stood before the king. Therefore, again following a spiritual impulse, he withdrew into an even more remote seclusion. The solitary gorge of the Cherith Brook in the midst of the Judean wilderness, located there in utter desolation, became his hermitage.

The land and its inhabitants were languishing in the drought and famine that he had predicted and apparently had helped to conjure forth following the divine command. All around, the world was burning up from the stifling heat of the oppressive, cloudless atmosphere. Yet, the feeling was far from the hermit that destiny had imposed on him an enforced continuance of his ascetic exercises. The thought of the people's suffering made him take all deprivations consciously upon himself as if they were his own free action. He suffered hunger not only for his own sake but for that of all the people. His soul became the focal centre of everybody's suffering: thus he experienced the great turning point that found symbolic expression in all occurrences.

The soul fruits that ripened in him through the consciously endured suffering far surpassed anything that he or any other Nazirite before him had achieved through ascetic exercises. While the earth, impoverished to the extreme, was no longer able to bestow its gifts upon human beings, the spiritual world above opened its portals to Elijah the more abundantly. Revelations and forces streamed into him that enabled him to feel nourished even in his physical being. Those who could accompany his experience with imaginative faculties of vision beheld this in the image of the ravens who flew to him to bring him food.

Many of the questions and thoughts that moved through the soul of Naboth-Elijah in his seclusion may have related to the Baal cult which the Phoenician princess had brought to Israel. He knew that it entailed an ominous seduction of the people, a demonic diversion from the important step that Israel was now supposed to take in the field of religion for the sake of all humankind. Nevertheless, the riddle of the spirituality, nurtured there, must have held him in its grip since the Baal-Adonis mysteries had originally truly possessed a genuine Messianic character. This may have been the reason that Naboth-Elijah finally exchanged the solitude of the Judean Desert for the populated, at other times so luxuriant Phoenician coast, travelling through the whole suffering land from south to north. Thus he arrived in Zarephath that was located between the splendid ports of Tyre and Sidon.

It was inevitable that here, in the sphere of the decadent Adonis cult's origin and realm of forces, the sensitive soul of Naboth-Elijah was drawn forcefully into powerful turmoil and trials. In the wilderness, he was exposed to the effects of suffering. Here, the demonic possession of spiritual opponents closed in upon him. He had to come to the realization that it would not suffice to find a link to higher powers through the endurance of suffering. Beyond that, it was a matter of preparing himself for utter abandonment and transformation of his being, for the authority of spiritual battle. The imaginative description of the Bible depicts this in images that seem to refer to external events. We hear of Elijah's encounter with the widow of Zarephath.

The experience of Naboth-Elijah that is concealed behind the pictures of this story represents a certain correspondence to what happened to Moses when he entered the region of the Jethro sanctuary after his flight from Egypt. Moses beheld seven maidens who came to the well in order to fetch water for the flocks; before the gates of the alien city, Elijah beheld the sorrowful widow gathering dry kindling in preparation of the last meagre meal. Moses helped the maidens to overcome the obstacles that tried to stand in their way until, at last, through them he found access to Jethro.[2] Elijah moved into the upper storey of the house and the widow, who, along with her son, had already prepared herself for death, experienced how her flour and oil became inexhaustible all at once. When the son then nevertheless died, Elijah could waken him from death.

Just like Moses' experience at Jethro's well, so the experience of Elijah before the gates of Zarephath was an inner event. In case of the widow who gathered dry kindling, as well as her son, it was no more a matter of outwardly approaching physical figures than in the case of the seven maidens, come to fetch water. Moses and Elijah, each in his characteristic way, in a spiritual mirror beheld his own soul in the process of transformation. While Moses could proceed inwardly from a wondrous wealth of soul, symbolized in the visionary image of the seven Muses or Graces, a last inner impoverishment and isolation had to represent the way for Naboth-Elijah. Whether a widow actually crossed his path outwardly through whom the picture of his own being became clear to him in spirit, or whether this image appeared to him purely within in meditative seclusion is of no great importance and can well be left open to question. Elijah experienced his soul as a widow who felt herself unable to go on. It was particularly the contrast to the world of the Baal cult that did not care to separate from the opulent soul wealth of the past that led him to the awareness that acknowledged the necessary nadir and low point in his being. But no less powerfully, there dwelled in him the presentient confidence in the divine power that was close to him even in misfortune and inner impoverishment. He had already experienced that at the Cherith Brook. As he beheld himself taking up his abode in the upper storey of the widow's house, Elijah affirmed his own widowed state and simultaneously, also found the faith-filled ascent to the powers that would guide him to their goals through all trials. The miracle of a spiritual feeding was repeated. Now, however, a completely new stage of experience was added. Naboth-Elijah passed through an inner self-transformation, through a death of the former 'I'-consciousness and a resurrection of the new, higher 'I.'

In the mystery centres of the ancient world — in the surroundings of Zarephath, such sites had been preserved in decadent form — the disciples had been guided through death and resurrection by the hierophants who placed them for three days into a condition resembling death, afterwards calling them to rebirth as inwardly transformed persons and leading them back to life. In Zarephath, Naboth-Elijah underwent something similar in total seclusion without the aid of a hierophant. For him and those who could gain a clairvoyant impression of his experiences, his own dying and re-arising was clothed in pictures reminiscent of the ancient initiation practices: Elijah beheld himself how he brought the son of the widow from death back to life through the life-warmth of his whole being. In his own soul life, he now knew of the presence of a divine force that could not only survive and overcome deprivation but also death. In Zarephath, Naboth-Elijah himself had became the resurrected 'son of the widow.' In him, the pure counter-image of the Phoenician Baal-Adonis initiation, grown decadent, had become reality.

At the Cherith Brook and in Zarephath, Naboth-Elijah penetrated in inner self-transformation to a power and sovereignty that enabled him to confront as a mighty spirit warrior the forces of chaos and demons that were beginning to spread in Israel. During his first appearance before King Ahab, the spirit and courage had come over him as if from outside. Now, he went into battle consciously as the confident master of the forces working through him. The drama, which up to then had been one of the inner soul, now emerged on the stage of outer life.

Certain of his spiritual victory, Naboth-Elijah knew nevertheless that when he confronted the Baal priesthood on Mount Carmel he would provoke hate-filled opposing forces that would not rest until they could annihilate him as an earthly personality. He could break the power of the priests who gave vent to their whipped-up ecstasy around the pompous temples and altars up there, but now, the direct counter-effect of a personality set in who had at her disposal mightier clairvoyant and magic faculties than did the priests of Baal: namely Queen Jezebel. Herself an initiated priestess of Astarte, the female deity beside Baal-Adonis, she was the Phoenician, demon-possessed mystery decadence in human incarnation. The look and suggestion of a sorceress emanated from her. When she uttered the fierce oath of revenge against the prophet, she knew very well that she was not speaking idle words. She also knew where to direct the blow. It was Jezebel who saw through the connection between Naboth and Elijah, owing to her clairvoyant ability. Her consort, King Ahab, still had too many humane qualities to be possessed by such passionate and unrestrained greed for power and hatred, to decide for merciless employment of magic potentialities. He had no idea that a humble Galilean in the immediate vicinity of his palace at Jezreel was identical with the prophet whose threatening countenance had already frightened him a number of times.

Naboth-Elijah let himself be guided by the insights, lighting up deep within his inner being, that were like directions of the deity itself. He became aware that he had not yet reached the end of his mission that he was to carry out on earth. The hand that was trying to strike out at him could not be allowed to take hold of him. He fled and finally arrived at the storm-surrounded Moses height of Horeb-Sinai. Here, he became clearly conscious of his historical mission. God no longer spoke to him as he once had spoken to Moses. He spoke to him in a more inward manner and Naboth-Elijah realized that with this a new age had begun.

A new faculty was gaining entry into the soul realm of human beings. The Sinai fire became an inward element. Through the power that would henceforth indwell him, man himself was to become a flame. Elijah was not supposed to be a prophet in the sense of doctrinally predicting something pertaining to the future. In his own being, he was to exemplify and inaugurate something that all humanity was gradually evolving towards. He had to turn the future into the present. Thus, he himself was the first great realization of the inner fire. The Sinai fire, still confronted by Moses in the burning thornbush and on the height of the law's revelation, had become one with Elijah, it had become man in him. His being blazed in the spirit, his destiny was to remain alive as a living, procreating seed of fire in humankind.

Thus, Elijah also learned to discern his mission within the Messianic predestination of his people. He was not to prophesy the coming of the Messiah, but to prepare the way for him. The power of faith, the fire of inner strength, of not being led astray through suffering and death was to be kindled in the human soul as a preparation for the Christ power itself, as an early dawn of the great sunrise. Elijah was the herald and bringer of this dawn. In him, the inner human god was arising.

The experience at Horeb and the prophetic outlooks resulting from it had to bring it about now that Naboth-Elijah saw the future destiny of the separated twelve tribes in a new light. Although he himself belonged to the ten northern tribes that now constituted the kingdom of Israel, he had to struggle through to the realization that only the southern tribes of the kingdom of Judah would be capable of nurturing the inner fire enkindled in him. Israel was too closely related to paganism, whose time would have come to an end even if the chaos of demonic decadence had not cast its spell over it. For the religious concentration that was now required, a soul condition estranged from nature was needed, such as had developed in Judah. It was Elijah who, as a non-Judaic northern Israelite, had to bestow on Judaism its specific mission.

Naboth-Elijah beheld the future of his own Israelite homeland as if it were one great cosmic conflagration. He even felt called upon himself by the inner deity to throw the torch into the house destined for doom. It was a legacy of doom of which he became the executor when he moved northward from Sinai-Horeb to Damascus in order prophetically to appoint Hazael as king of Syria, Jehu king of Israel, and Elisha his own successor. He was to speed up the development that was consummated when the Assyrian armies, the great spectre of the age, actually approached one hundred and thirty years later, destroyed Damascus and Samaria and carried the ten tribes of the northern kingdom into exile.

Now the earthly task of Naboth-Elijah had been carried out. The pile of wood was stacked; only a spark had to be thrown into it for the fire to blaze forth. Elijah knew that his own death would be this spark. Calmly anticipating what was coming, he ventured to his home — Naboth's home — in Jezreel. The queen took note of his return and laid her plan. The king's desire for Naboth's vineyard suited her perfectly. Naboth-Elijah knew what he precipitated when he rejected the king's demand. When the deadly stones were flung against Naboth, Ahab was as yet unaware that they struck Elijah. He only thought that nothing stood any longer in the way of his wish's fulfilment. Content, he ventured into the vineyard that now belonged to him. But here, a shattering experience awaited him: suddenly, he beheld the flaming form of Elijah before him, more overpowering than ever, but no longer tied at all to the human, physical form. Horror-stricken, Ahab became aware of the connection that had existed between the murdered owner of the vineyard, where he was standing, and the prophet whose form he beheld. All at once he realized what a devilish game Jezebel had played when she said she would help him obtain the desired vineyard. He felt as if lightning had struck his innermost being. A terrifying vision of horror unfolded before his repenting soul. Did the prophet allow him to look into his own future? The king foresaw his and Jezebel's violent death and the whole bloody tragedy that was now to break upon his house and his kingdom.

As Ahab's encounter with Elijah in the vineyard of the slain man demonstrates, the prophet's appearances did not cease after Naboth's death. But henceforth, when Elijah showed himself, destinies were thereby thrown off-course from their orderly direction, either, when he appeared as the messenger of doom as he did before Ahasiah, Ahab's son, or when he transferred his own soul being and spiritual authority to his disciple. Hardly anybody found out and knew that with this stoning, the human bearer of the Elijah genius had been killed, except for the two regents and Elisha who had been taken into his master's confidence. Anybody who did find out about it maintained the strictest silence. Thus, the people could not but believe in Elijah's survival — and he did, after all, continue to be effective with mighty spiritual power — until, finally, it was said of Elijah and the prophet's disciples that the prophet had ascended to heaven in a fiery chariot.

Once, a grandiose revelation occurred of the Naboth-Elijah drama, contained in the Old Testament only as a veiled secret, namely, in the tragedy of John the Baptist. As the Gospels state in all clarity, the preacher in the wilderness was the reincarnated Elijah. One cannot become more clearly aware of the moving mission of blazing sacrifice that this genius had to fulfil in preparation of the Christ event than by realizing how the dramatic sequence of the Elijah destiny is repeated in all details in John. It is as if this sequence of images could not have been deeply enough imprinted into the soul of humankind. In retrospect, through the comparison with the drama of John the Baptist, the Naboth-Elijah drama is once more brightly illuminated. Like Elijah, John was an entity who was at the same time human and superhuman, since he did not completely submerge in his incarnation. Like Elijah, John was a fire, resembling a roaring force of nature. Like Elijah, John was confronted with a pair of enemies; in the New Testament, the place of Ahab and Jezebel is taken by Herod and Herodias. Again, the hate-filled sorceress was the driving force. And in place of Naboth's corpse, crushed by stones, the plate with the bloody head of John confronts us. Each time, the murderous hand destroyed a still young life. John was thirty-one years old when he was beheaded. Naboth-Elijah was hardly any older when he met his death on earth. Like Elijah, however, John the Baptist also continued to be effective beyond death, thus foiling the intentions of the murderess.*

The Bible describes for us that when Elijah ascended in the fiery chariot to heaven he let his mantle drop down on the disciple chosen to be his successor. This does not indicate a physical occurrence any more than does the whole report of Elijah's ascension. This picture shows us that the request of Elisha is being fulfilled, 'I ask that your spirit continue to live in my soul like a second "I".'†

Already when Elijah made Elisha his pupil in Damascus and initiated him into his secret, it is said that he spread his mantle over him.

---

* After John was beheaded, the soul of the Baptist continued to be effective in the deeds of the Apostles' circle.[3]

† The customary translation, 'Let me inherit a double share of your spirit' (2 Kings 2:9) has originated from a misunderstanding.[5]

The 'mantle of Elijah' is a supersensory hieroglyph and just as significant for humankind's development of consciousness as the 'staff of
Moses.' Through a special miracle of Providence, Moses had at his disposal an etheric or formative-forces body into which, already at that
time, future faculties of humanity could be imprinted. He thus became
the herald of the self-imbued thinking-force and planted the staff of
freedom into the human being.[4] Elijah embodied a pioneering soul
impulse. His soul body arose from humanity's soul sphere like a tall,
pure sacrificial flame, enveloped completely by the angel-winged rule
of the higher world. This fire, however, was not formless and merely
atmospheric. It proceeded from a clear centre within the soul. Elijah
was the first-born of the power of faith which bestows on the soul the
concentrating and inwardly strength-giving centre of divine
indwelling. While Moses had inaugurated the beginning of freedom
for the earthly 'I'-being in the centre of the forehead along with the
force of thinking, Elijah enkindled the fire of the higher 'I' in the central being, in the heart, through the inner force of faith. The higher self,
the indwelling divine power, made the soul capable of love and
shaped the soul-body into the fiery mantle of protective love. The
'mantle of Elijah' was the spirit-pervaded soul-body of Elijah himself.
By placing it around his disciple, he relinquished to him the power of
his own soul, now kindling in him too the fire of faith.

When the request to ensoul him with his being's power was
directed by Elisha to the spirit form of the departing Elijah, he realized
that he first had to fulfil a condition. Only if he was capable of recognizing the secret and inner form of Elijah in his vision would he be
advanced enough to have his wish granted. How could he be given the
mantle without perceiving what it contained? And his soul was indeed
capable of lifting itself up to visionary insight. Deeply moved, he
uttered the words, 'My father, my father! The chariots of Israel and its
horsemen!' (2Kings 2:12). As puzzling as it seems to be, this sentence
has always been experienced as filled with magic power. It speaks so
directly and powerfully to the soul that one realizes only slowly how
little one comprehends it.

It can only be understood in the context of the mystery streams that
strove through systematic, step-by-step training for the transformation
of the soul forces and the attainment of a spiritual core of courage and
power in the human being. In all ages, imaginative concepts were

coined there in order to designate the stations of the inner path that had to be undergone. Let us follow the description of the seven main stages as known in the Mithras mysteries at the time of early Christianity, for there the names in question have come down to us in particularly classic clarity, especially in the writings of the Church father, Jerome. The goal of the Mithras worship was above all supposed to enkindle in the soul the torch of inner power and devout courage through the focus upon the contending and victorious sun hero, Mithras.

When the neophyte attained the first level of soul transformation, one designated him as a *'raven' (corax)*; for now he had become capable of receiving the message of the divine world. On the second level, the striving disciple withdrew completely into the secluded isolation of his own inner being. Out of the bottomless depths of his own being, he brought forth soul contents that no other human being could recognize in him from outside. His actual, true being had henceforth become invisible as if through a magic hood, and he was called *'hidden one' (occultus)*. On the third level he turned into the *'warrior' (miles)* of the spirit. Effects emanated from him now by means of which spiritual aberrations felt struck as if by a sharp sword. The fourth, middle stage was that of the *'lion' (leo)*. Here, a sunlike victorious higher power permeated the heart of the neophyte. The indwelling divine element bestowed on the centre of his being royal spiritedness and visionary power of illumination. The one who was initiated up to the fifth degree was called by the servants of Mithras, *'Persian' (Persa)*. Within other folk contexts, he would have been called, for example, a 'true Israelite' or a 'true Greek.' For on this level, the personal soul extended over that of the whole nation. In a special sense, the individual person became the bearer and instrument of the people's genius and could turn into a leader of his folk. On the last stages, the mystic disciple advanced to cosmic authorities and was designated as a *'sun hero'* or *'sun runner' (heliodromos)* and finally as *'father' (pater)*.

The main significance of Elijah's soul, blazing like a fire, was that in it were inscribed in exemplary manner for humankind the stages and fruits of purification and transformation. Naboth-Elijah was not merely by nature a person who could exercise such a far-reaching, atmospheric influence on the development of humanity. By bearing deprivation and suffering, through stern discipline and work upon

himself he had transformed his soul. The human Naboth-Elijah drama
had not been lived in vain. The living crowns of victories won and conquest of self were woven into the soul that Elisha saw ascend to
heaven.

At the beginning of the path, the visionary image of the ravens that
carried nourishment to him had lit up over Elijah. In the sense of the
Mithras mysteries one could say: Naboth-Elijah himself became the
'raven.' Then, in the experience at Zarephath that led to inner rebirth,
he became the 'hidden one.' On Carmel, he stepped forth mightily as
the 'warrior.' On Mount Horeb, when he penetrated to the revelations
of the god within, he became the 'lion.' As the 'true Israelite,' the
bearer of the folk spirit concerned for the future, he could and had to
interfere forcefully in the destinies of his people. And when Elisha saw
the fiery sun chariot before the open heaven, the sphere of the father
of the universe, he realized that the signs of highest perfection had
been inscribed into the soul being of Elijah: the soul of Elijah itself was
the chariot with the fiery horses; it had become the sun runner and was
now elevated to union with the cosmic father. In the exclamation of
Elisha, upon whom the mantle of Elijah descended, the final three
stages of a path, struggled for to the very end, were mantrically concentrated together: the genius of the folk of Israel, the spirit of the sun,
the sphere of the father were all mirrored in the mature, sacrificed soul
of Elijah: 'My father, my father! The chariots of Israel and its horsemen!' Thus, discernible in the image of the mantle, an impulse proceeded from the Elijah drama through history which prepared the
path for the power of Christ in the souls of human beings.

CHAPTER EIGHTEEN

Elisha: the Reform of the Prophethood

In the canon of the Old Testament, the great polarity between Moses and Elijah is given expression by the positioning of the two main groups of texts side by side, customarily designated as 'Moses and the Prophets.' The creative spirit of Moses is felt behind and above the multiplicity of the historical books. A new phase commences only at the point where the great number of prophets appears in the Israelite-Jewish history as well as in the Old Testament scriptures. Towering above the many great and not so well known prophets, however, *the* prophet stands out as their inspiring and ensouling genius, the mighty inaugurator of the whole prophetic movement, namely Elijah.

How did matters progress from the *one* prophet to the *many?* The appearance of Elijah himself was a historical event and to attempt to trace his origin from some previously existing movements would be a useless endeavour. Elijah appears in history as if he had emerged from sovereign, brilliant self-procreation. In a spiritual sense, it could be said of him that he was without father, without mother, and without a home. A fire burned and nobody knew who had kindled it. How could it be avoided that the flame would burn down and finally become extinguished? How could something of its blaze be preserved and carried forward into the future, even beyond the death of its first bearer?

Elijah knew very well why, of all the disciples and followers loosely grouped around him, he had to choose Elisha as his successor. Elisha did not stand alone. He was the highest ranking representative of a movement. Having been designated as the torch bearer of the prophetic Elijah-fire, the beginning of a whole movement was inaugurated, a tradition was established; a historical continuation and ongoing maintenance of the sacred flame was assured. The well-spring that had swelled forth in Elijah in unique fashion without origin found a river bed in which it could stream on and could turn into the broad river of the prophetic spirit life.

In Elijah's lifetime as well as in earlier centuries, many prophets existed in Israel. In the story of Saul and earlier, we have already encountered the communities resembling brotherhoods and guilds. In the course of time, the major part of the Israelite prophethood seems to have assumed a professional character. This alone would probably have been reason enough for the infiltration of much charlatanry and deceit. The members of the prophets' schools had become psychic practitioners, who, on account of their clairvoyant talents and deeper insights, were called in as advisors and helpers in the life of individual people and the state. In many instances, their craft consisted in an oracle technique which they exercised by placing themselves into a kind of trance condition while playing certain musical instruments, frequently also while dancing like a dervish.

Originally, a quiet, brightly shining flame had been enkindled in Israel's life through the establishment of this stream that was like a monastic order. In its unassuming, genuine periods of inception, Naziritism, inaugurated by Moses, still kept alive the waning light of clairvoyance through strictly arranged, ascetic exercises, nurturing the after-effects of the ancient sun-forces in the human body and keeping it free of all influences that went too strongly in the material, earthly direction. In Samson, the old sun hero nature of man had once more made an appearance in mythical dimensions of greatness. Increasingly, however, it became less and less possible effectively to guard the delicate, anxiously protected sun legacy against the developments that caused the human entity to turn into a terrestrial being and were leading him deeper into material corporeality. We saw how, in Samuel's and Saul's era, the prophets' schools resorted to the violent, agitating means of ecstasy and intoxication in order to maintain clairvoyant faculties. Along with this, the sun nature of ancient Naziritism was quite naturally lost. The nocturnal, somnambulistic realm of unconscious trance conditions came to the fore and bestowed on all these practices a lunar, sleep-walking element.

Then, under David and Solomon, when the life of Israel pushed its way with urgency into the busy development of external culture, this could not remain without effect on the prophets' schools. People sought the advice of a seer in completely new areas of life. An element of trade increased in the prophets' activities.

It was in this age that a certain movement must increasingly have come to the fore from among the guilds of prophets, representing a form of antithesis to Naziritism, namely, the community of the Sons of Korah. It too went back to the days of Moses, even though, at first, it had stood in opposition to his leading impulses. Here, however, instead of proceeding by cultivation of the ancient gift of clairvoyance, a premature schooling of the conscious soul forces, particularly those of the calculating intellect, brought about the possibility to develop prophetic insights and to pronounce oracular counsel. It appears that in these circles people also utilized the stimulating effects of music or certain foods and drinks, though the violent dervish-ecstasy was rejected. The Korah-side of prophethood were on colder soul paths than in the circle of those who traced themselves back to Naziritism. From the beginning, no warm sun element had existed among the Korahites but something that could be compared to the cold light of the moon. The two totally opposed movements, also those in between and transitional ones that must have existed in great numbers, came together in the lunar element.

Nazirites and Korahites distinguished themselves outwardly in a most extreme manner, since the former wore the hair on their heads and faces uncut, while the Korahites shaved themselves to the point of baldness (see p. 119). At the time of the kingdom's division, the prophethood must therefore have constituted a most characteristic segment of the people's life even by means of its conspicuous outward marks of distinction. On both sides, prophet natures of a genuine, spiritually high-ranking kind must by then have been very few. If they existed on the Nazirites' side, they probably remained in most cases in lonely seclusion and did not mingle in the commercial activity of external life. On the side of the Korahites, the earnest, unselfishly striving groups appear to have been active especially in the artistic realm. We have encountered them in the music and poetry of a significant part of the biblical Psalms.

By and large, prophethood had turned into a form increasingly devoid of content. A complete vacuum threatened it since it was on the verge of being merely a 'school,' an institution for acquiring all sorts of soul exercises, techniques and skills. The fact that these practices extended into the supersensory realm and bordered on fakirism could only conceal, not prevent the spiritual emptiness and the increase of the formal, psycho-technical element.

Elijah had nothing in common inwardly with this contemporary, professional management of the prophets' schools. He was a world unto himself. If, in his development, he underwent a number of disciplines similar to those of the genuine Nazirite hermits, this does not mean that he would have needed to borrow in any sense from the Nazirite tradition. The individual, however, whom he made his most intimate disciple after the experience at Mount Horeb, through whom he continued to be effective beyond his earthly death as his inspiring and overshadowing genius, had absolved the prophethood resembling a guild. Through Elisha, Elijah directed the soul impulse, enkindled by him, into the earthly stream of prophets' schools. The form that had grown empty was once again filled with a content, ensouled by a spirit fire. Sunlike procreative spirit again gleamed with creative sparks in the prophets' realm which had become dependent like the moon. It was Elisha who, out of the spirit of Elijah, was to bring about a reform of the prophetic movement in the direction of its original destination. The fire of the Messianic expectation and that of the soul state preparing itself for the coming of the Messiah was supposed to return to the Israelite prophethood the greatness and vision of the future that alone justified its existence.

Elijah chose his successor not from the ranks of the Nazirites but those of the Korahites. The Bible allows us to discern this in the scene in which the street urchins of Bethel call from the hill of the Jeroboam sanctuary to Elisha, saying, 'Go up, you baldhead!' (2Kings 2:23). In this is expressed the future-oriented, in the best sense of the word, modern character of the Elijah impulse. The Nazirite as well as the Korahite forms of the established prophets' schools had their dangers. Through the use of ecstatic conditions of intoxication, the ascetic, Nazirite side slipped only too easily into a form of consciousness belonging to the past. The Korah members, on the other hand, rushing ahead of their time, readily succumbed to the temptation of giving too much room to chilling, intellectual cleverness. Nevertheless, this second danger had in its favour that even those who succumbed to it remained masters over their consciousness. After the age of David and

Solomon, it was no longer tolerable if dimmed down states of consciousness were made the starting points of the spiritual life.

Naturally, a historical fulfilment of the Elijah impulse was by no means inherent already in the nomination of Elisha and his reform of the professional prophethood. Rather, this call and ensouling from above was far-sighted. Actually, for the time being, nothing happened except that after long ages of decline the prophetic movement regained its former position of esteem. It was due to this, however, that prophethood was prepared and dedicated to produce from among its ranks or receive into them all the lofty, brilliant spirits whom spiritual sight could see approaching. The path had been cleared for the epoch of the great prophets, which, like a miracle of Providence, is inserted into the history of Israel, namely, in the periods of its greatest outward decline.

In the very first deeds that Elisha accomplished after Elijah's demise, it became clear that a 'practical' spirit indwelt him, one that was oriented to the details of the physical plane. In Jericho, he purified the water of a spring by adding salt after the inhabitants of the city had asked him for help. Unlike Elijah, he was not *the* prophet but *a* prophet who made his skill available to the people just as did the other professional prophets. Likewise, Elisha followed the practices of the school in the methods of prophetically dispensing advice. When the kings of Israel, Judah and Edom planned to do battle against the disloyal Moabites, they suffered from lack of water and called the prophet. He, however, asked a musician to come and, only under the influence of the music, he was able to indicate how the difficulty could be rectified.

Gradually, however, a strange thing happened. It came to pass that, as time went on, all manner of demands were made of Elisha within the circle of the prophets itself. In the outward and inner experiences ensuing from this fact, images were entwined that appeared like a reflection and echo of Elijah's destinies.

The Bible weaves an imaginative veil over the events similar to the descriptions of what Elijah experienced in his seclusion at the Cherith Brook and in Zarephath. The reason for this might be the mystery character inherent in everything that took place within the prophets' communities that resembled religious orders. The stage of

Elisha's actions was a group seclusion, segregated from the world just as the stage of Elijah's experiences had been an isolated personal seclusion. Those who were witnesses of Elisha's activities were less concerned with the outer course of things than with what was achieved in the soul-spiritual direction. It was this that arose in imaginative pictures whose resemblance with Elijah's light astonished them.

It is said that the widow of a prophet came to Elisha, asking for help. Her creditor was going to take her two sons from her unless she paid her debt. Following Elisha's advice, together with her sons, she locked herself into her house where she not only had placed her own jar of oil but those of the neighbouring women. And lo, she could fill all the vessels from her own which proved to be inexhaustible. Now her distress was over. She could pay the debt and, henceforth, neither she nor her sons suffered the lack of anything.

Is this not like an altered version of what had occurred in Zarephath in the house of the widow? The fact that Elisha was overshadowed by the spirit of Elijah began to be revealed.

Now, while, behind the picture of the full vessels of the widow at Zarephath, a process was concealed that had run its course in the inner being of Naboth-Elijah, the picture of the full oil jars of the prophet's widow veils a process in the soul realm of the prophetic order. Elisha too experienced himself in the image of a widow; not, however, as an individual man but as a member of the school. The inner poverty, the spiritual vacuum of prophethood arose before him like a threatening spectre now that Elijah no longer was active among human beings. This insight drove him to seclusion and meditative contemplation. Within himself, he penetrated to the well-springs of prophetic life and activity from which not only he himself could receive abundantly but all those disciples under his leadership. The new ensouling of the prophetic stream was inaugurated.

As yet, however, only the first, more soul-like part of the Zarephath miracle had found its correspondence. The drama continued. In Shunem, Elisha encountered a wealthy woman who made available to him a chamber on the upper floor of her house. The prophet predicted to her the birth of a long wished for son; but the son did not remain alive. One day, when he was a few years old and had gone to be with his father among the reapers, he touched his head and exclaimed, 'Oh, my head, my head!' (2Kings 4:19). Upon his return home he died on his mother's lap. She immediately went to the prophet to beseech him for help. Elisha sent Gehazi, his servant, ahead of him to place his staff upon the boy. It was not until Elisha himself came, however, and prayed over the dead child, causing the warmth of his own life to flow into the body already grown cold, that life returned to it.

The resurrection of the son of the widow at Zarephath signified the breakthrough of the Naboth-Elijah soul to its higher self, the bearer of death-transcending life. The resurrection of the son of the wealthy Shunammite woman was the imaginative wording for the rebirth of the prophetic movement to which Elisha belonged. Despite its abundance of traditional spirit treasure, the creative forces of prophethood had reached a dead end. Even though Elisha had directed new soul forces with his impulse of inner intensification into the stream that was about to run dry, this could only temporarily produce the semblance of a genuine continuation of life. Particularly the Korahite segment of the prophets' communities bore spiritual death within itself. The use and cultivation of the intellectual head consciousness in their exercises could not help but lead into a cul-de-sac of cold soul death. The boy who cried out in pain, 'Oh, my head, my head!' is a deeply moving picture for the danger inherent in the one-sided spiritual life of the head. Intellectualism only seemingly produces spiritually alive thoughts; in reality, it gives birth to dead thoughts and pours chilling death into the soul realm. The peril could not be resolved by means of the school's skills: In vain, the servant, Gehazi, touched the boy with the prophet's staff. Only a total break with traditional custom, its transformation from the bottom up, the head element's infusion and ensouling from the direction of the whole human element could newly inaugurate the seemingly lost spirit future of prophethood's activity. What had died through the coldness of the head was reborn from the blazing warmth of the enthusiastic heart, willing to be selfless.

Elisha had to realize that, along with the spiritual future of the prophetic life, the Messianic future of Israel was at stake. Thus, he came forward as the reformer, conjuring forth the inner fire of Elijah for the re-establishment of prophetism, the fire by means of which he had first transformed his own spiritual life. He made his own soul-spiritual life-warmth pour into the body of the spirit-discipleship, already grown cold. A genuinely prophetic spirit henceforth blazed in the part of prophethood led by Elisha. The Elisha flame had found an altar on which it could continue to burn.

In a number of imaginative pictures, puzzling to begin with, the Bible continues to point to the spiritual reconstruction that Elisha carried out in the spirit of Elijah within the private circle of his pupils for the sake of the Messianic future. Thus, it describes how Elisha, along with his disciples, went to the Jordan in order to fell wood for the new construction of the prophets' school. One of them dropped their axe-head in the river, and Elisha made it float by means of a stick of wood. The disciples of the prophet were surrounded by all manner of images and signs that called their attention to the task, confronting them in the supersensory sphere, that they now had to fulfil.

There are pictures and experiences among them that appear only like first auspicious indications of a turn in the priestly direction that prophethood was to take one day. Curative, generously given effects were to take the place of the sensational oracle trade that could not really bring about a true change in human souls. Immediately after the miracle of the resurrection in Shunem, the prophet's disciples were gathered together, aware of the needs of that age. The following strange occurrence took place. A pot with vegetables was prepared before their eyes. Elisha cut wild gourds into it and gave the soup to the disciples to eat. A taste of death penetrated them. Then Elisha added flour to the pot and directed them to distribute the now well tasting meal to the people. They all sensed that this was a prophetic picture of the imminent destinies. They realized that they would have to guide the people through bitter suffering. The time would come, however, when, from among their midst, there would come those who would be allowed to bestow blessings, namely the priestly dispensers of divine salvation.

The sacramental vision of the future intensified. Obeying Elisha, loaves of bread were brought that they gave to the people around them to eat. And the whole multitude was sated and there was bread left. The disciples sensed the presence of the genius above them who enabled them to work in a priestly, bestowing fashion: the eternal priesthood of the genius of Elijah in their midst. A presentiment of the wondrous feeding had pervaded them which occurred later at the Sea of Galilee, where a group of disciples also gave out loaves of bread to the people gathered around them. Again, during this later

incident, as the genius of the priestly gift of the Elijah spirit, the soul
of John the Baptist, who had been beheaded by Herod, hovered over
them.*

The careful, behind-the-scenes work of reconstruction that Elisha
accomplished within the prophets' movement was in marked contrast
to his intervention in the external destinies of the nation. The
Messianic future that he served was not identical with the contemporary political interests of the kings of Israel. To try and preserve the
outward basis of the people would have signified sacrificing the
divinely willed future. For, if the ground is not ploughed up, the future
crop cannot ripen.

Elisha now fulfilled the remainder of the task that Elijah had
received at Mount Horeb. He unleashed a gruesome, apocalyptic chain
of events, a tempest that bloodily avenged Elijah's death. Israel was
involved in battle against Hazael of Syria (843 BC). Misery and confusion prevailed in the land. Elisha could only follow his inner dictates,
even if, thereby, he would perhaps cause the cup of suffering to over-
flow. Through one of his disciples, he had Jehu anointed as rival king
against the dynasty of Ahab's and Jezebel's sons. Jehu, who was at the
front as one of the leaders of the Israelite army, was the head of a religious party which had chosen as its mission the battle against the
Phoenician Baal cult. Right in the camp, he received the divine message that was the signal for the beginning of the revolution. At the
head of the troops that were loyal to him and paying no heed to the
Syrian enemies, Jehu stormed against the royal palace of Jezreel where
King Jehoram was convalescing, having been wounded in battle. Jehu
proceeded like a raving madman. His arrow pierced the king. He
ordered the servants to carry the body into the vineyard of Naboth
whose death was now to be avenged. Adorned with royal jewellery,
Jezebel appeared at the windows of the palace. Her own courtiers
pushed her to her death. An immense bloodbath followed: the heads
of seventy sons and grandsons of Ahab were stacked up by the city
gate. The Baal priesthood was totally annihilated; the house of the
kings of Judah who had allowed themselves to be drawn by the house
of Ahab into the seduction of Baal were also felled by the blows of raving Jehu.

* Chapter 6 of the Gospel of Mark reveals these secrets through its composition.[1]

The shattering reports concerning the events that broke out over Israel once Elisha had started the wheel of calamity rolling, remind of the conclusion of the Lay of the Nibelungen. As, there, King Etzel avenged the murder of Siegfried, the sun-hero, by means of a gruesome bloodbath, here, Jehu took revenge for Naboth-Elijah. A mighty twilight of the gods appeared on the stage of outer history as a human-subhuman drama. Catastrophes were unleashed that did not pave the way for a quick renewal. A whole world ended; indeed, it had to end. Only another hundred years and the northern Israelite kingdom, now being ruled by King Jehu (842–815 BC), would be falling victim to the onslaught of Assyria. Nevertheless, it was imperishable seed of the Messianic future that grew towards its historical unfolding within the womb of the inwardly renewed stream of the prophets.

If their ages are compared, Elisha and Elijah stand side by side in moving polarity. Elijah was young like the fire of soul that burned in him when Jezebel's hatred violently ended his earthly life. Elisha must have been nearly ninety years old when he died. By the deathbed of the old man stood Joash, the king of Israel.* Deeply moved, he broke into the same words that Elisha had once called out when he saw Elijah ascend to heaven in the fiery chariot, 'My father, my father! The chariots of Israel and its horsemen!' (2Kings 13:14). When Elisha breathed his last breath, the lofty genius, who had overshadowed and worked through him, revealed himself one more time.

---

* Joash, a grandson of Jehu, was king from 799 to 784. Ahab's death, which followed three years after that of Naboth-Elijah, occurred in 854 BC. Therefore, Elisha's activity as a prophet lasted from 853 (Jehoram) until approximately 790 BC.

CHAPTER NINETEEN

Abundance of Spirits:
the Prophet-Scribes

After Elijah's days, peace and tranquil prosperity never prevailed again in Israelite-Jewish history. Incessant disaster broke over the external existence of the people and if a few of the once closely united twelve tribes appeared to withstand the onslaught of suffering and enslavement, it was only a reprieve and delay prior to complete destruction. On the other hand, Elijah's and Elisha's influence proved to be the opening of gates from which the stream of a never-expected spiritual wealth poured forth. In times of the greatest outward peril, Israel-Judah became the meeting ground of a great assembly of enlightened and brilliant spirits who spoke and were experienced as messengers of the deity itself.

An era dawned at that time in which the whole earth seemed to glitter with stars of the spirit. In India, Buddha was teaching his disciples, freeing himself from the wheel of earthly incarnations; in China, Lao-tzu and Confucius coined ancient wisdom of life into new thought forms; in Greece, Heraclitus and Pythagoras brought forth the bright day of philosophic thought; in Italy blossomed the mythical beginning of Rome with its seven kings. The world-historical focal point of the marvellous gathering of spirits, however, was Israel-Judah, from whose womb came forth the lofty sequence of the prophets.

The prophets, whose names are inscribed in the Bible not only because mention is made of them in the various narrations, but because of the creative deeds that their scriptures represent, carried out the mighty religious transformation for which the flame of the Elijah genius had given the signal to the spiritual life of Israel.

From Abraham and Moses until Solomon, a spiritual life had been developed in Israel that was in harmony with the origin and ascent of the people and their culture. Although a number of battles and conflicts had to be weathered, the faith in the Yahweh deity again and again had found support and footing in the external historical development. The divine will obviously coincided with the vital interests of the people. It was believed that indications of the protective nearness and benevolence of Yahweh could be discerned in everything that finally led to the splendour and wealth of the Solomonic era.

The history of Israel-Judah that followed Solomon's time, however, was but an unbroken chain of catastrophes and trials. The nation disintegrated and, one after the other, its segments became the spoils of alien, conquering nations. It had to appear as if the Yahweh deity had abandoned its people. In this age of decline, the spiritual life of Israel and especially its religious convictions could not remain what they had been in the period of advancement. The religion of the Old Testament would have crumbled without the prophetic intensification and deepening of the Yahweh faith, begun by Elijah and taken up and continued by the prophet-scribes. It was no longer possible to look up and pray to Yahweh merely as the protective genius of the nation. One had to advance to the point of seeing through him into the deeper realms of the deity, into beholding a divine being who guided all of humankind. This was the goal to which Elijah and the prophets tried to lead their people. By calling for inwardness of soul, they pointed the way to the divine being who, even in the decline and suffering of nations and bypassing all national relationships, is close to the self in loving manner.

The significance of the prophetic turn in the Yahweh religion cannot be stressed enough. In the wilderness of Sinai, in a landscape that differed greatly from the major portion of the Promised Land in which the people settled and built up their culture in the ensuing period, Moses had implanted into the Israelites the feeling and devout veneration for the Yahweh deity. The transition from the desert to the fruitful land had to bring about the temptation to loosen the sternness of the Yahweh cult and to draw closer to the pagan nature religions; something that applied especially to those tribes assigned to the central and northern part of the land, the later Samaria and Galilee. This was the case even more inasmuch as the Moses revelation itself still represented a last phase of nature religion. Until Solomon, the inner history of Israel was determined by a slight surrender in regard to this temptation. Remaining within the spiritual territory outlined by Moses, people approached as closely to the pagan surroundings as was possible without crossing over the boundary.

After Solomon's death, however, this boundary was no longer maintained. As if limited already for too long to a religious constriction that no longer corresponded to its character, the northern kingdom in particular rushed and stormed away from the Law of Moses into a more nature-bound pagan attitude. Finally, even the kingdom of Judah, which in landscape was more closely related to the Sinaitic origin of the Yahweh cult and therefore had kept its faith more easily, was in danger of being pulled along into the pagan seduction.

Beginning with Elijah, it was against this danger that the counter-stroke of prophethood was directed. The Yahweh faith was saved not only by means of being directed back to its original Mosaic sternness, but, beyond that, by being subjected to an inward transformation. Even those remnants of the relationship to nature were discarded that had been contained in the teaching of Moses and had made it possible to seek for the divine outside in nature or in the outward destiny of the people. The prophetic impulse consisted in a totally inward intensification of the Yahweh idea.

Through Elijah, this prophetic impulse blazed forth on north-Israelite territory, called forth by the extreme pagan decadence which had come about there. The actual location for the prophetically recast Yahweh idea, however, was Judea. Destiny soon brought it about that this came clearly to expression outwardly as well. After the destruction of the northern kingdom by the Assyrians (722 BC), only the kingdom of Judah remained as the stage of continuing Old Testament history. Only now, the wilderness of Sinai, the birthplace of the Mosaic Yahweh worship, was truly replaced by the Judean Desert, the topographic correspondence of the prophetic Yahweh cult. Most of the prophet-scribes did in fact belong to the southern, Jewish segment of the nation; after all, almost without exception, their activity took place during the period when the northern kingdom no longer existed. Only a few of the prophets who appeared after Elijah and Elisha, such as Jonah and Hosea, still belonged to the northern, Israelite history. As a whole, however, the prophetic impulse was the soul of Judaism which emerged during the division of the kingdom as an independent national group.

It is no coincidence that we have texts within the biblical canon by the prophets of the age following that of Elijah. A spiritually essential element is expressed in them. In its scriptures, the prophets' movement continues the development that had already come to the fore in the Davidian poetry of the Psalms and the Solomonic books. It is part of the advance that had been attained in the step from the nocturnally dark ecstasy of Saul to the light-filled, thought-imbued and conscious wisdom of Solomon. The visionary consciousness of the biblical prophets does not precede thinking as did the ecstatic, somnambulistic soul condition of the prophets who beheld the future prior to the age of Elijah and Elisha. Rising above the sphere of thought, this consciousness possesses within itself the clarity and discipline of thinking, and to this fact it is able to proclaim the visionary content and inwardly perceived divine word in clear ideation as well as in artistic formation, through human words.

We have already mentioned that the change that occurred through the prophetic impulse in Israel's religious life and faith in God was based on a change that had occurred in the spiritual world itself.

During the age of Moses, the Yahweh form-forces of external earthly nature had, like a mirror, caught and reflected the spiritual, sunlike Christ light. This had given the Mosaic piety a lunar character, since the moon is indeed the mighty reflector of sunlight in the cosmos. In the human being as well, the lunar forces that are tied to the external, earthly body brought it about that the divinity was experienced. This is why the Law of Moses contains so many regulations that refer to outer, physical life. Among the organs of the body, it was specifically the brain that served the thought-imbued impulse of morality and piety, inaugurated by Moses, as a mirroring apparatus. In an especially extreme form, the nature of the moon element was inherent in the clairvoyant experiences that were nurtured in the prophets' guilds. Here, however, it was not the brain but above all the lower part of the human organism that served as a mirroring instrument. In reality, the ecstatic, somnambulistic element of the schooled prophets, which had also extended into Saul's nature, was of corporeal, not psychic origin. It therefore could not lead to clear conscious, supersensory perceptions but only to dim unconscious ones, reflected from the physical level into the soul. In all this, Yahweh was active, the regent of night.

Increasingly, in Elijah's time, the divine light that was reflected in moon-like manner from the mirror-realm of physical existence went out. In its place a shimmer of light became evident in a number of individuals, which lit up directly in the inner sphere of their self-aware soul. It must have seemed to these people, who were piously sunk in contemplation of their own inner being, as if a bit of a wondrous spiritual sunlight were trying to shine into their own heart. It was something completely different from the lunar light of intellectual thoughts that are tied to the brain, but also something quite other than the sultry lunar nature of somnambulistic ecstasy. This gentle illumination was added to the experience of thought as if from another side, but clear, thought-imbued consciousness was needed to pick up this dawning light. The head-thinking, which had become tranquil and pious, turned into an inner human mirror for the divine light, shining forth in the heart. The heart began to nourish the head with premonitions and thoughts that sprang from a divine source of light, generously giving of itself. The Yahweh forces with their nocturnal, lunar character, which are effective in the human brain and transform it into a marvellous mirror apparatus, ceased to occupy the foreground. A being announced himself who is the sunlike regent of day and who therefore makes himself known only to the soul of waking consciousness. In serving this being, the Yahweh element had to withdraw completely. The first-born of this now inward experience of God were the prophets. The prophetic scriptures abound in the miracle of a merciful sunrise in the soul realm:

> Arise, shine; for your light has come,
>> and the glory of the LORD has risen upon you.
> For behold, darkness shall cover the earth,
>> and thick darkness the peoples;
> but the LORD will arise upon you,
>> and his glory will be seen upon you.
> And nations shall walk in your light;
>> and kings in the brightness of your rising. (Isa.60:1–3B)

The prophets knew that it was the Christ being whose light they now saw arising in the soul sphere. They did not merely mention a future event when they spoke of the Messiah's coming. The sun, who before long was to make the moon fade completely before its mighty brilliance, was already present in them with its first miracles of early dawn. Their prophecies were not a miraculous prediction but a testimony to a light, already beheld. And when the prophets waged an increasingly radical battle against the nature sanctuaries of Israel's early era, they tried thereby to let humankind know: Do not look any more in the direction where the divine light no longer shines. Turn your glance around, change your attitude and follow the light to where it has journeyed. Christ has now moved into the soul realm, into the centre of the human being!

This answers our question concerning the position that Elijah and the great prophet-scribes occupied in the course of humanity's evolution of consciousness. The fact that the humanization of the consciousness deriving from the reflections of the ancient wisdom of the gods reached a certain culmination in David does not imply that the next level of this evolution could have followed immediately, namely, the new illumination and expansion of consciousness through the development of fully conscious, supersensory faculties of perception. It took not only centuries but a millennium before the element that had made its appearance in David as in a first-born could truly become humanity's possession; the consciousness of the struggling soul that has at its disposal merely human soul forces, intellectual thinking and artistic feeling.

Providence, however, also brought it about that in the Israelite-Jewish history, moving far ahead of the course of humankind's history, early realizations of future levels of consciousness lit up. It was as if encouraging images and ideals were to be set up in order to show humanity the path of the future. The picture of the harmonically attuned whole being of man was illustrated in Solomon. Then, the flame of the Elijah being blazed forth. Here, the only recently attained human stage seemed again to be overpowered directly by the breaking in of superhuman, divine forces. In reality, however, the Elijah figure represented the opening of a door through which, in future time, the evolving human being would eventually have to pass. Elijah not only brought down fire from heaven but also something of the future consciousness of humankind. The human being, who had proceeded from an ancient supersensory consciousness belonging to the gods, who now had arrived at the impoverished earthly consciousness tied to the brain and senses, was one day to ascend again to supersensory cognition, but then with all of his awakened self which, in the meantime, had been imprinted into his nature. It was the promise of this new spiritual consciousness, to which humankind was to mature in a still far distant future, that Elijah conjured forth on the level of historical life through the prophetic impulse ablaze in him. Jonah, Isaiah, Daniel and all the other great torch bearers of the Elijah spirit were not merely prophets by virtue of what they proclaimed but through what they were as well. The light that arose in their souls was an actually living prophecy of the future resurrection of humanity's consciousness. The faculty of deciphering present and future events in the spiritual world that was felt in them did not presuppose any ecstatic or trance-like interruptions of ordinary consciousness. They were geniuses of consciousness, an anticipation of a future goal of humanity, brought about by Providence.

According to what Rudolf Steiner brought out, the astounding miracle of the mighty gathering of spirits and the new, shining spiritual consciousness with which Israel-Judah was honoured during the times of its decline was based on a very special secret of destiny and Providence. It is described to us as a result of spiritual research, that while the Israelite prophets were not initiates in that particular incarnation, they had been privileged to undergo initiation in a preceding earth life. As a matter of fact, initiates from the most diverse, great spiritual streams of humankind were reincarnated among them. Now, destiny brought all of them together in the same period and nation in such a manner that the after-effects of the earlier initiation could blossom forth from their souls as an uncommonly gifted life of spirit.

> ... consider the prophets from Isaiah to Malachi, through Jeremiah, Ezekiel, and Daniel, and study what it [the Bible] relates of these figures. You will find that you cannot bring these prophets into the general scheme of initiation. Where does the Bible relate that the Jewish prophets went through the same kind of initiation as other initiates belonging to different peoples? It is said they appeared when the voice of God stirred in their souls, enabling them to see in a different way from

ordinary men, making it possible for them to make indications
as to the future course of the destiny of their people and future
course of the world's history ... The spiritual vision of the
Jewish prophets seems, so to speak, to spring from their own
genius ...

We find that the souls of the Hebrew prophets are reincar-
nations of initiates who had lived in other nations, and who
had attained certain stages of initiation ... it is as though there
were a gradual assembling of the initiates of other peoples
among the Jewish people, where these initiates appear in the
form of prophets. This is why these prophets appear in such a
way that their gift of prophecy appears to proceed elementally
from out of their own being. It is a memory of what they
acquired here or there as initiates. All this emerges, but not
always in the harmonious form it had in earlier incarnations,
for a soul that had been incarnated in a Persian or Egyptian
body would first have to accustom itself to the bodily nature of
the Jewish people ...

Thus we see the Jewish prophets gave their people many
spiritual impulses, which are often disarrayed, but nonetheless
grandiose recollections of former incarnations ... [This came
about because] the whole evolution of humanity had to go
through this passageway, so that what was achieved in its
parts over the whole world should be brought together in one
focal point, to be born again from out of the blood of the people of the Old Testament ... Like rays of light coming from different sides, streaming in and uniting in the center, the
incarnating rays of the various peoples were collected together
as in one central point in the blood of the old Hebrew people.[1]

The essential part in the initiation practices of antiquity was the
mystic disciples' undergoing of death and resurrection. During the
deathlike condition lasting three days into which the hierophant
placed the one who was being initiated, spiritual contents and
impulses were imprinted into the soul that had been liberated from
the body. As a new person, one who had attained to spiritual leadership, the pupil returned to life. In the experiences and writings of the
prophets, we find clearly definable and moving traces of how the
mystery of rebirth from the ancient initiation-destinies bore the fruits

of genius. In this incarnation, the prophets themselves did not undergo death and resurrection in the sense of the old initiations. It is due to the fact, however, that in earlier incarnations they had absolved mystic death and rebirth, conscious memories of this re-emerged as if by themselves in their lives. The experience of Elijah at Zarephath, namely the death and resurrection of the widow's son, is the archetypal example of this. The death of the Shunammite woman's son and his revival through Elisha also belong in this context, although this was mainly a reflection of Elijah's destiny. The grotesque images surrounding Jonah, of whom it is said that he remained for three days in the belly of a fish, derive, as we shall discuss in what follows, from the realm of ancient initiations. Experiences arise again as purely inward soul occurrences in a form resembling recollections and envelop themselves in the pictures or symbols of the once physically real events.

In the earlier destinies, the souls of the prophets had the profound experience of a life that survives dying, of a higher will that remains helpful, particularly in the trials of peril and death. It was this experience which, in this incarnation (as prophets), became the foundation of the inwardly sensed concept of God. It led to the conviction that the deity could be close to the human being even if nothing but misfortune and decline held sway in outward existence. The present inner power and faith of soul arose from the after-effect of the former process of rebirth. Scenes abound in which the prophets placed before the people proclamations testifying to their faith. We merely need recall Ezekiel's vision of the large field covered with bones of the dead, which is imbued with the miracle of resurrection.

The secret of death and resurrection has a changing importance in the various great epochs of humankind's history. In the ancient mysteries, death and revival existed as an initiation practice which was applied to a few, chosen as leaders. At the turn of time, in the death and resurrection of Christ, this mystery appeared on the stage of history in divine-human greatness and uniqueness so that, henceforth, all human beings have the choice of imbuing their own being with a soul impression of this mystery by means of pious surrender to the Christ-destiny. The prophetic images and experiences, in which the knowledge of death and resurrection arose as brilliant premonition and power in the souls of the great messengers of God, stand as the interim stage between the ancient initiation mysteries and the Mystery of Golgotha.

The personal destiny of the prophets, deriving from earlier incarnations, was in significant harmony with the present fate of their people. Was the inescapable decline that was breaking in over the external life of the people not the beginning of the fact that Israel as a whole now had to pass through a death and resurrection?

In numerous instances, it was probably the general suffering which, as in the case of Elijah or also in several other prophet-personalities, awakened the memory of their own earlier death and rebirth. The inwardly re-emerging initiation principle then turned into the organ of prophetic knowledge and speech, particularly the organ for the initiation through destiny into which the people had entered. The nation became the 'servant of Yahweh,' who experienced the story of his passion and made ready to pass through death and resurrection (Isaiah 53). Through the folk-destiny that was becoming transparent, the form of the longed for Saviour, the Messiah, finally appeared. Prophetic vision beheld that the Messiah would become the 'servant of Yahweh' in a very special way, namely that as the representative of all humanity, he would exemplify the mystery of suffering, dying and arising.

As yet, however, the age of the Messiah had not arrived. It was the people who were still Yahweh's servant. The national pre-stage of the Messiah mystery occurred. The prophets felt themselves placed in the midst of the coming mystery passion of Israel.

In the providentially preordained mighty gathering of spirits in Israel, which was the focal point of great simultaneous events spread out over the whole earth, we recognize the sign that a significant occurrence, preceding the Mystery of Golgotha, did indeed take place. The fact that, at that time, the shadow of the approaching Christ-destiny fell upon the sphere of the people's destiny, bestowed on the age of the prophets its lofty spiritual wealth. The Messianic configuration of destiny was to be realized in the people before it was revealed in the earth's destiny by the One.

CHAPTER TWENTY

Jonah: Breakthrough of the Prophet-Destiny

In his paintings in the Sistine Chapel in Rome, Michelangelo has tried to encompass the mysteries of the world's origin and future; the sacred-divine primal beginnings and movingly solemn last days of earthly creation. On the ceiling, the images of creation proclaim the divine origin of world and man. The pictures of Genesis, beheld by Moses' visionary retrospection in past ages and inscribed at the beginning of the Bible, unfold high above. Moving forward from the back of the chapel, when the visitor's glance penetrates to the front, the picture of the Last Judgment points to the separation of the spirits at the end of the earth's aeon, conjuring forth the prophetic spirit of John's Apocalypse which represents the conclusion of the Bible.

Between Genesis and Revelation, the exalted circle of prophets and sibyls unrolls. Their sight is not bound to the present. They look back and ahead; in the spirit realm, they decipher the letters of the past and the dawning images of the future. In them, Moses and John reach out and touch each other.

Michelangelo's artistic creativity was still aided by his wisdom-filled familiarity with the prophets' figures, something that has been completely lost to theological thinking of recent centuries. Five prophets, Isaiah, Jeremiah, Ezekiel, Daniel and Joel look down on us from the upper edge of the two long walls. On the two cross-walls, we find in each case only the figure of one prophet. Depicted as the oldest and the youngest, the two confront each other: Above the mighty portal, aged Zechariah, adorned in a flowing robe and casting his glance downward, reads in the sacred book of the past. Above the painting of the Last Judgment, the youngster, Jonah, disrobed and the fish by his side, looks up with a transfigured expression into the spirit heights that bear the future.

When we move in the pictures from Moses to John, from Genesis to Revelation, we move at the same time from the aged man to the youngster, the genius of youth and the future, who is placed before our soul in the figure of Jonah with the radiant look. The artist's wisdom directs us with a profound, silent gesture to the character of the prophet Jonah which resembles that of John.

Next to Christ himself, early Christendom did not know of any biblical figure that could typify the victorious, death-transcending faith that confronted the Caesarian environment more obviously than the prophet Jonah. No other subject has been depicted in the catacomb paintings and sarcophagus sculptures as many times as the sequence of scenes of the Jonah drama. The ship's crew cast Jonah, whom they consider the reason for the storm, into the ocean. The mighty fish, the sea monster, swallows him, then spews him forth again. Finally, as if it had just emerged from the hands of the Creator, the figure of the young man lies in the pumpkin arbour with a surprised, blissful look, fathoming distant divine secrets in the womb of the future. In these pictures, early Christianity found nothing but a symbol from the Old Testament for the death and resurrection of Christ. Concentrated in picture form, the whole mystery background of humanity for the Golgotha event was beheld in it.

There is perhaps no point where the enduring imaginary wisdom of the first Christians and the abstractly clever, yet basically helpless viewpoint of recent, theologically educated Christianity are further apart than here. For the enlightened intellect of people today, the story of the whale that swallowed the prophet and supposedly spewed him out again still alive after three days is nothing but a grotesque tale filled with clumsy impossibilities, which can at most be acknowledged as an allegory of the idea concerning death and resurrection, originating out of weird fantasy. Where the attempt is nevertheless made to save the biblical story, truly ludicrous results are attained in many instances. In the 1930s, for example, an American professor supported the theory that it could only have been a shark, since a whale's gullet is much too small to swallow a human being. Yet such explanations only serve to show up even more the absurdity of picturing this event in a physical sense.

It goes without saying that early Christianity had no reservations in acknowledging the truth of what the Book of Jonah depicted. People possessed the instinctive spiritual sensitivity, however, to interpret the scenes of Jonah's having been swallowed by a fish as a soul event rather than a physical fact of history. The manner in which the fish was depicted shows that people sensed that they were dealing with a completely different sphere than the one of earthly zoology in which exist whales and sharks. They painted or sculptured a legendary being, a sea monster, the leviathan, which is more dragon than fish, and thereby rose instinctively to the pictorial conceptions of supersensory events.

Over and over again, we must learn to recognize in what instances the biblical description weaves events in seemingly physical images into the occurrences of the external physical plane, events that did not take place outwardly but only in the souls of certain individuals. Only by making this distinction, it is possible to obtain from the biblical scriptures the truly lofty description of history, intended and contained in them. And only in this way can we avoid the mistake that modern theology has made especially in reference to the Book of Jonah. Since certain scenes are believed to be allegories, the whole book is considered to be allegorical and devoid of history.

Correctly understood, it is just the brief prophetic Book of Jonah that is of extraordinary value for insight into the history of the Old Covenant. Placed courageously into the context of the history of that period, it throws a bright, clear light upon the tense play of forces that existed in Israel during the age following Elijah's time shortly before the end of the northern kingdom. In the customary historical descriptions of the age of the prophets, it has almost become tradition to proceed from Amos and Hosea because it is believed that quite a concrete picture can be derived from the biblical scriptures concerning the personalities of these 'earliest' prophets. To place the Book of Jonah at the beginning was as far from the considerations of historic theology as was the idea to take it seriously in the first place. In reality, the Jonah text illustrates above all others the dramatic birth and beginning of the prophets' era and destinies.

After the bloody turmoil during which Jehu and his sons had

replaced the House of Ahab on the throne of the kingdom of Israel, the shock waves of the world-historical power struggles broke in upon the Holy Land even more threateningly. Alternating between fighting and allying itself with its Syrian neighbour, at times even degraded to a tribute-paying vassal of Syria, the northern Israelite kingdom trembled in face of the approaching Assyrian danger. Rare were the glimpses of light, the brief times of relief that interrupted the anxious suffering dominating the land. The reign of Jeroboam II (783–743 BC), a descendant from the house of Jehu, a hundred years after Elijah, is designated by the Bible as such a time when the fate of the people seemed to brighten. While describing the deeds of this Jeroboam, the Books of the Kings mention the prophet Jonah and thereby moves him out of the seemingly timeless sphere of myth into a quite concrete historical situation: Jeroboam 'restored the border of Israel from the entrance of Hamath as far as the Sea of the Arabah, according to the word of the LORD, the God of Israel, which he had spoken by his servant Jonah the son of Amittai, the prophet, who was from Gath-hepher. For the LORD saw that the affliction of Israel was very bitter, for ... there was none to help Israel.' (2Kings 14:25f).

Still during the reign of Jeroboam II, a ruler attained to power in Assyria who appears in history like a colossus and whose broad, black shadow falls into the Old Testament: He was Tiglath-pileser III, called by his Babylonian name in the Bible, 'Pul' (747–727 BC). With a few brief but gigantic steps, he completed the power structure of the Assyrian Empire by forcing the still partly independent vassal states of the Babylonians, Medes and Armenians completely under his rule. It was he who, soon afterwards, reaching out to Egypt as well, was to crush Syria and was to cast Israel into the darkness of inescapable doom.

It was shortly before this last, great advance by Assyria that the prophet Jonah received the divine direction to move to Nineveh and become spiritually active there (Jonah 1:2). In the context of the traditional interpretations of the story of Jonah, it was often thought that the name Nineveh had no concrete significance but was merely the designation of some large city. But this term designates Assyria, just as the city of Babel appears in the Old Testament as a collective expression of the neo-Babylonian kingdom at a later historical point in time. Nineveh, situated at the northern course of the Tigris river, evolved in that period to the capital and royal residence of Assyria, the giant stretching his limbs in northern Mesopotamia. At the time of Jeroboam II and the prophet, Nineveh had indeed become the embodiment of the monstrous spectre, threateningly arising on the horizon.

It is not difficult to imagine what fear and terror were released in Jonah's soul when he received the inner direction to go to Nineveh. The political inclinations and attitudes, prevalent in Israel at that time and also shared by Jonah, could only suggest strict avoidance of anything to do with Assyria. Nobody could dare venture into the abode of the monster itself. Would it not signify the arousal of the giant's wrath, the deliberate unleashing of the catastrophe which the people still hoped to avoid?

Jonah wanted to side-step the challenge that made itself felt so imperatively in his mind. He attempted an escape by boarding a ship in Joppa, destined for Spain. He wanted to flee to the extreme West in the face of the mission that called him to the East. The Bible relates that hardly had they left the coast behind when the ship was caught in a great storm which made continuance of the voyage as well as any return to land impossible. The navigators had to believe that the fury of the elements was the deity's reaction to Jonah's flight, a fact which he himself had admitted to them. Thus they cast him into the sea.

Here, the narrative continues in the puzzling pictures in which early Christianity recognized the primal mystery-drama of death and resurrection: A mighty fish swallowed Jonah, so it says, following the command of the deity itself. After three days and nights, the fish spewed him out, again obeying a divine order, and Jonah safely reached solid ground.

As means of imaginative descriptions, these pictures belong to the sphere of the initiation mysteries, namely, in the manner in which they must have existed earlier in the coastal regions of the Holy Land, where Jonah fell victim to the storm at sea. The cult of the god Dagon, whom the Philistines revered in the form of a mighty fish, was the external side of the mysteries, accessible to the people. It still remained in existence when the practice of initiation had long since reached and fallen into decadence. The deathlike initiation-sleep, lasting three days, was concealed behind the image that a human being spent three days in the belly of a great fish. It was the condition into which the mystic disciple of these mysteries was placed when the latter were still in their prime. The grave into which the mystic aspirant was laid during this time was the mouth of the earth; the earth itself was the mighty fish that swam in the cosmic ether.

During these three days, a psalm broke from Jonah's soul that in itself was a testimony to the fact that the sojourn in the fish's interior was in reality an experience of feeling himself immersed in the depths of the sea and the earth: 'Waters close in over me that reach to my very soul. The depth of existence yawns around me. My head no longer reaches above the waves. I have descended into the innermost part of the earth, where, out of the chasms, the mountains arise, and where earthly being is chained with eternal fetters.' (Jonah 2:5fB) The escape from the belly of the fish after three days is a picture for the resurrection in the mysteries which occurred when the hierophant awakened the disciple from the temple sleep and allowed him to arise from the grave.

What actually did take place in Jonah's life when he had proceeded on the abortive escape attempt? We need not assume that he somehow happened upon the confines of a mystery location where an initiation was conducted on him in the regular sense. Blows of destiny broke in upon him — outwardly, it was perhaps nothing more than the fact that, having been shipwrecked, he was exposed to the fury of the elements for three days — which brought upon his soul a mighty transformation, at the same time awakening in him the memory of an initiation, undergone in a former incarnation. It was as if the ancient destiny repeated itself once again in a different form and just as was the case then, Jonah emerged from the experience as a new, reborn human being. He had wanted to flee from himself and God, but, in a higher sense, destiny had directed him even more so to awareness of himself and recognition of his divine call.

The experience that Jonah underwent is the correspondence to Elijah's experience at Zarephath; it too was a dying and arising of the innermost essence of his being, of the Son of man. In Zarephath, Elijah himself was the son of the widow, now it was Jonah. Ancient theology did indeed sense and stress this connection, for it took up the legendary tradition that Jonah himself had been the youngster whom Elijah had awakened from death at Zarephath:

Rabbi Simeon said: 'We have the virtue of the just to thank that there is a resurrection of the dead. You discern this from the story of Elijah, the Tishbite. He went from mountains to mountains, from cave to cave until he ventured to Zarephath where the widow received him with great honours. She was the mother of Jonah, and from her bread and oil they all sustained themselves, Elijah, the widow and her son ...'[1]

After the dramatic experiences into which his escape had led him, Jonah understood that the divine will was wiser than the political opinion and sympathy of his contemporaries. He followed the inner charge, which he had become conscious of anew and much more forcefully at that, to set off for the Assyrian capital. He now interpreted the deity's will to mean that he was to appear in Nineveh in a militant fashion, thereby contributing to the doom of the formidable enemy and the salvation of his threatened people. He confronted the Assyrians as the herald of their city's and kingdom's impending doom.

But Jonah's appearance in Nineveh brought about a religious mass movement. The Assyrians experienced his words as if a fiery angel were speaking through him. Terror gripped the ranks of the nation that was just on the verge of making itself the undisputed ruler over the whole of Asia Minor. Greatly astonished, Jonah had to realize that the enemy nation was earning the right to survive by virtue of the introspection that it seemed to embrace. The threatening cloud of doom dissolved that he believed had been conjured forth over the Assyrians by himself.

Jonah was shocked, he had not intended that! Now he himself had contributed to the enemy's gaining a reprieve and gathering new forces. He could not understand God's tolerance. Anger arose in him. Abraham had once pleaded for the deliverance of Sodom and Gomorrah; Jonah pleaded with God for Nineveh's destruction or his own death. For the second time, he rebelled against the divine intentions.

In order really to penetrate to the meaning of the present and imminent world events, Jonah needed intensified inner courage. He had to lift himself up to a standpoint where he had overcome personal fear as well as the deep concern for the fate of his people. The outlook that the prophet finally fought to attain is indicated in a veiled and hieroglyphic style by the conclusion of the biblical Jonah book. There, we behold the picture in which culminate the sequence of scenes depicted on the walls of the catacombs and the stone slabs of the sarcophagi. Jonah lies in a bower, deeply sunk in meditation. A castor oil plant above his head protects him from the scorching heat of the sun. A worm bites into the fruit so that it withers and shrinks down. Jonah suddenly feels the cruel intensity of the sun's heat. In that moment, however, his meditative contemplation lights up in vision. The simple event of nature becomes his key to insight.

In order to understand what sort of insight the spirit of the prophet had awakened to, we must once again take into consideration the political situation and events of that time which then actually came to pass. Jonah came to the realization that his nation's destruction by the hand of the Assyrians was part of the divine intentions and that even behind this seemingly cruel decision by Providence a higher, divine will of love was concealed. As insignificant as this seemed to be, the withering of the fruit above his head which had shaded him became the image for the ending of Israelite life. When, following the divine command, he had taken up the spirit battle against Nineveh, he himself had contributed to the bitter misfortune that now was fulfilled over his nation. The Assyrians did not meet their doom; rather, they remained. They were therefore spared so that, when the time for it should come, they would crush the northern Israelite kingdom as the instrument of Providence. Perhaps it was the impression that the fiery words of Jonah made on them that worked in such a way that, now more than ever, they wanted to reach out and conquer Israel. Did Jonah not speak to them like an initiate who was in possession of mighty mysteries? And could the Assyrians not hope by usurpation of the land from where Jonah came to make themselves lords over these mysteries as well?

Mysterious are the paths on which God leads nations and human beings. Jonah became a prophet when he acquired the inner strength to look courageously into the abyss of doom that threatened his people without losing his faith in God again. At the same time, acquisition of this courage signified sensing the Messianic day which, one day, would dawn on yonder side of the darkness of night now breaking in.

After his return to the Holy Land, Jonah must have become the herald of a mighty apocalypse of that age. It must have been his endeavour to strengthen the souls so that they could bear the impending trials after he himself had struggled through to the inner apocalyptic courage. Only a little more than two decades after his appearance, the ten tribes of the northern Israelite kingdom were deported to Nineveh and the other cities of Assyria.

CHAPTER TWENTY-ONE

The Destruction of the Northern Kingdom

The battles and wars that the Israelite nation waged before and after David's age had all remained confined within the immediate surroundings of the Holy Land. Even the largest expansion of the kingdom under David and Solomon had not crossed beyond the basically still small territory of the Jordan land.

After the division of the kingdom, the balances of power possessed by the Israelite-Jewish kings diminished still much more. Now, however, world-historical dimensions entered into the history of the land due to the fact that Israel-Judah was directly drawn into the controversies of mighty empires and, as the land of the middle, in many instances represented the pointer on the scale.

In 854 BC, Ahab of Israel had fought near Karkar in Syria in the army of Ben-hadad II of Damascus against the armies of the Assyrian king, Shalmaneser III, in order to defend the independence of Syria and Palestine. In the following period, the Assyrians repeatedly had to desist from their designs on Egypt since, in order to carry them out, they first had to make sure of Syria and Palestine. The mighty kingdoms of Asia Minor and Mesopotamia did not cease from attempts to shake off Assyria's rule. Finally, the Assyrian will for power found an elemental, irresistible embodiment in Tiglath-pileser III. With strong assurance, he completed the political structure of the northern Mesopotamian empire. The Babylonians in the south, the Armenians in the west, the Medes in the east had to submit to him, seemingly for all time. Even the smaller kingdoms of the Syrians and Phoenicians in the north of Palestine were subjugated to him. The sphere of Assyrian power already bordered on the kingdom of Israel. The internal unrest in Israel itself, however, did not subside even in the face of the threat from outside. On the contrary, an irreconcilable controversy arose over the question of responding to the Assyrians with diplomatic accommodations or ultimate show of force. The faction of the Jehu dynasty, which still maintained rulership, was in favour of clever compromises. Against them stood the radical opponents of Assyria who thought of seeking an alliance with Egypt. A few months after the death of Jeroboam II (743 BC), his son Zechariah was deposed. The last descendent of Jehu fell victim to the hand of a murderer. His killer and successor, Shallum, leader of the radical party, was also slain a few weeks later. With Menahem (743–737), the more prudent group again ascended to the throne.

A joint attempt by Syria and Phoenicia to regain freedom (738 BC) gave Tiglath-pileser (Pul) the opportunity to move forward forcefully in the northern region of the Holy Land. Mighty deportations began. Many thousands of noble and skilled men from the insubordinate vassal nations were transported to Assyria. Of his own free will, Menahem of Israel acknowledged the sovereignty of the great conqueror and, through payment of high tribute managed to have his land spared:

> Pul the king of Assyria came against the land; and Menahem
> gave Pul a thousand talents of silver, that he might help him to
> confirm his hold of the royal power. Menahem exacted the
> money from Israel, that is, from all the wealthy men, fifty
> shekels of silver from every man, to give to the king of Assyria.
> So the king of Assyria turned back, and did not stay there in
> the land. (2Kings 15:19f).

For a brief time, the Holy Land was left in peace since Tiglath-pileser's presence was required in his homeland until the underground opposition and anger in the vassal kingdoms closest to Assyria had quietened down. Then, a spark of unrest from the preparations, undertaken in Syria for a revolt, ignited in Israel as well. The radical faction pushed for Israel's siding with rebellious Syria. Pekah, the charioteer of the king, was the leader of the radicals. He slew Pekahiah (737–736), the son of Menahem, and, after he had appointed himself king (736–730), concluded an alliance with King Rezin of Syria. In order to have a chance of success, Pekah and Rezin sought for further allies. Through the use of force, they tried to compel Ahaz, ruler of the small kingdom of Judah, which had remained relatively untouched by the gruesome chaos of events, to join their conspiracy. Ahaz, however, resisted and finally turned to Tiglath-pileser himself for assistance, sending him a part of the Temple treasure of Jerusalem as a sign of his submissiveness.

The Assyrian king hesitated no longer. With inescapable vehemence, the end drew near. Israel surrendered before any battle had even begun. Rezin's Syrians were defeated. After a siege of some duration, Damascus, the Syrian capital, fell in 732. Rezin was executed before the eyes of his people. Syria had now completely forfeited its independence and became an Assyrian province. The deportations begun earlier were continued on a massive scale and the Assyrians now penetrated deeply into the northern Israelite provinces: 'In the days of Pekah king of Israel Tiglath-pileser king of Assyria came and captured Ijon, Abel-beth-maacah, Janoah, Kedesh, Hazor, Gilead, and Galilee, all the land of Naphtali; and he carried the people captive to Assyria' (2Kings 15:29). Assyria had arrived at a decisive point in the realization of its plans. With the destruction of Syria, it finally had free access to the wealthy harbours of the Mediterranean Sea. With the conquest of Israel and the voluntary submission of Judah, the Assyrian armies for the first time could advance all the way to Egypt. The bridge between the two mighty empires had been thrown.

Suddenly, in the year 727, something unexpected occurred: Tiglath-pileser died. News of his death spread like wildfire through all the subjugated kingdoms. Everywhere, the hope of liberation gained ground. Shalmaneser V (727–722) who took his father's place in ruling the empire, would find it difficult to hold together what the mighty personality of Tiglath-pileser had forced together. Even Israel, whose throne was now occupied by Hoshea (730–722), exempted itself from its tribute. The armies of Shalmaneser marched into the land. Now, Israel's last hour had struck. Samaria, the nation's capital, was besieged. It almost seemed as if the new ruler of Assyria was lacking in the impact and momentum which could hold the many segments of the empire in submission. The Assyrian army, however, tolerated no relaxation. A military coup toppled the son of the great conqueror; one of his generals, a sinister, determined man of domineering character, ascended the Assyrian throne as Sargon II.

Samaria fell in the year 722. No more leniency could be expected. To the extent that the populace of the kingdom of Israel held any cultural importance, namely priests, members of the court, the aristocracy, the wealthy, twenty-seven thousand people in all were deported to Assyria and the cities of the Medes. Only the culturally insignificant inhabitants of the countryside remained. Among those that were left behind, however, care was taken effectively to extinguish the former national configuration. In place of the deported Israelites, Mesopotamians from the south, above all Babylonians, who had also been removed from their homeland by their Assyrian masters, were settled in the central region of the Holy Land. The foundation was thereby laid for the racially mixed population north of Judea, the Samaritans, who were so despised and avoided as an impure Israelite-Babylonian mixed race by the Jews of the period following the exile.

Through these events, the tragedy which had already begun to develop in a frightening way during the division of the kingdom following Solomon's death, had grown into an unheard-of historic catastrophe. The largest segment of the nation, which had split off at that time, therewith excluding itself from the Messianic future, was smashed utterly into splinters. Its expulsion through the might of destiny was completed. Later, when the remainder of the nation, the inhabitants of the small kingdom of Judah, was led into the alien land of Babylonia, a cohesion remained among the deported people so that a continuation of their common destinies and, later on, a return was possible. The ten tribes of the northern kingdom, on the other hand, were scattered into the winds and remained lost. The search for the 'ten lost tribes of Israel' runs through the ages like a never-silenced question concerning a profound mystery. Again and again, here and there, it was thought that their traces had been found. In reality, they had been absorbed into humanity in general and continued to be effective invisibly as a ferment of the totality of historical evolution.

Henceforth, less than twenty kilometres (thirteen miles) north of Jerusalem, lay the border of the Assyrian empire. Only a small area, the largest part of which was comprised of the Wilderness of Judah at that, had remained as the stage for the history of the Old Testament folk. It was — to make use of a picture from the books of the prophets — as if a tree had been felled and its trunk and the top that had reached far into the sky consigned to the flames so that in the realm of earthly visibility nothing remained of it. Only a dark stump still rose out of the earth from the root stock. It was questionable whether a living shoot could once again grow forth from this root.

For what purpose did the deity allow the misfortune to break in over Israel? Did it only intend to punish through annihilation? Or was it its aim to guide the people through difficult trials to new heights?

In the legend of Tobias, which numbers among the apocryphal texts of the Old Testament, a half mythical imaginative inkling of the positive aspect of the cruel suffering has found literary expression.

In it, we are transported to Nineveh and Ecbatana of Media, the two centres of the Israelite deportations. In both localities, we are spectators of the miseries that the Israelites had to suffer in the alien country. In Nineveh, devout Tobit visited the ranks of the afflicted as an unwearying comforter and helper; during the time of an especially cruel persecution, he buried the dead until, in thus serving others, the hand of misfortune took hold of him as well and he lost his eyesight. Like a second Job, he was exposed to the ridicule and reproaches of his friends as well as the distrust of his wife and he beseeched God for deliverance through death. In Ecbatana, the same prayer rose to heaven from the soul of Sarah, a relative of Tobit, who was beginning to lose courage in face of the blows of fate that struck her without cease. It was as if the spiritual and the soul element of the people, suffering in the alien land, had found embodiment in Tobit and Sarah. The prayers of the two were not answered to the letter. Instead, the archangel Raphael was dispatched to help both with his healing spirit.

In a youthful, gifted sense, Tobit's son Tobias was a picture of what remained to the people as hope for the future despite all misfortunes. Tobias left on a journey in order to fulfil the last wish of his father. This turned into a mystery path: Raphael, who designated himself as 'one of the seven holy angels who ... enter into the presence of the glory of the Holy One' (12:15), took him by the hand and accompanied him.

The youth walked along the banks of the Tigris with the archangel. Once, when he was washing his feet in the river, a big fish leaped up to swallow him, but Jonah's destiny did not befall Tobias. Following the archangel's direction, he caught the fish by its fins, pulled it to dry ground and, taking out the heart, gall and liver, carried them with him.

The journey continued. In Ecbatana, in the spirit of Raphael, Tobias freed the desperate Sarah from the demon of her misfortune with the heart and liver of the fish. The journey, which originally had seemed only to serve the collection of an old debt, turned into a bridal journey, for Sarah became young Tobias's wife. About midway during the return home, Raphael directed Tobias and Sarah through the ancient city of Laban, namely Haran, where, long ago, Jacob had courted Rachel. Back in Nineveh, old Tobit was then cured with the gall of the fish. His eyesight returned and more than that, the seer's eye opened in him. He beheld the future of Israel, the manner in which it would be fulfilled for the still surviving remnant of the people:

> O Jerusalem, the holy city,
>> he will afflict you for the deeds of your sons,
>> but again he will show mercy to you the sons of
>> righteousness
>
> ...
>
> For Jerusalem will be built with sapphires and emeralds,
>> her walls with with precious stones
>> and her towers and battlements with pure gold.
> The streets of Jerusalem will be paved with beryl and
>> ruby and stones of Ophir;
>> all her lanes will cry 'Hallelujah!'
>> and will give praise (13:9, 16–18).

In Tobit, even that segment of Israel which, long before its destruction, had surrendered its share of the earthly Jerusalem, advanced to the presentiment of the heavenly Jerusalem, to the realization of the existence of a future, for the sake of which even the worst suffering served its purpose.

The fish mythos of the Book of Jonah returns in the legend of Tobias in transformed manner. It is more human, less mythological, submerged more into the element of the fairy tale. The fish bestowed rebirth on the one it had swallowed. Through Tobias, it gave healing forces to those who suffered. In the Assyrian misfortune, Israel received a reflection of the Jonah mystery. Out of the sorrow in the foreign land, a spiritual force emerged for him who passed the trial which finally could even replace the lost homeland. Tobit, who, in the course of the Assyrian suffering, had turned blind, regained his sight through the power of the fish who allows us to sense the secret of death and resurrection. The earthly loss was compensated for spiritually. In its youthful genius and through divine, helping powers, the nation, which, on the earthly plane, had been shattered, gained the prospect over a spiritual future, even across the valleys of trials still to come.

After all, the whole of Israelite-Jewish prophetism is a fruit of the suffering, which the Assyrians, and later on the Babylonians, had caused to break in over the people. To this extent, the Book of Tobit is a pictorial motto for the epoch of the great prophets. Sorely tested and grown old, Israel regained its vision and was illuminated with the light of the youthful Messianic future in the prophets. This sentiment also permeates the healing of aged Tobit who turned into a prophet when the cover of blindness fell from his eyes.

The alien land guided the people back to their own origins. Was not the journey of Tobias, transformed by the archangel into a bridal courtship, a repetition of the journey which, long ago, was undertaken by Jacob to Laban? It is not without meaning that we see the returning Tobias pass through Haran, the city of Abraham and Jacob. Outwardly, Israel had lost its homeland, and would lose it even more, once Judah and Jerusalem lay in ruins. Spiritually, however, the homeland, the realm of origin and the patriarchs, was rediscovered together with the faculty of beholding the spiritual world. The prophetic consciousness is the metamorphosis, the higher octave of the ancient clairvoyance, which, in the age of the patriarchs, had been renounced. In the figure of Tobit, Israel looked out of the first exile into the second one and with it into the future that would grow out of it. The end of Galilee and Samaria, brought about by the Assyrian deportation, was a loss, a great sacrifice. The end of Judea through the Babylonian deportation would become the beginning of a transformation. The prophetic vision, the fruit of the great trial, turned into apocalyptic sight. The birth of the apocalypse announced itself. For the first time, through the death of the old, terrestrial Jerusalem, the image of the new, heavenly Jerusalem emerged: the rosy dawn of the new heaven and the new spirit-permeated earth. The mighty outlook of John's Apocalypse, with which the New Testament concludes, shone forth germinally in the figure of Tobit, who appears like the personification of the spirit of the great prophets.

CHAPTER TWENTY-TWO

Isaiah and Hezekiah:
Wealth of Revelation

The development of the tiny kingdom of Judah was a very quiet one after the division of the nation. Although Jerusalem still stood there in its Solomonic splendour, it was no longer a fitting expression for the spiritual life and mental attitudes that emerged ever more clearly in this southern part of the land. The Judeans could not help but compare their life with that of the ten tribes. Their awareness of the contrast caused them to take an even more watchful and reserved attitude, the more violently the waves of destiny surged to and fro in the northern brother nation.

How differently the royal rule developed in the two territories! In Israel, the sequence of the kings was determined by a series of bloody murders. There was hardly a single king of Israel who did not owe his power to the gruesome shedding of blood. Those who sat on the throne in Samaria did not hold the rudder of the storm-endangered ship tightly in their hand; they themselves were propelled into their places for a time by arbitrary agitated waves until the next wave swallowed them up again. The unstable vacillation between Egypt and Assyria, by means of which the contemporary upheavals found their way into the region, was mirrored in the course of revolutions and counter-revolutions.

In contrast to this, the descendants of David replaced each other in the office of king in undisturbed harmony. The dynastic sequence was not interrupted. Just as the fast change-overs in Israel were an expression of the chaotic present, the mystery of a sacred future expressed itself in the dynastic uniformity of Judea. The various generations of the ruling house as well as the whole nation were held together by the awareness that the great 'son of David,' the

Messiah, would eventually come forth from the royal lineage of David. Those who reigned in Jerusalem felt themselves to be not only kings of the present age but progenitors and preparers of the Messianic future.

Surely, the more serious and consciously alert individuals must have observed the development of the northern kingdom with abhorrence and consternation. If only the wild chaos with the hypnotic suggestions of its ostentation did not encroach upon Judah and Jerusalem! What else could be done but erect a barrier of prayer-filled inwardness in order to protect the as yet unfulfilled Messianic task, given Israel by God!

The anger over the pagan decadence of the northern tribes of brothers, their entanglement into the chaos of a world that was destroying itself, caused many a Jewish man of God to become a prophet. It caused him to predict the imminent end; to appear before the people as a preacher of repentance by calling for rejection of all things external and a radical inward intensification. The destiny of the people enkindled a spark in the inner being of these men which they themselves experienced as the will of God, bestowing a task on them. They designated and felt themselves to have been called and driven by God himself.

Judah's prophetic arousal in regard to Israel broke forth with special vehemence and diversity when, under Jeroboam II (783–743), the northern kingdom again experienced an unexpected temporarily recovery. Particularly the re-establishment of its wealth and splendour was experienced by the stern Judean faction as the sealing of Israel's inward faithlessness and thereby also its external doom.

During this time, which could be considered the hour of birth of the prophet-scribes' age — it was when Jonah's destiny ran its course in the configurations of the northern kingdom — Amos, the shepherd from Tekoa, also made his appearance. Amos was a stern herald of divine wrath and judgment. Although, being a man from the Judean mountains, he was a foreigner there, he still dared enter the centres of northern Israelite activities. He ventured into the courtyards of the palaces of Samaria and the bull temple at Bethel, chastised the ostentatious externalization of piety and morality, and presented pictures of imminent doom to the souls of the people.

It was also right after the death of Jeroboam II, during the reign of King Azariah of Judah (also called Uzziah, 779–740), when a fiery spirit, namely Isaiah, appeared in Judea of whom people had the immediate impression that he would one day be a supreme teacher who had at his disposal great inner wealth. To the surprise of the stern Jewish circles, his mighty admonition for repentance was not directed against the kingdom of Israel, fallen victim to pagan seduction, but against Judah itself. He went a step further and demanded that the much quieter, withdrawn Judah relinquish all its worldliness. He saw the waves of doom closing not only over Samaria but over Jerusalem. Judea had no reason to consider itself to be more pious than Israel and therefore lull itself into believing that it was safe.

> And the daughter of Zion is left
>   like a booth in a vineyard,
> like a lodge in a cucumber field,
>   like a besieged city.
> If the LORD of hosts
>   had not left us a few survivors,
> we should have been like Sodom
>   and become like Gomorrah. (Isa.1:8f)

We know almost nothing concerning the personal circumstances of the prophet's life. Isaiah's own nature and destiny receded completely behind the great supra-personal task bestowed on him by God as whose instrument he spoke to people. We do know of one experience, however, that transformed his being and also his activity through and through. The Bible describes it to us in the words of the prophet himself (Chapter 6).

It is customary to denote the mighty vision that overcame him in this instance as the 'call' of Isaiah. The Bible, however, makes it clearly evident that this important experience by no means signified merely the beginning of his activity. Perhaps we can compare it to the event that brought about such a radical turning point in the life of Johannes Tauler, the fourteenth-century Dominican from Strasburg. For years, Tauler had been involved in a most successful preaching career. The masses flocked to this famous orator. Then, one day, an illiterate man came to him and pointed out to him that despite their great cleverness his sermons did not originate out of a transformed heart. Tauler took the conversation with the 'Friend of God' so seriously that he withdrew for two years into seclusion for the purpose of stern, meditative exercises. Following that, when he once again spoke from the pulpit, he was a changed man and quite unheard-of new effects proceeded from his sermons. It is said that when he spoke again for the first time, forty people fell down as if dead. Henceforth, one could feel that Tauler was imbued by a direct relationship to the divine world.

Isaiah had already been active as an admonishing voice. Similarly to Amos, he had felt called upon to do so because of his inner divine spark, kindled through the people's destiny. An inner and clear obligation which yet remained general had asserted itself in him. Now, however, it was as if he had been drawn into the sphere of a burning fire and was completely changed and forged into a sword of the spirit. The transforming fire blazed forth from his own depth of destiny, similarly to how it had happened in Jonah's case. Actually, only now, the personal call of fate was added to that by the national fate.

Henceforth, Isaiah was no longer one of those prophetic preachers calling for repentance, whose numbers increased steadily. Perhaps he withdrew for some time into seclusion as did Tauler when the profound experience made clear to him to what extent his verbal activity had, after all, still flowed out of more superficial levels of his soul.

It was a mighty Temple vision that appeared to the trembling soul of Isaiah. The curtain concealing the Holy of Holies appeared torn, the portal before the divine supersensory world was thrown open. In the spirit, the sphere opened to him of which even the holiest inner sanctuary of Solomon's Temple was merely a symbolic indication. On the lofty heavenly throne, the prophet beheld the figure of the deity itself surrounded by the cherubim and seraphim, themselves totally representing the eye of the spirit, who struck up the great Sanctus of divine worship.

Isaiah felt as if crushed by this vision. How could anything mortal endure the light and fire of the immortal without being consumed? What would be left of him now that the dead, unchangeable element had been brought to his awareness so inexorably? The seraphic servants of God purified the word-bearing part of his being with burning coal. His human word was to become completely transparent for the spirit word of God. Despite its scorching glow, the experience already lost its crushing judgmental severity in the transition from the first terrifyingly powerful image to the purification of the word. Isaiah felt how a living divine element streamed into him. He was able to place himself at the service of the spiritual power as a messenger and instrument: 'Here am I; send me!' On a higher level, his prophetic mission had been renewed.

Yet he now became aware that his mission was a strange one: he was to harden the hearts of the people, make their ears deaf and their eyes blind, so that they would no longer be able to perceive with their eyes, hear with their ears and would even lose their hearts' comprehension. How was this puzzling task to be interpreted? Had it not been the fervent endeavour of the prophet to waken the people from their sleep, to open their eyes and rouse their senses for the true inner happening of the age?

It was a great mystery of humanity's evolution of consciousness that Isaiah perceived in his Temple vision. The stream of history took its course from past ages in which human beings had been gifted with organs other than the physical sense organs. They not only cognized with the physical eyes; a clairvoyant faculty permitted them dreamily to behold supersensory facts. Not only external sounds and noises reached their ear, an inward listening process led them to a hidden speaking and resounding. The heart that was still flesh and had not yet become hard as stone resembled an entrance through which the beings of a higher world could gain passage into people's soul realm. But for a long time, the old macrocosmic consciousness that still extended into the human being was becoming obscured. Only the last, stunted remains thereof lingered on in the souls.

In the mighty illumination into which his soul had been drawn, Isaiah recognized that even the last remnants of the ancient vision and hearing now had to die. It was made incumbent upon him to become the executor of this death sentence. The paradox was that in the experience through which he became clairvoyant, he recognized that humankind had to cease being clairvoyant. In him, a completely new vision broke through, anticipating a future faculty, which ensouled the prophets. Owing to this, however, it became frighteningly clear to him that before humankind could mature to the level of this new vision, the ancient vision had to die. Could the doom, which came to fulfilment over the northern tribes of the same blood, not have led to the insight now gained by Isaiah through the awakening of his soul? The pagan seduction that historically affected Israel did in fact proceed from the decadent remains of the ancient macrocosmic consciousness which had been preserved in the neighbouring nations. And the ten northern tribes could not have fallen victim to this temptation if they had not shared in an after-effect of the ancient clairvoyance.

Isaiah felt called upon to become the conscious teacher of the specifically Jewish awareness which, purified of all macrocosmic remnants, was to be exclusively of a microcosmic human nature. The annihilation of all atavistic elements, of all clairvoyant faculties of perception, was the contribution that Judaism, acting for all humanity which thereby had to pass through an absolute separation of consciousness from the supersensory in one of its members, was required to make to the evolution of consciousness.

The Mosaic Law's prohibition of the worship of images found its intensification, applying specifically to the Jewish people, in the divine task of Isaiah. The human being was to be thrown back to what the physical senses and his brain-bound intellect could tell him.

It was the correspondence, on the level of consciousness, of the impending destruction of the northern kingdom which was to be brought about by the prophetic activity of Isaiah. The axe was already placed at the root of the tree of visionary macrocosmic consciousness, which had to be felled so that nothing would remain of it except the root stock of the physical intellectual consciousness. The Assyrians were preparing to annihilate the northern kingdom. Basically, they did this as instruments of the divine will, for what they did was at the same time a picture for what Isaiah was to accomplish on the soul level, namely the limitation of Israelite life to the Jewish way of life by eradicating any form of closeness to nature and all cosmic presentiments.

The time of the experience concerning his new, higher calling was clearly established by Isaiah himself. It was the year 740, when King Uzziah (Azariah) died. Throughout the years, during which the surge of world events penetrated with increasing ferocity into Israel, coming increasingly closer to the borders of Judea, Isaiah was at pains to fulfil

his prophetic task. It seems as if he was sparing in his public appearances and remained active more in quiet, secluded circles. During
moments of great tension in the destiny of his people, however, he did
not hold back. When the kings of Syria and Israel, for example, tried to
coerce the Judeans to join in their alliance against Assyria, Isaiah went
before King Ahaz of Judea in order to strengthen his inner courage,
faith and steadfastness in the face of the Syrian-Israelite intentions.

Thirteen years after Uzziah's death, a king assumed the reign in
Jerusalem who himself was filled in the most vivid sense by the
impulse of the prophets: Hezekiah (727–699). In the field of religious
life, he began to implement a reform of the greatest magnitude. The
biblical report states:

> He removed the high places, and broke the pillars, and cut
> down the Asherah [Astarte]. And he broke to pieces the bronze
> serpent that Moses had made, for until those days the people
> of Israel had burned incense to it; it was called Nehushtan.
> (2Kings 18:4)

Along with Hezekiah's endeavours at reform, a cultic-religious
attitude began to emerge and crystallize, the like of which had never
before existed in humankind's history. Actually extending into the
forms of worship, a piety came into being that completely rejected
nature and depended exclusively on the inner essence of the human
being.

In Judea, corresponding to the desert landscape and its effects,
there had always been fewer nature sanctuaries than existed in the
middle and northern parts of the region. In the religious life of Judea,
the impulse that emanated from the ecstatic nature rituals had never
been as significant as it had been in the north. Everything took on a
more moderate character here. Nevertheless, in Judea as well, there
existed many sanctuaries in high places, sacred grottoes and groves;
after all, not only Mizpah-Gibeon but Jerusalem itself with its two
archetypal high places was a sacred hill and not only in pre-Israelite
times. Although the transfer of the main sanctuary from Mount Zion
to the Rock of Moriah was a first turning away from the ancient connection of the Yahweh cult to the ether-life forces of the kingdoms of
nature, Solomon himself had caused this beginning of a new attitude
to be ineffective by his introduction of the numerous alien nature rituals. Under Hezekiah, the radical struggle against all nature religions

began. Hezekiah was even determined not to stop short of the infusion of nature rituals dating back to Moses himself. He by no means envisioned a reform that merely consisted in returning to the point of departure. He followed an impulse that transcended Moses and possessed the courage to bring about something completely new.

It was the impulse of inward intensification proceeding from Elijah and continuing in the prophetic movement. We are probably not mistaken if we imagine that, without making a visible appearance to the people, Isaiah was the teacher and counsellor of the still young king. What the king undertook was the execution of the task that Isaiah had received in his Temple vision. It was after all the influence of the sacred trees and symbols, bestowing on the ritual life of Israel the macrocosmic touch and closeness to nature, which at the same time helped enkindle the remnants of ancient clairvoyance and other ecstatic soul faculties. Through their abolishment, the atavisms, whose annihilation had been entrusted as a duty to Isaiah, were deprived of their breeding ground. The symbol of the serpent had truly been a pictorial expression of the old, dreamy-clairvoyant soul forces.[1] Moses did place the erect bronze serpent before the people in order to take a first step in overcoming the atavistic dangers. As the bearer of the new prophetic impulse, Hezekiah, on the other hand, had to go further. The image of the serpent had to disappear altogether. Therefore, the sacred symbol that was preserved in the Temple in memory of the trials and miracles of the journey through the wilderness had to be sacrificed. Finally, any sort of symbolism had to be given up since it still always drew the devout soul to something outward. Humanity had to pass through an epoch in which, for the religious feelings, a terrestrial outer world did not exist. Through the realization of Isaiah's mission, the way was prepared for a thoroughly abstract inwardness, namely the specifically Jewish element.

Hezekiah became king the same year that Tiglath-pileser died. At that time, Damascus had already fallen; Syria was an Assyrian province. Israel had bought time through high payments of tribute but great numbers of Galileans had been deported into the foreign lands. The catastrophe broke out. Deeply moved, the Jewish people and their king were witnesses of the tempest that destroyed the tribes of their brothers. Through lightning and thunder, guided by Isaiah's advice,

Hezekiah executed his first actions as king. Ever since Ahaz, his pre-decessor, had himself called on the Assyrians for help in order to pro-tect himself against the Syrian-Israelite pressure, it could be supposed in Judea that as protector of the land Assyria might desist from a force-ful conquest. And in fact, the tiny region around Jerusalem was now left in peace for some time by the mighty, threatening nation which had become its close neighbour. Only a meagre remnant of the Promised Land henceforth bore the legacy of the patriarchs and the promise of the Messianic future.

Hezekiah was far from maintaining peace with Assyria through any compromises that would have been an infraction against the stern purity of the new prophetic cultural life. Despite his impotence, he gave Assyria clearly to understand that he considered himself an ally, not a vassal of Assur. It was inevitable that the ominous giant stretched out his hand towards the dwarf who dared claim for himself a free autonomous existence and whose tiny land always remained an unpleasant obstacle on the path to Egypt.

Hezekiah had been king of Judah for more than two decades when the troops of Sennacherib (705–681), who had succeeded Sargon II on the throne of the Assyrian empire, marched into Judea. Hezekiah still made the attempt to save the freedom of his land by delivering to the enemy everything that had remained in the palace and the Temple of the Solomonic gold and silver treasures, but he was unable thereby to bring the advance of the Assyrians to a halt.

Sennacherib's armies laid siege to Jerusalem. It seemed impossible for the city to hold out for long. Was the remnant of Israel that nur-tured the legacy really doomed to destruction even before the purifi-cation was completed that it had imposed on itself? The awareness of the Messianic mission and future arose fervently in the devout Judeans, now that everything, even the last remains, appeared to be in the process of being swallowed up by the abyss. In Hezekiah too, this concern burned like a fire. He was the present son of David. Perhaps the ardently longed for moment was no longer so far away when the mystery of the greatest son of David was to emerge. Had he, the king, not done what was in his power to purify the people and to prepare the way for the Messiah? What kind of demon was it that now stretched out its destructive paw with Satanic calculation?

Violent excitement gripped the people when the Assyrian troops surrounded Jerusalem. And Isaiah? Even if fear and concern were thereby only increased, could he do anything but unrelentingly direct the nation to the duties that accrued for it from the Messianic expectation? Untiringly, he also endeavoured to strengthen the inner courage and power of faith in Hezekiah and his people. It was, after all, the 'faith' that was the faculty newly growing in the souls to which the prophetic sermons were addressed in every case. 'If you will not believe, surely you shall not be established.' This was what Isaiah called out to his age (Isa.7:9).

A miracle took place. After a night during which the excitement had risen to fever pitch and the inhabitants of Jerusalem already believed that they were being engulfed by the flames and lightning flashes of judgment, they saw the army of the beleaguers suddenly withdraw as if gripped by panic and fear at the early dawn of morning? What had happened?

There exist traditions that claim that this night had been the one preceding the Passover festival, and just as the destroying angel had passed through the ranks of the Egyptians, erecting the gruesome image of death everywhere, he had now afflicted the ranks of the Assyrian army, and once again, the children of God had been saved from a great peril.[2] Others report that a mighty fire blazed forth between Isaiah and Hezekiah who were praying in the Temple, and that this fire then went its consuming way into the army of the enemy, spreading fear and death there.[3] Perhaps fire and smoke once more arose from the ancient depths of Jerusalem's gorges, revealing to the Assyrians the divine power fighting on the Jewish side. Perhaps, without any direct outward cause, the besiegers were frightened by visionary experiences. Whatever it was, spiritual powers now appeared on the stage who brought salvation to the Jewish nation when it had just seemed to be abandoned to inescapable doom.

Sennacherib's army commanders are reputed to have smiled with derision over the small size of the city when they first beheld Jerusalem.[4] So, this was supposed to be the 'centre of the world,' of which the people of all nations spoke in such glowing terms! Spiritually, however, Jerusalem and Judea were infinitely greater than their physical appearance suggested. During that mysterious night, the Assyrians had to become aware of that.

Still, the miraculous events were not over yet. At first, it seemed as if
fate were taking an even more ominous turn. The king succumbed to
a serious illness. His death appeared imminent. The people had been
saved; was the king now to die in their place? It was an illness without
a clear physical cause. Had the profound excitement and shock of the
preceding event exceeded Hezekiah's energies?

The prophet Isaiah was not present when the king became ill. He
practised a strange restraint.[5] Did he foresee the inevitable? People
searched for him and called him to the beside of the king, his disciple.
Isaiah could do nothing except confirm the imminent death of
Hezekiah, departing again silently. All at once, a great secret was
revealed to his soul. A completely new, unexpected light fell from it on
the illness of the king. He turned around and announced what had
appeared to him: three days hence, Hezekiah would recover from this
mortal illness. The Bible describes that he placed a poultice of figs on
him and indeed, the king who had already seemed to be a victim of
death, was cured three days later. The miracle of Jerusalem's deliverance was followed by that of the king.

Special circumstances must have been involved in the healing of
Hezekiah. Otherwise, the Bible and ancient theology would not have
seen in it an even more astounding influence of the spiritual world
than in the deliverance of the besieged city. A mystery emerged that
was rooted deeply in the womb of destiny. As in the case of Elijah and
Jonah, the death and resurrection of initiation in former incarnations
threw its reflection into the destiny of a present life owing to the shattering impression made by the nation's fate. The illness of Hezekiah,
lasting three days, was nothing but the karmic echo of the three-day
mystic death, undergone at one time in the temple sleep. Just as the
hierophant then stood as the guide of the soul by the side of the sarcophagus of the mystic disciple, so the prophet Isaiah now stood by
the king's bed of suffering. He who at first had to assume that this illness would lead to death now all at once recognized its inner nature
and meaning. And while this dying and reviving took place as an
actual event beside Isaiah, he himself became a participant in this mystery. He underwent Hezekiah's destiny as if it had been his own. Once,
when he was still in the bloom of his life, the mighty, transforming
Temple vision had taken hold of him. Now, in the maturity of old age,
the fate of Hezekiah came to him of which he was more than a mere

witness. The deepest mysteries of destiny illuminated his soul like flashes of lightning. It was as if thick coverings had been taken away from his eyes.

The biblical description turns imaginative and hieroglyphic where it touches upon the secrets of the Hezekiah destiny that is so like an initiation. It says that as a sign of the recovery that was to occur three days hence, Isaiah had indicated to the king that the shadow on the sun dial of the Temple would run backwards by ten steps. And supposedly, what the prophet had predicted did come about. This account does not point to an outward event but the content of what Hezekiah underwent during the three days as transformations of soul. Much more happened than the recovery of a hopelessly ill individual. After his recovery, Hezekiah was a different human being from before his sickness. As a reborn one, he became master over faculties that otherwise do not obey the will of man. Hezekiah won a share of the inner solar forces in the same manner as did Joshua long ago. It is now as if he also had been given the power to say: 'Sun, stand still!' Legendary tradition subtly points to the relationship that tied the destiny of Hezekiah to the sun nature of Joshua. It reports that Hezekiah, seeking for the meaning of his newly acquired life, asked:

> Am I still needed to proclaim ... the miraculous deeds ... of the
> holy one? Are they not already known from one end of the
> world to the other? Did the sun not stand still once before in
> the sky in broad daylight so that the glory and the might of the
> Lord was revealed to all the people?[6]

Within the Israelite-Jewish history, the death and resurrection of Hezekiah was a revelation from the mysteries pointing into the future. The prophets and their disciples knew that one day humanity's fundamental mystery of death and resurrection, carefully guarded in the initiation centres of the ancient world, would emerge openly, namely in the destiny that the Messiah would undergo on the earth. In Hezekiah, an early shadow of the future Messianic destiny fell into the preparatory history of humankind. The old rabbinical traditions coarsened this and stated that even at that time the possibility existed of the Messiah's arrival: 'The Lord intended to make Hezekiah the Messiah and Sennacherib was to be Gog and Magog.' But because Hezekiah did not intone the song of praise that God had expected of him a voice resounded: 'The secret is mine ... I know why I do not yet allow the time to begin.'[7]

Within the old Testament development, the figure of Hezekiah indicates a significant stage. It is not a coincidence that those who wanted to bring this to expression pointed to the Messianic secret that lingered around this king to a special degree. The reality of what occurred in the days of Hezekiah was situated more in the realm of the supersensory than on the physical plane. Only from the Messianic aspect of history can the importance of this time be truly discerned.

Behind and above the Israelite-Jewish folk history the Messiah history progressed in the spirit realm. The destiny of a deity had been approaching the earth since ancient beginnings. From sphere to sphere, the Christ being descended. Always, the mystery of death and resurrection designated this path; for Christ always had to die in one sphere in order to be able to shine forth in the next. Reflections and rays of presentiment fell on to the earth from this mystery. A first great epoch had been the one when the coming divine being still sojourned high above in the heavenly realms in the deepest mystery-womb of the world. In that time the accompanying earthly correspondence, whereby human beings united themselves with the Messianic sphere, was initiation which, carried out in utmost secrecy, imparted the mystery of death and resurrection. Later, a completely new epoch of humankind was to begin, namely, when, for the purpose of incarnating as a human being, the Christ being would arrive on the earth. Then, the mystery of death and resurrection was to emerge completely out of the confines of secrecy and become an open fact of history, accessible to all, imprinting without initiation ceremonies the seal of the spirit into the souls of those who would unite themselves with the being and destiny of Christ.

The Old Testament development represented an interim stage between the first and the third epoch, between the mystery religions of the ancient world and Christianity. The sphere of the folk-spirit destiny turned into the transit-stage of the Christ destiny. A people, who were 'chosen,' because the approaching Christ being hovered over them and increasingly moved into their soul realm, became bearers of the mystery of death and resurrection. Something that earlier was only the fate of a god and later would be the destiny of one individual, now became the fate of a nation.

Herewith, the first step of disclosing the mystery was reached. The principle of dying and reviving, however, did not immediately appear fully visibly on the physical plane. It can be deciphered from Israel's history only as the secret inherent element. Especially in the age when the reflection of death and resurrection from the Christ sphere arrived on the stage of the people's destiny, there were individuals among the prophets who not only stood within the dramatic events simply through their existence at that particular time. They were also capable of consciously recognizing this inherent Messianic element in the people's destiny, of interpreting and proclaiming this transition of the mystery from the world of the gods to that of human beings.

We have already spoken of the kind of karmic preparation that the prophets brought along for the fulfilment of this task. The divine destiny that was moving into the folk sphere was met by a quite definite human destiny. On the second level of the development, the initiation memories from the times of the first epoch now became for the prophets an organ for perceiving the mystery symbol of death and resurrection in the destiny of their nation. The fate of their people in turn became transparent to them for what was to come in the future: the earthly incarnation of the Messiah.

A very special process now entered the Messianic history. With the shattering of the northern kingdom, the future-bearing folk-soul sphere was compressed into a much smaller area. This shrinking could not remain without effect on the destiny of the Christ-being who hovered over the people in the spirit realm. The Messiah entity had to narrow down its circles and make its entry into the smaller body of the remaining segment of the nation. The Christ exchanged the totality of the Israelite environment for that of Judaism. In the supersensory realm, an Old Testament version of Christ's entering Jerusalem took place.

The Christ being's progression to a new phase of his journey was an event that could not become evident directly on the physical plane. In the soul-spiritual periphery of the destinies of the Hebrews, however, it called forth significant flashes and surges of forces, a concentration of happenings that appear like miracles to us since they are of theophanic nature, revelation-bearing signs of the higher, invisible events.

In order to clarify what is meant here, the New Testament scene of the healing at the Pool of Beth-zatha can serve as an example. The Gospel of John describes how the periodic surge of the healing spring was accompanied, indeed caused by a supersensory process. An angelic being permeated the water's element. Nobody who stood there could perceive the angel and his approach with physical senses. All that could ever be seen was the agitation of the water. It was a similar occurrence when the Christ being entered the Judaism of Jerusalem after the destruction of the northern kingdom. There too, the 'angel' was not beheld, only the agitation. The cause for the visible effects was what occurred in the supersensory sphere. And the theophanic play of forces, actually the effect of the step taken by Christ, appeared in the experiences that motivated the Assyrian army suddenly to terminate their siege and, above all, in the strange initiation illness and healing of King Hezekiah. In the indicated passage through a death and resurrection by Hezekiah, the approaching Christ mystery was mirrored especially clearly in earthly visibility. At this instance, the king was the personification of the Jewish people into whom the Christ being carried down the destiny of initiation. Such an urgency was inherent in the approach of Christ that it also seemed as if, above the nation that now was to be his corporeality, he rushed towards incarnation in a single human being. The ancient traditions are not so wrong when they said that Hezekiah had almost become the Messiah. In any case, Isaiah, who stood by the side of the king, trying to help him, beheld in him how the people's innermost destiny took on form and became a real prophecy of the Messianic event. From the experience of Hezekiah, Isaiah could decipher what he had to express in words as a prophet, as an interpreter of the contemporary events and herald of the future.

Through his powerful experience of sharing in the world-historical spiritual event, a great transformation had occurred in the soul of Hezekiah. The king himself had turned into a prophet just like his aging teacher and adviser who stood by his side. In his inner being, rich treasures of the spirit had all at once been released. The secrets of humankind's future were opened to him. The two streams seemed to flow into one another: the one of the kingship which at the same time was the bearer of the Messianic heritage, and prophethood whose task it was in a spiritual manner to prepare the paths of the Messianic future. A wondrous identification of the political and spiritual guidance of the people as it had existed in David and Solomon lit up once more in Hezekiah.

Soon, however, it was to become evident that the king was not completely master over his blessed destiny. What he had experienced had not sprung from his own inner endeavours, it had been caused by an extension of the spiritual folk-destiny into his individual being. He did not pass the test when it became a matter of properly guarding the mysteries that had been revealed to him.

News of the strange withdrawal undertaken before Jerusalem by the Assyrian troops spread throughout the lands. Thereby, Assyria's position of power was shaken more than through an outward defeat. Right away, the vassal states entertained the hope of liberation from the Assyrian yoke. Particularly in Babylonia, which was gradually beginning to awaken to an awareness of itself and started to free itself from Assyria, the report of the events in Jerusalem must have made a deep impression. In addition, news of the miraculous recovery of the Jewish king must have gone out into the world and been received eagerly by the nations of the Orient, because among them, a frequently sensational, coarsened feeling for the initiation secrets was still alive. It may have been that a rumour spread through the world of that era that the small Jewish kingdom, whose ruler was reputed to be a lofty initiate, had broken the power of Assyria through mysterious powers.

Soon, delegates of the Babylonian king, Merodach-baladan, arrived in Jerusalem in order to win Judea for an anti-Assyrian conspiracy. The Bible specifically indicates that the report of Hezekiah's illness and recovery had been a reason and also the pretext for this delegation. Only in hidden images do the biblical books recount what happened next. It is said that the king showed the Babylonians all his treasure chambers. It is obvious that he could not have been flaunting material wealth because after the numerous deliveries of palace and Temple treasures to the Assyrians, Jerusalem must have been impoverished regarding its gold and silver. Indeed, how could little Judea have impressed rich Mesopotamia with its treasures! Concealed behind this pictorial report is the fact that the king had been induced into allowing the Babylonians a glimpse into the mysteries of the spirit and

prophetic wisdom of which he had gained a share through his theophanic experience resembling an initiation. The traditions outside the
Bible indicate the spiritual meaning of the treasure houses by saying
that Hezekiah also showed the messengers of Merodach-baladan the
tablets of the Law of Moses.[8]

When Isaiah heard what the king had done, divine wrath broke
forth from him. He stood before Hezekiah like a judge and prophetically conjured forth the image of Jerusalem's doom: this very
Babylonia, to whom the secrets of Jerusalem had just been betrayed,
would soon usurp the power of the Assyrians and then also come to
destroy the city of God. It had not been long since the Assyrians had
annihilated Israel and deported its people to an alien land; soon, the
Babylonians would do likewise with Judah. In the shadow of the first
deportation, the spectre of the second already arose on the horizon.
To the antagonism of Nineveh-Samaria was added the other of Babel
and Jerusalem. Hezekiah had to realize that he himself had sown the
seeds of doom. He had aroused the desire in the enemy who was still
acting like a friend to reach out his hand after the life of Judah. He
had repelled the Assyrian danger but conjured forth the Babylonian.
Just as Jonah had once betrayed to the Assyrians in Nineveh by
means of the spirit speaking through him what could be gained
through a conquest of Samaria, Hezekiah had now called the attention of the Babylonians, craving for the secrets of the mysteries, to
what lived in Judea. The difference was that Babylon's envy and
desire had been aroused through Hezekiah's weakness and fault,
whereas the people of Nineveh had been given reason to listen
through what Jonah, obediently following the divine command,
spoke in their midst. At that time, destiny held sway, now, guilt.
Thus, from the miracles of a new closeness to God, the germ of the
final calamity emerged.

Not long after these events, Hezekiah died. Isaiah's life too seems
to have ended soon afterwards. It says that Hezekiah's successor, King
Manasseh, who cancelled all the religious reforms of his father, had
Isaiah killed in the course of a bloody persecution with which he tried
to destroy the prophetic movement. Hezekiah was the last of the kings
who was buried on the Mountain of the Old Covenant, Mount Zion,
near the tombs of David and Solomon. It testifies to the great significance accorded Isaiah as the teacher and adviser of the king that he

was the only person, not of royal rank, whose grave found a place beside the kings of Judah.[9]

From early on, surging in the tempests of cosmic judgment, shining in the rays of the future world renewal, the book of Isaiah has posed a difficult riddle to theological contemplation. Between Chapters 39 and 40, it is divided so clearly into two parts that generally the conclusion was reached that there were two books not related to each other, originating from two different authors and periods, that were merely placed together at some time under the same prophet's name. Today, it is even considered 'scientifically proven' that although the first thirty-nine chapters are ascribed to the prophet Isaiah, the figure of a great unknown individual stands behind the grandiose, sweepingly poetic second part. It is believed that by giving the nameless one, who seems to tower over the actual prophet Isaiah, the name 'Deutero-Isaiah,' an adequate solution of the great riddle has been found. One who has really been moved by the wisdom and the wondrously exacting conformity dominating the structure of the biblical scripture cannot, however, be content so quickly and interpret something so intimately linked together by the Bible as the side-by-side appearance of two unrelated texts, fitted together merely by coincidence.

It would be an injustice to minimize or cover up the riddle inherent in the difference of the two segments of the book. Even the style changes completely. Following the thirty-ninth chapter, the Book of Isaiah swells to such rich abundance of sounds that in the so-called Deutero-Isaiah must be recognized one of the most wonderful poetic high points of the Old Testament. If this is a matter of two authors, the second is one of the greatest geniuses of poetry.

Nor can the fact be ignored that in the second part of the text quite concretely presupposes a historic situation which in many instances only took place much later, almost two centuries after the days of Isaiah and Hezekiah. An individuality seems to be speaking who, together with the deported Judeans, was awaiting imminent liberation in Babylonia. The Persian king Cyrus, who then actually brought an end to the Babylonian kingdom of Nebuchadnezzar and Belshazzar and permitted a segment of the Jews to return to the Holy Land, is so clearly designated as the 'eagle from the north and east' (Isa.46:11*B*), even called by his name, (for example, Isa.44:28 and 45:1) that more recent theology, which no longer believes in concrete prophecies, could imagine no other possibility than that the second part of this scripture originated from a contemporary of Cyrus.

We could now enter point by point into a discussion of the Deutero-Isaiah hypothesis. Here also, it is preferable, however, to attempt a positive description of the solution of this problem as we have always done in our studies.

In order to comprehend the possibility and nature of the description of history confronting the reader in the prophetic books, it is necessary to point from another aspect to the secret of history, existing in the epoch of the prophets, mentioned already a number of times. Between Elijah and Isaiah, in the days of Jonah and Amos, there is a turning point in humankind's history, the importance of which can, however, only be recognized if one does not merely undertake a straight, linear but a cyclic contemplation of history, thinking in 'cycles of time.'[10] This turning point contains much more than just the founding of Rome (747 BC). A new epoch began because the spring equinox moved from the constellation of Taurus to that of Aries (747 BC). Anthroposophy calls the epoch of evolution beginning at that point the Fourth Post-Atlantean Epoch. The fourth era of time, however, is the very middle, since time progresses in the rhythm of the number seven. The middle period of historic humanity commenced. The prophets were the first-born of this central point of time. And the great lights in the heaven of humankind that began to shine forth just then in such great number, namely, the seven kings of ancient Rome, the great artists and philosophers of Greece, the Buddha in India, the great teachers in China, they all formed a wide circle, beginning with the prophets, which was illuminated everywhere by the light of a world-historical sunrise.

The middle of time stood under different laws and constellations from the historical epochs before and afterwards. The miracle of this midpoint of time consisted in a very special correspondence between the sphere of the archetypes, holding sway above all events on the earth, and the sphere of terrestrial images and realities. The personalities and events on earth formed symbols and figures during the midpoint of time in which the structures and laws of the supernatural worlds became evident more clearly than at other times. Earthly history was more than ever a projection and shadow-image of what took place in the higher spheres. During this time, when the spring equinox was in the sign of Aries (about 747 BC to AD 1413), the physically visible constellations of the stars and the 'signs' of the zodiac, understood in a more spiritual sense corresponded; that therefore, the 'horoscope,' conceived of in 'signs' for any event of this period possesses an especially high degree of truth. It is due to the fact that along with the birth of the fourth post-Atlantean epoch, the dynamic middle-epoch in the evolution of humanity commenced, the age of the prophets, the time between Elijah and Ezra, between the founding of Rome and Pericles, was an age of archetypal history. People will one day learn to utilize this insight as an important key for the history of this epoch. They will realize, for instance, that it was wrong to dismiss the first seven kings of Rome as mythological, unhistorical figures. They were real contemporaries of the prophets, but history was at that time so completely pervaded by celestial figures and compositions that it is easier to assume mythical poetic tales than historical reports.

In the Israelite-Jewish history of this era we observe how the events of the physical plane took on an apocalyptic character. The pictures and dramas of supersensory events recorded in John's Apocalypse appeared to be imprinted on terrestrial occurrences. A kind of apocalypse of history began to emerge in the days of Isaiah. At first, the Assyrian-Israelite tension, expressed in the confrontation of the two capital cities, Nineveh and Samaria, dominated the events. Then, however, the new tension rose on the horizon which was now purely archetypal and apocalyptic: Babel-Jerusalem. In the days of Jeremiah and Daniel there appeared a physical fulfilment of the mighty dramatic contrast which forms the conclusion of John's Apocalypse where the harlot Babylon, who is cast into the abyss, is contrasted with the celestial Jerusalem, descending down to earth. In the delegation of Merodach-baladan, the harlot Babylon, apocalyptically speaking, was distantly announced for the first time. And Hezekiah did not see through the temptation.

The prophetic scriptures of the Old Testament are filled with apocalyptic nuances. We saw a beginning of that at the end of the Book of Tobit, where the image of the 'New Jerusalem' surfaced; in the contemplation concerning Ezekiel and Daniel we shall find the apocalyptic stream in great abundance. It is possible in the Old Testament to interpret the apocalyptic pictures in a historical contemporary sense, hence relating them to physical, terrestrial facts. This is because the age of the prophets and the Babylonian exile was indeed filled with archetypal, apocalyptic history. In that age, the gods inscribed the apocalypse, later written by John into a book on Patmos, on to the earth itself with the stylus of historical evolution.

It is apparent from this, however, that merely interpreting the apocalyptic element in the prophetic books through the history of that period does not suffice. Since, in that age, the terrestrial images coincided with the heavenly archetypes, we still must not ignore the archetypes. The events that took place on earth were a physical replica of events which recur in all ages in the spirit sphere and the soul realm.

The possibility of true prophecy and prediction is alien to modern thinking because it knows nothing of the world of archetypes. This is the reason for theological hypotheses such as the one which has the second part of the Book of Isaiah originating only during the last period of the exile. Since the apocalyptic sphere of the archetypes lay open to a prophetic genius like Isaiah, he was able to behold the confrontation of the two cities, Jerusalem and Babylon, when there was as yet no mention of the possibility that the Babylonians would one day destroy Jerusalem.

Particularly in a time of archetypal history, a spiritually awake individual had to be aware of what the future would entail. Through single terrestrial events, he saw into the archetype realizing itself in them; this at the same time allowed him to sense the future actualization. Thus, Hezekiah's destiny became transparent to the prophet for the archetype of the Christ destiny which would have to become reality only in his own time through the nation's death and resurrection and, in the future, in the death and resurrection of the Messiah. If a prophetic spirit intoned the psalm of the vicarious suffering of the servant of God (Isa.53:4): 'Surely, he has borne our griefs and carried our sorrows,' he uttered a Messianic prophecy even if his reference to the servant of God indicated King Hezekiah or the Jewish people who had been deported to an alien land. What Hezekiah had suffered, what the people were yet to undergo, all these were but reflections and fulfilments of the same archetype; they were prophecies come true of what would eventually come to be, namely, the earthly destiny of the approaching lofty being, sent by God. The reason that Cyrus, the eagle of liberation, is mentioned specifically by name in the Book of Isaiah before the suffering had even commenced from which he would one day free the people, is due to the fact that figures like Cyrus, the Persian, or even Alexander the Great later on, were simultaneously terrestrial projections of apocalyptic archetypes. Just as the author of the Apocalypse, John, proclaims the white horseman (Chapter 19), who will complete the fall of the harlot, Babel, so, the prophet of the Old Testament mentions the sun-hero* who, like an eagle, came flying down from the north and the east and toppled the power of Babylon.

There exists a hypothesis concerning John's Revelation that represents a certain parallel to the Deutero-Isaiah theory. Just as the second part of the Book of Isaiah is placed in a later age following that of Isaiah, so the Apocalypse is dated to an earlier time, preceding that of John. It is said that clearly an old Jewish text, which refers back to the period of the exile and the tension between Babel and Jerusalem and later had merely been infused a little with Christian elements, can be discerned in this last book of the New Testament.[11] In the final analysis, all these theories are nothing but the fruits of a materialistic world view. One who can take into account the existence of a supersensory world as representing the sphere of the archetypes and the possibility of prophetic seership as the reading in this realm of primal images, will comprehend that it was possible as early as the age of Hezekiah to speak of the Babylonian servitude and the New Jerusalem. He will also understand why, in the age of early Christianity, when Jerusalem was already destroyed and nothing of Babylon could be seen rising over the desert sands any more, the great dramatic antithesis of Babel-Jerusalem was nevertheless still placed before men's souls.

How is the riddle, posed to us by the duality of the Isaiah scripture, resolved? After having recognized the central and archetypal significance of Hezekiah's illness and recovery, we can decipher the solution from the biblical text itself. The initiation-like Hezekiah drama is placed at the dividing line that separates the two parts of the book, differing from each other so fundamentally. It must therefore also contain the secret of the duality.

Right in the middle of the report about the king's experience of rebirth, a psalmlike hymn is added, just as was the case in the descrip-

---

* The name 'Cyrus' comes from the Persian word that denotes the sun divinity.

tion of the Jonah destiny. Just as did Jonah, Hezekiah here describes his descent into the subterranean depths of death in a psalm of initiation. Conspicuously, Hezekiah's words are introduced by means of a most emphatic title: 'This is the book of Hezekiah, king of the Jews, who had been sick unto death and has recovered from the sickness of death' (Isa.38:9B). After the conclusion of the Psalm, only the recovery of the king and his conduct in regard to the Babylonian emissaries are briefly reported. Following the reply given by Hezekiah to Isaiah's ominous prophecies, the great second part of the Isaiah book continues directly as if the king, having returned to life, continued to speak: 'Comfort, comfort my people ... Speak tenderly to Jerusalem ... prepare the way of the LORD ... And the glory of the LORD shall be revealed.'

Attention to the subtle compositional indications of the biblical scriptures, makes evident that the title of the Hezekiah Psalm is relevant far beyond this Psalm. It seems to attribute the whole second part of the book to Hezekiah or it appears at least to bring it into a close connection with him. One thing is certain: the mightily intoned poetic and prophetic stream of the chapters that now follow (40–66) is presented to us as the divine abundance that has been unearthed through the Hezekiah drama. It matters not whether it originated from the soul of the king turned prophet or Isaiah's soul that had been drawn into the transformation, or whether it was the fruit of their co-operation. Now, the name Deutero-Isaiah becomes meaningful, although in a sense other than the customary one. Even if Isaiah, to whom the first part of the book is credited, did record the second part as well, he was no longer the same person when he wrote it; through the lightning flash of initiation that had struck next to him, he had turned into the 'other' Isaiah, the Deutero-Isaiah.

The whole Book of Isaiah now stands before us in its spiritual form and structure, ascending through the same four stages, Annunciation, Offertory, Transubstantiation, Communion, as does the Christian Eucharist. In the first twelve chapters, Isaiah is the great teacher. All the highlights of a higher knowledge, also those referring to the Messianic future, light up in the form of teachings. Then, up to Chapter 35, the mighty end of the world of ancient soul forces is unrolled as they are embodied by the nations other than the Jewish one. Vials of divine wrath a-plenty are poured out. The specific Isaiah-task of felling the tree of ancient vision is executed. The stage of suffering and sacrifice has to be absolved. Then, in the Chapters 36 to 39, a dramatic, historical report is inserted: the drama of the miraculous Easter-like salvation of Jerusalem and its king takes place before our eyes. That is the transubstantiation. Now, the breakthrough has been accomplished, the view is open. And in the wide stream of salvation prophecies unfolding in the Deutero-Isaiah chapters, the bright light of God already becomes visible which one days is to shine forth in the world of human beings. The sound of the glory, of the spirit light revealing itself, is intoned again and again: 'The glory of the LORD has risen upon you' (Isa.60:1). The picture of the heavenly Jerusalem, as beheld by the seer John at the conclusion of the Bible, shines forth above the paling, although not yet destroyed earthly Jerusalem: 'The sun shall be no more your light by day, nor for brightness shall the moon give you light by night; but the LORD will be your everlasting light' (Isa.60:19). The picture of the celestial city is intensified here also to the vision of the new creation: 'For behold, I create new heavens and a new earth; and the former things shall not be remembered or come into mind' (65:17). The Book of Isaiah, having undergone the transformation, the transubstantiation, concludes in the song of songs about a communion between heaven and earth.

CHAPTER TWENTY-THREE

The Reformation under Josiah: Purification of the Temple

After Hezekiah's death, many opponents arose against the prophetic impulse. The successors of the great king, Manasseh and Amon, not only did everything in their power to undo the reforms demanded by the spirit of the prophets, more than ever throwing open all gates to the infiltration of paganism. They also provoked persecutions of prophets. Along with Isaiah, many prophets and proponents of their spirit died a martyr's death.

In the year 622, however, a hundred years after the destruction of Samaria by the Assyrians, the flame of the prophetic impulse which had already appeared to have died down blazed forth mightily once more. King Josiah, having ascended to the throne in the year 640 as an eight-year old boy, became a disciple and adherent of the prophets' party from early on. When he had reached adulthood, he made himself into an instrument of Judea's religious purification in an even more radical measure than Hezekiah.

He started out with something that was more a symbolic act. He had Solomon's Temple freed of extravagant additions, thus restoring it to its original simplicity. Plans for the execution of a radical reformation may well have begun developing in Josiah's and his counsellors' minds, when a strange act of Providence came to their aid. During the construction work on the Temple, workmen found a sacred text dating from antiquity, a 'Book of the Law' (Torah), which, in the form of commandments given by God, expressed the inward-pointing Yahweh impulse in classic form as if it had been written down explicitly in order at this very moment to serve as the expression of the prophetic reformatory aims.*

In solemn manner, Josiah had the whole text read publicly in order that a relentless mirror of their religious behaviour be held up to the leaders of the nation and the inhabitants of Jerusalem. Then Josiah went into action. The religious life in all of Judea was thoroughly cleansed; all vestiges of heathen elements were eradicated.

One must read the brief biblical description concerning Josiah's purging in order to realize, in the first place, how inundated Jerusalem and its vicinity had become at that time with decadent pagan nature rituals and their atavistic effects eight decades after Hezekiah and Isaiah. It is astounding to see all that was possible within the closest confines of Solomon's Temple. Jerusalem appeared to have become the focal point of all religious streams of Asia Minor, which, now that their time was over, had only assumed even more intense and violent forms.

> And the king commanded Hilkiah, the high priest, and the priests of the second order, and the keepers of the threshold, to bring out of the temple of the LORD all the vessels made for Baal, for Asherah, and for all the host of heaven; he burned them outside Jerusalem in the fields of the Kidron, and carried their ashes to Bethel. And he deposed the idolatrous priests whom the kings of Judah had ordained to burn incense in the high places at the cities of Judah and round about Jerusalem; those also who burned incense to Baal, to the sun, and the moon, and the constellations, and all the host of the heavens. And he brought out the Asherah from the house of the LORD, outside Jerusalem, to the brook Kidron, and beat it to dust and cast the dust of it upon the graves of the common people. And he broke down the houses of the male cult prostitutes which were in the house of the LORD, where the women wove hangings for the Asherah. And he brought all the priests out of the cities of Judah, and

---

* It is very likely that Deuteronomy, the Fifth Book of Moses, is referred to with this book. More recent theology utilizes the story of its discovery to determine the date of origin of Deuteronomy in its own manner. It is believed that the priests under Josiah were themselves the authors of the text. Then, to bestow on it more emphasis, they invented the tale of the coincidental discovery in the Temple.

defiled the high places where the priests had burned incense
from Geba to Beer-sheba ... And he defiled Topheth, which is
in the valley of the sons of Hinnom, that no one might burn
his son or his daughter as an offering to Molech. And he
removed the horses that the kings of Judah had dedicated to
the sun, at the entrance to the house of the LORD ... and he
burned the chariots of the sun with fire ... And the king
defiled the high places that were east of Jerusalem, to the
south of the mount of corruption, which Solomon the king of
Israel had built for Ashtoreth the abomination of the
Sidonians, and for Chemosh the abomination of Moab, and
for Milcom the abomination of the Ammonites. And he broke
in pieces the pillars, and cut down the Asherim, and filled
their places with the bones of men.

Moreover the altar of Bethel, the high place erected by
Jeroboam ... he pulled down ...

Moreover Josiah put away the mediums and the wizards
and the teraphim and the idols and all the abominations that
were seen in the land ... (2Kings 23:4–8, 10f, 13–15, 24).

The newly pagan Jerusalem of Manasseh did not lack grandeur
and monumentalism. There was the entrance to the Temple area
with the golden chariot of King Helios in front of which the horses
of the sun reared up. In the Temple courtyard, the altars of the stars,
the zodiac and the planets stood in a circle. In the interior of the
Temple belonging to the god without image, the image of the goddess Isis-Astarte (Ashteroth), who bestows splendour and fruitful-
ness, was attended and decorated by the temple harlots who were
dedicated to her. All around the city on every high place, there were
temples and altars, towering stone sun monuments and trees dedicated to the moon, sites of ecstatic-orgiastic rituals. In the valleys,
for example in the Hinnom Valley or Valley of Hell, sites existed of
gruesome, black-magical blood sacrifices. The intoxicated urge of
Manasseh that expressed itself in such a return to the magic streams
of the past may have found support in the political condition of Asia
Minor.

Esarhaddon, who had become ruler of the Assyrians following the
assassination of Sennacherib, had made up for all the fluctuations of
Assyria's power, and through the conquest of Lower Egypt had

expanded the empire to its zenith. Since the time when King Ahaz had called for its support and since Sennacherib's attack on Jerusalem had failed in such a strange manner, Assyria, thus enlarged, remained the protector and ally of the small kingdom of Judah. Since support from Egypt for the purpose of doing damage to Assyria was no longer a consideration, the source of mistrust was eliminated with which the giant state had always looked upon the tiny nation it protected. Under Manasseh, Judah was safer than ever before. What could be more expedient from a political standpoint than to adapt itself in regard to religious activities as well to the rituals of the great heathen ruling empires?

Manasseh must in fact have succumbed to an infection from Assyria's ominous intoxication with power and blood-lust. He too is reputed to have sacrificed his first-born son on the gruesome Topheth, the fire altar of the black-magical Molech rite. And with what Caesarian feelings of triumph he must have watched the blood of the prophets and their followers run down the altars of the stars, erected by him, the son of Hezekiah!

As quickly as the last rise of the Assyrian power had occurred, just as suddenly followed its final collapse. Already during the rule of Esarhaddon's son Ashurbanipal (669–626 BC), Egypt again threw off Assyria's yoke; the powerful vassal kingdoms of the East rebelled one after the other. Above all, Ashurbanipal's death was the signal for the long-planned defection of Babylonia (625 BC). Nabopolassar, the founder of the neo-Babylonian kingdom, which was soon to replace Assyria in the latter's position as the leading power, allied himself with Media against Assyria.

Along with the sudden increase of Assyria's power into gigantic dimensions, the infatuation with paganism in Judah quickly subsided. This was why it was possible that after his early ascent to the throne, Josiah soon grew up as a disciple of the prophets. His reformatory efforts in the year 622 were benefited by what the signs of the time seemed to proclaim. Did not the fall of the giant, Assur, have to be an admonition for introspection? Did not the winds of war threaten especially to engulf the Holy Land and Judah, now that the battles of the allied Medes and Babylonians raged against Assyria? And would the approaching trials of destiny find the people inwardly armed?

Josiah's reformation, introduced with the reading of God's Law and the solemn attestation of the people, appeared for history as a mighty destruction of images. The followers of the prophets allowed nothing to remain of what could be a reminiscence of the cultic life up to now. They did not even stop before the ancient nature sanctuaries of the people, which, without particular leanings in the direction of other nations' religions, existed everywhere in the land. It was as if anything that was an external feature of religious life had to disappear. Henceforth, outside of Jerusalem, not only were there no longer any sites of worship, no priests were there any more. What did remain in that case?

Under Josiah, the prophetic impulse, pressing towards introspection, found its radical realization in that all religious life of the Jewish people was concentrated upon the Solomonic Temple, which had been restored to its original simplicity. This concentration in favour of an abstract introspection, the result of which was an early form of what has arisen in modern times as extreme Protestantism, actually represented a historical peculiarity. A whole world of religious practice was wiped out without people having anything to replace it with. Places of learning resembling the later synagogues did not yet exist; likewise, the profession of the scribes was non-existent whose concern it would have been that religious instruction be dispensed around the land. The people outside Jerusalem's confines had to become orphaned in a religious sense, for they were by no means mature enough simply to produce on their own the religious introspection striven for by the prophets. From an overall viewpoint, despite the land's small size, it was hardly possible for a person to make a pilgrimage frequently to the Temple in Jerusalem.

Josiah's definitely violent reformation would inevitably have resulted in an extreme setback, if the blows of destiny that could be termed the Golgotha of the Jewish people had not broken in now with full force. The purification from all pagan elements were like a bath that somebody, having received a harsh sentence, undertakes before he is led away to prison or his execution. The restoration of the Temple to its former simplicity took place only shortly before its destruction and resembled the words of dedication that the priest utters over the sacrificial animal bound on to the altar in order to receive the death blow.

With his iconoclasm, Josiah was actually the creator of that form of Judaism which, in the age following the exile, developed its abstract spirituality and religion and carried it out into the world.

The closer time moved to the end of ancient Jerusalem's existence, the more clearly recognizable a pattern became in the course of history, who, more than anything else, allows us to sense the structure of the archetypal sphere behind the outward appearance of events. It is the pattern of correspondences and homologies between the history of the Old Testament people and the earthly life of Christ as pictured in the New Testament. Both biographies, that of the people and that of the one individuality, follow the same spiritual laws, pass through the same stations of inner development. The only difference is that the circle is drawn more tightly from the first to the second biography: the circle of the god descending from heaven to earth.

In the life of Jesus it signified an important decision when, for the last time, he started on the solemn path 'up to Jerusalem' and bade a final farewell to the paradisal heavenly world of Galilee and its lake. When the spatial circle of his destiny was concentrated on Judea and finally upon Jerusalem, this signified the entrance into the arena of the last, extreme struggle. The solemn determination to the very end, the heroic tensing of will actually brought about a new and higher degree of incarnation for the Christ being. Seen from the viewpoint of the spirit, the entrance into Jerusalem was a powerful sealing of the physical incarnation, a last and most profound taking hold of and entering into the earthly and mortal corporeality. This was the reason why the sensitive souls of the people and disciples broke into hymns of praise when they witnessed actually quite a common scene of a man riding into the city on a donkey. For, there extended into them something of the theophanic flashes of light and play of forces that accompanied this humble event in the supersensory realm. They were touched by the Christ event involved in the Jesus happening. It was as in the case of the waters of the Pool of Beth-zatha where the angel remained invisible but the agitation of the waters that he brought about came clearly into view. Here, this agitation was represented by the ecstatic excitement of the populace.

We have discussed the Old Testament correspondence to the

entrance into Jerusalem. It is expressed in the miraculous events that took place in Jerusalem in Hezekiah's and Isaiah's time. The destruction of the northern kingdom and the deportation of the tribes dwelling in Galilee and Samaria had preceded this. The genius of the people had been forced to bid farewell to the etherically rich meadows and fields in the Palestinian north, contracting its circles to the stern wasteland of Judea. Together with the folk genius, the Christ being, having arrived in the folk sphere, made his entrance into Jerusalem. The sparks of spiritual beacon-flames and the effervescence of the soul world's forces drove off Sennacherib's troops who were besieging the city and illumined the souls of Hezekiah and Isaiah. Just as in the New Testament the sphere of forces surrounding the entrance into Jerusalem became visible through the death and resurrection of Lazarus, so, in the Old Testament, they became evident through the initiation-illness and recovery of Hezekiah.

In the first three Gospels the purification of the Temple is reported as the first deed which, taking extreme measures, Christ carried out after his entrance into Jerusalem. He turned over the tables of the money changers and drove the vendors and buyers out of the realm of the sanctuary. The correspondence to this in the Old Testament was the reformation of Josiah. It was the purification of the Temple that embraced the whole land and its people. Here too, the parallel extended into the deepest levels. When Christ drove the money-changers out of the Temple, he did not do this in order to restore the house of God to its sacred purpose. He resembled a forester who cuts a mark into the bark of a tree about to be felled. Through the purification of the Temple, Christ abandoned it to its destruction which did follow not long after this. So, the reform of Josiah was basically a process of preparing the people for their great destiny of sacrifice. Three decades later, ravaged Jerusalem stood in flames and the troops of Nebuchadnezzar razed Solomon's Temple to the ground.

In the New Testament, the events following the act of the purification of the Temple rushed towards the dark hour of Golgotha. The broad, all-encompassing implication of this outwardly unassuming event is announced in the three figures of Pilate, Herod and Caiaphas, who, like emissaries of three mighty streams of humankind, were participants and witnesses of the decisive moment. Where the Gospel points to single personalities, whole nations are represented in the Old Testament. The three great empires of the world, Assyria, Egypt and Babylonia, still linked shortly before in an artificial union by the grip of power, suddenly appeared in a new grouping. Assyria's star declined. With the help of Egypt, which only gave a faint impression of its former greatness, Babylonia usurped the world dominion of the Assyrians. Nineveh was destroyed. But then the Babylonians turned against Egypt too. The Assyrians were forced to fight together with them against the army of Pharaoh Neco. It so happened that the armies of the three powerful nations, who represented the world-historical background to the Jewish people's story of passion, collided on the battlefield of Megiddo, a site so pregnant with history. King Josiah, who, like the Assyrians, was compelled to fight with his troops in the ranks of the Babylonians, was killed in the battle (of the year 609). This sealed Judea's fate. First, it came under Egyptian sovereignty. Pharaoh Neco dethroned Jehoahaz, the son of Josiah, and took him along to Egypt as his prisoner. In his place, he appointed Eliakim, another of Josiah's sons, as king, in whom he believed he had found a willing tool, and changed his name to Jehoiakim. Then, however, the Babylonians were successful in defeating Egypt.

Nebuchadnezzar (604–562), the son of Nabopolassar, completed the work begun by his father and with a few powerful strokes drew together the neo-Babylonian kingdom, which in power and greatness was equal to the Assyrian kingdom of Esarhaddon. When the king of Judah, Jehoiachin (the son of Jehoiakim) in the belief that he still had Egypt's support, refused the payment of tribute to the Babylonian ruler, Nebuchadnezzar's army approached. Jerusalem was forced into surrender. In the year 597, the king along with many thousands of Jewish leaders, was deported to Mesopotamia.

Still, Jerusalem remained. A third son of Josiah (Jehoiachin's uncle) was installed as king by the Babylonians under the name Zedekiah. Again, Judah sought protection against the Babylonians from Egypt and dared loosen itself from Nebuchadnezzar's rule. The final blow of annihilation then fell. A new terrible siege commenced around Jerusalem. The city was taken, plundered for a month, destroyed and finally burned down (in the year 587). Solomon's structures, including the Temple, fell victim to the flames. King Zedekiah was forced to watch his sons being brutally torn to pieces. Then his eyes were put out as if one intended to extinguish the bright spirit flash of the Messianic nation. Along with all the inhabitants of Judea who had any cultural significance at all, he was led in chains to the alien land of Babylonia. The Golgotha hour of the Jewish people had been fulfilled.

CHAPTER TWENTY-FOUR

Jeremiah and Baruch: Passion

How the gold has grown dim,
    how the pure gold is changed!
The holy stones lie scattered
    at the head of every street.
The precious sons of Zion,
    worth their weight in fine gold,
how they are reckoned as earthen pots,
    the work of a potter's hands!
    ...
The crown has fallen from our head;
    woe to us, for we have sinned!
For this our heart has become sick,
    for these things our eyes have grown dim,
for Mount Zion which lies desolate (Lam.4:1–2, 5:16–18).

The lamentations and prophetic utterances by Jeremiah allow us to listen to the melody of the great passion of the Jewish people and their pain. Jeremiah was the individuality who, owing to his profound sensitivity, could turn his soul into the focal point of all the troubles and suffering which had afflicted the Messianic people. When the agony over the darkness of night engulfing humanity evoked from his soul the plaintive words: 'Cursed be the day on which I was born! The day when my mother bore me, let it not be blessed!' (Jer.20:14), the soul of the people went through its Gethsemane hour.

On the northern edge of the city of Jerusalem, not far from the Damascus Gate, is a large, dark natural grotto. Since the entrance to the extensive subterranean halls, which are called Solomon's Quarries, is located quite close to the cave, it too most likely belongs to the system of gorges and grottoes which long ago lent ancient Jerusalem its character. According to tradition, this is the grotto in which Jeremiah, his soul weighed down by suffering, gave vent to his songs of lamentation and prophecies. It is not a far-fetched thought to feel that one is standing in a place that is an Old Testament correspondence to the Garden of Gethsemane in the New Testament.

It was under Josiah's rule — the king was still young and the great reformation was only in a quiet state of preparation — that a youth of the party of the prophets was noticed who observed silence most of the time but from whose soul shone forth unusually mature benevolence and wisdom. He descended from an ancient lineage of priests from Anathoth, a place located in the region of the former high sanctuary of Gibeah. The people among whom he lived must have realized with what fervour of feeling young Jeremiah followed all the events of that time, although he kept away from the strata- gems of the reformatory party members who, together with the royal court, were laying their plans in Jerusalem. In 628 BC, at the age of about twenty, the same age as the king, Jeremiah made his first appearance.

Strange occurrences caused Jeremiah to break his solemn, heavy silence. Presentiments that resembled fleeting, disappearing memories arose in his heart like the breath of a distant, sacred age. He felt as if he knew from his innermost experience how closely connected the sphere of divine forces and beings had once been to humankind. Merely the fact that present-day humanity had moved so far away from the ancient nearness to God filled his whole being with a deep sadness akin to homesickness.

This feeling of a loss suffered by all humankind fashioned in him the fertile ground for vividly experiencing the stirring destinies of the present. He could have remained standing on the sidelines in complete resignation. Yet again and again, he did not yield to this danger. Did not the knowledge that there had once existed a living bridge between the world of God and the world of men place an obligation on him? Each time when his will would have been translating into action, the memory-like presentiments became perceptible in his mind. He felt as if he beheld himself in ages of long ago, standing at sacred altars involved in priestly actions, ever and anew rebuilding the bridge between above and below which threatened to collapse. Then it seemed to him as if he would only continue a former activity if he were to go before the people and proclaim to them the divine presentiments that he harboured within. As yet, the knowledge of his youthfulness held him back. The tension, however, in which he participated in the events of the age, became ever greater.

Still, the day came when the call of the inner experience became so clear and peremptory that he could no longer resist it. Perhaps the turn in his life when he was twenty-one was the reason. He himself described how the divine call within his inner being made itself heard:

> Now the word of the LORD came to me saying,
> > 'Before I formed you in the womb I knew you,
> > and before you were born I consecrated you,
> > I appointed you a prophet to the nations.'
> Then I said, 'Ah, Lord GOD! Behold, I do not know how to
> > speak, for I am only a youth.' But the LORD said to me,
> > 'Do not say, "I am only a youth";
> > for to all to whom I send you you shall go,
> > and whatever I command you you shall speak ...'
> Then the LORD put forth his hand and touched my mouth;
> > and the LORD said to me,
> > 'Behold, I have put my words into your mouth'
> > (Jer.1:4–9).

From the beginning, the prophetic faculty in Jeremiah was linked to the feeling of former initiate and priestly destinies. The underlying destiny, reaching back far into the past, and the predestination of the Old Testament prophethood arrived at awareness in feeling. He brought it with him through birth that he is pictured as an old man, when in fact he emerged with his divine task while still a youth. In the classic paintings of the prophets with which Michelangelo framed the ceiling of the Sistine Chapel, Isaiah is depicted as a youthful, fiery spirit, who looks up into the future-bearing heights with an enthusiastic expression. Jeremiah, the old sage, on the other hand, lets his head, adorned by a long beard, rest heavily in his hand, and oppressed by grief and pain he looks down to the ground. Isaiah still possessed a young spirit when, in old age, he stood by the bedside of King Hezekiah. Jeremiah's soul sank its roots deep into the ground of the past when the youth broke his silence.

The grief and pain in Jeremiah's soul did not remain dull and blind. It did not culminate in hopeless desperation. In absorbing the suffering of the people completely into himself as if it flowed out of his own destiny, the prophet became capable of discerning its meaning. He recognized that just as there is night between two days a painful age of darkness and distance from God must lie between humankind's former closeness to God and a future new illumination. And in the misfortune that drew together over Jerusalem, he beheld the approach of history's inevitable dark hour of midnight. Thus, he became the indefatigable preacher who admonished his people patiently to take upon themselves their suffering and bondage. More than through the word, he was effective through the example of his own being. Anyone who was not blinded by fanaticism could see how Jeremiah himself obeyed this admonition, although the heart of no other person bled as much as his. Supportive forces like those of a benevolent father who, with tears in his eyes, consoles others, emanated from him.

The hardness of the hearts around him, however, was great. Only a handful took seriously the destiny of the people. Even among the adherents of the prophetic movement there were many who believed that they could determine the will of God through the radical ritual reformation and thus change destiny. The selfless willingness to empty the cup of suffering completely was hardly to be found anywhere. And the illusion of being capable easily to escape the nation's hour of Golgotha all too often disguised in the garment of courage that impatiently designated anybody as a coward who, like Jeremiah, was convinced that one had to resign oneself to the misfortune.

After the decline of Assyrian power in 625 BC, the political illusion increased greatly, but as long as Josiah reigned, it appears that Jeremiah held back with his proclamations. After all, he could not participate actively in the ritual reform which was not free of fanaticism and soon was usurped by the egotism of Jerusalem's high priests. Only after Josiah's death in 609, under Jehoiakim's rule, Jeremiah came forward more forcefully. Perhaps it was only then that he, the forty-year-old, transferred his dwelling place from Anathoth to Jerusalem.

The idea of an alliance with Egypt, which had already caused such self-deception and confusion in the northern kingdom prior to the latter's destruction, began to exert its power of delusion on Judah as well. Jehoahaz, who initially had succeeded his father to the throne, had not allowed himself to be deluded by the hope placed in Egypt, although he was not a follower of the prophets' faction. He had been dethroned by Pharaoh Neco and had been led away to Egypt as a prisoner. Jehoiakim, king through the grace of Egypt, actually was hostile to the prophetic movement. Under him, a setback in the religious reform occurred similar to the one under Manasseh after Hezekiah's death. His mania for construction, whereby Jerusalem was once more to acquire a new appearance, brought an end to the puritanical simplicity and sternness of Josiah. It was inevitable that this pomposity also encroached upon the rituals.

No longer could Jeremiah formulate his sermons of the divinely willed inevitability of suffering and decline in a consoling manner, he now had to word them in a militant way. Thereby he risked his life. Often, he resorted to a pictorial, dramatic action in order to indicate to the people what was imminent and to admonish them to practice introspection. Thus, he once called together a number of elders and priests in the Valley of Hinnom at the site of the gruesome Molech altar, and before their eyes smashed an earthen flask. With this action, he not only placed a symbol of the threatening destruction of the kingdom of Judah before the people, but more than that, revealed the apocalyptic image of the mighty approach of a power that could not but shatter all ancient blood ties and communal forms.

When, in the year 597, the storm of the Babylonian army had already swept over Jerusalem for the first time, Jeremiah still did not find an audience. He again brought a symbolic picture before the leaders of the people. He himself had placed a heavy yoke across his shoulders, not only to indicate the impending bondage of the people, but to call for the patient acceptance and endurance of the bitter destiny. He preached to deaf ears. One from the ranks of the prophets themselves tore the yoke from his shoulder and broke it in two before their eyes.

Jeremiah's path was that of a martyr. In the stations of his suffering, the passion of the folk genius, concealed behind the external
aspect of events, found a human reflection. When he held up the symbol of the broken flask to the people in the Valley of Hinnom, it was the
priests who took hold of him and, painfully put in the stocks, he was
exposed to the ridicule of the gaping crowd by one of the city gates.
This was only one example of the tortures that were inflicted on him
constantly.

Through no form of spite and persecution could Jeremiah be
silenced any more. And since he was not alone in his efforts, his lips
were not silent even when he was thrown into the dungeon. One of
the helpers who stood by him was Baruch. If we knew only what the
Book of Jeremiah tells about him, we would imagine him as nothing
but the prophet's scribe. We shall see that he was more than that.
When, under Jehoiakim's rule, Jeremiah was held prisoner for some
duration, Baruch recorded the prophetic addresses and hymns that he
had heard from the mouth of Jeremiah and read them to the people in
the courtyard of the Temple. This caused great excitement. Finally, the
book was taken out of Baruch's hands and brought before the king.
Jehoiakim's reaction could only be Caesarian fury. He tore one page
after the other out of the reader's hands, cut it into bits and threw
them in the fire. By a miracle, the king's command to kill Jeremiah
and Baruch was not obeyed. Again, by another miracle, Baruch was
able once more to write down all the divine words that already had
seemed lost.

When Nebuchadnezzar's army had conquered Jerusalem in the
year 597 and had humiliated Judah with the deportation of many
noble Judeans, people really should have begun to listen to
Jeremiah. For what he had foretold had now actually taken place.
Yet, the report that the Babylonians had departed because they had
heard of the approach of an Egyptian army fuelled the old illusions
even more vehemently. Even Zedekiah, whom Nebuchadnezzar had
appointed king, was soon won over to the idea of joining in with the
Egyptians. Despite the urgent warnings by Jeremiah, he concluded
an alliance with the Pharaoh against Babylonia. Right away,
Nebuchadnezzar's troops were at hand and threatened to besiege
Jerusalem.

Despite this fact, the pro-Egyptian faction did not give up. It was decided to do away with the relentlessly admonishing one. Men from the party of the prophetic reform movement lent themselves to raising the accusation of high treason against Jeremiah. They claimed that they had caught him just as he was about to desert to the Babylonians and threw him into a dungeon from which nobody returned alive. Jeremiah would have perished there, if Zedekiah, who was by no means as certain as the agents of the Egyptian alliance had made it appear, had not fetched him secretly in order to ask his advice. The king did not dare let him go free completely, but he at least placed him in less severe confinement. Immediately, Jeremiah began anew to utter his prophetic warnings and admonitions. Now his opponents forcefully gained control over him and threw him into a well filled with mud.

Another helper of the prophet emerged from the background. The Ethiopian, Ebed-melech, who occupied a position of some rank at the king's court, brought Jeremiah, who was already struggling with death, back to life.

In the meantime, Jerusalem's fate ceaselessly ran its course. The increasingly perilous trials of Jeremiah seem to reflect the approaching catastrophe. The Egyptian relief army could not help. Again, Zedekiah, who had heard that Jeremiah had been saved, sent for the prophet. Jeremiah advised him to surrender to the Babylonians, for avoidance of the catastrophe was by no means possible any longer, only a mitigation of its severity. The king did not have the courage to prevail against the fanaticism of the people around him. The siege increased in severity. Finally, the Babylonian troops broke through; the pillage of many weeks ensued, the total destruction and burning of the city, the slaughter of Zedekiah's sons, his blinding and the people's deportation to Babylonia.

Nebuchadnezzar ordered that Jeremiah be spared, perhaps because he had found out that Jeremiah had unceasingly protested against Judah's affiliation with Egypt. The biblical report shows us the prophet in the vicinity of Gedaliah, the governor, who had been installed by Nebuchadnezzar. Gedaliah was close to Jeremiah in spirit. It is possible that the Babylonian king's choice fell on him on the prophet's advice. It was like calling to mind a sacred time and destiny when, since Jerusalem was no longer inhabitable, Gedaliah transferred his seat to the ancient holy Gibeah heights of Mizpah, where the tabernacle had stood until the days of Solomon and where the tomb of the seer Samuel appeared to be the grave of a whole world of divine grace.

The spell of the Egyptian illusion was not even broken among the pitiful remnant of the Jewish people who, robbed of all their leaders, had to fall back to an indigently vegetating rural existence. Thus it came about that Gedaliah and Jeremiah, who could have taken up leadership over the external and the inner life, only met with rejection. Even now, when he shared all deprivation with the remaining populace, Jeremiah did not cease his admonitions to accept the difficult fate. He could not prevent those in sympathy with Egypt from hatching a plot; they murdered Gedaliah and fled to Egypt with the majority of the Judeans who as yet had not been deported to Babylonia. Jeremiah kept faith with his people, regardless of how brutally they acted toward him. He even joined in the flight to Egypt which he had done his best to prevent.

Now, nobody remained in the land who could have kept alive the spark of the future. The failure of all his fervent efforts and the utter submergence of the Messianic nation into the darkness of an alien land must have weighed heavily on the soul of the prophet. The second book of the Maccabees shows us a moving scene: Jeremiah, who, unbeknown to the others, had saved the most sacred treasures of the Temple from the flames, travels with the fleeing people on the path of Moses' journey in the opposite direction to Egypt and secretly hides the holy symbols in the rocky gorges of Mount Nebo, from whose summit Moses had once beheld the Promised Land when he led his people out of Egypt into their homeland. Was this not a final burial of all hopes? No, it was just this that gave Jeremiah the strength to empty the cup of suffering and pain to the last drop so that at least he could fathom the meaning of this misfortune and could know that an Easter morning would one day have to follow the night of Golgotha.

It is reputed that in the end Jeremiah was stoned by his own people in Egypt. His martyr's death was no worse than all the suffering that he had lived through already, since, through all loneliness and persecution, he maintained the consciousness, which he knew coincided with the consciousness of the folk spirit itself.

Jeremiah is the classic example for the fact that true selfless pain does not diminish the soul but makes it great. Hardly any other among the Old Testament prophets has been experienced in such a human way encompassing all humankind. There exist a great number of traditions that ascribe to his life's destinies a much wider sphere of action and horizon than the Bible allows us to discern. Perhaps this does really indicate periods of his life of which we know nothing otherwise. Quite certainly, what comes to light through them is that, especially in Jeremiah's case, extending far beyond the spatially limited external biography, the folk genius' sphere of destiny was perceived.

If one takes these traditions into consideration, either as imaginative accounts of soul-spiritual facts or as indications of unknown journeys, then, Jeremiah is the first in a sequence of great wanderers who, beginning with that time, were at pains to bestow breadth and momentum to the spiritual life of humankind. One must place the figure of Jeremiah, coming to life in these reports, beside such travellers as Pythagoras, Apollonius of Tyana or Paracelsus in order properly to sense what was developing in it.

In the life of Pythagoras (*c.* 582–490 BC), who was young when Jeremiah was an old man, the motif of the wanderer, which in the prophet's life only became slightly visible through mythological mists, appeared clearly on the physical plane. In both their lives, one can clearly see how it is the impact of destinies extending across from former lives which urges them on with a cosmopolitan drive into the wide world.

After he had been a disciple of Thales and other great teachers in the Greek cities of the coast of Asia Minor, Pythagoras was guided by his destiny into the realm of the mysteries of Tyre. In the temples on Mount Carmel, in front of which Elijah had called down fire from heaven three hundred years earlier, the priests of Baal-Adonis initiated him for three years into their secrets. A ship, on which he once sought refuge without knowing its destination, brought him to Egypt. He is reputed to have been a pupil of Egyptian temple wisdom for over two decades. Then, when the armies of the Persian king, Cambyses, conquered Egypt (525 BC), Pythagoras found himself among the prisoners who were deported to Babylonia. There, he is still supposed to have encountered the teachers who transmitted the wisdom of the mystery centres to the Jewish prophets and leaders during their exile. Only then, did Pythagoras himself become the founder of a mystery school and community in southern Italy and Sicily.

In most instances, the broad cosmopolitan radius inherent in the first half of Pythagoras' life is attributed by the traditions, which emerged in all the different locations, to the latter part of time in Jeremiah's life. A very strange legend exists, for example, in England, considered nevertheless by many as an indication of historical facts. It relates that, following King Zedekiah's blinding and deportation, Jeremiah is supposed to have made a pilgrimage with two of the king's daughters to England and Ireland in order to wed them to the kings of the land. According to the same traditions, the oldest British and Irish kings supposedly descend from the Jews.* One of the daughters of Zedekiah, Thara or Tamar by name, was given by Jeremiah in marriage to Eochaidh, the legendary first king of Ireland, the other to the one who was king of the Britons at that time. The name Tara Hill, which exists to this day near Dublin, is traced back to the fact that Queen Thara, the daughter of Zedekiah, was buried there.

As fantastic as such traditions may sound, it would be equally wrong to deny them any historical content from the first. Spanning oceans and continents, the mystery streams of antiquity without question had much more lively contact with each other than historical research has hitherto been willing to assume. In particular the Hibernian mysteries of the Irish island were certainly not only known to Asia Minor already in very ancient times but also had a relation to the wisdom centres over there. It has also often been recognized[1] that in the legendary story of a priest of the Hibernian Apollo, named Abaris, who supposedly appeared before Pythagoras in order to bring him a gift of his god, the fact is concealed that emissaries of the Hibernian mysteries journeyed in those early times to the wisdom centres of the south. Though there may be even another form of truth to it, the saga of the Jewish descent of the first Irish and British kings could well be an indication that, concerning especially the Messianic future of the tribe of Judah, there may have existed an understanding

---

* The twin sons of Judah, Joseph's brother, were Perez and Zerah. David and all the subsequent kings of Judah descended from Perez. Two of the five sons of Zerah are supposed to have become the forefathers of the British and Irish kings; the ancient Irish line is traced back to Calcol, the old British ruling dynasty to Dara.

between the prophetically knowledgeable individuals in the Holy Land and Hibernia's initiates. And it is certainly an idea worth pondering to imagine that in his concern for the seemingly lost Messiah secret, Jeremiah, the witness of the Jewish doom, could have turned to the Hibernian mysteries, an idea which, even if thought through only as a possibility, would illuminate something of the inner aspect of the events of those days.

Frequently, there are also indications that Jeremiah is supposed to have appeared in Central Asia. And these wanderings are occasionally placed in that span of time left open by the biblical Jeremiah text between the calling of the prophet under Josiah and his appearance under Jehoiakim. The ancient Rabbinical schools give an answer to the question, why, during Josiah's reform, people did not turn for advise to Jeremiah, by indicating: 'Besides, Jeremiah was not present at that time because he had departed to bring back the ten tribes.'[2]

Strangely enough, alongside the biblical indications that Jeremiah remained in Judea with the remnants of the people and then went with them to Egypt, a tradition also appears that he accompanied those who were led away to Babylon and had been a comforter of the people in exile. Apocryphal writings show Jeremiah in Babylonia.[3] One wonders how it is possible that such contradictory descriptions could have come about concerning the last major part of Jeremiah's life, especially since the biblical report was well known in the circles from which these writings of Baruch originated. The question is not solved by concluding that only one of the two possibilities can be correct, that Jeremiah either remained in Jerusalem or went to Babylonia. What appears to be an irreconcilable contradiction must here be an indication of deeper secrets. It also does not completely explain the origin of the reports contradicting the biblical narration to say that even if Jeremiah remained behind in Jerusalem, he was present in thought, feelings and through letters in the midst of those banished to Babylon. It becomes evident in all clarity that Jeremiah was experienced as a personality in whose biography there still existed many secrets because in its background profound mystery contents were pressing toward revelation. People instinctively felt that the radius of this human being's destiny was exceedingly great embracing all the ancient, cultural realms. And perhaps this great individuality, imbued

with the experience of former lives on earth, did after all travel on journeys which the Bible does not mention.

The mystery backgrounds of Jeremiah's life is also revealed by the
figures who emerge nevertheless as companions and souls linked
with this utterly lonely individuality since earliest days: Baruch and
Ebed-melech. The Bible always veils mystery elements carefully and
mentions the two aides of the prophet almost incidentally so that they
can almost be overlooked. But the above-mentioned apocryphal text
allows one to sense the deeper secrets of destiny linking Jeremiah
with Baruch and Ebed-melech in wondrously clear, poetic imagina-
tions.

Reminiscent of fairy tales, but in a transparent style, we are told
how Jeremiah and Baruch climbed atop the city wall at night, following a divine command, when the Babylonian army was surrounding
Jerusalem. They heard the sound of trumpets and beheld angels
approaching with burning torches to lay fire to the city. Henceforth
they knew that even if it appeared outwardly as if the Babylonian
troops were the destroyers of Jerusalem, in reality it was God himself
who used the enemy as an instrument and allowed his sanctuary to go
up in flames.

At the same time, it was revealed to Jeremiah what to do. With
Baruch, he went into the Temple to save the sacred signs and imple-
ments. Before their eyes, the earth received them. And they entrusted
the key of the Temple to the rays of the sun when day had dawned. As
they were still sitting and weeping, pouring sand on their heads and
chanting dirges, the enemy troops already entered the city, causing
destruction.

Before daybreak, Jeremiah had sent Ebed-melech, the Ethiopian,
into a vineyard outside the city to fetch figs for the sick. Baruch lay
down in a grave in the Kidron Valley and angels came to show his
soul, unencumbered by the body, the secrets of all the events in mighty
apocalyptic pictures. Jeremiah himself left for Babylon together with
the imprisoned people.

During the heat of noon, Ebed-melech arrived at the vineyard, sat
down in the shadow of a fig tree to rest a little, and fell into such a deep
sleep that he only awakened after sixty-six years. When he returned to
the city, with the basket still filled with fresh figs, everything appeared
strange and unknown to him. To no avail, he searched the streets and

houses in which his people had lived until an old man told him about what had taken place and that since long ago Jeremiah was suffering with the people in the foreign land. Ebed-melech then realized that a miracle had happened to him.

An angel guided him to the grave where Baruch still rested. When the latter noted his friend's approach, he rose and they embraced each other with tears of joy. By an eagle, they dispatched a letter to Jeremiah in Babylonia, announcing to the banished people that the hour of their return had come. Just as Noah greeted the dove which proclaimed the end of the Flood with the olive branch, so, in the midst of the waiting people, Jeremiah greeted the eagle.

Jeremiah led the people back to Jerusalem and in the courtyard of the Temple, a time ensued of singing hymns of praise and gratitude. Something deeply moving then occurred. Just as he had ventured with Baruch and Ebed-melech to the altar, Jeremiah sank to the ground, his soul leaving the body.

> And a voice resounded: 'Do not bury him! He still lives and
> his soul will return to his body' ... So they remained around his
> tent for three days and held council at what hour he might
> arise. And after three days, his soul returned again into his
> body. (Rest Baruch 9).

The old prophet arose and broke into the overwhelming hymn of a great Messianic prophecy. Hard of heart, however, the people objected and stoned the newly risen one. In deep sorrow, Baruch and Ebed-melech buried Jeremiah.

Especially in this text, it is important to go beyond the initial superficial impression of something fantastic. The text itself does, after all, make it evident that it does not mean to describe physical historic events. What it does convey to our feeling is how Jeremiah was surrounded and enveloped by soul images of bygone initiation experiences. In the cases of Elijah, Jonah and Hezekiah, the Bible itself shows us how these individualities were drawn into processes of dying and re-arising which were true memories of former initiations. In the biblical description of Jeremiah's destiny, we only behold the martyrdom and suffering which were like a constant knocking on the portal of the mystery of death and resurrection. On the other hand, the apocryphal text presents the prophet, under the shadow of the martyr's imminent death, in soul images directly undergoing death and rebirth after three days. In passing through the after-effects of initiation, Baruch and Ebed-melech here stand by Jeremiah's side. They are more than his accidental helpers. They share the karmic sources from which originates his greatness of spirit.

Ebed-melech, the Ethiopian, was carried across the periods of doom by a mystery sleep. The motif of a long sleep forming a bridge from one epoch to another indicates experiences through which memories of former earth lives arise in the soul which thinks that it is awakening from a deep sleep.

Baruch is described to us as one who, under the impression of the doom befalling the people, awakened to apocalyptic vision. Even if previously he had been merely an aide and scribe of the prophet according to the Bible's report, now the fruit of former soul destinies blossomed in him; he himself turned into a prophet who beheld the Apocalypse. It is as if he could see into the events taking place in the present with spirit organs that were once awakened in his soul through initiation in ages of the distant past. It was then that he was laid in a grave and while his body appeared dead, his soul had arisen to body-free vision in the spirit worlds. Now, a number of fateful, shattering events had taken place which made possible an inner connection to the former experience of being placed in a grave. The imaginative text describes this as if Baruch had spent the period of the exile in a grave where he was constantly informed by angels concerning the events that were taking place.

What we have noted in the figure of Hezekiah, namely, that the circle of illumined spirits in Israel-Judah during the period of external decline extended far beyond the great number of the biblical figures of the prophets, we now see again in Ebed-melech and Baruch. Just as a whole number of personalities pass through the story of the Passion in the Gospels about whom we hear far less than about the disciples, but who appear like emissaries of other mystery streams, such as Joseph of Arimathea, Nicodemus, Simon of Cyrene, so, other great unknown individualities joined the prophets, who took the place of the Apostles, in the story of the people's passion. Baruch in particular, under whose name two lengthy apocalyptic books have been preserved, accompanied the events prior to and after the Golgotha-hour of the Jewish nation like a guest from a mystery centre gifted with clear vision.

The Hebrew name 'Baruch' is synonymous with the Latin name

'Benedictus' which means 'Blessed One.' Whether we recall the great significance which Benedict of Nursia had for Western Christenity as the founder of the Benedictine Order, or whether we have in mind the figure of Benedictus, who strides through Rudolf Steiner's Mystery Dramas as a messenger of the mysteries, in either case, it allows the wealth of figures of Jeremiah's age to light up from a specific aspect when we realize that, in Baruch, a Benedictus figure of the Old Testament also belonged among them.

The mystery backgrounds that become visible in the spatial radius and the human surroundings of Jeremiah's life were those of the people themselves. Higher destinies had guided the people during the age of the Patriarchs into the distant foreign land and bestowed on it an overall human significance, especially in their hour of greatest degradation. Loftier destinies now also turned the people into a focal point for such a rich abundance of illumined spirits.

CHAPTER TWENTY-FIVE

The Babylonian Exile: Spirit Encounters

A peculiar law of history is in our opinion expressed in the fact that in all periods, the life of certain nations and cultures received its tension and stamp through a north-south duality and polarity. The Greek civilization was born in and out of the tension between Athens and Sparta; the culture of Germany is unthinkable without the mutual fructification of the southern and northern Germanic tribes.

The most concentrated and archetypal realization of this duality was exhibited by the nation of the Old Testament, namely in the initially united and then dividing polarity of the northern Israelite and southern Jewish tribes. Here, lending it even more emphasis, the historical and human differentiation had its supportive basis in the classic polarity between Galilee and Judah. And something of the inner mathematics of world history itself can be glimpsed at work when it is observed how the separated Israelite duality was destroyed, also by a dual world turned hostile, namely the Mesopotamian culture which had split apart into the Assyrian and Babylonian realms. The northern Israelite kingdom fell victim to the northern Mesopotamian Assyria; southern Israelite Judah found its end under the blows of the southern Mesopotamian neo-Babylonian kingdom.

Through many centuries, Assyria had slowly but surely developed into a vast empire and had definable structures within the chaos of nations and races which had originated in Asia Minor since the long-lost flowering of Babylonia in the time of Gilgamesh. During the summit of its power, Assyria's armies had crushed the kingdom of Israel. Then, the surprisingly quick ascent of Babylonia had ensued. The southern Mesopotamian rulers took advantage of the difficulties which Assyria encountered when it became important to hold together this widely extended kingdom composed of the most alien elements.

Almost overnight, Assyria fell from its position of power. A hundred years after the Assyrian troops had destroyed Damascus and Samaria, Nineveh too lay in ruins.

At the time when only the southern part of Israel had remained, the south of the Mesopotamian region became the starting point for the formation of the imposing neo-Babylonian kingdom. The fact that Judah was in the end so utterly destroyed by the Chaldean armies was a misfortune which was not really due to Nebuchadnezzar's plans of conquest but originated from the blind fanaticism of the pro-Egyptian Jewish faction. The first defeat of Judea and the deportation of a select group of Jewish cultural representatives which followed in the year 597 BC would have sufficed for the plans of the Babylonians. And it is clearly discernible how, after the fall of rebellious Jerusalem ten years later, it was only out of necessity that Nebuchadnezzar, having hesitated for a month, gave orders for the total destruction of the city and Temple as well as the sweeping deportation of the people.

Assyria and Babylon certainly differed as to their spirit. The Assyrians, a militant nation of conquerors with a sinister will nature, were of a violent, cruel ruthlessness in their quest for power. All religious and cultural elements and aspects belonging to the mysteries were for them only means for the purpose of ruling. In Babylonia, the ancient Mesopotamian and Sumerian basis with its sensitive spirituality still made itself felt distantly. As opposed to the will nature of Assyria, Babylonia possessed a strong impulse of feeling. On that account, however, it was less capable of creating firm and clearly outlined political structures. In contrast to the harsh tendencies of social forms in the north, the life of southern Mesopotamia was also determined by amorphous, relaxed elements.

The founders and rulers of the neo-Babylonian kingdom were bearers of cultural rather than military impulses. Above all else, it appeared as if, coming from the mythical ages of the Babylonian construction of the Tower, an unceasing will to build continued to live in them. When Nabopolassar began with the reconstruction in his capital city of the mighty step-sided tower, Etamenanki, he himself lent a hand together with his sons, Nebuchadnezzar and Nabushumlishir, in laying the foundation stone and the initial construction work. And on the quite numerous tablets of praise that we have of the forty-two-year reign of Nebuchadnezzar, we find any number of inscriptions in which the king recounts his accomplishments in regard to constructions. Inscriptions that commemorate his great military successes do not exist. Babylonian life was also filled with the decadence and corruption which had long since overtaken the Oriental mystery streams. There was no longer any question of a pure spiritual striving. Everything was dominated by the ambition and power struggle of the ruling class. The ambitions of the rulers, however, were directed towards building up an imposing and all-embracing cultural accomplishment. We must picture Nebuchadnezzar to ourselves as a complete cultural despot.

The sources of spiritual life had already become much too sparse and uncertain to impose Babylonian culture on the subjugated nations. Therefore, it was sought to concentrate in Babel and the other centres of the land everything possessed by these nations of religious and cultural traditions and arts in order then to make them subservient. Just as Imperial Rome later on gathered together as in a Pantheon the rituals and mysteries of the conquered lands in order to increase the divine radiance of the Caesars, so it appears to have been in Nebuchadnezzar's Babylon. The foreign gods were not done away with. Instead, it seemed possible to place them in the service of Babylonia's own god, Marduk.

When alien tribal groups were led away from their homeland and settled in Mesopotamia, the main purpose was therefore not always to utilize them as slave labour but to make use of their intelligence and cultural abilities. This is particularly true of the banished Jewish people in Babylonia. Especially during the first deportation in the year 597, those Judeans had been selected from the start who were suited for a cultural fermentation and enrichment of Babylonia. It is significant that the prophet Ezekiel was among those who were deported at that time. It was only from the second, much more extensive deportation that greater numbers were most likely pressed into slave labour for the colossal constructions of the king. In general it was not in the interest of the ruling nation to treat the Jews like slaves and to hold them back in an unfree condition without property of their own. On the contrary, it appears that although they had hardly been able to take any of their native possessions along, a number of the banished Jews eventually attained to a certain standing in Babylonia in the course of time.

The world of Babylonia could not have helped but make an impression on the Judeans deported there, despite the fact that they were filled with sorrow over the loss and destruction of the sacred homeland and that a faith devoid of images stood before their souls as an ideal.

Once before, when it only began to develop into a nation and to have a history, Israel had been submerged in a great and abundant temple world, namely in Egypt. There, however, it had been enveloped by a surrounding world which, having still originated from ancient clairvoyance, was more a creation of the gods than of human beings. In Babylon, the impression of imposing greatness could not be separated from that of a strange mixture. Although deriving now only from traditions, elements of revelation and creations of the human will were fused together. The feeling that they were confronting an impure union of divine and human aspects, of heavenly and earthly things soon caused the apocalyptically visionary souls of the prophets to speak of the 'harlot of Babylon.'

Nevertheless, the city of Babylon in particular, which had at that time been newly reconstructed in ostentatious greatness, must have aroused the amazement of the Judeans when they arrived in the land of the conquerors after a trying journey of many months. The excavations directed by Koldewey shortly before the First World War brought to light the countenance of Nebuchadnezzar's capital city from the desert sands. And the segment of the monumental avenue 'for the procession of the great Lord Marduk,' which has been erected in the Pergamon Museum in Berlin, gives many people in our time an idea of what the Jews beheld during their exile.

This magical 'street of Babel' ran from the eastern side southward along the towering complex of Nebuchadnezzar's Palace. It was twenty-three metres (75 feet) wide, paved with huge stone slabs and framed on both sides by a wall that was seven metres (23 feet) high. In the walls on either side, an endless sequence of lions, majestically moving along and magically embedded out of raised enamel tiles, met the eyes of one moving southward in the procession. Egypt's avenues of the sphinx along which moved the processions of the priest in ancient time from Luxor to Karnak, were bordered by marble sculptures of rams which, in static divine tranquillity, were encamped in the wide open landscape of the Nile, emitting sentiments of primal, eternal paths and laws. The lions on the walls of Nebuchadnezzar's street with their glowing eyes, their teeth showing in their wide open mouth, were images that struck into people the terror of a life filled with dangers and tensions. A magic almost bordering on the naturalistic emanated from them which had to be faced with forces of courage. Only the unearthly gleaming colours of the tile glaze bore the senses beyond the sensory sphere. Between the yellow of the lions, wondrous shades of blue and green spread out. A lapis lazuli blue of a most intense hue was interrupted by still, white lotus flowers.

The processional path, which made such a powerful impression because the walls did not allow any view of the surrounding world, led to a great double-structure, the Ishtar Gate. Bulls and dragons resembling serpents and griffins made of bronze stood in front of the gate and, like the lions of the street-walls, were fitted as regularly repeated tile-relief figures into the broad frontal wall of the pylon structure. South of the Ishtar Gate the magic avenue continued to the great Marduk sanctuary, E Sag Ila.

In the northern part of the city, underneath the Hill of Babel crowned by a momentous figure of a lion, a royal palace was situated. And in the area marked off by the tall city wall, constructions abounding in towers, the mighty temple complexes around the broad towers of the ziggurats, represented actual cities within the city. By contrast to this magic splendour, how humble the Solomonic structures that had been Jerusalem's pride must have seemed to the Judeans! What were the sparse gardens north of Mount Zion, even if they were called paradises, in comparison to the world wonder of the Hanging Gardens of Babylon, which Nebuchadnezzar had constructed for his Median wife, Amytis? And what admirable mastery over the elements could be observed in the extensive constructions of walls, dams and canals, through which the waters of the Euphrates River, slowly flowing along in a mythical, dreamy manner, were directed either over desolate areas or held back from marshy terrain!

With few insignificant exceptions, the Jewish exiles nevertheless were not overcome by the world of Babylonia and did not allow themselves to fall under its spell. Instead, the miracle occurred that only now, in the alien land, did they really find themselves.

In general, the deportation of subjugated nations resulted in a process of denationalization, a separation from the folk genius holding them together. This was particularly the case because the folk soul experience was in most instances bound tightly to the landscape and nature of the homeland. By virtue of the topographic condition of Judea, Judaism, which was not rooted so much in the ground of its region, could not really lose its folk unity through being uprooted. The northern tribes, whose own nature had been strongly tied to the ethereally rich world of Galilee and Samaria, had been completely robbed of their cohesiveness through the Assyrian deportation and had become assimilated in the predominating nations. The Judeans, on the other hand, fared like a person with little awareness within the narrow circle of his home and who comes truly into his own only when he is led out into the wide world.

The rich cultic and ceremonial life around Babylon's temples and palaces did not represent a temptation for the Jewish character. It was so alien to the faith striven for by the prophets and their followers that instead it rather emphasised the contrast and thus led to self-awareness. In beholding Babylonia's temples, it was even easier for the Jews to adhere to their own faith which lacked temples and to give it expression, than it had been at home where those who lived in Jerusalem had been able to cling to the Temple of Solomon, whereas the others could only avail themselves of the abstract idea of inwardness.

It was different in the case of what was nurtured in Babylonia as a form of science, still closely bound up with religious teachings. In this area, Judaism received an important stimulus from its rulers. The Jews were not compelled to adhere to the teachings of Babylonia's religious life; it also seems that hardly any pressure was put on them to participate in the Marduk and Ishtar rituals. On the contrary, it appears that since it was not unusual to engage foreign teachers, a number of leaders of the prophetical Jewish life were welcomed and listened to in the Babylonian schools for scholars. The Babylonians also possessed an institution which was suitable for fulfilling a requirement of Jewish life. It was the profession of scribes that seems to have been organized somewhat like certain Jewish prophetical schools.

Since any ritualistic activity was impossible for them and on principle was far from their mind since the destruction of the Temple in Jerusalem, the Jews were in need of developing a similar profession. It was the exile in particular that confronted them with the necessity to give increased attention to the doctrinal, theological side of the religion handed down to them by their fathers. As a means of religious exercise, only the word remained to them, be it in the form of the prophetic sermon or by reading and interpreting the holy scriptures. This was why the foundation was laid in Babylonia for the principle of the synagogue, the house of teaching, which, after the reconstruction of the Temple, was to bestow its form on the religious life of the Jews in the homeland as well as in foreign countries. That this was done on the model of and perhaps even in co-operation with Babylonian cultural life can be discerned from the fact that at the end of the exile the Jews actually had at their disposal the profession of scribes which they designated with the same term as was customary in Babylonia. The Babylonian scribes were called *sapiri,* the Jewish ones, *sopherim* (*grammateis* in the Greek New Testament). Whole branches of imaginative Jewish theology, abounding in pictures and legends, seem to have found their origin in Babylonia through the exchange with the local temple scholars. It is therefore significant that an important segment of the ancient collections of teaching and stories is called the 'Babylonian Talmud.'

The exile turned the Judeans into a religious unity capable of life. And what had to be experienced initially as a tearing apart of the folk community, the separation of the culture-bearing part from the dependent rural population, in the end result proved to be an opportune destiny. Those who had been led away were a select group and therefore found it easier to produce the national and religious cohesiveness which Judaism after the exile actually possessed.

The real secret of the Babylonian captivity, however, is found on a deeper, hidden level. In the foreign land, the Messianic people were to experience an extraordinarily important spiritual encounter. Rudolf Steiner has placed this encounter before us as a concrete fact. He states that the cultural leaders of the Jews who had been banished to Babylonia met and listened to an initiated teacher there, who, in the spiritual guidance of humanity, radiates the brightest light. The same individuality, who in ancient times was active as the original Zarathustra, the lofty teacher of sun-wisdom of the oldest Persian cultural period, who was later to reincarnate in the figure of Jesus of Nazareth as the human bearer of the Christ entity, became the teacher of the prophets in Babylonia.

In the sanctuaries that were known to and frequented by the wise men among the Hebrews during the captivity, ... in the Mystery-centres in the regions around the Euphrates and the Tigris ... the reincarnated Zarathustra was teaching. ... in his incarnation as Zarathas or Nazarathos he became the teacher of the captive Jews who knew of the sanctuaries existing in those regions.[1]

An important supplement of this communication is that 'in the centres of learning in ancient Babylon' this Zarathas or Nazarathos had also been 'the teacher of Pythagoras.'

The great teacher is mentioned numerous times in the ancient traditions. Immediately, however, a probing uncertainty occurs in these mentions which make it obvious that veils of secrecy have always been woven around this figure. Clement of Alexandria, who still presented his Christian theology from the knowledge of the Greek mysteries, said in connection with the contemporary text of a neoplatonist: 'In his book about the Pythagorean symbols, Alexander reports that Pythagoras is reputed to have been a disciple of the Assyrian, Nazarathos. Some say that this was Ezekiel; but this is not correct as we shall show ...'[2] In his *History of Nature* (30.1), Pliny says that Zarathas had been a magician from Media.

The confusion of Nazarathos with the prophet Ezekiel, which Clement of Alexandria rejects — the detailed refutation which he promises has unfortunately not come down to us — is encountered frequently in the legendary Jewish traditions: 'According to the view of a scholar of history, Pythagoras received the secret [of soul migration] from the prophet Ezekiel who was his teacher. In one of his epistles, one famous teacher of the church positively contends that Pythagoras had been a Hebrew'[3] At first glance, it sounds like vain fantasy on the part of the rabbis to claim Pythagoras' teaching and Greek philosophy as their own in this manner. In most cases, the supposed encounters also cannot coincide in time.* And yet, in their frequent distortions, these traditions are an indication that the Jewish prophets in Babylonia together with the Greek philosophers were

---

* The Jewish teachers at one point have Plato, who was not a contemporary of Jeremiah, say the following: 'I was in Egypt with Jeremiah. At first, I mocked him and what he said. In time, however, I received the insight that his words were those of a living god. Then I told myself that he was a sage and prophet.'[4]

disciples of one and the same teacher. The great gathering of spirits all over the world, which made Buddha, Confucius, the great spirits of Greece and the prophets of the Old Testament into children of the same age, had had a centre in that mysterious Mesopotamian teacher that could draw together forces from distant peripheries. Hellas and Judah met face to face: guided there by the most diverse destinies, they journeyed through whole continents in order to listen to an unassuming teacher, who yet towered over humankind.

If, in the midst of the exile's deprivations and misery, this spiritual encounter, bestowed there on the Jewish people, is seen shining forth, attention is also drawn to a wondrous figure of Providence in the totality of the Israelite folk destiny. Twice, and both times in a foreign land towards the end of a banishment,* the mysterious figure of an initiate emerged out of the background in order to be the teacher of the Messianic people. At the end of the Egyptian captivity, Moses, and through him the whole nation, became disciples of Jethro in the Sinai region; toward the end of the Babylonian exile, the prophets and through them all of the people became pupils of Nazarathos in the teaching centres of Mesopotamia.

The submerged connection between the Israelite-Jewish development and a wisdom-stream of humanity is revealed in the above. We have said that in Moses a metamorphosis of the first Zarathustra impulse was active and that in an incarnation of that age, in or behind Jethro, the Zarathustra individuality may perhaps even have intervened in the Israelite folk-destiny.[5] Ezekiel and the other prophets of the exile had to transform what they received in the form of wisdom from the reincarnated individuality of Zarathustra into piety for the people. A people and a human being encountered each other again and again on their journeys. Each seemed to seek the other. And behind the paths of the people, who were twice led through misery and unhappiness into an overwhelmingly alien land, the hidden impulse seemed to be that their genius felt attracted by a light that it sought and wanted to follow. One day in the future, a real finding of each other was to follow all these searchings and their encounters. This original teacher of humankind, the most mature human soul, who,

---

* The encounter between the Israelite prophets and Nazarathos must fall into the last part of the exile, if Pythagoras, who, according to tradition, only arrived in Mesopotamia in 525 BC, still found the great teacher present there.

from outside, had spoken through Jethro to Moses and through Naza-rathos to the prophets, would himself incarnate among the sons of David in order to prepare and offer himself up as the vessel to the divine being who was striving towards becoming man.

The whole of pre-Christian history is a searching and gradual find-ing that took place between humanity and the Christ-being descend-ing from heaven. The seeking and finding between the people of the Old Testament and the Zarathustra individuality are the human reflec-tion and preparation for that superhuman striving to come together. In Babylon, the prophets actually saw and heard the one towards whose renewed coming they directed the inward eyes of the people, for it would be the last preparation of the path for the coming of the Christ himself.

At one point, Rudolf Steiner characterized the stage, represented by the age of the prophets and specifically the spiritual encounter in Babylonia in the course of the Old Testament, by explaining further what he had said concerning the age of Moses and David (see page 00). In the Old Testament, the path is outlined which the sun wisdom, turned into earthly wisdom, traced in a step-by-step reflection toward the sun in ancient time. Just as Moon, Mercury and Venus are inter-mediates between earth and sun, so the reflecting wisdom, which had become terrestrial and was to become sunlike again, underwent a Moon, Mercury and Venus stage. In Egypt, the children of Israel were submerged in an after-effect of the ancient sun wisdom and thereby had received into their earthly wisdom the impulse of reflection. The Moses wisdom represented the passage through the moon stage. The Davidic culture was an Old Testament version of the Mercury or Hermes stage.

> On the returning path towards the Sun the wisdom of Moses was to advance to the Venus stage. Hebraism reached this stage at the time when the Moses-wisdom ... was destined to unite with an entirely different element, with a stream of wis-dom that had come from the other direction.

> Whatever rays back from the Earth into space encounters Venus on the path to the Sun, and during the Babylonian cap-tivity the wisdom of Moses encountered the wisdom that had made its way over from Asia and was presented in a modified form in the Babylonian and Chaldean Mysteries. This contact

was made during the time of the Babylonian captivity. Like a
wanderer who, having started from the Earth with a knowledge of what the Earth is, had passed through the region of
Mercury and arrived in the region of Venus in order there to
receive the light of the Sun falling upon Venus, so did the wisdom of Moses absorb what had proceeded directly from the
sanctuaries of Zoroastrianism and was being continued in a
modified form in the Mysteries of the Chaldeans and
Babylonians. It was this that the Moses wisdom received during the Babylonian captivity, thus assimilating wisdom that
had made its way to the region of the Euphrates and the
Tigris ...[6]

[We see] how the wisdom of Moses made still closer contact
with the Sun wisdom during the time of the Babylonian captivity, when Zarathustra himself, then bearing the name of
Zarathas or Nazarathos, was the teacher of the Hebraic
Initiates during the captivity.[7]

A significant light falls on the strength of feeling and soulfulness of
the prophetic proclamation if we recognize in it the Venus stage of the
spirit of the Old Testament. After the regions of Moon, Mercury and
Venus there follows the approach of the Sun's reflection itself. The new
sun stage was realized when the Zarathustra individuality, the eternal
bearer of the ancient sun wisdom, was himself incarnated among the
Hebrew people in Jesus of Nazareth and, as Jesus, fashioned himself
into the vessel of the sunlike Christ-being.

The rule of the neo-Babylonian kingdom was only of brief duration.
Hardly half a century had passed since Nebuchadnezzar's armies had
destroyed Jerusalem, when he who took the power over the Orient
away from the successors of Nebuchadnezzar made his entrance into
Babylon (539 BC). Just as the Babylonians had done with the Assyrians,
the Median-Persian group of nations, who had already co-operated in
the fall of Assyria, now dealt with the Babylonians.

For a decade and a half already, the nations of Asia Minor and,
along with them, the Jews enduring the exile, had observed with suspense and expectation the ascent of the eagle who now settled down
upon Babylon and took possession of it. From the beginning, the figure of the Persian King Cyrus had been seen and experienced as sur-

rounded by a mysterious divine mission. Had one of the gods perhaps descended in him once more to the earth? Or whence originated the victorious, youthful sun-radiance of his nature? For the childhood and youth of Cyrus were surrounded by miracles and secrets. Motivated by strange dreams indicating his successor, Astyages, the king of the Medes, had given his daughter Mandane, his only child, in marriage not to a Mede but to a man from the ranks of the subjugated Persians by the name of Cambyses. When, however, Mandane gave birth to a son, obeying additional prophetic dreams, Astyages ordered the child to be abandoned in the mountains. The shepherd who was supposed to slay the infant raised it in place of his stillborn son. Even at an early age, his royal nature emerged in the boy, Cyrus. Destiny favoured him and when his true origin had become known, he soon ascended to rulership of Persia and, overthrowing his grandfather Astyages, he liberated his country from Median servitude. In 553, Ecbatana, the capital of Media, fell into his hands. After the surprising victory of Sardis (546), where he defeated the armies of the neighbouring kingdoms who fought against him under Babylonia's leadership, Babylon anticipated an attack. The banished Jews awaited him as their God-sent liberator.

When, in 539, greeted by the priesthood of weakened Babylon itself, Cyrus entered the city of Nebuchadnezzar, he aroused the amazement of the world by the attitude with which he began his reign over the Orient. He did not allow the rich conquered city to be plundered and destroyed. Instead, he went to the temple to pay homage to the gods of the land and to offer sacrifices to them. He bowed down before Marduk in a way hardly ever done by the Babylonian rulers. He did not raise the claim that the Persian gods had been victorious over the Babylonian deity. In the foreign name of Marduk, he recognized the sun spirit whom he as a Persian served under a different name and he could say to those he had vanquished: Your god himself has called me. Alongside Susa and Ecbatana, Babylon was declared a residence of Cyrus, who now unified an empire that was larger than Assyria had once been.

A closeness to people and a humaneness appeared on the scene with Cyrus, the like of which the Orient had not known since the days of the Utopian, Akhenaton. Without forfeiting even the least of his victorious impetus, Cyrus employed a universal positivity and justice which nowhere led him to become an oppressor of an alien religious movement. Just as he was capable of recognizing and acknowledging the spiritual reality of the Babylonian god, Marduk, so he appears to have had an understanding for the Yahweh worship of the Jews whom he encountered in Babylonia. For, as early as in the year 538, he gave the order to prepare for reconstruction of the Temple in Jerusalem and dispatched fifty thousand Jews to their homeland to bring to realization the goals connected with it.

This aroused great jubilation among the exiles. They saw Cyrus as their liberator and thought they recognized in him an early dawning actualization of the Messiah mystery. Yet, nothing had really happened except that, instead of the Babylonian, a Persian alien rule had commenced. Those who were returning to Judea were basically Persian colonists in their own homeland and were not sent there for their own sake, but for the purpose of the reconstruction of a destroyed city and its temple. Through the quake of the events of the day still roaring past them, the Jewish people sensed the dawn of their Easter morning.

The figure of Cyrus is truly a great historical riddle. We owe the reports concerning him to the great historians of Greek antiquity, above all to Herodotus and Xenophon. Is it not surprising that the Greeks could not do enough to sing the praises of Cyrus, even though his closest successors threatened to engulf the Greek world in the dark waves of Oriental nature and plunged it into the hardships and battles of the Persian wars? At a time when the tempests of these wars still re-echoed in the minds of men, the great Greeks wrote down their numerous epic descriptions of the fates and deeds of the Persian, Cyrus, which, like Xenophon's *Cyropaedia*, were actual precursors of the later Alexander romances and, similar in manner to these, sang the praises of a ruler as if he had been a god.

A solution to the puzzle of the enthusiasm which Cyrus' figure aroused among Jews and Greeks, despite the fact that he was the despot of Judah and the forerunner of the Greek enemies, is probably only found by considering glance to the mystery of the great teacher, to whom the Jewish prophets listened shortly before Cyrus' appearance there, and whose pupil, later on, was Pythagoras. At the time when Cyrus commenced his majestic flight like an eagle, a wondrous blossoming of cultural life was bestowed on his homeland of Persia. A teacher appeared among the Aryans of the Iranian mountain country in whom the spirit of the original Zarathustra, the inaugurator of the ancient Persian culture, seemed to have returned. He appeared in the name of Zarathustra himself and was active as a reanimator and reformer of ancient Zoroastrianism. In a profusion of marvellously poetic hymns, he expressed the ancient solar wisdom of life in contemporary language and thought forms. The Gathas of Zarathustra, the oldest part of the Avesta that has come down to us as one of the most beautiful fruits of Oriental wisdom, are in fact poetical works that are contemporaneous with the writings and songs of the biblical prophets. Their creator belongs in the first rank of the great spirit gathering which distinguished that period across the earth.

The problem of Zarathustra or Zoroaster has confronted historical research for ages. The Greeks saw in him a figure of long ago. On the other hand, it is clear that the author of the Gathas of Zarathustra belonged to the sixth century before Christ. Certainly, this contradiction is not resolved by delegating the opinion of the Greeks into the realm of fables. One will have to think of two figures: the first Zarathustra, and a towering personality of the sixth century who was either an incarnation of the Zarathustra individuality or at least one who renewed the spirit of Zarathustra.

We probably do not go wrong if we assume that Cyrus had been a disciple of this great spirit, be it that this Zoroaster was still alive and himself stood by the side of the rising royal genius as his teacher and advisor, or that the great reformatory movement already existed for several decades and Cyrus was educated along its lines. If Cyrus was in possession of a living knowledge of Ahura Mazda, the great spirit being of the sun who through millennia was journeying to the earth, the king's humaneness and positivity towards the various religious movements of antiquity is understandable, because, in that case, he was able to see through the countenances of the gods as through masks and behold the countenance of the One who was to come. From this direction, the Messianic radiance that the Jewish prophets saw in him becomes comprehensible.

We have arrived at a question which probably contains one of the greatest, but also loftiest problems of the history of the last pre-Christian centuries. How do the two individualities, the Zarathustra of the Persian Gathas, and Nazarathos, the initiated teacher of the prophets and Pythagoras, relate to one another? The idea that it could be one and the same personality is intriguing and indeed cannot be rejected outright. Perhaps, before coming to Babylonia towards the end of the exile, Nazarathos was active in Cyrus' homeland and only moved to the Mesopotamian temple sites after Cyrus, having commenced on his victorious campaign, had rushed ahead of him into the centre of the world of that time. It may also be that the Zarathustra individuality had already called to life the mighty Iranian reform movement from which Cyrus received the direction of his impulses, either in a previous incarnation or through a disciple inspired personally by him, before he then incarnated as Nazarathos. We shall leave this question open. But even though it has not been answered, it allows us to sense the spiritual backgrounds of mysteries which work through the history of the final part of the Babylonian exile as well as the beginning of Cyrus' reign.

CHAPTER TWENTY-SIX

Ezekiel: Premonitions of Easter

Like the fourfold sequence of the Gospels in the New Testament, the fourfold arrangement and sequence of the 'great' books of the prophets, which the canon of the Old Testament places at the head of the prophetic scriptures, is no coincidence. As with the Gospels of Matthew, Mark, Luke and John, with the Books of Isaiah, Jeremiah, Ezekiel and Daniel, the figure of a cross is outlined that points to the four heavenly corners of the soul realm.

Initially, one might assume that the arrangement of the four texts was simply according to the chronological sequence of the figures of the prophets. Isaiah belongs to an age more than a hundred years preceding the Babylonian exile. When Jerusalem was destroyed, Jeremiah had already been active as a prophet for forty long years and survived well into the era of the exile. Ezekiel, younger than Jeremiah by more than two decades, belongs among those who, ten years before the destruction of the Temple, were deported to Babylonia together with King Jehoiachim. He appears to have died only a short time before Cyrus conquered Babel. As the Bible reports, Daniel was led to Babylonia at the same time as Ezekiel, but he was at that point still a small boy. About twenty years younger than Ezekiel and without having made the return journey, he was still a witness of Cyrus' reign.

The chronological order of the first prophetic scriptures is, however, unimportant in comparison to the spiritual order expressed in its sequence.* Only because the age of the prophets was an epoch of archetypal history in which the Spirit of the Age itself inscribed cosmic-mathematical signs and figures into the course of history, the historical and the spiritual structure synchronize. The karmic universality that

---

* It is obvious from the arrangement of the twelve shorter prophetic books, where age is ignored, that the Bible's concern was not directed to the chronological sequence.

characterizes the whole Old Testament prophetism is here brought to a fundamental denominator. If, through their previous earth lives, the abundance of prophets is like the gathering of messengers from all of humanity's mystery streams, Isaiah, Jeremiah, Ezekiel and Daniel seem to stand in the history of the Old Covenant like the emissaries of four great spiritual kingdoms coming from the spiritual West, South, East and North. And the four texts named after them represent a step-by-step path similar to the one we saw emerge in the structure of the Book of Isaiah, namely, as if a sacred rite were being celebrated that passes from the annunciation to the offertory, transubstantiation and communion.

With clear objectivity, lifted above the level of his personal life, Isaiah spread out the wealth of his wisdom that was permeated with the fire of heaven. He was the great teacher and herald. At the time of Jerusalem's destruction and the Babylonian captivity, when Jeremiah, Ezekiel and Daniel were living, people must have looked back to Isaiah as to the one who, out of inexhaustible riches and as if he were a last mediator of the divine wisdom, had for the first time unfolded the universal prophetic picture. Regardless of whether his hymns and words existed as written texts or whether they were still passed down orally from generation to generation, they were taken like a primal gospel of prophetic teachings.

If Isaiah was the teacher, Jeremiah was the sufferer. What streamed out of his lofty soul in feelings was more important than the content of his preaching. In him, everything was experienced in the most personal sense. In his life, he exemplified for his people the pain that was suffered by the folk genius of the people itself. In him, the nation's path of sacrifice became human, even though the majority of people deluded themselves concerning the true nature of the events in which they were involved. The offertory followed the annunciation.

Jeremiah was an offspring of an old lineage of priests, banished, however, since Solomon's age. He descended from Abiathar who, together with Zadok, was high priest in David's time. Since Abiathar protested against the violation of the right of the first-born incurred in Solomon's ascent to the throne, he was banished to Anathoth, with only Zadok remaining as high priest. Ezekiel also came from a very ancient family of priests. His forefather, however, was Zadok, the first high priest in Solomon's Temple. Thus, as a member of the hereditary

Temple aristocracy of Sadducees, he occupied a high priestly office when, together with the other prominent and noble members of his people, he was selected by Nebuchadnezzar for the first deportation. Ezekiel was the priest among the four great prophets. The mood and attitude that he had fostered when he still conducted the sacred rites in the Temple of Jerusalem accompanied him into the foreign land. In the face of the Babylonian temples and the opulent rituals that were observed there, he let his mind wander back to the courts and halls of the sanctuary at home, and in his spirit he participated in the prayers and offerings that rose to heaven there. For ten long years, he could thus participate. As he did this, however, he could see in his spirit how the dark clouds of doom massed together more and more over the holy height of Moriah until, finally, word reached him that his cherished Temple along with the whole city had fallen prey to the flames.

Then, the great multitudes of the second deportation arrived in Babylon and Ezekiel had to work in their midst. Through the priestly nature of his being and activity he himself had to be a temple for the people deprived of their temple. From the prophetic images beheld by his soul, he fashioned a sacred temple in the minds of his people. He proclaimed the great Messianic turning point, the longed-for transformation. The new Jerusalem, the new temple, became the content of his prophecy. In the midst of suffering, he henceforth pointed to salvation, to the true home in the midst of the foreign land. The prophetic words of Ezekiel must have affected the banished people during the exile as if the offerings on the altar shone forth in the aura of the divine presence. The teacher and the sufferer had been followed by the priest, annunciation and offertory had been followed by the transubstantiation.

Like Joseph once upon a time in Egypt, Daniel rose to royal honours at the king's court of alien Babylonia, grafting the spiritual impulse of prophetic Judaism on to the decaying tree of Mesopotamian life. He was the apocalyptic spirit among the prophets, the bearer of a royal courage of spirit who even dared venture into the midnight-dark sphere of the opposing forces in order to raise the enchanted gold of the spirit there. The boundary between this world and the world beyond was lifted and the apocalyptic communion of spirit experience opened as the last stage of the mighty fourfold phenomenon.

The prophetic scriptures of the Old Testament by no means display a contrived structure. On the contrary, they represent a most unusual form of poetry within world literature because they alternate between hymnlike, poetic highlights and frequently still confused and unformed sequences of obscure utterance. It is as if a trace of the atavistic-ecstatic form of prophecy, customary in the earlier prophets' schools of Israel where men spoke in tongues, was still recognizable in the remnant of formlessness attached to these texts. Out of the deep, subconscious levels of the prophets' souls, the images and words poured forth as if, in them, divine, spiritual beings of a higher world were proclaiming their thoughts and will. The I-imbued light of consciousness illuminated what thus emerged, received it and coined it in human thoughts and words. Thus, harmony and accord held sway between the religious and artistic productivity of the prophetic personality and in what streamed into them as the imaginative and inspired element of inward vision and hearing. Nevertheless, on occasion, the wealth of what was being received appears to have overtaxed the conscious, thought-filled faculty of receptivity. Then, an oracle-element of twilight filtered into the prophetic words.

The 'I' of the prophets was conscious enough to become the expressive interpreter of the revelation, yet it was still sufficiently delicate not to stand in the way in a distorting manner. We owe it to this peculiar supersensory origin of the prophets' scriptures that, unintentionally, in the structure of the texts, as if deriving from the mathematics of the higher world, compositional elements and architectonic figures are reflected. This is the reason that in the priestly style of the Book of Ezekiel, more clearly than in that of Isaiah, there comes to light the fourfold stage which also comprises the spiritual consistence of the first four prophetic scriptures. Here too, proclamation, offertory, transubstantiation and communion follow one another.

The awakening of Ezekiel, the priest, to prophetic vision resembled the opening of a curtain. By the waters of Babylon, the mighty cherubic visions flared up before him. He read in them as if in an open book.

On the Babylonian temples, Ezekiel had everywhere observed the monumental, sphinx-like figures which, completely or partly, expressed the mystery of the world's fourfold element through the symbol of the four beasts: lion, eagle, bull and human being. As a member of the family of high priests, he was aware of the beings of

the cherubim, represented in the image of the four beasts, members of
the loftiest angelic hierarchies who bear heaven as if at the four corners of a mighty supersensory realm. In the Holy of Holies of
Solomon's Temple, they had been depicted in visible form, carrying
the invisible throne of the deity above the Ark of the Covenant. And
just because he knew about the image of the cherubim and the four
beasts as the only secret and wordless replica of the invisible realms
of being, concealed to the eyes of all human beings by the curtain in
the Temple of Jerusalem, the Babylonian sculptures and reliefs again
and again must have given rise in Ezekiel to the feeling of profana-
tion, a betrayal of the mysteries. The incompatibility between the
Babylonian temple world and the spirit of the Jerusalem Temple
became glaringly clear to him.

Then the moment arrived when his inner eye opened. And what
did he behold? The spiritual reality, of which the Assyrian and
Babylonian life created grandiosely externalized images, whereas it
was symbolized chastely and mysteriously in the secret room behind
the veil of the sanctuary, appeared itself in its overwhelming radiance
of fire. The cherubic sphere flamed toward him, in which the images
of the four beasts permeate each other and everything is in powerful
activity and motion, as if it were a rushing of wings and a blazing of
fire and lightning. A multiplicity of fiery wheels, which 'were called in
my hearing the whirling wheels' blazed forth, penetrating each other
in sparkling turns and pulsations (10:13). These wheels are organs of
vision. As he awakened to his vision, Ezekiel simultaneously beheld
the soul organs of his own supersensory being with which he saw.
They turn like whirls of light. The eyes of the cherubim met with the
spirit eyes of visionary man. The cherubim are beings who consist
totally out of the fiery light of spirit vision, 'full of eyes in front and
behind' (Rev.4:6). Ezekiel beheld a most profound cosmic mystery in
recognizing that the figures of the cherubim carry the throne of the
highest divine being. That which is eternally at rest is borne by the
sphere knowing no sleep and no stillness, the sphere where all movement and activity of the universe originates — all the way to the suns
and constellations, themselves nothing but cosmic phenomena of the
cherubic fire wheels become visible. Only one who struggles through
the fire of evolution and consuming true life can and may sense the
divine throne's world of rest.

Thus, behind earthly misfortune and doom that come into being where the sparks of the wheels of divine life fall, there dwells the concealed, resting and never wavering meaning, the will of the Enthroned One. In the mighty cherubic vision, Ezekiel beheld how burning coals from the sphere of the evolving elements were scattered over Jerusalem (Chapter 10), and he comprehended the throne-secret even behind the trials of his people. This was the mighty Gospel-vision which was shown to him as if behind a curtain drawn away. That was the content of the book in which he read but which, as represented to him in the spirit experience, he had to eat and take into his being like fire in order to understand it.

With the idea of the historical effects emanating on the earth from the sparkling fire of divine life, the floodgates of the spirit were opened from which the weighty second part of the Book of Ezekiel poured forth. As yet, Jerusalem and the Temple were still standing. Ezekiel, however, saw how on the altar of events involving humanity a great sacrificial act was beginning. In the fire of cosmic wrath, a whole world would end. The hour of Golgotha had come for the nation of the Promise, and all around, the waves of disaster were engulfing the old decaying world.

It has often been thought that one could divide the prophets into heralds of salvation and doom. This is a quite unrealistic abstraction. The end of the world stood before the seeing soul of all the prophets as the great sacrifice that had to precede the transubstantiation. The universal principle of death and resurrection had been deeply inscribed into their own being, and they therefore could recognize the expression of divine purpose and will of salvation even in the decline of their people.

In Ezekiel's case, the transition from prophecies of doom to hymns of grace occurred in an especially classic manner. Ezekiel was, after all, the prophet of transformation, of the great priestly transubstantiation that God would one day bestow on humankind's history in the future. He was the prophet of doom until the Temple fire and the deportation of the whole nation had actually taken place. From then on, his sight penetrated through the fiery clouds and beheld the future salvation.

The transformation and salvation of the world would take its start in the human being. A time eventually was to come when humanity's hardness of heart, which resulted in the extinction of all ancient spirit faculties — Isaiah still had to bring about an intensification of this extinction — would lose its oppressive force. Thus, the deity said: 'A new heart I will give you, and a new spirit I will put within you; and I will take out of your flesh the heart of stone and give you a heart of flesh' (Ezek.36:26).

The view towards the Easter morn of humankind, of which the liberation of the people could only be a first instalment and symbol, enlarged into a mighty vision: 'The hand of the LORD was upon me, and he brought me out by the Spirit of the LORD, and set me down in the midst of the valley; it was full of bones ... there were very many upon the valley; and lo, they were very dry.' The prophet had to go before the gruesome field of death as the messenger of new life: 'So I prophesied as I was commanded, and lo, as I prophesied, there was a noise, and behold, a rattling; and the bones came together, bone to its bone. And as I looked, there were sinews on them, and flesh had come upon them, and skin had covered them.' And the prophet had to call upon the wind to breathe its breath into the still lifeless bodies: 'So I prophesied ... and the breath came into them, and they lived, and stood upon their feet, an exceedingly great host.' (37:1f,7f,10)

The Easter drama of transformation in which the prophet was included in his vision threw open the portals of a whole world. Now, Ezekiel stood in the midst of a new creation, in a cosmos of salvation, partaking in the abundant blessings of a mighty communion.

A lofty figure of an archangel, fashioned as if of pure bronze, appeared to him, in his hand the line of flax and a measuring reed, and he walked before him, determining the dimensions of the new Temple and the new Jerusalem. And lo, everything that he measured came into being forthwith in brilliant glory. The portals, courtyards and halls of the sanctuary arose.

> And behold, the glory of the God of Israel came from the east;
> and the sound of his coming was like the sound of many
> waters; and the earth shone with his glory. And ... the glory of
> the LORD entered the temple by the gate facing east, the Spirit
> [wind] lifted me up, and brought me into the inner court; and
> behold, the Glory of the LORD filled the temple. (43:2–5)

Sacred order spread out around the new Temple. Finally, the stern figure with the measuring reed led the prophet once more to the gate of the Temple and from the sacred rock (did not antiquity secretly call it the stone of libation?) under the threshold, there flowed a spring of water that spread out in the land into a wide river, at the banks of which grew the most wondrous fruit-bearing trees. It was as if the lost paradise with its life-giving streams had newly arisen. All that was lost returned. Around Jerusalem, the land took the form of rays into the harmony of the twelve tribes, which, in outer life, had long since been torn asunder and scattered to the winds. Finally, the holy city with the twelve gates stood before the visionary eye: on each gate, the name of one of the twelve tribes was inscribed, and the city itself received its new name: 'Here is the LORD.'

The misunderstanding that the prophet finally turned into the organizer and lawgiver of the theocratic constitution which the people were to adopt after their return, has been linked particularly to the last part of the Book of Ezekiel. It is believed that the specifications, which are indeed worked out in all details, were intended directly as instructions for the earthly reconstruction of the Temple and the people. In reality, however, the profound culmination of Ezekiel's book represents a full breakthrough into the apocalyptic sphere. Even if the later reconstruction of the Temple should have coincided in some aspects with descriptions given by Ezekiel, the prophetic scripture here is still meant in an apocalyptic sense and presents pictures which reach far beyond the history of the physical Jerusalem and the Jewish people in beholding the spiritual future of humankind. It would certainly have been illusory to undertake a new sectioning of the land for the twelve tribes in a physical sense, since there was no longer any possibility for the reunion of the former national configuration.

In the first and the fourth parts of his book, Ezekiel reached the same spiritual realities which later on appeared also to the vision of the seer at Patmos. Ezekiel's text is therefore permeated with an abundant sequence of parallels and correspondences with John's Revelations. As yet, Ezekiel's sight was not directed to the opposing spiritual powers and the great battles which the apocalypse of John indicates to us as well. In this respect, Daniel will be completing the text with his militant vision. If, however, the solemn pictures of the gods' existence and the new creation, lifted above any controversy, are considered by themselves in John's Revelations, we arrive at those segments which Ezekiel and John have in common. They are the cherubic four beasts at the throne of the eternal one, the angel with the golden measuring line in the Temple, the heavenly Jerusalem with the twelve gates and the stream of the water of life. In his apocalypse of grace, Ezekiel not only reached beyond the deprivation of the captivity, but beyond the narrow confines of the physical history of the people of Israel as well. He attained to a view of the 'eternal Israel,' of which the Apostle Paul spoke later on, and which, just like the 'heavenly Jerusalem,' has significance for all humanity. The image of the 'new Jerusalem' dawned in the Book of Isaiah. Here, through Ezekiel, it rose in strong and concrete details on the heaven of the future. The breakthrough to the Messianic and apocalyptic vision of the spiritual future of humankind was the most beautiful fruit of the Babylonian period of suffering.

CHAPTER TWENTY-SEVEN

Daniel: Michaelic-Apocalyptic Elements

The Book of Daniel could be called the *Faust* of antiquity. Like Doctor Faustus towards the end of the middle ages, the prophet Daniel was experienced as an embodiment of the turn of time ensouled by the daring of the new spirit of the age. The admiration and astonishment at the classic style of the scenes and visions in the Book of Daniel as well as over the never-ceasing life in these pictures extended into the sphere of early Christianity and far beyond it into early Christian theology.

In more recent theology, however, the Book of Daniel fared like the Song of Songs and other scriptures that are especially significant from a spiritual standpoint. The special esteem of former times was now followed by special disregard. It was believed that almost all historic validity had to be denied this text which was considered a late product of the period of the Maccabees. And in fact, historical criticism is offered a number of points of attack. The Book of Daniel is not uniform even as far as its superficial literary form is concerned: it starts in Hebrew, but at the beginning of the second chapter it changes into Aramaic. Furthermore, it does not appear to place great value on historical accuracy, for, by its mythic legendary style, it takes considerable licence with historical facts. Finally, anyone who wishes to relegate the figure of Daniel from history into the realm of myths can appeal to the Bible itself. The prophet Ezekiel (14:14) mentions Daniel along with Noah and Job as a righteous one who seems to belong to a remote past age.

Among the prophetic texts, the Book of Daniel occupies a position similar to that of the Samson narrative of the Book of Judges within the historic texts. Everywhere, the imaginative elements of the style go beyond descriptions of the external course of events and enter into the realm of sagas and fairy tales. No more than in the story of Samson, however, is there reason here to deny Daniel's historical validity. If the description resorts to imaginative means, it need not contain merely thought-up occurrences that never took place. Instead, it can well be the case — and this is especially true of the great classic power of imagery of the Book of Daniel — that the reported set of facts reaches so far into the supersensory and the realm of mysteries that a description other than the imaginative and legendary kind would have to remain inadequate.

In the Daniel destiny, something of the mystery-background of the Babylonian exile becomes visible even within the Bible itself. Through the figure of Daniel we perceive how in Babylonia, behind the events of the more political foreground, esoteric streams of humanity encountered and fructified each other. The rulers of that age thought that they were making history, but in reality they were only instruments of destiny and had to do no more than create the opportunity for encounters which bestowed on that period the character of a spiritual new beginning.

The Bible relates that in the year 597, Nebuchadnezzar chose a number of noble youngsters from Israelite aristocracy to be page servants at the Babylonian court. It is said that the four youths were given new Babylonian names and received instruction in the script and language of the land. Then, as if this were the main thing, mention is made of the wine and dishes that were prepared for them. In order to serve the king, they had to be vigorously handsome.

Just here where it seems that the description is getting lost in trivialities, an imaginative element, veiling everything, is entwined into the narrative. In reading it, one has to change viewpoint a little to detect the emerging resemblance to fairy tales. The fairy tale that tells us how Hansel and Gretel are fed and fattened with all sorts of delicious foods by the witch appears to be on an entirely different level, and yet contains a certain pictorial parallel to the report that the four youths were to enjoy the wine and dishes of the king for three years. Behind the pictures of what was eaten and drunk, forces were concealed that bound the spiritual element to the body. Through a variety of manipulations pertaining to Babylonian mystery education, to which, among other things, belonged the establishment of a certain manner of diet, the attempt must have been made to arouse these forces in Daniel and his three companions.

It says that the boys declined to partake of the foods and drinks they were served. They succeeded in prevailing on the chamberlain, who had been charged with their upbringing, to allow them their own form of diet for a time and to observe the results. They ate purely vegetarian foods and drank water instead of wine. And behold, the chamberlain soon had to admit that they surpassed all the youths, who were being raised in the Babylonian manner, in handsomeness and strength. Here, the Bible allows us clearly to discern that what is indicated with food and drink, handsomeness and bodily strength refers to soul-spiritual disciplines and results. The youths were not only handsome, they exhibited 'learning and skill in all letters and wisdom,' and more than that, Daniel proved to be one who 'had understanding in all visions and dreams' (Dan.1:17). Thus, it came about that the youngsters were permitted to follow their own path of development during the whole time of their Babylonian upbringing.

Two completely opposite soul and mystery disciplines encountered each other here. A schooling that utilized Dionysian means even in the matter of diet corresponded to the Dionysian body bound spirit of intoxication to which the Babylonian civilization owed its origin. Only when this schooling was first applied to the youths, it became quite clear that Daniel and his friends had already been involved at home in a spiritual training and discipleship, for they followed the ascetic direction of the Nazirites who completely abstained from meat and wine. And the Babylonian taskmasters had to discover to their amazement that the Nazirite discipline not only exhibited the same but far better and more genuine results than their own. A rich life of wisdom and great familiarity with the realm of the supersensory blossomed forth in the Judean youths, especially in Daniel. A spirit showed forth which Babylonia would have to confront, not in a giving but in a taking attitude.

The spirit of prophetic Judaism could not exercise its fructifying influence of the despotic foreign land without its bearers having to pass through battles and suffering. Especially in martyrdom, however, the triumphant superiority of the soul-spiritual power, which had developed in Daniel and his companions on their inner paths, proved itself. The Book of Daniel presents to us archetypal pictures of the victory of the spirit over all suffering and martyrdom in the stories of the fiery furnace and the lions' den.

After they were already occupying high offices in Babylonia, Daniel's three companions were accused of having refused the worship, demanded of them, of a golden idol that had been erected by Nebuchadnezzar. As punishment, they were to be thrown into the fiery oven. The blaze was fuelled to such a degree of heat that the tormentors themselves were incinerated by it. The three Judeans, however, who were thrown chained into the fire, remained unhurt. And the miracle intensified: When he looked into the flames, the king saw, not three, but four figures, who, free of their fetters, moved about without the blaze being able to do them harm, and 'the fourth appeared as if he were a son of the gods.' Nebuchadnezzar placed the Judeans into still higher Babylonian offices and strictly forbade any defamation of their god.

As mythology relates to us, at the same location, a millennium and a half ago, Abraham had been tossed by Nimrod into the fiery oven when he refused to co-operate in the construction of the Babylonian Tower. Of him too, it says that he was able to pass unharmed through the flames as if he walked about under blossoming trees.[1]

The similarity of the Daniel stories to the pictures of fairy tales continues: The witch stokes the fire in the oven so as to bake Hansel and Gretel in it, but she herself becomes a victim of the blazing flames. In Abraham as well as in Daniel's companions, the existence of a mystery trial becomes discernible through the imaginative description. The ancient world knew of punitive measures which were externalized initiation procedures and included a sort of divine judgment. Through the manner in which the inner power emerged of those on whom such punishments were carried out, people recognized whether they were guilty or not and what spiritual importance was due them. From the souls of the Judeans, this baptism by fire brought forth higher spiritual faculties than existed even among the initiates of the land. Now, the desire to utilize the capabilities of these foreigners arose even more in the Babylonian leaders.

A mystery still surrounds the fourth figure whom Nebuchadnezzar beheld in the flames. Was it a genius who protected the tested ones like a guardian angel? Or was it perhaps the spirit form of the one who otherwise was always united as the fourth with his companions, namely Daniel? These two possibilities were not so far apart. The scenes possess imaginative value even if, to a large extent, physically tangible reality underlay them. Taken pictorially, Daniel and his three friends were part of a unity, as if they were physical projections of the soul forces of thinking, feeling and will that gather around the genius like an 'I.' In the fairy tale as well, Hansel and Gretel, taken as one, are a whole human being, spirit and soul that have assumed form and mature together. We saw Isaiah working in a twofoldness united with King Hezekiah. Jeremiah is viewed by the apocryphal traditions in a threefoldness since Baruch and Ebed-melech stood by his side. Daniel is represented as the superior member of a fourfoldness by the Bible itself. He was actually the bearer of the spirit that proved itself in the Babylonian trial by fire. Therefore, even though the narrative does not mention him, he did participate in the martyrdom which turned into the release of spiritual faculties.

Whereas the three companions were seemingly in the fiery oven without Daniel, he appeared to be without his friends in the lions' den. Time had gone by. Daniel had become one of the highest lords in the Median-Persian sphere of rule. The king, here called Darius, wished to place him over the whole kingdom, 'because an excellent spirit was in him.' (Dan.6:3). The underlings were jealous of the foreigner. They urged the ruler to introduce a Caesarean cult which concentrated all religious veneration on the royal throne. Thus, they could prosecute Daniel for his prayers that were directed to Jerusalem. In vain, the king himself intervened to save Daniel. When the sun went down, he was thrown into the lions' den. The miracle took place: The protective genius came to Daniel's aid and the lions turned tame before the spiritual force, the nearness of which they sensed. When the sun rose again, Daniel went unharmed to meet the king who had been afraid for him all through the night. The accusers were thrown to the lions who immediately tore apart the welcome prize. Daniel as well as the deity proclaimed by him were paid the highest homage. The Bible specifically adds that Daniel now entered the sphere of the Persian king, Cyrus, the rising eagle (6:28).

Again, something that was supposed to have been a martyrdom had turned into a mystery trial and stage of inner development, thereby changing into a still higher confirmation and freeing of spiritual power. Just as Samson once proved himself to be the ruler over all lower forces by vanquishing the lion, so, in a still higher sense, Daniel now absolved the lion trial: it was as if from his soul a sound had emerged that tamed all ferociousness as did the harp of Orpheus.

Since ancient times, the Median-Persian nations had experienced the sun lion as their sign, thereby bringing to expression a special relationship to the royal cosmic forces of the sun. The fact that Daniel attained mastery over the lions between the time the sun set and rose again must have appeared to the Medes and Persians as an indication that he was in possession of their own highest mysteries and spirit secrets. They had tried to punish him for false worship; now, he stood before the people as the embodiment of their own temple principle, that of worshipping through the power of the lion. Daniel headed those who experienced the destiny of the prophets in themselves. Outward events of fate affected him like the recapitulation of initiation experiences absolved in former lives on earth, and indeed, the spirit fruits of ancient mystery discipleship had ripened again as if through magic.

On the walls of the catacombs and on the sarcophagi, alongside the destiny of Jonah, the first Christians have repeatedly depicted the two Daniel-mysteries: the three young men in the fiery furnace and Daniel in the lions' den. The inkling of a connection with the Babylonian and Persian mysteries was brought to expression by depicting those undergoing the trials with Persian Mithras caps on their heads, their hands raised in prayer to the spirit. In the days of the Caesarean persecution of the Christians, the martyrdom of the age of the prophets, which had been like a divine judgment, had long since been coarsened into cruel blood sacrifices. In Nero's gardens, the martyrs really burned as living flames and in the arena of the Colosseum they were truly torn apart by the lions. Yet, to recall the spiritual victories of Daniel again and again gave early Christianity the certainty of the inner power that overcomes all death.

The Babylonian and Persian destinies of Daniel had many similarities to the Egyptian fate of Joseph. As Joseph once interpreted the dreams of the Pharaoh, Daniel read the dreams of Nebuchadnezzar. He could even interpret the first dream anew out of the spirit since it had slipped the king's mind. What all the temple sages and seers of Babylonia were incapable of doing, Daniel could do.

The king had beheld a tall shining image, frightening in its power. Formed like a man, it extended up to heaven, the head fashioned of gold, the breast and arms of silver, the belly and thighs of bronze, the legs of iron, the feet a mixture of iron and clay. By powers without hands, a huge stone was torn loose from cosmic heights and thrown down shattering the weak feet of the image. The figure collapsed and gold, silver, bronze and iron were scattered 'like the chaff of the summer threshing floors, and the wind carried them away.' The stone finally grew into a great mountain that filled the whole earth.

The interpretation which Daniel added to the dream was more one that applied to the history of that age than one that exposed the archetypes contained in it. If we take a look at the latter which are valid in all ages, the dream represents a complete world history. It shows the evolution of humanity beginning from the cultures that still proceeded from the pure sun-gold of clairvoyant sight and continued to the increasingly earthly developments that finally became more and more disunited and mixed. Finally, like a bolt of lightning, the 'I'-impulse strikes, shattering all the old forms, and, having initially resembled a large boulder, grows into a mountain and at last into a whole world.

Nebuchadnezzar's second dream adds another picture which, in a classic manner, demonstrates even more the decline of the ancient forces. A tree, very tall and strong, stood in the midst of the land extending up into the heavens and spreading out to the ends of the earth. All creatures lived on the fruits that grew on the tree's branches. Then, a holy guardian came down from heaven and commanded the tree to be felled, sparing only the root-stock that still remained in the ground. Again, it was only Daniel, in whom 'was the spirit of the holy gods,' who was able to interpret the dream. Dismayed, Daniel realized that the felling of the tree was to take place on the person of Nebuchadnezzar himself just as was indicated by the shattering of the image fashioned of gold, silver, bronze and iron. Again, it is a matter of penetrating through the contemporary interpretation, pointed out by the biblical report, to the archetypal level. Once, when he was still in possession of the ancient cosmic consciousness of the gods, the human being himself resembled the world embracing tree. And it was inherent in evolution itself that in the end, only the root-stock of head-bound thought consciousness remained from the tree of ancient soul existence. In the Book of Isaiah, the picture of a stump with roots appears that alone remains after the felling of the tree and from which, later on, the shoot of a new life is to emerge (Isa.6:13 and 11:1). What head-thinking is in relation to the old cosmic consciousness, was the tiny Judean nation, the root of Jesse, among the peoples of antiquity. The felling of the tree refers to the divinely willed spiritual impoverishment of humanity that has to precede a new awakening.

The dreams of Nebuchadnezzar that Daniel interpreted were similar to those of the Egyptian Pharaoh which, more than a thousand years earlier, Joseph had explained. They all proclaimed the necessary end of the ancient clairvoyant civilizations, all were prophecies of the twilight of the gods that was coming upon them with increasing strength. In the Pharaoh and in Nebuchadnezzar, the ancient world dreamed of its own impending death.

As happened to Joseph in Egypt, Daniel was elevated in Babylonia to high spiritual and political positions of leadership. As was the case earlier in Egypt, a doomed world in Babylonia, afflicted by tremors and spectres of the gods' twilight, sought to lengthen its life by the inclusion of the Israelite-Jewish spirit. The fateful destiny, however, could not be stemmed. There came that mythological midnight hour, heavy with significance, of the feast of King Belshazzar. The banquet in the royal castle in Babel was suddenly interrupted by the appearance of a ghostly script on the wall. Nobody could interpret the mysterious signs until Daniel was fetched. He translated the script: Babylon's end had come, for it had been weighed and found to be too light. The same night, the king of Babylon was murdered.

In the chapters in which the Book of Daniel speaks about the fall of the Babylonian and the rise of the Median-Persian power, especially large numbers of 'historical inaccuracies' are found which are apt to cast doubt on the historical value of the description. Actually though, nothing unhistorical is related. Instead, the events that took place are represented in a veiled form because they were pervaded by mysteries. One already begins to see through the veil if it is realized, for instance, that the names of the kings are exchanged. Although the names mentioned in the Bible do exist, the kings who are referred to by the Book of Daniel are given other names by historical tradition.

History knows of a Belshazzar who was king of Babylon when Cyrus made himself the ruler of the land. He ruled in place of his father, Nabonidus, who, having no interest in politics, had abdicated in favour of scientific indulgences. The ghostly scene concerning the feast of Belshazzar, related to us by the biblical scripture, does not refer to the last king of Babylon but instead, as the Bible itself states, to the son of Nebuchadnezzar who reigned under the name Evil-Merodach (562–560 BC) and was killed when the priests of the moon sanctuary of Haran staged a revolution in favour of Nabonidus.

Likewise, the Median king, Darius, who is mentioned in the immediately following story of the lions' den, does not refer to the Persian king, Darius, who, as the second successor of Cyrus, reigned over the latter's kingdom (521–485 BC). The Bible makes it clearly discernible that this Darius is a contemporary of Cyrus who was king before Cyrus conquered Babylonia. Perhaps the Bible even referred here to the Mede, Astyages, who was finally toppled by his grandson, Cyrus.

The names Belshazzar and Darius obviously were very common names of that period so that it was easily possible that they were in use as second names of the individuals referred to. But why does the Book of Daniel resort to such disguises?

We observe that Daniel in a significant manner was involved in the events which later led to replacement of the Babylonian power by that of Persia. Although he occupied a high ranking influential post in Babylonia, he went over to the courts of the Median and Persian kingdom when Babel was not yet in the hands of Cyrus. From the beginning, people there heeded what he had to say and allowed him to have great influence on the leadership over the nations. The Bible expresses this in the words: 'So this Daniel prospered during the reign of Darius [at the Median court] and the reign of Cyrus the Persian' (Dan.6:28).

Obviously, Daniel was living in Ecbatana at the court of the Median ruler when Cyrus entered the city in the year 553 and placed Media under Persian jurisdiction. Then, from the vantage point of Cyrus' closest surroundings, Daniel may well have watched the majestic, eagle-like rise of the king. Daniel was not with the captives of his own people in Babylonia. Instead, he may have been present in the year 539 as one of the advisors of Cyrus during the entry into Babylon. The Bible states: 'Daniel experienced the first year of King Cyrus.' This surely indicates the year after the take-over of Babylonia when the Judeans received permission to return and reconstruct the Temple.

This possible and most probable course of history immediately indicates the significant connections that determined the inner structure of that period. We suddenly recognize Daniel as a personality who not only stood in the centre of the world of that time but must even have exercised a decisive influence on the course of the various folk destinies.

It is also obvious for outward historical research that, to a large extent, spiritual impulses affected Cyrus' politics. In the concealed background of the rise of Cyrus, experienced almost in a Messianic sense, we already saw emerge the figures of leaders who possessed towering greatness. We encountered the great spirit who, as the author of the *Gathas* of Zarathustra, had brought about the reformation and renewal of Zoroastrianism in Persia at that time. We also came upon the figure of the great teacher, Nazarathos or Zarathas — perhaps identical with the above reformer — who was the reincarnated Zarathustra himself. Now, the Bible also shows us the prophet Daniel among the figures to whom the spiritual impulse of Cyrus is traced. After that ghostly hour in the palace of the biblical Belshazzar, did Daniel himself perhaps depart in order to direct the paths of Cyrus in such a manner that the latter could then enter Babylonia as the liberator sent by Providence? If historical tradition allows us to discern that the Babylonian priesthood and inhabitants joyfully greeted the victorious Persian king, must we not assume that the political events were spiritually prepared by men such as Daniel?

Last but not least, the idea arises that a close relationship and cooperation must have existed between the great teacher Nazarathos and Daniel. Some years before the return of the Jews, Nazarathos appears to have arrived in Babylonia from the Median-Persian region where Daniel sojourned at that time in order to turn into the teacher, first of the Jewish prophets living there and later, of Pythagoras. At that point, Daniel may have remained where Nazarathos had previously been active. Perhaps, where he had formerly been the disciple, he was now the teacher in Nazarathos' place.

Again, it is enough merely to touch upon the possibilities that exist here for forming conceptions concerning the mystery backgrounds of the Babylonian exile. And again, it suffices that even by raising the questions we begin to sense the wide-branching configuration of spiritual impulses, encompassing many nations, into which Daniel in particular was placed, since, of all the prophets, he most of all transcended the confines of his own people. It would be a most interesting and fruitful endeavour to gather the single references of Daniel's biography, inserted merely as indications in the flow of descriptions, into a dramatic totality of a novel. The result would be a larger-than-life biography. A figure would arise before us in clear outline, who, since he was at the same time available to the mystery backgrounds as a mouthpiece and instrument, was not only one who, as a member of a deported slave nation in the subjugating foreign land, had risen to high honours. Instead, he was one who helped shape the destinies of nations and kingdoms over vast territories. As far as the background is concerned, Daniel was a companion and herald of the loftiest initiated leaders of humanity. In the foreground, he prepared the way for the Persian King Cyrus, who was overshadowed by Messianic lights of the future.

In every epoch which, according to the calendar of the mighty archangel cycles, stands under Michael's sun leadership, there exist a number of such larger-than-life biographies: alongside that of Daniel, for example, those of Pythagoras, Cyrus, Plato and Alexander the Great, which were subsequently recorded in super-historical, half-mythical descriptions. The Golden Legend depicts the destinies of the world traveller Pythagoras. Then we have the Cyropaedia, in which Xenophon describes the life and reign of Cyrus. We have the legendary traditions that first show us Plato as a youth on the Island of Aegina, having been sold there as a slave, later in Egypt in a thirteen-year-long mystery-discipleship in Heliopolis. Finally, we have the Alexander saga in varied form all the way to the Middle Ages. One could speak here of 'Michaelic biographies.' As bearers of the Michaelic spirit of the age, human individualities rise beyond human dimension so that their biographies turn into a direct expression of the superhuman archangel history.

Daniel not only interpreted the dreams and visions of others. His soul itself penetrated to the most significant visions. The second half of the prophetic text could be entitled the Daniel Apocalypse. Especially in the second part of the Book of Isaiah and in the case of the prophet Ezekiel, we have seen how prophetic sight arrived at a certain apocalyptic element. The images of a solemn divine earth-future lit up: the heavenly Jerusalem, the new earth and the new heaven. In Daniel, a completely new impulse appeared within the apocalyptic realm. To the visions of divine perfection that radiated tranquillity were added the frightening and shocking images of opposing powers. Visionary sight dared venture into the ominous abysses of evil and gained the power of spirit battle. In Daniel, seer-ship broke through to the sphere of the Michaelic spirit, at the portals of which it had knocked in growing strength. It was as if the sword-wielding archangel himself had slashed the curtain concealing the maws of the dragon. For the first time, there grew in Daniel like a seedling what is contained in John's Revelations as images of evil deities, militant drama and tension. The tranquil world of Ezekiel's Temple visions found its complement. Thus in Ezekiel and Daniel, the two streams were present that were to unite one day in the Apocalypse of John.

The first great vision of Daniel is that of the mighty four beasts. It is, however, not that of the cherubic four beasts of lion, eagle, bull and man, presented in the beginning to Ezekiel's seership and appearing in greatest purity and clarity in John's throne-vision (Rev.4–5) — although lights fall from there on the first of the four of Daniel's beasts, which resembles a lion with eagle's wings, a human heart and feet. Then, however, the gruesome spectral elements intensify all the way to the fourth beast. Into the divine fourfold beast, the demonic twofold beast intrudes of which John's Revelation speaks (Chapter 13) and which had already surfaced in the books of ancient wisdom (for example, in the great Book of Enoch, Chapter 60, and Job 40) under the names Leviathan and Behemoth.

Above all, in Daniel's vision of the four beasts, picture elements appear in the foreground that make it possible to sense the soulless, cold, life-destroying breath of the Ahrimanic power (Behemoth): the iron teeth of the fourth beast, devouring things around itself and crushing everything with its claws. It is as if, here, Daniel was resorting to his spiritual kinship with Persian wisdom which had designated the sinister power opposing the sun genius as Angra Mainyu (Ahriman). The spiritually militant disclosure of the evil power, partic-ularly the principle of darkness, was something that Daniel had in common with the Zarathustrian teaching which had been renewed at that time. Courageously, Daniel turned his seer's glance into a future of humankind when the fourth beast will make the attempt to stamp out all feelings for sacredness and to create a completely profane, soulless world of machines.

The continuation of the gods' twilight which was increasingly becoming demonic was also referred to by the subsequent visions of Daniel. At one point, Daniel beheld a ram emerging out of the darkness at the bank of a wide river. From the west, a he-goat with an ominous horn between its eyes raced up to the ram, struck it, broke its horns and trampled upon it. The harsh destructive one then became magnified exceedingly and, rising all the way to heaven, tore down the stars and destroyed all the sanctuaries on earth.

The archetypal meaning of this frightening vision of the future is the following. Soon, even the last remnant of the ancient, still clairvoyant knowledge and with it the legacy of the old, pious closeness to the spirit will perish before the ruthless thirst for power of the cold head-intellect. The last spiritual organ withers, the two-petalled lotus flower which, like spiritual ram's horns crowned the forehead of Moses[2] and gifted the human being with inklings of divine-spiritual cosmic relationships. Instead, the human forehead produced the pushy, injurious horn of calculating thinking, lacking in reverence and love. Heaven loses its constellations; all that is left are orbiting, phosphorescent bodies of gas. No more room is left on earth for what is holy.

Through the archangel Gabriel, Daniel received a contemporary interpretation of the vision. He was to recognize the Median-Persian element in the figure of the ram, in that of the he-goat from the west the element approaching from Greece.

In the Babylonian, Median and Persian Orient, there did exist a last clairvoyant civilization, having emerged from the forces of the 'ram.' As opposed to it, Greece experienced the wondrous dawn of the thinking European spirit. How was it possible that the Hellas of a Heraclitus and Pythagoras could show itself in the image of a beast that tears the stars from the heavens and destroys all the sites of worship? Daniel's prophetic sight penetrated so far into the darkness of night that he could also discern far-distant developments of which hardly the first germ had appeared. One day, the great demonic danger of soulless cold will emerge from the head thinking, born in Greece, namely, when the words of Aristotle will be forgotten which said that the capacity of marvelling must be the beginning of all philosophy. Then, the Ahrimanic power will rise up, and machines and statistics will execute their suggestive power over humankind's life of knowledge.

Daniel, who may have made a major contribution towards the reconstruction of the Temple in Jerusalem, unfolded an apocalyptic view of the future which made it clear that the rebuilding of the sanctuary by no means indicated the end of all misfortune and that, only then, the evil power would go forward to its greatest triumphs. Mysterious cycles of time will be fulfilled and as they take their course, it will come about that the first destruction of the Temple will be followed by a second, worldwide one. A demonic desecration of the holiest is imminent for humankind: the 'desolating sacrilege' will be erected where the deity itself was supposed to dwell.

Daniel coined an important biblical image when he spoke of the 'desolating sacrilege.' This prophecy by Daniel is referred to in the New Testament. In the apocalyptic instructions which Christ imparted to his disciples on the Mount of Olives before his imminent death, he said: 'But when you see the desolating sacrilege set up where it ought not to be ...' (Mark 13:14). It was frequently thought that here the Book of Daniel referred to a specific historical event, namely, the erection of his Caesarean statue by King Antiochus of the Seleucids in the Holy of Holies in the Temple (168 BC). And the prophetic text does indeed unfold detailed historical descriptions in the ninth and eleventh chapters which in some instances fit so exceedingly well with the age of the Greco-Persian wars, the figure of Alexander the Great, and the epoch of the kingdoms of the Diadochi, especially the Syrian rule of the Seleucids opposed by the Maccabees, that it is understandable why theology could hit on the idea of dating the origin of Daniel's scripture as late as the age of the Maccabees.* Once again, however, we have above all to reclaim from his apocalypse its archetypal value. A contemporary fulfilment of the prophetic visions can at most be one of many realizations and embodiments of the archetype beheld in them.

Daniel foresaw the battles and confusion that would occur in the spirit region and on earth as consequences of the clash between the

---

* In the case of this quite generally prevalent theory, the assumption is taken as a basis that no concrete prediction of the course of history could exist. A prophecy is considered genuine if it was not fulfilled. If the biblical scriptures do contain predictions that correspond to an actual later event, one likes to explain them as *vaticinia ex eventu*, meaning, having been invented after the fact, and their origin is then dated according to the events, the prophecies of which they claim to be.

ram and the he-goat, between the ancient pious world-view and the dawning soulless Ahrimanism. The anti-Christian impulses will arise. The temple of the human being will be profaned inasmuch as the ego-tistical lower 'I' will make its place there instead of the divinely inspired genius. The living, organically developed culture will be dis-torted to the mechanistic civilization in which not the divine, but the idol of numbers and money will reign. As the spiritual power, the Antichrist himself is the 'desolating sacrilege' in the single human being as well as in the larger social configurations. Here, the Greek Bible employs an expression which is much clearer and more drastic than the customary translation: $\tau o\ \beta\delta\epsilon\lambda\theta\gamma\mu\alpha\ ^{\prime}\epsilon\rho\eta\mu\omega\sigma\epsilon\omega\varsigma$ *(to bdelygma erêmôseôs)* 'the abomination of isolation.' The splitting apart of all sup-portive structures of social communities, the egotistic principle, will begin to go about like a mighty demon when, in its pursuit of knowl-edge, humanity subscribes entirely to intelligence that has turned com-pletely into an earthly, calculating force.

The history of the last pre-Christian centuries, from Cyrus through Alexander the Great to Antiochus Epiphanes and the Roman Caesars, is like a reflection on earth of the archetypes that Daniel placed before us, especially in the segments concerning the 'desolating sacrilege.' The archetypal character of history is extensive at the beginning of the fourth post-Atlantean cultural epoch (see p. 263) between the age of Isaiah, the founding of Rome and early Christendom.

Cyrus was the embodiment of an ideal ruler, which Pharaoh Akhenaten (Amenophis IV) had attempted to anticipate in an abstract manner and Alexander the Great no longer was able to completely ful-fil, namely, out of purely human ability to lead the nations in the same way as the higher gods precede the hierarchies serving them. After Alexander's death, chaos broke out under the Diadochian rulers, the Ptolemies in Egypt and the Seleucids in Syria. The demonic egotism of the Caesars installed in the place of the gods spread its spectral influ-ences over the whole world. From Antiochus Epiphanes to Nero and Caracalla, the counter-image of true rulership became reality. The 'des-olating sacrilege' assumed human form. When the Seleucid, Antiochus Epiphanes, desecrated the sanctuary in Jerusalem's Temple by erecting his own statue as a divine image, this was not as yet the fulfilment of Daniel's prophecy. Through the symbolizing power of world history, a physically tangible, historically concrete prophecy was added to the prophecy that had been beheld and coined in words. A mighty spiritual battle of future humankind was foreshadowed in events that took place like warnings of the gods on earth. As through a window, Daniel looked through the history of the centuries directly before him into the larger developments that humanity would be in danger of falling victim to in future time. Distantly, a mighty Temple desecration and destruction was starting. The spectre of the Antichrist, the 'monster of desolation,' was rising.

His courageous advance into the pits of evil now gave Daniel a deepened view for the Christ-mystery. Even the Messianic prophecy, which had sounded humanly consoling in Isaiah and in Ezekiel merged completely with the general prophecy of salvation about resurrection and the new temple, turned apocalyptic in Daniel. Penetrating through the sphere of the four beasts, metamorphosing into the Ahrimanic direction, the visionary soul broke free to the view of the figure of the Son of man who approaches on the clouds of heaven. Here, the presentiment and knowledge of the coming one was replaced by the direct view of him. The spiritual surroundings of the earth were already darkened and filled with thunderous clouds. Nevertheless, Daniel beheld the divine shining being flashing through, the being who was preparing to assume human form and had approached closely already.

In a similar form as the seer John (Rev.1) saw Christ after the Mystery of Golgotha, preparing his Second Coming, Daniel now beheld him at the point when he was readying himself for his First Coming:

> I lifted up my eyes and looked, and behold, a man clothed in linen, whose loins were girded with gold of Uphaz. His body was like beryl, his face like the appearance of lightning, his eyes like flaming torches, his arms and legs like the gleam of burnished bronze, and the sound of his words like the noise of a multitude (Dan.10:5f).

Even now, the entity whom the seer had thus beheld intervened mightily in history; setting things straight, striving forward, it held sway above the heads of people. And now Daniel became aware that a mighty helper placed himself at the side of Christ in the spirit realm. Amazed, Daniel recognized a profound secret of his age. The archangel Michael, who until then had been the folk spirit of the

Israelite-Jewish people, rose up to a leadership encompassing nations and humanity in so far as he became the militant servant of the approaching Christ being. Daniel heard the Shining One in the white garment speak himself: 'There is none who contends by my side against these except Michael' (10:21).

It is an important spiritual fact that at the beginning of the seventh pre-Christian century, after the destruction of the northern kingdom of Israel, a Michaelic epoch had commenced. As spiritual science teaches it — and already Trithemius von Sponheim describes this in his works — seven archangelic beings take turns assuming the work of time spirits. During the age of Isaiah and Hezekiah, as it occurred in the last third of the nineteenth century, a Gabriel epoch was replaced by a Michael age, which then continued through the period of the Babylonian exile and of Cyrus, approximately until the death of Alexander the Great.

The fact that humanity entered upon a Michaelic age had far-reaching consequences for the people of the Old Testament. The entity whom Israel had sensed since the days of the patriarchs as the folk genius above them rose up beyond the single folk sphere. The people relinquished their protector and leader to all of humankind. When he became aware of this secret, Daniel may have been shocked and have asked the question whether there was perhaps a connection between the external decline of the people and the elevation of Michael. Were the outward misfortune and captivity not perhaps the darker shadow of a greater light, the tragic side effects of an added spiritual force and task? For some time, the archangel of Israel had been active beyond the realm of his people. Was it this that made all the world experience the Persian King Cyrus like a human incarnation of the Michaelic time spirit, even though the Jews waiting in exile believed rightfully that they were united in an especially close way with the Michaelic power?

Christ and Michael are the theme in which the Daniel apocalypse culminates. The elevation of Michael, the ascent of the terrestrial people to the spiritual Israel, and the lofty all-human mission of preparing an abode on earth for the Messianic light was proclaimed to him with all clearness.

> At that time shall arise Michael, the great prince who has
> charge of your people. And there shall be a time of trouble,
> such as never has been since there was a nation ... And those

who are wise shall shine like the brightness of the firmament;
and those who turn many to righteousness, like the stars for
ever and ever. (12:1,3).

Finally, Daniel beheld a wide stream. On the bank beyond as well
as on this side stands a figure. On yonder side, Christ shines forth, the
figure in the white garment with the golden girdle. On this side stands
Michael, who calls across the stream to the greater one and asks him
concerning the time of the expected events (12:5ff). No image more
classic than this could conclude the Michaelic text, the Faustian book
of antiquity! The Christ being has drawn near. But as yet, the wide
stream separates us. The archangel Michael stands on the river's bank
on this side as the spokesman of humankind. His only desire is to prepare the way for the One who is to come. It is almost as if we could
hear him sadly say the words that are also expressed by the beautiful
Lily in Goethe's *Fairy Tale:* 'Oh, the bridge is not yet built!' This was
what called forth the Faust-like activities and movements of spiritual
beings in the age of the mighty spirit-gathering that shone forth in all
segments of humankind and particularly in prophetic Judaism: A militant, progressive being, Michael, the archangel, willed to construct the
bridge over the stream for the Christ.

CHAPTER TWENTY-EIGHT

Ezra: Final Forming

When, for the purpose of the Temple reconstruction, Cyrus returned the Temple treasures that had originally been taken to certain of the Jewish people, and permitted their return in the year 538, the spell of the exile had been broken but the people did not regain their freedom. Led by Zerubbabel, they journeyed to their homeland as Persian colonists. Only a few of the very old people among them had in their youth consciously absorbed into their souls an impression of the land of the fathers. The great majority of the others, especially the men who were in the prime of life, had been born in Babylonia.

The reconstruction of the Temple met with difficulties. Controversies among those involved in the building, the interference of the foreigners, especially the Persian officials, who, after the death of Cyrus (529 BC), gave free reign to their antipathy, delayed the undertaking until, in the year 515, under the rulership of the Persian king, Darius, the dedication of the Temple could at last take place.

The Jews who had remained behind in Mesopotamia followed the course of events with great concern. They soon realized that the new Judean colony was developing in a dubious way. People who had not been filled with and guided by the stern spirit of prophetic Judaism had rushed to join the first return migration. The true Israel and the awareness of its Messianic mission only continued to live on in the foreign land. What was coming into being in Jerusalem and Judea was only seemingly a restoration of what had been lost. In the same way as those initially deported to Babylonia at the time of Nebuchadnezzar had looked upon the others left in the homeland around the Temple, so those still remaining in Mesopotamia viewed the life now developing around the newly arising Temple. There were great prophetic natures, such as Haggai and Zechariah, who were active in Jerusalem, but their words were heeded no more than those of Jeremiah after the first deportation. And just as those in Babylonia who were concerned had gathered around the prophet Ezekiel in the years between 597 and 586, so, a few decades after the first return migration, the people rallied around a significant figure of a leader, namely Ezra.

The more they watched those who had returned to the homeland lose awareness of the stern folk mission and submerge into the alien neighbouring nations, the more closely the Judeans in Babylonia banded together, faithfully adhering to the Law. While the foreign world had already helped to bring Judaism to self-awareness during the actual exile, in the face of the dangers that they saw arising in the homeland, people now felt called upon even more, in order never to lose it again, to secure their own religious life through forms that were as clearly defined as possible. In the person of Ezra, there emerged for Judaism a superior reformer, capable of expressing and shaping ideas, through whom it received its final valid form. Although crushed by blows of fate, it was nevertheless preserved in a condition capable of sustaining life until the arrival of the Messiah.

While the Persian wars were raging, in which the proud young nation of Greece defended itself with heroic courage against the onslaught of the ancient world which the new rulers of Babylonia and Israel attempted to carry westward, Ezra prepared his reformatory work.

Like Ezekiel, Ezra descended from the lineage of the high priests of the Zadok sons, who later developed the religious faction of the Sadducees. During the age, however, when all priestly activities had ceased in the people deprived of their Temple, he devoted himself with all his energies to the detailed development of scribism. The Bible calls him 'the priest, the scribe, learned in matters of the commandments of the LORD and his statutes for Israel' (Ezra 7:11). Scribism was nurtured among the Judeans in connection with the Babylonian schools of wisdom in order that one had a replacement for the Temple rites in the Bible's words which were read aloud and interpreted. Through the universal, keen spirit of Ezra, this scribism was elevated to a high level of perfection.

The most fundamental deed that Ezra had to accomplish here was the creation of the Old Testament canon. From among the vast, disorderly profusion of holy scriptures that circulated everywhere among the Jews, he selected those that henceforth were to pass as an essential part of the Bible itself. He bestowed on them the final and, at the same time, stern and distinct form which they required for ritualistic use and fitted them together into a spiritually corresponding composition. In this endeavour, there was no room for arbitrariness; only a person who possessed the faculty of recognizing and distinguishing spiritual elements to a high degree was capable of accomplishing this. It was not only a question of discerning which of the texts really originated from divine revelation. For there were naturally a great number of scriptures in which, although they had come from sources higher than merely those of human perception, the imaginative pictorial character predominated, not having been put under the control of the I-imbued, form-giving and inspired consciousness.* The texts that only reached up to the imaginative profusion of pictures could only be part of the apocrypha of the Holy Scripture, not of the Bible itself. The existence of a genuinely inspired impulse was the prerequisite for inclusion of a scripture in the biblical canon, for only thereby could a text be accessible to clear conceptual comprehension. Ezra would not have possessed the spiritual sovereignty and authority necessary for establishing the Bible canon, if he himself had not been master over imaginative and inspired consciousness. Thus, he became the one who had to draw the final line under the spiritual development of the Old Covenant. It was now no longer a matter of evolving upwards to new heights of revelation but to fashion the remainder of the Messianic people, together with the spiritual possession bestowed on them, into as pure a vessel as possible for the expected divine, Messianic being and to preserve it as such until the time would be fulfilled.

A second spiritual inauguration by Ezra, which like no other was suited to bestow on post-exilic Judaism its form and cohesiveness, has eluded external historical traditions, because it concerns the esoteric life; it can, however, be deduced in all clarity from the course of developments. This was the establishment of the order of the Pharisees. As

---

*   Here, the underlying view is that an undifferentiated dogma of inspiration does not suffice for a comprehension of the biblical scriptures. The threefoldness of supersensory perception, described repeatedly by Rudolf Steiner, namely, imagination (in pictures), inspiration (in words) and intuition (direct essence), must be utilized here for the question of how the biblical texts originated. Only those scriptures have been included in the canon of the Old and the New Testament, where the inspired element was added, at least in its inception, to the imaginative element.

is true of the Essenes, we only have reports of the existence of the Pharisees in the age of the Maccabees. But in the case of esoteric communities resembling religious orders, it is always wrong to date their origin from the time in which the first public mention is made of them. The fact that esoteric groups are spoken of before all the world is a sign that their genuine period of flourishing is already over and has been replaced by a time of decadence and externalization. And in fact, we see how, in the age of the Maccabees and even more so during Jesus' time, the order of Pharisees hardly exhibited anything any longer of its spiritual-occult origin, having instead fallen victim to the fanatical arrogance and pedantry which turned the Pharisee almost into a ridiculous figure.

The word 'pharisee' means 'the segregated ones.' It could well have been that their community began its fermentative activity as an esoterically trained élite group at just that time when the whole of the Jewish people, in order to save their Messianic task, had to turn more than before into a group of 'segregated ones,' namely, after the exile was over.

Ezra's important position within Jewish scribism has always been recognized. He was not the first scribe. But within the long-existent circles of the Sopherim, he represented a decisive new beginning, the infusion of a new spiritual substance into their institution. Everything points to his having founded among the scribes a choice group resembling a religious order so as to incorporate his reformatory impulse into the theological establishment. In seclusion, by means of their strictly prescribed occult training, this select group was actively to maintain a stream of direct apocalyptic spiritual experience.

The Pharisees have carefully kept secret the esoteric character and content of their order. Yet, here and there, something leaked out. There exist traditions of the ten degrees of holiness which were striven for on the path of the Pharisees' exercises: first, the stage of the one who learns (the student), who acquired discretion through a detailed study of the law; second, the novitiate, designated by the symbol of the apron; third, the stage of freeing oneself of sin (of purification) through carefully outlined washing and baptism with water; fourth, celibacy, the detachment from sexuality; fifth, the stage of inner purity and discipline of thoughts; sixth, a still higher degree, the content of which could not be indicated; seventh, the level of gentleness; eighth, abhorrence of all sin; ninth, the stage of holiness; tenth, the faculty of healing the sick and resurrecting the dead.[1]

Although ensouled from the beginning by a completely different spirit, the structure of the Pharisees' order appears to have resembled the order of the Essenes, concerning which we also have no external reports earlier than the age of the Maccabees. Doubtless, the order of the Essenes goes back much further and probably also owed its strict form to the age of that final preparation towards the end of the exile.

The two tightly organized religious communities, determining the inner countenance of post-exilic Judaism to such a great extent, namely, the Essenes and Pharisees, were the continuation and heirs of the monastic streams active in Israel's spiritual life since the age of Moses. They most likely originated directly from the latter. The duality of the Nazirites and Korahites reappeared again in them. These two groups, outwardly recognizable by the fact that the Nazirites, like the clergy of Greek Orthodox Christianity, let the hair on their head and face grow long, whereas the Korahites, like the Roman Catholic clergy, adhered to the principle of tonsure,[2] distinguished themselves inwardly as well. The Nazirites underwent a soul training predominantly involving the heart and feelings, whereas the Korahites were directed more to thinking and the will. Until the time of the judges, both orders had remained mostly in the background, something that was advantageous for their inner cohesiveness despite the absence of stern forms of organization. They emerged during the time of the kings in connection with the activity of the various prophets' schools. In the age of the prophets and the exile, they appear to have been dangerously caught up in formlessness and dissolution which necessitated a reorganization with strict disciplines. Thus, the order of the Essenes may have originated through a concentration and reform within Naziritism, that of the Pharisees through the same efforts within the Korahite groups.

One could term the Pharisees the Jesuits of late Judaism. The comparison also fits in so far as Pharisaism, after an initial period directed towards spiritual aims, like the order of the Jesuits, quite soon became the bearer and unscrupulous advocate of a fanatical political impulse. A polarity existed in the Essenes and Pharisees similar to that within the monastic orders of the Catholic Church between the Benedictines and Jesuits. The contemplative and meditative element which

Benedict of Nursia implanted into his order had its correspondence in the contemplatively withdrawn life of the Essenes. The active endeavours of educating the masses which, emerging out of occult training, were established by Ignatius of Loyola in his order, resemble the activity exercised by pharisaism after the exile in Judaism in order to bring about the 'isolation' of all alien and impure elements. Ezra was the inaugurator in the institution of the Jewish scribes of the select esoteric group which emerged historically in the order of the Pharisees. The same sovereignty of spirit that enabled him to give the Holy Scripture its final form turned him also into the creator of an Order.

In the year 458 BC, the Persian king, Artaxerxes Longimanus, dispatched a new group of returning Jewish settlers to Judea. The fact that he entrusted its leadership to Ezra shows that the great scribe had confidence and recognition even among the Persian leadership and centres of wisdom. Having arrived in the homeland, Ezra stepped among his people as the stern reformer. Just as the priests, belonging to the prophets' party, had done during the age of Josiah, so he too proceeded now. He called the people together and read and interpreted to them the ancient texts containing the Law of the fathers. While the purification of the Temple from foreign cultural elements had been the goal then, now the radical cleansing and segregation of the people themselves from all alien intermingling was demanded. The prophetic reformation of the age of Josiah was now followed by that which Ezra undertook in the name of the first and still genuine Pharisee impulse. The principle of marriage within the ethnic confines was proclaimed as a strict law; any marriage with members of other tribes was declared invalid and prohibited. It must be understood that Ezra did not yet link the fanatic political aims, connected with them in later times, with his reformatory measures. He was guided by the outlook towards the Messianic mission and future of his people. A strict purification and concentration, carried out even in regard to the blood relationships, appeared to him to be the spiritual-physical prerequisite so that the Messiah being, having drawn very near, could incarnate in the people chosen by it.

Although he himself belonged to the aristocracy of the priests serving at the Temple of Jerusalem, after his return to the homeland Ezra was primarily concerned with establishing the institution of synagogues. In order that the concentration of all actual ritual activities on the one Temple, begun by the prophets, could remain in force, there had to be houses of teaching everywhere in the land, as well as in Jewish settlements outside Judea in the Diaspora where, under the guidance of the scribes, the reading of the scripture could be practised as a kind of substitute for the ritual. Later, in the days of Jesus and the apostles, a hate-filled, jealous controversy had developed between Temple and synagogue which became clearly apparent in the contrast of the two factions of the Sadducees and Pharisees. In Ezra's age, this difference did not yet exist. Ezra was a Sadducee and at the same time the spiritual leader of Pharisaism and scribism. Nobody has done more than he for the first bold and exact structure of synagogue life, which represented the foundation for the teaching activity of scribism and the Pharisees' work in the people's education.

The reorganization of the state was something Ezra left to others who were striving to work in the same spirit as he was. They accomplished what they did on their own. They either occupied the position of a Persian governor themselves or they were the advisors of the latter. The most evident harmony between Ezra's religious reform and the political reconstruction of the state occurred when Artaxerxes Longimanus, who favoured Ezra's endeavours, appointed Nehemiah. Filled with Ezra's spirit, this man was able to be active for fifteen years (445–430). In the new construction of the city walls and gates of the holy city, he created an outward symbol for the segregation and concentration of Jewish life executed inwardly by Ezra. When Ezra and Nehemiah had completed their work, Judaism of the post-exile era had received the stern imprint of its appearance and form. As small as it may have appeared after all the blows of fate, the house had been built and made ready, into which the great longed-for One could move.

If we knew nothing more about Ezra except what the canonic texts of the Old Testament relate concerning him, we should perhaps consider him a great organizer. His actual greatness of spirit, however, and his connection with the mysteries would remain concealed from us and we would have to confront with great doubts and reservations the traditions, according to which he was the creator of the Bible canon, the esoteric scribism and the institution of synagogues. In reality, we know much more about him through a book ascribed to him, which, in late Judaism and the early age of Christianity, was more important than the biblical Book of Ezra. It places him in the ranks of the Old Covenant's great prophets and heralds of the apocalypse. It is the so-called Fourth Book of Ezra,* the most widely circulated apocalyptic scripture of antiquity and, next to the Book of Daniel, *the* apocalypse of the turn of time. Here, the fountain of higher insight and perception is revealed out of which alone Ezra could accomplish his organizational and reformatory work.

At the end of this book, Ezra himself explains how he has partaken of the loftiest revelation at the end of his life:

> And on the next day, behold, a voice called me, saying, 'Ezra, open your mouth and drink what I give you to drink.' Then I opened my mouth and behold, a full cup was offered to me; it was full of something like water, but its colour was like fire. And I took it and drank; and when I had drunk it, my heart poured forth understanding, and wisdom increased in my breast, for my spirit retained its memory; and my mouth was opened ... (2Esd.14:38–41).

After Ezra has dictated his revelations day and night for forty days to five scribes for the chosen teachers of his people, he is taken up and for ever more is named, 'writer of the loftiest, divine knowledge.'

The reason that the Fourth Book of Ezra is a classic is because it is the summation of all the struggles by the prophets' age concerning the meaning of suffering and the efforts for attaining the inwardness of life with God.

At the beginning stands the weighty question asking why Zion has to become desolate whereas Babel is blossoming in full abundance. Is Babel not just as sinful as Zion? The divine messenger replies to the torturous question of man by directing his glance through a variety of allegories concerning the superficiality of things

---

* The scriptures attributed to Ezra are numbered in the following way: the first book of Ezra is the Ezra text contained in the Old Testament. The second book is called the Book of Nehemiah. The third book is the expanded, freely rendered Greek version of the first Ezra book, called the First Book of Esdras in the Apocrypha. The fourth book is the great apocalypse, the Second Book of Esdras. Aside from these there exist smaller apocalyptic apocryphal writings, designated as fifth and sixth books of Ezra.

into the deeper levels of existence. 'Go, weigh for me the weight of fire, or measure for me a measure of wind, or call back for me the day that is past.' says the archangel Uriel to the questioning and seeking Ezra (2Esd.4:5).

> Do not think that you receive a reply to the difficult riddles that oppress you if you merely go by the outer appearance of the senses. After all, you do not even understand what is closest at hand; how can you hope to fathom the secrets of destiny without penetrating behind the veil of the senses?
> (4:9–11*B*)

Israel's suffering and doom is only the beginning of great trials that will have to be undergone by humankind before salvation can appear:

> If you are alive, you will see, and if you live long, you will often marvel, because the age is hastening swiftly to its end. For it will not be able to bring the things that have been promised to the righteous in their appointed times, because the age is full of sadness and infirmities. For the evil about which you ask me has been sown, but the harvest of it has not yet come. If therefore that which has been sown is not reaped, and if the place where the evil has been sown does not pass away, the field where the good has been sown will not come. (4:26–29).

Man wishes to know the times when all this will take place; he is troubled by the concern whether new postponements will occur. Uriel says to him:

> 'Go and ask a woman who is with child if, when her nine months have been completed, her womb can keep the child within her any longer.'
> ... 'In Hades the chambers of the souls are like the womb. For just as a woman who is in travail makes haste to escape the pangs of birth, so also do these places hasten to give back those things that were committed to them from the beginning.'
> (4:40–42).

Man dares ask one last question: how does the period of grace compare to the past? 'For I know what has gone by, but I do not know what is to come.' The answer is given in pictures:

> ... a flaming furnace passed by before me, and when the flame had gone by I looked, and behold, the smoke

remained. And after this a cloud filled with water passed before me and poured down a heavy and violent rain, and when the rainstorm had passed, drops remained in the cloud.

And he said to me: '... for as the rain is more than the drops, and the fire is greater than the smoke, so the quantity that passed was far greater; but drops and smoke remained.' (4:48–50).

Man is not left without an answer in his struggles for insight, but the reply each time is so eschatological and apocalyptic, and rouses so many presentiments concerning life that it necessitates even more profound contemplation and further seeking. It is as if in the interchange of questions and answers between Ezra and the archangel something shines through of the apocalyptic quest for wisdom by esoteric scribism, which was supported by certain soul exercises. The rabbinical dialectical theology of later times which always started by raising a question of doubt appears to be nothing but a thinned out, humanized continuation of the apocalyptic element unfolded by this book for Ezra.

The visions in which the questioning soul receives the answer from the spirit-world become increasingly powerful and dramatic:

... the days are coming when those who dwell on earth shall be
seized with great terror, and the way of truth shall be hidden,
the land shall be barren of faith. And unrighteousness shall
increase beyond what you yourself see, and beyond what you
heard of formerly. And the land which you now see ruling
shall be waste and untrodden, and men shall see it desolate.
But if the Most High grants that you live, you shall see it
thrown into confusion after the third period;
And the sun shall suddenly shine forth at night,
    and the moon during the day.
Blood shall drip from the wood,
    and the stone shall utter its voice;
the peoples shall be troubled,
    and the stars shall fall.
... There shall be chaos also in many places, and fire shall often
break out ... And at that time men shall hope but not obtain;
they shall labor but their ways shall not prosper. (5:1–12)

Again and again, the question arises: All creatures have their habitation, why are the Chosen People the only ones who are so homeless? Indicating a profound riddle of life, the angel answers and says:

> There is a sea set in a wide expanse so that it is broad and vast, but it has an entrance set in a narrow place, so that it is like a river. If any one, then, wishes to reach the sea, to look at it or to navigate it, how can he come to the broad part unless he passes through the narrow part? Another example: There is a city built and set on a plain, and it is full of good things; but the entrance to it is narrow and set in a precipitous place, so that there is fire on the right hand and deep water on the left; and there is only one path lying between them, that is between the fire and the water, so that only one man can walk upon that path. If now that city is given to a man for an inheritance, how will the heir receive his inheritance unless he passes through the danger set before him? (7:3–9).

Through all doom, the coast of a new world becomes visible which represents the meaning of all suffering and allows Ezra to recognize the revelation of divine love even in the most difficult trials:

> For behold, the time will come, when the signs which I have foretold to you will come to pass, that the city which now is not seen shall appear, and the land which now is hidden shall be disclosed. ... For my son the Messiah shall be revealed with those who with him, and those who remain shall rejoice four hundred years. And after these years my son the Messiah shall die, and all who draw human breath. And the world shall be turned back to primeval silence for seven days as it was at the first beginnings ... And after seven days the world, which is not yet awake, shall be roused, and that which is corruptible shall perish. (7:26–31).

Zion appears to the seer like a lamenting woman, sunk into deepest sorrow. After long times of barrenness she had finally given birth to a son. Then, however, misery has closed in:

> '... I brought him up with much care. So when he grew up and I came to take a wife for him, I set a day for the marriage feast.
>
> 'But it happened that when my son entered his wedding chamber, he fell down and died. Then we all put out the

lamps, and all my neighbours attempted to console me ...'
(9:46–10:2).

Ezra attempts to confront the mourning woman:

... behold, her face suddenly shone exceedingly, and her countenance flashed like lightning, so that I was too frightened to
approach her ... behold, she suddenly uttered a loud and fearful cry, so that the earth shook at the sound. And I looked, and
behold, the woman was no longer visible to me, but there was
an established city, and a place of huge foundations showed
itself. (10:25–27).

Mighty spirit battles finally take place before the visionary sight of
Ezra until the figure of the Son of man breaks victoriously through the
clouds. The Coming One shows himself, in whose service Ezra is
endeavouring to arm his people through stern forming for the difficult
dark times of transition.

CHAPTER TWENTY-NINE

The Book of Esther:
Breakthrough of the New Spirit

Owing to their nature and the place where they are found, the Book of Ruth and the Book of Esther, the two brief texts that were included in the Old Testament canon under the name of women, signify one of the most beautiful and transparent miracles in the architectonic structure of the Bible and the history depicted in it. The two groups of the historical books of the Old Testament end in them. The Book of Ruth signifies the culmination of those scriptures that describe the historical development up to the end of the age of Moses. The Book of Esther is an epilogue of the books dealing with the age of the kings and prophets.

Although themselves included among the historical books, both these texts were always taken as pearls of poetry and distinguished by special festive ritual use. Together with the Song of Songs, Ecclesiastes and the Lamentations of Jeremiah, they form the content of the sacred festival scroll, the Megillah.

Nothing can more clearly bring to awareness the difference of two historical periods and spirits of time than the dissimilarity of sound and content holding sway between the Book of Ruth and that of Esther.

Ruth, the pious, devotion-filled gleaner moves across open country evoking feelings of a pristine home. What could be more homelike than Bethlehem with its warm, golden aroma of ripening wheat and bread? Although coming from a foreign land herself, Ruth changes through the Bethlehem magic into the bearer of the maternal life ensouling the tranquil region. Esther, the Judean wife at the colourful, rich court of the Persian king, is like the personification of humankind, abandoned in homelessness and the alien world pregnant with danger. Placed into the spiritual battle against the demons of the strange land, she helps the good spirit of her people to gain the victory.

In Ruth and Bethlehem, Israel's history came to rest after the Egyptian exile, the journey through the desert and the battles of the age of the judges. The Promised Land became home for the people. The time could commence, the fruits of which would be the inwardness of the pious heart.

In Esther, the final, lasting homelessness of the people became complete. The Babylonian exile continued and was intensified to the eternal Diaspora, the dispersion into the world. Only a brief and in the end not lasting reconstruction of the outward folk community could develop from the return of a part of the exiled populace. Would the Judeans, living in exile and surrounded by hostility and persecution, be able to remain bearers of the same spirit which once ensouled them in their homeland? The story of Esther's and Mordecai's victory over the opponents gave the Jews an encouraging example and allowed them to sense the deeper, divinely willed meaning of their dispersion; it opened a view to the most unheard-of secrets of the historical development.

In Susa, at the court of Xerxes (who is called Ahasuerus in the Bible) there dwelled among the Jews who could not return to the homeland, Mordecai, a Benjaminite from the same tribe from which Saul had come long ago. He had living with him as his ward the young, orphaned Esther. Her radiant beauty was the reason why Esther, along with other maidens, was destined for the royal harem and soon was elevated to the favourite consort of Xerxes. A man occupied the office of chief royal councillor who in reality was the evil spirit of the court. He was Haman, a descendant of the Amalekite king, Agag, the sparing of whom had been the cause of Saul's incurring a great sin. Haman managed to become a focus of a private Caesar-worship next to the king, perhaps owing to his membership in a decadent sphere of initiation and rituals, and to demand cultic expressions of honour from the whole court. Mordecai, who, since Esther's elevation, dwelled in the closest vicinity to the royal palace, refused to pay the required homage to Haman, thus bringing upon himself the unrelenting hatred and persecution of this adversary. Haman had found out that Mordecai belonged to the Jewish strangers and he succeeded in having the king issue an order for a bloody persecution of the Jews, which was to erupt on a certain date in all the parts of the great kingdom. Only because Mordecai had once saved the king's life by uncovering a conspiracy, Haman did not dare eliminate his enemy immediately. He did, however, prepare for this blow: tall gallows were erected on which the hated one was to die.

Although she was risking her life by doing this, Esther appeared before the king without having been summoned. By revealing that she herself belonged to the persecuted people, she was successful in unmasking Haman's duplicity and evilness and to foil his designs. The command for the mighty persecution of the Jews was rescinded. Haman ended on the gallows which he had constructed for Mordecai; the king appointed Mordecai to the office which Haman had previously occupied. The Jews in the kingdom were categorically placed under protection against their antagonists.

This story must not be interpreted in the sense of the misunderstanding, later connected with it, when a fanatical Jewish nationalism appealed to it and, failing to recognize its imaginative style of the scripture, saw nothing more in it except the recorded memory of warding off the first Jewish pogrom.

The Book of Esther itself contains a subtle but clearly discernible indication, surely experienced originally quite vividly, that it wished to reveal important spiritual backgrounds and secrets of history's course in legendary images. The names that are being mentioned are throughout the names of the gods from the religious realm of the nations among whom the Jews lived in their diaspora. Mordecai is Marduk, the sun genius, whom the Babylonians revered, but to whom Cyrus, the Persian, also paid homage when he moved into subjugated Babylon. Esther is none other than Astarte or Ishtar, the feminine deity of the Phoenician-Babylonian Orient. In certain Phoenician and Mesopotamian regions, Haman was the customary designation for the Baal-Adonis deity. (In Carthage, for instance, the trinity of gods, who were named Isis, Osiris and Horus in Egypt, Astarte, Baal and Eshmun in Sidon, were called Tanit, Baal-Hammon and Eshmun.[1]) The other names in the Book of Esther are also clearly of mythological nature. One could think that in the seemingly clear earthly event nothing but gods and their divine opponents had emerged from the spirit realm in human form in order to make themselves bearers of a dramatic historical action on earth. The deity of external sense radiance turned demonic, Baal-Hammon, was the hate-filled villain. Marduk, the shining one, arose against the principle of evil in the figure of a Judean, robbed of his homeland. And the virginal-maternal goddess Isis-Ishtar, as Esther, simultaneously degraded and elevated as the slave and consort of the foreign ruler, stood on the side of Marduk.

It is an apocalyptic image which is unveiled to us in earthly dramatization. John's Revelation presents it to us in its twelfth chapter. Before the image of the woman who appears in the sky, the dragon lurks threateningly until the archangel Michael steps forward, vanquishes and topples the adversary.

Mordecai, the human Marduk, stands at the same time for the Michaelic power. The harmony of the Babylonian name, Marduk, and the biblical Michael figure is the secret of the Book of Esther and the militant element reflected in it. According to the apocryphal Additions to the Book of Esther, in a dream which showed him all the earthly elements in furious uproar, Mordecai himself beheld his victory over Haman in the image of a battle with a dragon (Ad.Est.6), thus touching closely upon the Michaelic archetype realized in his earthly experience.

We cannot point to the archetypal mythological content of the Esther story without immediately confronting a strange and puzzling question. But it is this question that opens to us the amazing view of the mysteries of humankind which are secreted into the unassuming brief biblical text in which the historical description of the Old Testament ends.

How was it ever possible that Judaism of the age following the exile, which, more than at any other time of Israelite history, segregated itself from all pagan influences, called its national heroes, Mordecai and Esther, by names of heathen gods? Would the name Marduk not conjure forth the image of the sacrilegious and tragic Tower of Babel after the Jews in Babylon had for so long witnessed the magnificent Marduk processions whose goal was the ziggurat which had taken the place of the legendary tower? Did not the name Astarte remind them of all the dark Jezebel abominations against which Elijah had called down the fire from heaven?

The mythological table of names in the Esther book only becomes comprehensible if it is realized that in it, a mighty and progressive spiritual self-awareness of post-exilic Judaism is expressed. An inner attitude becomes evident which was no longer satisfied merely to mark itself carefully off from the sphere of paganism. Instead, it even proceeded to put its own character in the place of the heathen gods. The names of the Babylonian gods, Marduk and Astarte, had turned into empty hulls. Having gone through the trials of the exile, Judaism felt spiritually strong enough to fill the empty forms newly with its own content. In Mordecai and Esther, the folk spirit and the folk soul of the Israelite-Jewish people had taken the place of the old gods.

The archangel, 'who has charge of your people' (Dan.12:1), was Michael. This was the secret that determined the pulse beat of the whole epoch, namely, that this archangel of the sun, who until then had been the genius of the Old Testament people, had spiritually stepped into the place of the Babylonian sun deity, Marduk. Michael was truly present as Marduk.

In the history of religion, people's attention has been drawn to the great similarity of the Marduk deity with the figure of the archangel Michael. The identity did not, however, exist from the beginning but was instead the result of a mighty, although quietly conducted, victory over the heathen surroundings. Outwardly, Judea was crushed and enslaved by the Babylonians. Spiritually, however, the vanquished were victorious over their victors. Their folk spirit Michael, the ruler of the spiritual sun forces, the militant guardian of the hidden, Messianic sunrise, beginning to light up the soul realm of human beings, now stood where once the Marduk-being had stood who had dwelled more in the external sun radiance. The Baal force in the form of the dragon was crushed under his feet. It was Marduk, turned into Michael, who found in Mordecai a human replica, an earthly bearer.

Perhaps, in the period after the exile, when the story of Esther had not yet succumbed to the brutality of political interpretation, there were not many people who were capable of more than a dim feeling for the secrets contained in the names of this text. And yet, everything was actually already contained in the triumphant self-awareness that said, 'We, the vanquished ones, are spiritually the victors!' For us, who are trying to decipher the language of these secrets for our modern thinking, the same mystery of the prophets' age is revealed which we had already encountered in discussing the Book of Daniel.

In the circle of the archangel epochs entwined in the course of humankind's history, it was Michael who ruled in the age of the prophets and the Babylonian exile. Outwardly, this era was painful and chaotic, inwardly, on the other hand, it was pervaded by the pulse of mighty forces that changed destinies. The archangel Michael, who as the folk spirit had accompanied and directed the Old Testament development up to the time of the destruction of the northern kingdom, had ascended to the rank of Time Spirit, to be regent over the whole of progressing humanity. He ceased permeating only the narrow confines of the Jewish people with his forces, extending his sphere of action far and wide. Outwardly, the people fell from their position of wealth and freedom and were dispersed into the wide world. But this was only the earthly shadow of the spiritual course of events behind which stood the powerful, victorious increase of the sphere of action now attained by the genius of the people as the Time Spirit. The pious Jew, who was inwardly strong enough to see through the illusion of their outward captivity, sensed in the unassuming pictures of the Book of Esther something which might be expressed thus: 'The spirit who ensouls us has toppled the old gods and has assumed rulership over those who appear to be ruling. Michael, the spirit of our people, is the true Marduk. The soul of our people is the true Ishtar. Although outwardly we may live as homeless ones in the Diaspora, spiritually we are elevated to the true leaders of our age in Mordecai and Esther.'

When Judaism of the age following the exile rigidified in fanatical nationalism, it lost the truth of the Book of Esther although it now began to refer to it in grand style. It had ceased to understand that it could remain true to its original Michaelic spirit only if it kept in step and selflessly turned into the nation of all humankind.

In the course of the Christian era, the inspiring power of the archangel Michael has led to the most wonderful heights of spiritual culture. Towards the end of the nineteenth century, as during the age of the prophets, the archangel Michael ascended from the level of folk spirit to that of Time Spirit. Today, he places before humankind a task similar to the one actually posed to the Jewish people after the exile and clothed in the images of the Book of Esther, namely, to serve the Michaelic power, soaring up like an eagle and changing destinies in the midst of a chaotic age.

References

Chapter 1

1 *Genesis,* pp. 142–49.

Chapter 2

1 See *Genesis,* pp. 91f.

Chapter 3

1 See *Moses,* pp. 173f.
2 See *Moses,* pp. 191–93.
3 See *Moses,* p. 187.
4 See *Moses,* p. 167.
5 See *Genesis,* pp. 155ff.
6 The Bible mentions 'Gibeon' at one point (1Chr.9:35–39), at another (1Sam.10:26) 'Gibeah' as Saul's hometown.

Chaper 5

1 See *Moses,* pp.107–10.
2 See Goethe, *The Fairy Tale.*
3 Steiner, *Building Stones,* (April 17 & 19, 1917).

Chapter 6

1 See *Genesis,* p. 129.
2 See *Moses,* p. 210.
3 Gorion, *Sagen,* 5:126f.

Chapter 7

1 See *Moses,* p. 128f.

Chapter 8

1 Midrash of the Divine Wisdom, Jellinik, Beth hamidrash 5.63f, Vienna 1873
2 Jalkut on Gen.28:22.
3 See *Genesis,* p. 34.
4 See *Genesis,* p. 40.
5 See *Genesis,* p. 109f.
6 Brocardus, *Locorum terrae sanctae accuratissima descriptio,* 1283.
7 Furrer, *Wanderungen durch Palästina,* p. 29.

8   Mommert, *Topographie des alten Jerusalem,* Vol. 1, p. 68.

9   See *Moses,* p. 71f.

10 See *Moses,* p. 73.

11 See v. Orelli, *Durchs heilige Land.*

12 *Bellum Iudaicum,* 6.1.1.

13 Mommert *Siloah,* 1908.

14 J. Murphy O'Connor, *The Holy Land,* p. 100.

15 Gorion, *Sagen,* 5:131f.

16 Judg.6 and *Moses,* p. 178.

17 *Moses,* p. 209f.

18 See *Genesis,* p. 123f.

19 See *Genesis,* p.113f.

20 Such as, for example, J. Jeremias: *Golgotha.*

Chapter 9

1   See *Moses,* 32ff, 81ff.

2   Steiner, *Gospel of St Matthew,* (Sep 2, 1910) p. 48.

3   Concerning the imaginative meaning of the Bathsheba episode, see also
Bock, *Evangelium: Betrachtungen,* Vol. 2. Ch. 14.

4   Gorion, *Sagen,* 5:143f.

Chapter 10

1   See *Moses,* pp. 127–29.

2   See *Moses,* p. 193.

Chapter 11

1   Gorion, *Sagen,* 5:155f.

Chapter 12

1   Gorion, *Sagen,* 5:155f. Yedidyah means 'beloved of God;' Solomon means
'bearer of peace;' Ithiel means 'with me is God;' Jakah (Jakeh) means
'fear of God.'

2   Gorion, *Sagen,* 5:190. Kohelet means 'preacher,' 'teacher.'

3   Steiner, *The Christ-Impulse,* (February 8, 1910).

Chapter 13

1   See Breasted, *History of Egypt.*

2   This is the title of a study by Th. Friedrich that is still valuable today
(*Tempel und Palast Salomos*).

3   For instance, Kurt Moehlenbrink, *Der Tempel Salomos.*

4   See *Moses,* pp. 20–22.

5   Herodotus, *Annales,* I, 2:44.

6   Schlegel, *Philosophische Vorlesungen,* 2:494.

7   Artistically formulated in Albert Steffen's drama, *Hieram und Salomo.*

Chapter 14

1 From the song, 'Der Winter ist vergangen.'
2 From the song, 'Wie schön blüht uns der Maien.'
3 A detailed analysis of the Song of Songs, together with a translation of the text, is found in Emil Bock's, *Das Evangelium. Betrachtungen und Übersetzungen*, Vol. 1, chapter 13. (translated in the *Christian Community Journal*, 1953, Jan–Feb).

Chapter 16

1 Steiner, *Gospel of St Luke*, (Sep 20, 1909) p. 118.
2 Steiner, *The Gospel of St Mark*, (Sep 17, 1912) p. 44.
3 Franz Werfel, *Die schwarze Messe*, a fragmentary novel.
4 See *Moses*, pp. 80f.
5 See *Moses*, pp. 101–3.
6 Steiner, *Apocalypse of St John*, (June 26, 1908) p. 161.
7 See *Moses*, p. 127.

Chapter 17

1 In the lecture 'Der Prophet Elias' (Dec 14, 1911) in *Wendepunkte des Geisteslebens*. The insights gained through this lecture form the main basis of this as well as the preceding chapter.
2 See *Moses*, pp. 88f.
3 See *Caesars and Apostles*, pp. 190ff.
4 See also Steiner's lecture 'Der Prophet Elias' (Ref. 62 above).
5 See *Moses*, pp. 101–3.

Chapter 18

1 For a more detailed description see the chapter concerning John the Baptist, in *Caesars and Apostles*, pp. 190ff.

Chapter 19

1 Steiner, *The Gospel of St Mark*, (Sep 16, 1912) pp. 26–28.

Chapter 20

1 Gorion, *Sagen*, 5:224.

Chapter 22

1 See *Moses*, pp. 105–10.
2 Gorion, *Sagen*, 5:264.
3 Gorion, *Sagen*, 5:265.
4 Gorion, *Sagen*, 5:260.
5 Gorion, *Sagen*, 5:267f.
6 Gorion, *Sagen*, 5:266.
7 Gorion, *Sagen*, 5:265f.
8 Gorion, *Sagen*, 5:270.
9 Pseudo-Epiphanius, *Vitae prophetarum*.

10 See *Genesis*, pp. 11ff.
11 Adolf von Harnack often presented this theory in reference to the theologian, E. Vischer of Basle.

Chapter 24

1 See Creuzer, *Symbolik und Mythologie.*
2 Gorion, *Sagen*, 5:482.
3 The Paraleipomena of Jeremiah, also called the Rest of Baruch, preserved in Ethiopic, Armenian, Slavic and Greek. See Harris, *The Rest of the Words of Baruch.*

Chapter 25

1 Steiner, *The Gospel of St Matthew*, (Sep 2, 1910) p. 49.
2 *Stromateis* 1.15.70.
3 Gorion, *Der Born Judas*, 3:215.
4 Gorion, *Der Born Judas*, 3.
5 See *Moses*, pp. 30, 136.
6 Steiner, *The Gospel of St Matthew*, (Sep 2, 1910) pp. 48f.
7 Steiner, *The Gospel of St Matthew*, (Sep 3, 1910) p. 65.

Chapter 27

1 See *Genesis*, p. 99.
2 See *Moses*, pp. 40–43.

Chapter 28

·1 See Mead, *Fragments of a Faith Forgotten.* Reference is made there to ancient sources which, unfortunately, are not identified.
2 See pp. 119 209; also *Moses*, p. 193.

Chapter 29

1 See W. Graf v. Baudissin, *Adonis und Esmun.*

Bibliography

Baudissin, Wolf Graf von, *Adonis und Esmun*, Leipzig 1911.

Bock, Emil, *Caesars and Apostles*, Floris, Edinburgh 1998.

——, *Das Evangelium. Betrachtungen*, Urachhaus, Stuttgart 1984.

——, *Genesis*, Floris, Edinburgh 1983.

——, *Moses*, Floris, Edinburgh, and Inner Traditions, New York, 1986.

Breasted, James Henry, *A History of Egypt*, London 1906.

Brocardus de Monte Sion, *Descriptio Terrae Sanctae*, Magdeburg 1587.

——, *A Description of the Holy Land*, Vol. 12 of Library of Palestine's Pilgrim's Text, London 1896.

Creuzer, Fr. *Symbolik und Mythologie der alten Völker*, Darmstadt 1810.

Friedrich Th. *Tempel und Palast Salomos*, Innsbruck 1887.

Furrer, Konrad, *Wanderungen durch Palästina*, Zürich 1865.

Gorion, Josef bin, *Der Born Judas*, Leipzig 1916–20.

——, *Die Sagen der Juden*, Frankfurt a.M. 1913–1927.

Gressmann, Hugo, *Mose und seine Zeit*.

Harris, J. Rendel, *The Rest of the Words of Baruch*, Clay, London 1899.

Jalkut, S. *Midrasch Sammlung*, Berlin 1926.

Jellinek, Adolf, *Midrasch ele Eschera.* Leipzig 1854.

Jeremias, Joachim, *Golgatha*, Leipzig 1926.

Mead, G.R.S. *Fragments of a Faith Forgotten*, London 1900.

Moehlenbrink, Kurt, *Der Tempel Salomos. Eine Untersuchung seiner Stellung in the Sakralarchitektur des Alten Orients*, Kohlhammer, Stuttgart 1932.

Mommert, Carl, *Siloah. Brunnen, Teich, Kanal zu Jerusalem*, Leipzig 1908.

——, *Topographie des alten Jerusalems*, Leipzig 1902–7.

Murphy O'Connor, J. *The Holy Land*, Oxford University Press 1986.

Orelli, C. von, *Durchs heilige Land.* Basel 1878.

Press, London 1972.

Riessler, Paul, *Altjüdisches Schrifttum ausserhalb der Bibel.* 2 ed. Kerle, Heidelberg 1966.

Schlegel, Fr. *Philosophische Vorlesungen*, Windischmann, Bonn 1837.

Steffen, Albert, *Hieram und Salomo*, Dornach 1933.

Steiner, Rudolf, *The Apocalypse of St John*, 4 ed. Steiner Press, London 1977.

——, *Building Stones for an Understanding of the Mystery of Golgotha*, 2 ed. Steiner Press, London 1972.

——, *The Christ-Impulse and the Development of Ego-Consciousness*, Anthroposophic Press, New York 1976.

——, *Gospel of St Luke*, 3 ed. Steiner Press, London 1964.

——, *The Gospel of St Mark,* Steiner Press, London, and Anthroposophic Press, New York 1977.

——, *The Gospel of St Matthew,* Steiner Press, London 1965.

——, *Turning Points in Spiritual History,* Steiner Publishing, London 1934.

——, *Wendepunkte des Geisteslebens,* Steiner Verlag, Dornach 1964.

Index of Biblical References

Index